BORGES

A Life

Also by James Woodall

In Search of the Firedance: Spain through Flamenco

BORGES

A Life

James Woodall

A Member of the Perseus Books Group

This book was first published in Great Britain in 1996 by Hodder and Stoughton under the title *The Man in the Mirror of the Book*. It is here reprinted by arrangement with Hodder and Stoughton.

Library of Congress Cataloging-in-Publication Data

Woodall, James, 1960–
  [Man in the mirror of the book]
  Borges : a life / by James Woodall.
    p. cm.
  Originally published: The man in the mirror of the book. London :
Hodder & Stoughton, 1996.
  Includes bibliographical references (p.   ) and index.
  ISBN 0-465-04361-5 (cloth)   ISBN 0-465-00724-4 (paper)
  1. Borges, Jorge Luis, 1899–1986—Biography. 2. Authors,
Argentine—20th century—Biography. I. Title.
PQ7797.B635Z965   1997
868—dc21
  [B]   96-47671

98   99   00   01   RRD   10   9   8   7   6   5   4   3   2   1

For Petra Wend

Contents

List of Illustrations

Francisco Borges Lafinur. (*Courtesy of Colección Jorge y Marion Helft*)

Francisco Borges's English wife, Fanny Haslam. (*Courtesy of Helft*)

Leonor Suárez Haedo de Acevedo. (*Courtesy of Helft*)

Isidoro de Acevedo Laprida. (*Courtesy of Helft*)

Georgie's father, Jorge Guillermo, in 1895. (*Courtesy of Helft*)

Jorge Francisco Isidoro Luis Borges Acevedo, aged three. (*Courtesy of Helft*)

Norah Borges, Georgie's sister, in 1910. (*Courtesy of Helft*)

Leonor Borges in 1911. (*Courtesy of Helft*)

The Borges family on their arrival in Switzerland in 1914. (*Courtesy of Helft*)

The changing face of the Ultraist poet: a 1921 portrait, one from 1923. (*Courtesy of Helft*)

Jorge Luis Borges in 1924, shortly before his second return from Europe to Buenos Aires. (*Courtesy of Helft*)

Four years later: Borges with Sergio Piñero, Carlos Mastronardi and Guillermo de Torre. (*Courtesy of Helft*)

Sur prepares for launch, 1930. (*Courtesy of Helft*)

Borges with Haydée Lange, 1939. (*Courtesy of Helft*)

Borges with Adolfo Bioy Casares, 1942. (*Courtesy of Helft*)

Borges with Estela Canto in March 1945. (*Courtesy of Helft*)

Borges and Leonor, December 1962. (*Courtesy of Helft*)

The couple arrive in Britain in February 1963. (*Courtesy of the British Council*)

Borges with Alberto Moravia in 1981 and with Bianca Jagger in 1983. (*Courtesy of Frank Spooner Pictures and Camera Press respectively*)

Borges in Paris, January 1983. (*Courtesy of Frank Spooner Pictures*)

With María Kodama. (*Courtesy of Frank Spooner Pictures*)

Borges in Palermo, Sicily, May 1984. (*Courtesy of F. Scianna/ Magnum*)

Jorge Luis Borges nine months before he died. (*Courtesy of F. Scianna/Magnum*)

Acknowledgements

No biography of Borges could be written without the help and support of those who knew him in Buenos Aires. My first thanks are therefore to Borges's widow, María Kodama, for her willingness to share some of her life with Borges with me. On my two visits to the city, she gave graciously of her time. In November 1994, during my second visit, she was particularly pleased to show me round the (then embryonic) Borges Foundation, which she has set up as a museum and as a centre of study into her late husband's works.

Norah Borges de Torre shared some memories of her brother with me, too, on my first visit to Buenos Aires in late 1993. I am also grateful to her son, Miguel de Torre, for his interest in this project.

Adolfo Bioy Casares remains one of Argentina's most distinguished men of letters, and was full of wit, and many memories of his old friend, when I met him in his eighty-first year. I am indebted to his efforts on my behalf when talking of Borges, with whom he shared half a century of literary and conversational life.

Quantities of information came from Elsa Rivero Haedo, whose memories stimulated some important areas of this book; her friend Carmen Valdés kindly introduced me to two uncollected items of Borges from the 1940s.

Alicia Jurado and Vlady Kociancich both filled in vital gaps. I am grateful to the former for some crystalline memories, and for answering correspondence of mine in 1995 (as did Elsa Haedo – the only two people from Buenos Aires who chose to correspond with me on the subject of Borges); and to the latter for letting me see an unpublished transcript of a talk she gave on Borges and Bioy in London in 1992.

María Esther Vázquez gave me some valuable insights into the character of the man she knew just as he was achieving world fame, during conversations in 1993 and 1994. Esther Zemboraín de Torres Duggan, an old friend of Borges's, was also ready to talk freely about her collaboration with him, in November 1994. Estela Canto, who wrote a book about Borges's relationship with her in the mid-1940s, was my most provocative interviewee, though sadly I wasn't able to visit (or thank) her on my second trip to Buenos Aires, as she died in mid-1994.

Sari del Carril was generous with time, documents and books at Borges's publishers, Emecé, in 1993 and 1994. Erika Escoda helped in all manner of ways; to name just one would do injustice to her multifarious generosity.

No biographer of Borges would dare omit from his research the San Telmo Foundation; Jorge Helft, the collection's owner, and his wife Marion provided essential information, and a much-appreciated photocopying and photographic service in November and December 1994. I must also thank Solange Sanguinetti for allowing me to peruse some fascinating Borges manuscripts, some unpublished, in 1994.

Others in Buenos Aires who have helped me in direct and indirect ways include: Roberto Alifano, Alejandro Bianchi, Santiago Hutton, Gloria López Llovet de Rodrigué, Margaret Murray, Teddy Paz, Andrés di Tella, and Jorge Torres Zavaleta.

Particular gratitude – not a big enough phrase – goes to Mercedes Capurro, who of everyone I've known in Buenos Aires is the most daring; at a crucial moment of my research, and at considerable inconvenience to herself, she took me in as her guest, and my debt to her is incalculable. Her mother Helena and aunt Elsita were similarly tolerant. In a few weeks in 1994 they all did more than anyone to make working conditions for me remarkably straightforward, when they could have been hell.

In Britain, I must begin with an anecdote.

In September 1993, I was sitting on the steps in front of the Royal Albert Hall, queuing for a Prom. Simon Rattle was conducting, and my thoughts drifted back over thirteen years to my time at Oxford, where I met Rattle, then on sabbatical and attending a series of seminars given by my tutor at Christ Church, Christopher Butler. It didn't seem inconceivable that Christopher would be at the Prom. At the very moment this thought entered my head – and in one of those freaks of connective coincidence that surely would have impressed Borges – Christopher strode into view with his wife.

I greeted them, and told them about this book and an imminent visit to Buenos Aires. After the concert, Christopher introduced me to his oldest friend, Paul Woddis, who had spent many years in Argentina. The upshot of this was that Paul and his wife Helena put me in touch with the families Mulville and Barbosa, whose help – particularly Marilyn Mulville's – over accommodation in Buenos Aires in October 1993 was profoundly appreciated. Arriving in a city the size of Buenos Aires knowing nothing about it is a forbidding experience; Butlers, Woddises, Mulvilles and Barbosas all made the experience less a trial than an easy landing.

And although this is not quite the right place to mention him, his being a colleague of Christopher Butler's at Christ Church, and my former tutor in Anglo-Saxon, makes the temptation irresistible: Richard Hamer was the only person Borges was absolutely determined to see during his 1971 visit to Oxford. (Chapter Nine explains why.) A quarter of a century after he met Borges and sixteen years after he taught me, Richard was good enough to recall his dialogue with Borges (even if he couldn't remember where it took place!). Moreover, the translating of the inscriptions on Borges's gravestone in Geneva could not have been done without his help.

Norman Thomas di Giovanni was professionally as close as anyone was to Borges in his life: more by default than by design, this American-born writer, translator and editor became Borges's personal assistant in 1968, and subsequently assured for many of his writings a place in the English-speaking world from that date on. His time with Borges was not prolonged – di Giovanni left Buenos Aires in 1972 – but their association was remarkably fertile.

In the first instance, di Giovanni (who now lives in England) gave me a great deal of help with contacts in Buenos Aires; and the chapter in which his time with Borges figures largely could not have been written without his patient answers to my many queries. He also helped greatly with many fine points of detail on the proofs.

Richard Cohen must be thanked for coming up with the idea

of a new biogaphy of Borges in early 1993; Roland Philipps at Hodder and Stoughton saw it through to completion with patient professionalism, while Angela Herlihy coped valiantly with the manuscript, photographs and sundry deliveries. Jason Wilson at University College, London, was supportive with contacts in Buenos Aires and, amongst other things, patient with his loan of Emir Rodríguez Monegal's 1978 biography of Borges, long out of print in its original English edition, as well as other books. I am also grateful for his comments on the manuscript.

Jane Woodall, my sister-in-law, kindly allowed me to continue using her computer to get this book launched, and must have been as relieved as I was when I bought my own. Keith Amery gave me briskly professional advice in making this acquisition and, when I ran into the predictable teething difficulties of a computer illiterate, was long-suffering – including having his expertise called upon from Argentina in November 1994 when I couldn't get into the software. My brother Edward read an early draft of some of the chapters, as well as the proofs, and made many encouraging remarks.

Martin Pope has more than once come to the rescue in my writing life with supplies of BBC videos. Though I remembered seeing David Wheatley's 1983 'Arena' documentary on Borges, it was essential I see it again – and in 1993 Martin didn't fail me. He and his wife Claire have also been helpful in many other intangible ways during the writing of this book.

Others who have helped are: Dawn Bates, Guillermo Cabrera Infante and Miriam Gómez, Lorraine Estelle, Carlos Fuentes, Andrew Graham-Yooll, Michael Jahn, Barney Miller, Humphrey Price, Nicholas Shakespeare, Peter Straus, and George Weidenfeld.

Claire Diamond has been especially kind at Canning House's Hispanic & Luso-Brazilian library in Belgrave Square. I am also grateful to Jennifer Booth for making available the Tate Gallery Archive's file on Borges's 1971 Institute of Contemporary Arts talks.

A particular debt is owed to Victorine Martineau, Head of Archives at the British Council in London, for unearthing a rich file of material relating to Borges's visits to Great Britain in 1963, 1964 and 1971; this was a last-minute find, and proved a priceless source of information for those visits, each of which was subsidised to some degree by the Council.

My thanks also go to Caroline Tonson-Rye for her expert copy-editing. Her knowledge of Spanish, and careful attention to the original manuscript's weaknesses and inconsistencies, were an essential part of getting the book into shape.

Any errors are my sole responsibility.

Further afield, Anne-Solange Noble, Hector Bianciotti and Héloise d'Ormesson in Paris, and Maarten Asscher in Amsterdam, helped deepen the French dimension of this biography; in particular Javier Marías in Madrid did the same from the Spanish angle. In the same city, I must thank Marcos-Ricardo Barnatán. In New York, Alane Mason brought to my attention Miguel de Torre's memoir of his uncle, first published in English in the *New Yorker* in 1993; and I must thank Susanna Porter for her help in New York in November 1993.

Also in New York, Alastair Reid, one of Borges's first English translators, came through with some indispensable documents and information; this was in addition to the time he put aside for me during a visit he made to Britain in mid-1995.

In Jerusalem, where in March 1995 Mario Vargas Llosa received the same prestigious literary prize as Borges did in April 1971, the Peruvian agreed to spare time in a packed schedule to talk to me about the writer he acknowledged (though he is not alone in this) as the master of Latin American letters.

This book was written in a period of peculiar financial strain. After signing the contract, I received help from the Society of Authors, and remain grateful for their support. Christopher, Sally and James Codrington alerted me to the existence of a low-interest loan scheme at the City of London's Samuel Wilson Loan Trust: without the Trust's or indeed the Codringtons' help, I would not have been able to continue work on this biography.

Perhaps the most important benefactors of all are my parents, Deirdre and Antony Woodall. The financial brick walls I ran into in the two and a half years it took to research and write the book were more numerous than I care to remember. My parents' willingness to help at a time of upheaval for them, and at the bleakest fiscal moments for me, was salutary, and way beyond the call of duty.

Special thanks, finally, are due to Victoria Scott at Aitken, Stone & Wylie, who undertook an elaborate financial service for me in October 1993, just before my first visit to Argentina; and last but by no means least, to her boss, Gillon Aitken, who gallantly agreed to become my agent at a time when no one else would, and who, more than anyone, was responsible for getting this book off the ground – and believed in it.

Copyright Permissions

For permission to quote from the published works of Jorge Luis Borges, the author would like to thank the following: María Kodama and the Estate of Jorge Luis Borges; New Directions Publishing Corporation (New York)/Penguin Books Ltd (London) for extracts from *Labyrinths* (New York, 1962); and Norman Thomas di Giovanni for the English translation of many extracts from Borges's prose and poetry in this book (see A Note on Texts Used, pp. 279–80, and Bibliography, p.307).

For permission to quote from works other than Borges's, the author is grateful to the following: Gallimard for the use of material (translated by the author) from Jean-Pierre Bernès's commentaries in the Pléiade *Borges: Oeuvres complètes*, Volume I (Paris, 1993); Espasa Calpe and the Estate of Estela Canto for the use of extracts (translated by the author) from *Borges a contraluz* by Estela Canto (Madrid, 1989); Thomas Colchie and the Estate of Emir Rodríguez Monegal for the use of material from *Jorge Luis Borges: A Literary Biography* by Emir Rodríguez Monegal (New York, 1978); and V. S. Naipaul for the use in Chapter Six of two extracts from *The Return of Eva Perón* (André Deutsch, 1980).

Foreword

It astonishes me how often in the English-speaking world today the name 'Jorge Luis Borges', pronounced correctly* – or even incorrectly – is greeted with bafflement. When I began work on this biography in 1993, I was specifically asked, by people who might have been expected to know something about Borges, two questions: first, when are you going to visit him? Second, he did write *One Hundred Years of Solitude*, didn't he?

Borges would have loved both gaffes – indeed, could have put them in one of his stories. A writer who is dead but is universally believed to be alive, and who writes the most famous South American novel of all time but under another name – García Márquez, say – is just the sort of literary joke Borges revelled in.

As I was leaving Buenos Aires after my first trip, a friend made a promise: if he bumped into Borges, he would of course let me know. It sounds a facetious joke, yet it is in the spirit of paradox that runs through Borges's fiction: a ghost is more real than the living person. '. . . he suffered from unreality . . .', he says of Herbert Ashe in 'Tlön, Uqbar, Orbis Tertius'; 'once dead, he is not even the ghost he was then.'[1] Buenos Aires encourages one to think like that, as it must have encouraged Borges to write what he did. A city of multiple crossroads, of streets that seem to intersect at mathematically repeating points, Buenos Aires might have been invented by one of those mysterious labyrinth-builders who have

* Hór-hay Lew-ýss Bór-haeyss.

become not just fictional but mythological prototypes, defying time and space at the heart of the Borges universe.

Of course, Buenos Aires has a modern metropolis's problems and pleasures. It is filled with writers and artists and politicians and business people contingent to nothing Borges created or wrote about, and who don't necessarily care for him. But it is almost impossible to get away from him. My first twenty minutes in Buenos Aires were spent in a taxi fielding questions from a young driver intent on knowing whom I was going to see, and did I know María Kodama?

Well, no I didn't, but I came to know her a little. She married Borges just before he died. A measure of Borges's omnipresence there can be taken by the fame she enjoys. After our first lunch together (in the restaurant named after her, 'María K'), we were walking towards the new Borges Foundation in calle Anchorena when she was greeted by a lady.

'María Kodama,' she said, 'you don't know me, but no matter' – whereupon she kissed María lightly on the cheek, and went on her way.

The gesture was indicative of the *porteño* public's respect for this elegant and strikingly youthful widow, and of its affection for Borges. She is his walking monument, a living recipient of the love the writer searched for all his life, and found only in old age, with her.

Whatever María stands for, Borges needs no monument. Indeed, there isn't a single one of him in Buenos Aires, neither plaque nor statue. It is a situation that could do with some improvement, but Borges is part of Buenos Aires's natural history.* He walked through the city openly and without fear for decades. One *would* feel quite comfortable bumping into him in the calles Florida or Maipú, still. Above all, no one in Buenos Aires is surprised you want to talk about him.

* * *

* In October 1995, El Centro Cultural Borges opened in central Buenos Aires: a space with exhibition rooms, a collection of first editions, photographs and so on – welcome, but not quite the same thing as a monument. Borges would probably have been embarrassed by the idea of a statue. As he told Victoria Ocampo in 1967 (referring to Argentina's great liberator San Martín): 'The statues of San Martín, the effigies of statues of San Martín, the anniversaries, the floral tributes and – why not say it? – the style of the panegyrists have somewhat distanced me from this notable'.[2]

Such ubiquitousness notwithstanding, any biographer of Borges is hamstrung by two things: the scant material available on his early life; and the almost complete absence of letters. The first is best dealt with by recourse to the memories and memoirs of those, still alive, who were good friends – now less than half a dozen. The best source for anything about Borges, his mother, died in 1975, though luckily some material was caught and put into print by people who were fond of her, such as the writer Alicia Jurado. In general, Borges's first sixty years were lived modestly, with a marked lack of the adventure you might expect of, or hope for, in a major writer living his next twenty-five in the glare of world fame.

The lack of letters is partly explained by Borges's blindness – he wrote very few* – and partly by ill winds: like his manuscripts (those that still exist), the few caches of letters that might otherwise be biographical primary-source material have been scattered across the world, and are either in the hands of private collectors – some of whom, like Jorge Helft, permit consultation – or are apparently untraceable. Such, it seems, is the case with those written by Borges to his friend Maurice Abramowicz from Spain; if they come into the possession of the estate they will no doubt be published at a later date. (See Chapter Two for details of Borges's correspondence with his friend from Mallorca in 1919, Jacobo Sureda.) No access to any existing papers was granted by the estate for this biography. Anyone interested in this subject will find a fuller explanation in the Epilogue.

Beyond such obstacles lies a further difficulty. Borges lived most of his life alone, and in his head. Indeed, a large proportion of it was spent day-dreaming – or if not that, then in its opposite, insomnia, where many of the constructs and distortions of his short fictions were invented. The only record we have of this activity is his published writing, and occasional comments he made in the countless books, written by others, of 'Conversations With . . .'.

A concerted autobiographical pronouncement did come in a 1970

---

* Apart from expeditions to the Argentine provinces and once or twice to Uruguay, Borges stayed in Buenos Aires for nearly forty years (1924–61); he was thus in daily contact with his friends and family either in person or by telephone, and had no real need to write letters.

essay which, though as entertaining as any of his fictions, and just as wonderfully written, is neither especially intimate nor, given Borges's track record as a hoaxer, entirely reliable. Moreover, by 1970, Borges had evolved a spirited, brilliant and self-concealing relationship with 'Borges', the world-renowned writer and seer whom his fans, including most of the citizenry of Buenos Aires, hailed as a kind of literary Caesar.

Borges played with him, sometimes as a fatigued old prof., sometimes as an imaginary 'other', sometimes as the ironic alter-ego he so usefully came to be. Because of this, there is little in the essay that points to the nervous, shy, emotionally myopic young man that Borges was before he became famous.

Before 'Borges' came 'Georgie'. This was how he was known for years to friends and family. The name is a straight anglicisation of the Spanish 'Jorge', and the English strain in his family was never far from either his mind or his writing. He wrote some poems in English, though it is largely through the Spanish verse of the 1920s that we have access to the younger man.

In later years, he suppressed, edited and excised his first writings, much as W. H. Auden did, and much to the frustration of anyone trying to trace a path through Borges's chaotic bibliography in search of biographical data. A first edition of *Fervor de Buenos Aires*, his first book of poems, or of *El tamaño de mi esperanza* (The Dimension of My Hope), a book of essays written in the mid-1920s, have for years been gold dust for Borgesians – *Fervor* would probably fetch $5,000 on the open market today; Borges even claimed to have gone around Buenos Aires bookshops buying up every available copy of such books so as to destroy them.[3]

Borges was a rigorous fixer of his own canon, and tampered with his poetry from decade to decade. This says much about the attitude of the self-patented older man towards the younger literary aspirant. Georgie was in fact a surprisingly idealistic chap, with a florid prose-style he later came to abhor. Self-editing – some might call it self-censorship – of this kind is not an uncommon pattern among writers, particularly great ones aware, like Borges, of their probable standing in posterity.

The clearest all-round picture of Georgie is still to be found in Emir Rodríguez Monegal's *Jorge Luis Borges: A Literary Biography*. Published in English in 1978, it was the only full-length biography of Borges attempted before his death, and as such merits close attention.

Rodríguez Monegal bears a similar relationship to his subject as Herbert Gorman did to James Joyce. Until Richard Ellmann's biography appeared, Gorman's work was the most immediate available on Joyce's life. Like Joyce, Borges was sceptical of biography. Joyce put much of his life, as lived in the world, into his work; Borges, far more sedentary than the Irishman and living purely through and for literature, put much of his into recorded conversation and reminiscence.

Like Gorman's, Rodríguez Monegal's is a deeply flawed book: toiling Borgesians in Buenos Aires have counted 'at least sixty errors' (a phrase I have heard more than once – errors which I trust have not been reproduced in this account). Also, Rodríguez Monegal, who was no intimate of Borges's, takes an obsessively psychoanalytical view of the man. Borges was interested in all kinds of psychology, but read Jung rather than Freud; if he had had to swear by anyone, it would probably have been William James. A Freudian – and in Rodríguez Monegal's case even Lacanian – reading of Borges as a child and young man creates only a construct of him, not a portrait. Rodríguez Monegal's writing is also rather humourless, a cardinal sin when dealing with so witty a man as Borges.

It is none the less a valuable document, and it would be an injustice not to acknowledge my debt to its intelligence. It has, perhaps more often than I anticipated at the outset, served as a useful reference book for piecing together some of my own material. Particular use has been made of what is really an eyewitness account of Borges's almost pathological reaction to Perón, offering the most immediate and memorable writing in the book; because I have found no better documentary material for the period straight after 1945, I have quoted liberally from this section of the biography (see Chapter Six, pp.156–8).

Rodríguez Monegal's pages are also full of textual analysis. That in itself is not a fault, but anyone coming to this biography looking for the same will be disappointed. Occasionally, I have plundered some of Rodríguez Monegal's acuter observations to consolidate one aspect or another of Borges's writing. More often than not, however, I found Rodríguez Monegal's commentary too strict.

While I felt considerable improvement could be made on

Rodríguez Monegal in straight *biographical* terms, I have deliberately avoided detailed textual analysis of Borges's work. There is no shortage of autobiographical references in his prose, poetry and essays, and where appropriate, quotation from them has been made. The temptation to speculate biographically over writing so gnomic and teasing as Borges's is great, and would in my view lead a biographer down many an over-analytical blind alley. Borges must have been written about almost as much as Samuel Beckett, especially in the United States, and it seemed to be beyond this biographer's brief to join a Babel-like industry for which he is ill-qualified.

Equally, I would not wish to pretend to match Borges's gargantuan range of reading. 'First and foremost,' he said, 'I think of myself as a reader, then as a poet, then as a prose writer.'[4] He had an insatiable and indiscriminate appetite for books from an early age, and was able to store up in his memory what seems like several lifetimes of reading before he went completely blind in his late fifties. Thereafter he could draw on a deep well of fiction, poetry and philosophy which served him amply for the rest of his life, and turned him into one of the most allusive writers of all time. If it seemed necessary to know more about Bishop Berkeley or Spinoza or Avicenna, none of whom I've read, then an encyclopaedia was reached for. Borges would have approved; much of his learning was gleaned from the Eleventh Edition of the *Encyclopaedia Britannica*. Ultimately, there seemed no point in trying to beat Borges at the game he was best at.

For all that, I believe this to be the first biography in English since Borges died. As I write, many others are being prepared, not just in English. Borges is read the world over, though, as this book will make clear, he cannot yet be read complete; and just as there is confusion and obfuscation over the state of his writings in both Spanish and English (less so in French, oddly), so there is over his life.

There are many people who today guard his reputation jealously, and who wish to promote 'their Borges'. If this book succeeds in anything, it will I hope be in painting Borges as he was, offering a picture as frank as it is accurate.

Introduction

Jorge Luis Borges has been dead ten years. The decade has seen little diminution in the reputation he gained for himself long before he died. His status as a literary giant is taken for granted.

In the 1960s, Borges joined that pantheon of twentieth-century masters which already numbered Samuel Beckett, Patrick White and Hermann Hesse in its ranks. Recently, the American critic Harold Bloom has placed him in a long list of authors from Western civilisation without whom we would somehow be less spiritually enriched (the two others Bloom places directly alongside him are the Chilean Pablo Neruda and the Portuguese Fernando Pessoa).[1]

Borges was almost certainly more read twenty years ago than he is now; what was unique about him was the immediacy of his influence on a new generation of writers – that is to say, post-war and post-Modernist – who wouldn't have heard of him much before 1961, or, if they read French, before 1951 at the earliest. Through a small body of work, patchily translated, he transformed not only the way people wrote fiction, but what they wrote and thought about it. The catchword 'Borgesian' is now, and has been for some years, as overused in literary parlance as 'Kafkaesque'.

Borges never wrote a novel, and published in a long life – he died aged eighty-six – as much poetry as prose. In the Spanish-speaking world, he is considered a master of its richly poetic language in a line that begins in the seventeenth century with Luis de Góngora and Francisco de Quevedo. Quevedo was a hero of his; and Borges, in Buenos Aires, felt as much akin to the greatest Spanish writer of them all, Cervantes, as a Castilian might.

For all that, his reputation was slow in coming. In Argentina, he was as well known from 1946 onwards for a vocal and uncompromising stance against the dictatorship of General Juan Perón as he was for having written *El jardín de senderos que se bifurcan* and *El Aleph* – Borges's two major books of stories from the 1940s.

He was probably even better known as a critic and writer of articles, as an associate of the great *littérateuse* of the day, Victoria Ocampo, and as a close friend of a writer who really was quite well-known in Argentina, Adolfo Bioy Casares.

Only when Borges began to be translated into French in the mid-1940s was the way cleared for his future European renown. When he shared the Formentor Prize with Samuel Beckett in 1961 for *Ficciones*, first published in 1944 in Buenos Aires and containing all the stories of *El jardín* along with six new ones, Borges's hour finally came (Beckett's had come nearly a decade before with *Waiting for Godot*). Borges was soon to be transported into the Anglo-Saxon world – the USA most especially – on the back of a curious book called *Labyrinths*, which Borges had not actually put together.

The oddest thing about *Labyrinths* is that the two stories he had written with the word 'labyrinth' in their titles were left out.* Twenty-three others, culled from the original Spanish editions of the stories, were included, along with a selection of short prose pieces, giving a flavour of Borges the essayist.

The idea on which *Labyrinths* was based was taken from a book originally compiled and published by Roger Caillois in France in 1953, though the French *Labyrinthes* was quite different from the English collection in that it contained just four stories.† *Labyrinths'*

---

* 'Abenjacan el Bojarí, muerto en su laberinto' ('Ibn Hakkan al-Bokhari, Dead in His Labyrinth') and 'Los dos reyes y los dos laberintos' ('The Two Kings and Their Two Labyrinths'): both texts were first collected in the second Spanish edition of *El Aleph* (1952), and eventually, in English, in a 1971 Cape edition, entitled *The Aleph and Other Stories*. (See A Note on Texts Used, p. 279.)

† Caillois had first taken on translations of Borges, officially, in 1944, publishing French versions, by Néstor Ibarra, of the stories 'The Lottery in Babylon' and 'The Library of Babel' in his magazine *Lettres françaises*, which he ran in exile in Buenos Aires. The first *ever* appearance of a piece by Borges in French was in fact on 15 April 1939, in a journal called *Mesures*; entitled 'L'approche du caché', the translation was again the work of Ibarra.

appearance in English translation in 1962 (following hard on the English-language *Ficciones*, published in the same year in honour of Borges's winning of the Formentor Prize) was the first important publishing event in Borges's life outside Argentina: the book sold consistently well (unlike *Ficciones*) and he began to be read on both sides of the Atlantic in the world's most widely spoken language. Even though it was only a miscellany of Borges, and as such unrepresentative of his work over forty years, *Labyrinths* became the touchstone of Latin American literature in the 1960s. It became fashionable, and the leading text in a school soon to be called 'Magic Realism'.

This term had been coined by Franz Roh in 1924 to describe the German paintings of the 'Neue Sachlichkeit' – New Objectivity.[2] The Cuban writer Alejo Carpentier then appropriated it in the late-1940s, calling it '*lo real maravilloso*'. He applied it to the strange writings of a number of Latin Americans; their fiction mirrored the turbulent and fantastic history of their continent. For Europeans, it seemed to break the boundaries of narrative realism, heralding a new vision of reality.

Borges was certainly strange, fantastic and new. He was also Argentine, and Carpentier's term was later swept up for international consumption; Magic Realism, a sort of campus shorthand, soon became a trendy genre, and Borges had always defied genres, and always will – and would not have known how to be trendy. When García Márquez's *One Hundred Years of Solitude* was published in 1967, Magic Realism had found its true exemplar. Here was a writer of tropical sensuality, of wild imaginative reach, of Caribbean celebration; his lush style and abundant fictional sleights-of-hand fully answered Carpentier's suggestion of exuberant anti-naturalism.*

Borges stands out, and chronologically ahead of Magic Realism, both because of his Argentineness, and the singularity of his innovations. He was acclaimed throughout the 1970s as Magic Realism's founding father, but this was to obfuscate his real importance: as a decidedly *Argentine* writer who had produced an austere new literature out of multiple traditions.

---

* The Colombian novelist in fact shares more in his carnival attitude towards fiction with the Bahian Jorge Amado than with anything Borges wrote; Brazil and the northern countries of South America share a cultural rapport which is lacking in their relationships with Argentina.

He was as steeped in the poetry of his Argentine predecessors, gaucho traditions and *porteño* slang as he was in the stories of Henry James and the novels of Franz Kafka. He admired the prose style of the Mexican humanist Alfonso Reyes as much as he did the thought of Schopenhauer. Of his Spanish, the Peruvian novelist Mario Vargas Llosa has said:

> Borges's prose is an anomaly, for in opting for the strictest frugality he deeply disobeys the Spanish language's natural tendency towards excess. To say that with Borges, Spanish became intelligent may appear offensive to other writers of the language, but it is not ... in Borges there is always a logical, conceptual level to which all else is subservient. His is a world of clear, pure, and at the same time unusual ideas that, while never relegated to a lower plane, are expressed in words of great directness and restraint.[3]

This hardly sounds like a formula for Magic Realism. In fact, it describes exactly one of Borges's main virtues: his ability to create extraordinary universes with a furtive, almost cheeky economy of style. His narratives exhibit a desire to divest language of literary sumptuousness; Borges's magic avoids tricks and elevates the literary-critical joke to new heights. And he created his universes not in steamy equatorial climes – and with barely a nod towards Paris – but in monkish, often sleepless solitude in a politically darkened Buenos Aires.

Borges the Argentine was a self-consciously modern yet for most of his life deeply unselfconfident writer, whom the world discovered before his countrymen did – and you could almost say before he did. He always held his work, his stories above all, in low esteem. Yet his ludic brilliance came as a salve for cultures – France, Britain, the United States – where Modernism had run its course and left their literatures dry.

Borges fed into, and was inspired by, a bewildering number of literatures. English was the language he considered literature best in, poetry above all. Paradoxically, he first read Cervantes in English translation. As a boy, it was English writers, not all of them considered major – Robert Louis Stevenson, Lewis Carroll, H. G. Wells – who made a decisive impact on him.

Throughout his life, particularly when he went blind, it was Rudyard Kipling and Gerard Manley Hopkins he would like to have read to him. Because of his education in Geneva, he was taught in French; German he taught himself, by reading Heinrich Heine. In his late fifties, as he was going blind, he embarked upon a most unusual act of auto-didacticism by teaching himself Anglo-Saxon – which in turn led him to Old Norse.

If this makes Borges sound like fussy campus material – all pens in the pocket, folders flying and leather elbow-patches – nothing could be more misleading. He was introspective, and perhaps wilfully lonely in his years of struggle as a writer in the 1930s and 1940s, but you wouldn't expect the creator of Funes the Memorious or the Aleph to be a Hemingwayesque man of action or Lawrentian Lothario.

Borges's arrival on the North American campuses in the early 1960s gave him a new, public identity. He became global property. When John Updike published an essay about him in *The New Yorker* in 1965, it was to announce Borges as a kind of literary El Dorado. 'The belated North American acknowledgement of the genius of Jorge Luis Borges proceeds apace,' Updike began. Against the 'dead-end narcissism and downright trashiness of present American fiction,' he wrote, Borges offered in his work 'intelligence less rare in philosophy and physics than in fiction'. Moreover, he was 'delightfully entertaining'.[4]

Borgesian gold-diggers and critical frontiersmen quickly proliferated; Borges was adopted as a quasi-North American author in the country most capable of absorbing the new and the strange. Little matter that Buenos Aires was a hemisphere, and multiple cultures, to the *south*; at least it was still '*American*'!

The adulation finally rubbed off back home. In the late 1960s, Argentines began for the first time in his career to sing plaudits to Borges, even if they didn't read him. His international standing was a source of great pride to a country whose literary output had, until Borges, been studiously provincial. Borges gave Argentina a firm place in the Latin American boom.

Apart from Che Guevara, and Juan Perón, whom Borges loathed, this blind *porteño* remains the most famous twentieth-century Argentine. The fact that Borges was famous in Britain, the USA and France long before Argentina took much notice of him says a lot about Argentina as it then was. For just as Borges was being circulated in French, Perón was doing enough damage to his country – from 1946 to 1955, to be precise – to last the rest of Borges's lifetime. It became a wretchedly philistine place.

Borges, the epitome of *lettré* civilisation, was to have a contro-versial relationship with his nation's governments until his death; his dying only a few years after Argentina's political fortunes began to improve, for the first time in over half a century, was perhaps more his country's loss than his own. More pointedly, he chose to die not there but in Geneva.

Borges was no conventional patriot; nor was he exactly a democrat. He was a bibliophile, a lover of foreign tongues and philosophical paradox, an intellectual of world class who effortlessly transcended origins he never repudiated. He loved the outside world looking in on him, partly because in practice he couldn't see it. In his later years, he made himself unpopular with the political left because his professed conservatism lay uneasily with Argentina's murderous regime of the 1970s and early 1980s. He certainly did himself no favours by welcoming the arrival of the military in 1976, which was really his way of saying a final farewell to Peronism. What the left later failed to notice was that Borges could see little of the mayhem – oppression, torture, bodies – the generals brought with them either.

That Borges refused, in the eyes of politicised anti-Borgesians, to speak out against the generals in the way they feel he should have is still a sore point. It has long been fashionable to vilify him for being right-wing. Such people may still boycott his fiction, or talk his reputation down; it may also be convenient for them to overlook a statement he made on 28 April 1980 to the Madrid correspondent of the Buenos Aires daily, *La Prensa*: 'I cannot ignore the serious moral problem created in the country by terrorism and repression. I cannot remain silent in the face of so many deaths, so many disappearances.'[5]

A month later, a further anti-government statement followed: 'On this government, I have no influence. This is a nationalist government, and I am not. They are Catholic, and I am not even sure that I am a Christian; and if I were, I would not be a Catholic. I have no posts. I am a free man.'[6]

Borges would not be drawn; he might have said too little too late, but he was also too free a spirit, and too changeable in his reactions to the moment, politically, for the simplistic verities of ideological conviction. We won't learn much about Borges by examining his politics, except that he liked to confound and annoy.

Borges's attitude towards Peronism is, by contrast, a means of understanding aspects of both the writer and his country. There will be plenty to say about this in the context of Borges the public figure. The private man, however, was an odder, more elusive, sometimes more quixotic, occasionally sadder individual than has hitherto been admitted in most official accounts of his life.

Borges was always in love. His feelings were rarely if ever reciprocated, and this caused him pain throughout his life. It was not pain he spoke about, and he wasn't good at talking about love. There is little of it, either, in his work. It wasn't his métier, though it was in his temperament.

Borges resembles here most closely those eighteenth-century men of Sensibility – such as one of his favourites, Samuel Johnson – whose learning and intellectual ebullience, and the rigour of their professional writing lives, somehow weighed heavily against their success in love. Melancholy is endemic in Johnson; so it is, perhaps better concealed, in Borges – particularly his poetry. Many women were attracted to him, intellectually; few, if any, wanted to go to bed with him. And however much Borges may have wanted to go to bed with them, the chances are that he had absolutely no idea how to go about it.

He was born in the dying years of the Victorian era, and often referred to himself as '*un ser victoriano*', a Victorian person. He loved women's company and, in later years when he couldn't see them, their voices; but he was shy. He was also steadfastly protected from the permissiveness that began – with as much energy in Buenos Aires as in Paris or London – in the 1920s. His mother, Leonor Acevedo, played an unusually important role in his life; one of the more eccentric aspects of Borges – and there were many – was that even as a man of sixty and seventy, he was living with and being tended to by his mother.

She was of *criollo* descent, proud of 'warrior antecedents', who lived until the age of ninety-nine. For only one period of her life, during her son's three disastrous years of marriage in the late 1960s, was she separated from Borges; when the marriage was over, he returned to the maternal fold until Leonor's death five years later. This was how Borges chose, or, because of his condition as a blind writer, had to live. There was, disappointingly, nothing Oedipal in it. Nor is there anything to suggest his mother cramped his style; there was little style to cramp. He lived quietly, without great riches, had no extravagant habits – he neither drank nor smoked – and he did more or less what he wanted.

More important than any psychological burden Leonor might have imposed were the services she provided. She had been accustomed to dealing with a blind man from early in the century; her husband Jorge Guillermo Borges had inherited a condition which led to detached retinas, from his English mother, Fanny Haslam. Leonor therefore had had to cope with a husband who increasingly was unable to work and support his family. It was second nature for her to look after a son whose unworldliness, comparable to her husband's, required her to be bank manager, amanuensis, agent and eyes rolled into one.

Leonor was, of course, a foil for Borges too. His ineptitude in relations with women could take refuge behind a domestic structure that no one had the impropriety to break. This was later bolstered by his international status as intellectual guru, keeping the hounds more or less at bay.

After his mother's death, Borges became almost public property. People hoped, quite nakedly, to feed off his mind. Borges possessed one of the most formidable literary intelligences of the twentieth century. Lionisation of it in the 1960s turned in the 1970s to tacit squabbles over ownership.

The list of camp followers, men and women, beating an 'exclusive' path to the flat in calle Maipú was long. Many succeeded in prizing 'conversations' or 'dialogues' out of him, which were invariably turned to journalistic or literary profit; Borges was one of the most interviewed writers in history. His promiscuity in front of a tape-recorder or notebook was legendary but ambiguous: on the one hand, he rarely deviated from a proven formula – wit, word-play, favourite authors, lament for Argentina, all subtly modified to provide one interlocutor after another with the same material; on the other hand, Borges's talk was a way out of blindness, and – crucially – another form of writing.

Blindness came not as a shock to Borges but as an inevitability.

It was in the family. He had always had bad eyesight, and expected the worst. He accepted the condition stoically. As he told Richard Burgin in 1969:

> ... it might be said that there is a certain benefit in being unable to read, because you think that time flows in a different way. When I had my eyesight, then if I had to spend say half an hour without doing anything, I would go mad. Because I had to be reading. But now I can be alone for quite a long time ...
> I think I am able to live with a lack of occupation. I don't have to be talking to people or doing things ...[7]

The eloquent stillness of the seer, the resignation of the sage – and, when drawn, the unceasing chitchat of a master writer: the combination was an alluring one. Borges perfected his communicative techniques over many years of practice, relying on tremendous inner intellectual strength, and polishing an image with which he knew questioners and admirers alike would comply.

For Borges blindness was a shield. Behind it, he could nurture a persona the world avidly sought out and devoured. His astonishing memory – his chief asset in coping with blindness – and, generally, his privacy were left intact. Details of neither his sentimental life nor his friendships, with people such as the writer Manuel Peyrou and poet Carlos Mastronardi, are to be found in books of 'Conversations', for example; but Borges was both a sentimental and a sociable man, and when he wasn't alone – which was a lot – he gave plentiful evidence of these traits, the latter in particular, amongst those he knew best.

The journey from 'Georgie' to 'Borges' was a long one. Though he retained throughout his life his essential characteristics – conversational expansiveness, a wide circle of friends, sexual timidity, an unquenched thirst for learning – there were multiple Borgeses.

There were the adolescent European experimentalist, high on Walt Whitman and crafting derivative verses in Switzerland during the First World War; the pugnacious pamphleteer on behalf of Ultraism, a quasi-Expressionist movement in early 1920s Madrid; Borges the editor; Borges the poet; Borges the librarian, anti-Peronist, teacher and lecturer; Borges the political stirrer; Borges the conservative; and, of course, Borges the inventor of fantastic tales, the introverted fabulist who in mid-century gave the world tantalising, post-Modern fictions before post-Modernism was thought of. But he still somehow remains mysterious. Borges was incapable of promoting himself, and had no monetary ambitions whatsoever. He read, and wrote – in that order – because that was what he had always done, and always would do. Fame was a pleasant and occasionally bothersome by-product.

He never wrote autobiographically about the women he loved, though one of the most significant recipients of his affections, Estela Canto, did turn to the pen; her book, *Borges a contraluz* (Borges in Silhouette) (1989), has divided opinion amongst Borgesians. Some say that her depiction of Borges as little short of impotent is correct, others that his amorous difficulties should never have been written about at all. Whatever the case, the affair, conducted in the 1940s, was an emotional disaster from Borges's point of view.[8]

He was poor, too, for most of his life, and only began to make money from his North American lecture tours. These led in 1967 to the second most significant event in his 'Anglo-Saxon' publishing life: a meeting at Harvard with Norman Thomas di Giovanni.

Di Giovanni worked with Borges in Buenos Aires for five years. He became his first major translator into English, and tirelessly spread the Borges cause in the United States – from where work other than the overcited *Labyrinths* began to be known in England too: *Historia universal de la infamia* (*A Universal History of Infamy*), Borges's first book of half-stories published in 1935, *The Aleph and Other Stories* (including the 'Autobiographical Essay', which di Giovanni persuaded Borges to write in answer to public curiosity about his life), *El informe de Brodie* (*Doctor Brodie's Report*), *El libro de arena* (*The Book of Sand*), and *Selected Poems*, amongst other volumes.

Di Giovanni can be credited with getting Borges to write again. He appeared at a time when both age and renown had induced a certain sloth in Borges. He was writing poetry – dictating it, rather – but seemed to have lost the taste for the radical fictions which had made him so famous.

Translation was for both men a creative act, particularly given Borges's refined understanding of English, and this energy happily sparked off *Doctor Brodie's Report*. It was written, said Borges, because 'so many people were imitating me that I decided I should try and imitate myself'. Five years later came *The Book of Sand*, a collection which, compared to most of Borges's fiction, feels tired, as if it were borrowed Borges. It was his last book of stories.

For many years, as his comment on *Doctor Brodie's Report* implies, Borges lived and indeed worked through his reputation as 'Borges'. However bothersome it could be, fame was there to be enjoyed, and Borges enjoyed it graciously. To the last, he wrote poetry, and obstinately considered himself a poet, when everyone who wasn't an *aficionado* of Argentine literature but who loved Borges thought of him as a great storyteller.

His best stories, however, were written between 1938 and 1953. If I agree with John Sturrock's assessment of Borges's poetry, that it is 'thoughtful, tight-lipped, and perhaps a little dull',[9] it is because I, like many others, can neither resist nor escape the more powerful and lasting impact those stories made, and still make half a century later.

One of the aims of this book is to clarify the obscurity of the life Borges had lived up until that moment when, at around the age of forty, he altered forever the universe of fiction, and – as he might have put it – the fictions of the universe.

Part One

The Mirror

About my literary creed, I can assert what is expressed in a religious sense: it's mine in so far as I believe in it, and not because I've invented it. Truly, I think making such a postulation is universal, even in those who manage to contradict it.

This is what I postulate: all literature is, finally, autobiographical.

Borges in 1926
('Profesión de fe literaria', *El tamaño de mi esperanza*)

Chapter One

1899–1914

Quiet Days in Palermo

The country that Borges was born into in 1899 was new. Centuries of
Spanish rule in Argentina had ended only eighty-three years before,
with the Congress of Tucumán in 1816. The middle of the nineteenth
century was then riven by frontier and civil wars, in which members
of Borges's family on both sides had been engaged. Many made their
way, memorialised or transformed, into his poems and stories.

Manuel Isidoro Suárez, born in 1799 and the grandfather of
Borges's mother, Leonor Acevedo, was one of the greatest of his
warrior antecedents. He fought in most of the wars of independence
in the early 1800s – in Chile, Peru, Uruguay – and excelled under
Simón Bolívar. He was also associated with the Unitarians, those
who opposed the dictator Juan Manuel de Rosas and his Federalist
faction (in spite of the fact that Suárez was a second cousin of
Rosas's): this conflict and Rosas's reigns of terror until 1852 were
to mark mid-nineteenth-century Argentina rather as Perón and the
generals were to in the mid-twentieth.[1]

Suárez settled in Uruguay, marrying in 1834 a woman from a
local patrician family, called Jacinta Haedo. An immediate relative
of hers – Jorge Luis's great-great-uncle – was another military

man, Miguel Estanislao Soler, who had fought alongside the great Argentine liberator, General San Martín, and became governor of Buenos Aires in 1820. The Suarezes had a daughter, Leonor Suárez Haedo, born in 1837, who married a man named Isidoro de Acevedo Laprida, who himself took part in the wars against Rosas. Back in a more settled Buenos Aires, their daughter Leonor, Borges's mother, was born in 1876.

Acevedo Laprida was related to Francisco Narciso de Laprida, the man who had convened the 1816 congress of Tucumán, declaring the 'United Provinces of South America' free of Spain. He ended badly in 1829, being hunted down by Federalist gauchos (basically cowboys)[2] and killed. His body was never found.

About him, as about Suárez and Acevedo Laprida, Borges wrote famous poems, and recalled them frequently throughout his life.[3] His mother's line was thickly populated with military men, and something of their nature came out in Leonor's campaigning character.

His father's side was not lacking in similar figures: Borges's grandfather Francisco Borges Lafinur was at least as colourful as Suárez. Born in 1832 in Montevideo, Uruguay, he was already in the wars at the age of fifteen. He fought under a famous general, and later president, Justo José de Urquiza, at the Battle of Caseros (1852), which marked the final defeat of Rosas. Later he fought in Paraguay, and in frontier wars in the south and the west.

This full-blooded, martial Argentineness was mellowed by Lafinur's choice of wife: an English woman called Frances Haslam.

Born in 1842 in Staffordshire of Northumbrian stock, she came to be in Argentina because her elder sister Caroline had married, Borges tells us in his 1970 'Autobiographical Essay', 'an Italian-Jewish engineer named Jorge Suárez, who brought the first horse-drawn tramcars to Argentina, where he and his wife settled and sent for Fanny'.[4] Unfortunately, Suárez's business ventures failed completely; but Caroline was made of doughty stuff, and earned a living by teaching English. She became the model of the intrepid Madame Dubois in Borges's father's short novel, *El caudillo*, published in Mallorca in 1921.

The English women's father was a certain Edward Young Haslam, son of a Northumbrian Methodist priest and married to a Quaker called Jane Arnett. He had got a doctorate at the University of

Heidelberg, and later edited one of the first English journals published in Argentina, the *Southern Cross*. He was also distinguished for having appeared in the pages of the British medical journal *The Lancet*, as the recipient of an innovative operation performed on his eyes: his condition, unfortunately for his daughter, her son and then her grandson, was, like colour-blindness, heritable.

In Paraná in 1870, the capital of the province of Entre Ríos – where Haslam died eight years later – Fanny met Francisco Borges, now a colonel in the army, heading a regiment charged with putting down a gaucho insurrection. Borges rather fancifully has Fanny seeing him on horseback from the 'flat roof of her house' defending Paraná with his soldiers, and both falling in love at a ball that same night. They married a year later, celebrating the wedding in Caroline's house in Paraná.

The young couple were very happy, and had two boys: Francisco, who followed his father into the military, and Borges's father, Jorge Guillermo Borges, who was born in 1874. But the marriage was cut short. Francisco Senior got entangled in late 1874 in a byzantine political plot hatched between the then president, Domingo Sarmiento, and General Bartolomé Mitre. During the latter's failed military uprising, Colonel Borges, at the end of his tether, rode on his horse at the battle of La Verde towards the enemy lines, arms across his chest, and was hit by two bullets. They were fired, notes his grandson, by a Remington rifle. It was the first time such a weapon had been used in Argentina. The colonel died two days later, his last words being: 'I have fallen in the belief of having fulfilled my duty and my convictions, and for the same principles that I have fought all my life.'[5] His second son was just seven months old, his widow not yet thirty.*

This was Borges's ancestral mythology. The lives of these warrior grandfathers constituted the fabric of the evolution of Argentina. It was a raw and brutal world, and years later was to filter through into some of Borges's more dramatic and realistic stories. Yet because this world was more myth than fact, tales of derring-do passed on by his grandparents like an incantation, the young Borges's

---

* Resourceful, like her sister, Fanny soon offered board and lodging, in Buenos Aires, to young North American ladies who had arrived in Argentina to teach English.

fictive imagination was amply fired. He was, early, led away from concrete history towards the taller, more abstract stories for which he became so famous. Of his forebears, he added in the 'Essay', 'this may account for my yearning after that epic destiny which my gods denied me, no doubt wisely'.[6]

As for his literary formation, the counterbalance to the highly coloured heroism of the Suarezes and Lapridas and Borgeses, it was in fact the Haslam line, passing through his father, that was to have the most decisive bearing on the young Jorge Francisco Isidoro Luis Borges Acevedo.

The first three names corresponded to those of his father and grandfathers, the fourth to a Uruguayan uncle, a diplomat called Luis Melián Lafinur. The writer was born on 24 August 1899, at calle Tucumán 840, a month premature. But Georgie, as he was quickly called, grew to be as healthy a baby as he was to be throughout his adulthood, markedly free from illness or disease – barring a near-fatal accident in 1938 and the terrible eyesight inherited from his father.

The house in calle Tucumán was small, flat-roofed, in the middle of Buenos Aires. Jorge and Leonor, who had married in 1898 – five years after meeting – were, as was quite common in those days, still living with the bride's parents (Leonor had been born in their house). The newly-weds were not rich, but they were not that poor either.

Jorge had qualified as a lawyer in 1895. Though bright and successful, he was not earning enough to buy a house in the same part of town as the Acevedos. Isidoro Acevedo was already infirm, having retired from the military years before. He was to die in 1905, Borges claiming thereafter to have known very little about him, though he remembered his death, and some details of his life, in a poem dedicated to Isidoro: 'I was a boy, who knew nothing then of dying; I was immortal, / and afterward for days I searched the sunless rooms for him', the poem ends.[7]

Leonor became pregnant again a year after Georgie's birth, and a daughter, Norah, was born on 4 March 1901. Moving somewhere bigger had become imperative; the calle Tucumán house had only two bedrooms. Before Norah's birth, Leonor Suárez helped the young family buy a house at calle Serrano 2135/47, in a relatively obscure suburb called Palermo. It was here that Borges's life, and his memory, began.

Had his father been older or further advanced in his career, the family could no doubt have moved to somewhere more fashionable. Palermo was not that, but it was cheap. It was also rough, a neighbourhood notorious for gangsters, knife-fighters and tango dancers (at this point in its history, the tango was still considered low-class and libidinous: it was the music of the brothels). Palermo was, in a word that Borges was to use frequently in his early essays and to which he was to attach such poetic suggestiveness, an *arrabal*, a slum.

Except it wasn't quite that either, not, at any rate, as Borges explained in the 'Autobiographical Essay', 'in the American sense of the word. In Palermo lived shabby, genteel people as well as more undesirable sorts. There was also a Palermo of hoodlums, called *compadritos*, famed for their knife fights . . .'.[8]

Palermo was where Buenos Aires ended, an equivalent of Paris's Montmartre at the same period. There was nothing special or notably dangerous about it. Downtown *porteños* would know straightaway if you tried to disguise your residence in Palermo by talking of the 'Northside'. The Palermo Borges later became interested in was of a much earlier period, the mid- to late-nineteenth century, when it was colonised by Italian immigrants, and really was a hive of fighting and dancing.* He wrote about it in his first full-length prose-work, *Evaristo Carriego*, published when the author was thirty-one and steeped in the vivid mythology of his home city: a past rather than a contemporary Palermo was always a prominent leitmotif in Borges's evocations of Buenos Aires.

The house the family moved to was one of the few two-storey buildings in the street. It was large, old, with spacious rooms, two patios, a balustraded terrace overlooking a garden containing a hawthorn bush and a red windmill which squeaked when water was drawn from it. The family was a tight unit, rarely venturing out of their own domain; social life was confined behind closed doors, climaxing every fortnight when friends would be invited for tea between five and eight o'clock.

Elsewhere in the street the houses were single-storey, without

---

* It was named not after the Sicilian capital, but after Juan Domínguez de Palermo, who had an estate there in the early sixteenth century. The estate was eventually taken over by Rosas, and in 1875 it became a park.

garden or their own supply of water. The locals were uncultured, not quite of the same class as the Borgeses, and mainly of Italian extraction – 'shabby genteel'. Neither Italian nor Spanish forebears were considered signs of cultivation in Argentina at the time; it was far classier to be of French or English origin, and the Borgeses of course scored well in the latter pedigree.

Englishness explains much of the oddity of Borges's early life. He grew up fluent in both English and Spanish, but Jorge's propensity for things English in general, and English literature in particular – Arnold Bennett, George Bernard Shaw, H. G. Wells – were the abiding cultural impulses for his son from the start. Georgie's first spoken language was English. And it was Fanny, after all, who was a daily presence; Colonel Francisco was already family legend.

Leonor, on the other hand, was neither a linguist nor intellectual. She was a stylish dresser, as photographs of her at this period show: all long skirts and wide hats. One of Borges's friends decribes her as a 'nineteenth-century beauty, an absolute belle of the *belle époque*. As the years went by, she simply became more and more modern, with short skirts and wonderful French perfume. The development of society at this time could be represented through her changes.'[9]

In later years Borges was generally proud of his mother, and deferential to the memory of her ancestors. However, in one unguarded moment, during a 1967 interview with Jean de Milleret, he said: 'The Acevedos are incredibly ignorant' and later added, talking of his parents' relationship, 'It was my father who had an influence on her and not the reverse. My mother was a young woman of a good Argentine family and my father was a liberal and cultivated man: his mother was English and a protestant; he had a good library at home. I must say that he lived, intellectually speaking, in a more complex world than my mother.'[10]

This was Borges fondly remembering his father, already thirty years dead. It was not quite accurate of him to paint a picture of his father's 'influencing' his mother: Leonor may have been intellectually less well-endowed than Jorge and, of course, she was receptive to his reading and ideas. She certainly learned her English through him, though not well until the late 1920s. There is no doubt Jorge knew more and was better educated – quite normal for a late-Victorian couple, and in a country which would place only belated credence in women's education (women won the vote in 1947, one of the few great reforms passed by Perón). But the clear impression from most of what Borges said about his early life (and it wasn't that much), and indeed from what he *didn't* say, was that Leonor was in charge, at home and in every practical matter.

Her background was Catholic, solidly middle-class, deeply Argentine. Her world view was that of a conventional Latin woman – with entrenched certainties about the importance of family, womanhood, and sartorial appearance – and she became a conventional Latin mother, imbuing her son with filial attitudes appropriate to their culture: loyalty to the point of deification, an irresistible tendency to 'put Mother first'. As another of Borges's many female friends put it to me when talking about his relationship with Leonor: 'A characteristic of Argentine males is to hide behind the desires of the mother.'[11] Borges was no exception. In later years, he perfected this disappearing act to serve his purposes more than adequately; Leonor was always a force to be reckoned with when it came to Georgie's best interests.

Jorge's culture stood in stark contrast to his wife's, and perhaps explains why they remained so interested in each other – and why their brainy son was soon to exhibit such easy multiculturalism. The religious atmosphere in the household was predominantly Catholic, with Leonor a worshipper and Jorge, though nominally Protestant, defiantly agnostic.

There may have been Jewishness, too – from the old-world strain, pre-nineteenth-century immigrant. When Borges first visited Portugal, he looked up his two family names in the telephone directory. He found that 'those who were not Borges were Ramalho or Acevedo!'[12] 'Borges' was indeed Portuguese in origin: Jorge Luis's great-grandfather, Francisco de Borges – the colonel's father – was born in Portugal in 1782. The name had long had Jewish associations; Acevedo, which might have been Jewish too, was derived from Pedro Pascual de Acevedo, a Catalan merchant who came to Argentina in 1728.

Thus the ancestry was colonial, mercantile, non-aristocratic: quintessentially New World. As Borges wrote in 1934, when anti-Semitism in Argentina was rearing its head, 'Our inquisitors are seeking Hebrews, never Phoenicians, Numidians, Scythians, Babylonians, Huns, Vandals, Ostrogoths, Ethiopians, Illyrians, Paphlagonians, Sarmatians, Medes, Ottomans, Berbers, Britons,

Lybians, Cyclops, and Lapiths.'[13] To counter the anti-Semite bug, Borges deployed encyclopaedic facetiousness – a favourite ruse.

Jorge was a good man, but not a steady one. He worked hard as a solicitor at the Tribunales, and he liked women; though not exactly a philanderer, he set no great store by marital fidelity. He was also, contradictorily, a frustrated intellectual. He supplemented these needs by teaching psychology, a subject that had always interested him, in English at the Institute of Living Languages. But it was Leonor's 'Argentineness' in a household of Anglophile intellectuals and dreamy artists that sustained them. When it became clear her husband was going blind and could no longer work, that her son was impractical and her daughter even more so, she would need every fighting instinct she could muster.

The two young children were well cared for. The house in calle Serrano was a sanctuary from the teeming life outside (it no longer exists). Fanny Haslam was always at hand, and was family first-storyteller. Borges remembered in later life that one of the first books she introduced him to was the Presbyterian Bible. In 1903, meanwhile, an English governess, Miss Tink, was hired to help around the house, and to perfect Georgie and Norah's English. She did not live with the family, but came to calle Serrano in the afternoons; Georgie adored her, and listened to her lessons with his arms round her neck.[14]

Another curious aspect of Borges's childhood was that he didn't go to school until he was nine. One reason was to avoid putting him in contact with contagious diseases, such as consumption. At home, Miss Tink was clearly an important surrogate teacher, along with his grandmother, but Borges had nothing to say about Miss Tink in later years. The first mention of her comes in Alicia Jurado's 1964 biography of him, and she had found out about her from Leonor.

About his delayed schooling, Borges was more forthcoming: '. . . my father, as an anarchist, distrusted all enterprises run by the State'[15] – a bald statement of fact; Borges senior, as an agnostic, also objected to the idea of his children being indoctrinated with the state religion. Jorge's political and religious individualism remained consistent throughout his life. Democracy was fledgling in Argentina at the time: politics was a matter of connections, your region, your tribe – and though the Unitarian-Federalist dichotomy had been politically resolved, it would not have been emotionally flushed out. It was more sophisticated not to pin one's ideals to local politics, but to underline one's individuality by being as European as possible. To some extent, the same is true in Argentina today.

Jorge's anarchism, derived from the evolutionary theories of the English writer Herbert Spencer, was complemented by his literary appetite. He passed both tendencies on to his son, who luckily took to literature first. (Borges's own 'anarchism' would be one of the marks of his politically conservative old age.) The Palermo house library was a much richer education for the pre-scholastic Borges than any school could have been. It was here that he had his first taste of books, the objects with which Borges was to develop his most intimate relationships. 'I have always come to things after coming to books,' he said in 1970.[16] Throughout his life, he was fond of listing his favourite authors, and it is impossible to overestimate the influence his father's library had over him.

In a separate room in the Palermo house, the books stacked on shelves behind glass, the library was full of English literature. He and Norah had been read to in English from an early age, by both Fanny and Miss Tink, and as soon as the young Georgie could read for himself – at around the age of four – he was attacking the library.

The first novel he read, he said, was *Huckleberry Finn*. Then followed Captain Marryat, H. G. Wells, Edgar Allan Poe, Longfellow, the Brothers Grimm, Robert Louis Stevenson, Dickens, Cervantes – in English – Lewis Carroll, and *A Thousand Nights and a Night*, in Richard Burton's translation.

Borges refers to the so-called 'obscenity' of the latter in his 'Essay' and therefore having to read it 'hiding up on the roof';[17] Emir Rodríguez Monegal, keen to find evidence of early sexual awakening, also makes much of the 'erotic significance' of the illustrations, and Burton's 'explicit notes, which never tired of discussing some of the most fashionable perversions of the Near East'.[18] Borges, whose visual imagination was always superseded by a verbal one, probably just did not remember the pictures or the perversions; even if he did, the eroticism *per se* did not rub off until very much later. Strangeness did. The effect of the stories – short, fantastic – and the spell of such splendid storytelling itself, appealed, just as did the endlessness, and timelessness, of *Don Quixote*.

More prohibited, and perhaps of even greater impact, was the epic *Martín Fierro* by the nineteenth-century poet-hero José Hernández (1834–86). This is a long narrative poem about a gaucho warrior, a kind of Tennysonian idyll in Castilian celebrating pampas* life. Hernández became the national poet of Argentina, and cast a long shadow across any Argentine poet keen to keep to Hernández's gauchesco idiom and working in the 1920s – Borges's first poetic era. He includes *Martín Fierro* in a number of books in Spanish he read in his father's library – books about outlaws and gauchos – as well as Domingo Sarmiento's *Facundo*.[19] Leonor prohibited Hernández because he had defended Rosas in the Unitarian-Federalist wars, and was therefore an affront to everything her ancestors had fought for. So the young Georgie read him 'on the sly'.[20] He couldn't have become an Argentine writer without doing so.

Other writers he tucked into were Dumas, George Moore, Jack London, Kipling and, amongst the English poets, Shelley, Keats and Swinburne, whose work Jorge could recite by heart. It is impossible to know with what depth Borges read all these: judging by the way he recollected them throughout his life, everything did sink in – perhaps unconsciously. Even to become familiar with such a wide range of names (to say nothing of individual books) was a remarkable achievement for a boy. In 1969, he said that it was *Huckleberry Finn* and 'the *Quixote*' that stayed closest to him into old age.[21]

Georgie's lexical precociousness was his way of learning, of responding to the bookish overtures of Fanny, Miss Tink and his father. It was a crucial part of his primary education, though eccentric in so far as he was pitched in at so indiscriminate a level.

There were reference books too: the *Encyclopaedia Britannica* and *Chambers*. Much of Borges's later learning was gleaned from such books, and his mature prose often parodied the style of a dictionary entry. Alicia Jurado, Borges's first biographer, reports that his childish awareness of dictionaries produced an amusing compound word: Fanny used to read to Georgie from the bound volume of issues of an English magazine, which became known as the '*leccionario*' – a cross between '*diccionario*' (dictionary) and '*lección*' (lesson).[22] In an unformed but agile verbal mind, Borges was already inventing conceptual puns.

---

* Pampa means plain; see p.23.

What was all this reading leading to? Science and maths were apparently ignored, classics were reached only through accounts of the great myths, and history was family mythology. Borges's training at this stage was a paternal imposition; he was to say in later years that his father's library was the 'chief event' of his life, which was true as far his literature was concerned – and Borges came to believe that life, his life, was literature. Other 'events' – love and politics, for example – were always subordinated: it was his way of dealing with the profound impracticality induced, at a very early stage, by such single-minded dedication to the imagination.[23]

Books were Borges's touchstone for reality, how he interpreted the world; reading was his first skill, his chief inheritance, and the foundation of a scattershot education. To set such store by his father's library was Borges's assertion of an identity others might have defined by race, creed or gender.

Another discovery, another reality, of childhood is, of course, one's own face. Looking into a mirror in a bathroom or parents' bedroom is visual evidence of one's physical existence – the ocular proof. For Borges, this bodily reflection was from an early age a source of acute discomfort. It became a phobia; when mirrors lost their infantile terrors they became emblems in his universe of the other, of the double, of what could happen on the other side of reality.

To Richard Burgin in 1967, Borges confessed to 'being afraid of being repeated' as a child – a curious obsession with the vertiginous experience of self-multiplication in a mirror.[24] Borges hated it, just as he was later to hate the idea of being taken out of his self – whether through drugs, drink, or sex. Borges's greatest fear, of a loss of self-possession, began with this most unorthodox shying away from physiognomic reproduction. Both in his life and in his writings, he exhibited something unusual in a twentieth-century artist: a principle of anti-narcissism. Its roots were in the Palermo home.

'I was always afraid of mirrors,' Borges said in 1971. 'I had three large mirrors in my room when I was a boy and I felt very acutely afraid of them, because I saw myself in the dim light – I saw myself thrice over, and I was very afraid of the thought that perhaps the three shapes would begin moving by themselves . . . I have always been afraid . . . of mahogany, of crystals, even of limpid water.'[25]

* * *

Calle Serrano was a liberal household. What discipline there was came from Fanny, who, with Miss Tink to help, occupied herself with the two children. Grandmotherly discipline tends to be remembered with greater affection than parental – it is significant that Borges remembered little if anything about his mother or father's scolding of him as a child. He was quite an obstinate little boy, and Leonor remembered, even if he didn't, how difficult he could be at the zoo.

Opened in 1892, this was close by and is still a prominent, if run-down, feature in Palermo today. To go there with mother was a treat for the two Borges children; in those days, it was a superb zoo. It smelt, Borges later wrote, 'of candy and tigers'.[26] Georgie loved tigers, and drew them at home incessantly. Locking on to them, spellbound, when he was out with his sister and mother, he would refuse to leave. He could get, as Leonor recalled, alarmingly fierce when told to go. If he carried on refusing, Leonor would confiscate his books: the perfect punishment for a burgeoning bibliophile.

On another occasion, Georgie had to be locked in his room he got so cross about leaving the zoo – too soon, in his opinion. If he admitted that he hadn't meant to react so, he would be let off. He insisted that he *had* meant it, underlining his defiance with a Spanish pun: '*lo hice* con *querer*' – I did it *meaning* to do so (the usual Spanish expression is with *sin* – without – i.e. not meaning to do so). From the start, words were his sliest weapon.

Generally, however, Borges inherited his father's kindness of spirit, and his mother's powers of concentration. 'Lying down on his stomach on the floor . . .' Leonor recalled in 1964, 'he would draw tigers . . . he moved to prehistoric animals, about which for two years he read all he could get hold of.'[27] He also played happily with Norah in the garden, which, along with the library, was magical terrain.

There was the red windmill, and a palm tree; under it, Georgie and his sister acted out their games, playing with two imaginary companions, Quilos and The Windmill. These phantoms were invented in the place of friends – there was a singular lack of them for the Borges children, caused largely by their not going to school. 'When they finally bored us,' Borges said of these two playmates in 1970, 'we told our mother that they had died.'[28]

Norah was a lively girl, less sedentary than Georgie, and she played the dominant role in their fairy-tale games: she was the queen, he the prince, following her whims or instructions. They were an inventive pair: Alicia Jurado has a particularly charming image of their travelling 'to the moon in a missile built by folding a red silk Chinese screen, embroidered with golden birds and flowers, into which they tumbled after sliding down the banister of the staircase'.[29]

Summer months – December to March – which can become unbearably hot in Buenos Aires, were spent on the other side of the Río de la Plata – the River Plate. This is the vast, slow, muddy river whose southern bank contains the port of Buenos Aires; various suburbs then look over it up to the delta at Tigre. The northern bank is the beginning of Uruguay. Its capital Montevideo, older, more run-down than Argentina's, was a day's ferry journey from Buenos Aires.

Francisco Haedo was a cousin of Leonor's. He lived with his family in the Villa Esther, in a place called Paso Molino, part of outer Montevideo. The Haedos' daughter, Esther, became a good friend of Georgie and Norah, and was the one child who participated in their flights of fancy, including the foundation of a secret society called The Three Crosses. The cousins remained close well into adulthood.

Jorge was freed for the summer holidays from the Tribunales every February. The family passed the vacation in long, lazy days in the garden of the Haedos' villa, or on the nearby beach of Capurro. In the river, Georgie learnt to swim – perhaps the most important thing he learnt in childhood after reading. Swimming was the only physical activity he had any propensity for, and he was good at it: strong, fearless, coordinated.

Another summer destination was Adrogué, a town to the south of Buenos Aires. Today, it has been engulfed by the city and little of it remains as it was in Borges's childhood. The family first rented a house with a red-tiled roof in an open square, where the smell of eucalyptus was pervasive, and later stayed in a hotel called Las Delicias. It was a neo-classical building, fronted by a portico with columns, adorned, in the niches, with carvings of semi-naked nymphs. 'Wherever I am in the world,' Borges said in 1969, 'all I need is the smell of eucalyptus to recover that lost world of Adrogué, which today no doubt exists only in my memory.'[30]

He was right. The hotel was demolished in the 1950s, but Borges had by then incorporated it, and aspects of the Haedo villa too, into various stories: 'Tlön, Uqbar, Orbis Tertius', 'The Shape of the Sword', 'The Immortal', and most memorably in 'Death and the Compass', where the Adrogué hotel becomes Triste-le-Roy, the setting for the tale's chilling denouement.

In 1908, the idyll was shattered. At the end of March, Georgie was sent to school. It was a state school in a neighbouring street, calle Thames – named not after the English river but an Argentine general of the previous century. The school was one of the type founded in the late nineteenth century as a result of Domingo Sarmiento's cosmopolitan passion for the educational systems of the United States and France – representative of a desire to get away from the primitive nationalism which was Rosas's legacy. If Jorge Borges had provided an eccentric education for his son thus far, it was as nothing compared to what Georgie now faced.

The school, far from being a civilised extension to the cultured atmosphere of calle Serrano, was full of tough Palermo boys; they took one look at this soft-faced, bespectacled, stammering boy in ridiculous clothing – an Eton collar and tie – and knew they had a victim. He was bullied mercilessly, and must have felt as if he had been actively thrown from the Borges sanctuary into the hostile streets it had for so long protected him from.

Jorge's overweening influence can be seen here. Sending Georgie to school dressed like an Eton boy was his most ill-considered decision with regard to his son: this was Europeanism – a very high-class image of it – taken too far. Pupils of Georgie's age at the calle Thames school would not have known where Europe, let alone England, was; yet here was a compatriot, or so they would have seen him, with nice manners and speaking a language – English – they had never heard, who arrived in their midst, and was immediately placed above them, in fourth grade. A boffin uninterested in sport or brawls, who wore glasses, read books and stammered, was not going to thrive.

He did not. There is no evidence that Borges learnt much from his Buenos Aires schooldays, other than some rudimentary lessons in survival, his first words of *lunfardo* – Buenos Aires slang – and certain facts about the heroes of the Argentine past: the liberator San Martín, General Manuel Belgrano, and Sarmiento himself.

Georgie's teacher, a Señor Agüero, noticed the short-sighted pupil's talent for writing, and reportedly said, 'The best essay is always his.'[31] He moved on to secondary school in 1912 and, according to Leonor, did have one friend who went with him – Roberto Godel, of French extraction, though nothing of him remained in Borges's adult memory, nor in any records.[32] This school, the Colegio Nacional Manuel Belgrano, was on avenida Santa Fe, near the junction with avenida Pueyrredón. Georgie completed just one year there.[33]

His real education continued at home. His father started discussing philosophy with him when Georgie was ten, he introduced him to chess, and presented little illustrations of mathematical theory, Zeno's paradox about the hare and the tortoise, and the problems of memory – how a recollection can only refer back to the last one, which has been drawn from a previous one, and so on: proof that memory was, in effect, non-existent, led to nothing, was a hall of mirrors. Georgie was already being inducted into the kind of epistemological scepticism that would lie behind so many of his great fictions.

Another side to his education came in the form of his father's friends. As he reached adolescence, Georgie had open contact with a succession of bohemian types who were to colour his imagination as much as his father's library. These were men who brought something of the rackety, proletarian flavour of Palermo into the Borges household: a human embodiment of the violent, promiscuous world Georgie and Norah were so sheltered from in their capsule of Victorian domesticity.

It was a world he depicted in his monograph to one of these friends, *Evaristo Carriego*, published in 1930. The first chapter of the book is the most ample description Borges ever devoted to his childhood environs: a place of slaughterhouses, late-night bars, muleteers and smugglers. Carriego, a minor popular poet, lived near the Borgeses, and came by most Sundays after the races to talk and share a glass or two with Jorge. He was a greater conversationalist than writer, and to that extent typified a certain self-educated, restless, literary dilettante that appealed to Borges Senior – he himself, though outwardly bourgeois, harboured aspirations to being the sort of free spirit the poet seemed to represent.

Carriego died of consumption in 1912, aged thirty, and he had such an important effect on Borges that at approximately the same age in the late 1920s, Borges attempted a biography of him. It was a text largely based on pre-adolescent memories. The book, though a failure as biography (it is closer to being a memoir), is a culmination of Borges's mythification of a Buenos Aires he never knew. But it was always a vital one to him. Borges introduces into the book a Palermo mentor of Carriego's, Nicolás Paredes, 'the true Argentine in all his glory'[34] – someone today we would call a mafioso – whom he knew; in old age, Borges used proudly to tell friends that he, Jorge Luis, was once 'the friend of a murderer'.[35]

Other rough-cut characters also passed by. There was Jorge's cousin Alvaro Melián Lafinur, a poet who became a member of the Argentine Academy of Letters – he was *au fait* with the tango and a frequenter of brothels, and avuncularly taught Georgie a thing or two; and there was John Tink, a real *compadrito* and a cousin of Miss Tink's; and Macedonio Fernández, a maverick café philosopher who had read law with Borges Senior. Georgie cultivated him when the Borgeses returned to Buenos Aires in 1921, and wrote adoringly of him in the 'Autobiographical Essay'. All these figures and images were to emerge in Borges's early writing maturity. Europe and a new intellectual horizon lay ahead. But what of even earlier scribblings?

Borges's mother said in 1967 that at the age of six he announced to his father that he wanted to be a writer. Borges corroborated this in 1970 when he said that he 'first started writing when [he] was six or seven'.[36] The first known jotting in fact dates from 1904, when he wrote out the words: 'Tiger, Lion, Papa, Leopard'.

Two years later, in what he called 'very clumsy English',[37] he filled a dozen pages of a notebook with jottings on Greek mythology – the Golden Fleece, Hercules, the Labyrinth – plagiarised probably from Lemprière's *Classical Dictionary* and which are now lost.

Also lost, and from around the same time, came a short play called 'La visera fatal' (The Fatal Helmet) – not a bad title for a boy who, years later, would turn the business of titles into an epigraphic art. It already sounds Borgesian. The piece, an attempted imitation of Cervantes, was written in 'old Spanish', according to Leonor, and was a few pages long.[38] According to Victoria Ocampo, it was rather in the style of a novel, *La gloria de don Ramiro*, by a popular writer of the day, Enrique Larreta, also a friend of Jorge's. Borges some years later wrote on the manuscript: 'Over-melodramatic and ridiculous effects. Too many crimes.'[39]

In 1909, Borges published his first work. It was a Spanish translation of Oscar Wilde's 'The Happy Prince'. Alvaro Lafinur found it so perfect that he arranged for it to appear in a Buenos Aires paper called *El País*, signed 'Jorge Borges'; friends of Jorge – *padre* – assumed it was his. For years, Leonor kept the cutting glued in a copy of her uncle Wenceslao Acevedo Laprida's doctoral thesis. Next to it was glued a manuscript of a story, signed 'Jorge Bores' (*sic*) and written by Jorge, called 'The Garden of the Golden Cupola'; Borges occasionally referred to it as 'The Golden Cupola' – but the word 'garden' probably stuck, too, for use over thirty years later in the title of his first major book of stories.

From 1912, finally, we have what Jean-Pierre Bernès calls Borges's 'first story without referential literary antecedents': 'El Rey de la selva' (The King of the Forest). It features, not surprisingly, a tiger, and his fight with a panther. As they fight, an arrow shoots into a nearby tree trunk. The tiger retires to his den. After a night's sleep, the tiger is shot with an arrow by a man in a blooded black coat. The story was signed 'Nemo', possibly after Jules Verne.[40]

It is a brief, assured, colourfully imagined anecdote, unsophisticated in subject matter but mature in style; above all, controlled. Control, at times an almost fanatical discipline, was the abiding feature of all of Borges's great prose.

By 1914, things were not so bright for the Borges family. Jorge was forty, theoretically in mid-career, but rapidly going blind. He had been forced to retire in 1911, aged thirty-seven, when he could not read the papers he was supposed to sign. His children's Argentine education was proving to be inadequate. Norah, gifted with pen and paper, was flighty; Georgie was under-achieving in class and needed stiffer academic discipline.*

A cure for Jorge's eye condition and an upgrade to European standards of learning remain the most obvious motives for the Borgeses emigration. For Leonor, it would have been a wrench – from friends and family, above all – but also an adventure; likewise for Leonor Suárez, Leonor's mother, who was to come with them

---

* One malicious interpretation of the Borges' sudden departure to Europe was that Georgie was also a compulsive masturbator, and that his parents wanted to sort that out too; there is no evidence to back this up.[41]

to help look after the children. For Jorge it was a necessity – he had found a doctor in Geneva to operate on his eyes – but also a late tasting of the gentleman's European Grand Tour, delayed since his graduation. Given the strength of the Argentine peso, which meant it would be cheaper to live in Switzerland than in Buenos Aires, there seemed no reason to delay any further. Fanny would join them later.

For the children, sailing to Europe was the apotheosis of their childhood trips through time and space. For Georgie, in particular, the European years were to be the catalyst for producing the writer he knew he would be from an early age; without Europe, he would have been both less Argentine, and less universal.

Chapter Two

1914–1921

Europe, and the
Fervour of Reading

୨୧

Argentina was wealthy in the early part of the century. Dairy and meat products were the heavy industry of the ranches, or *estancias*. Throughout the nineteenth century, the pampas, the great plains in the Argentine hinterland, had been successfully exploited by landowners – *estancieros* – so that the country's wheat, wool and above all refrigerated beef, generally to be transported across the Atlantic, were the most sought-after in the world.

The *estancieros* were from traditional Argentine families, often with upper-class French and English forebears. Their fortunes were specifically Argentine, as expressed in the might of the peso, then – perhaps surprisingly in the light of the notorious spirals of inflation in Argentina's post-Second World War economy – one of the strongest currencies on the globe; the habits and cultural inclinations of such Argentines, however, were European – which is why so many of them spent so much of their money in Europe, and took back with them Continental social mores and architectural configurations to give Buenos Aires an air of Paris or Milan.

The Borgeses were not abundantly rich, though Jorge had substantial savings, as well as a generous pension from the Tribunales; he and Leonor also received good rent from the letting of the calle Serrano house. On their voyage across the Atlantic in February 1914, their fellow passengers included the type of Argentine family which transported its favourite cows, in case the European species wasn't up to much. Jorge, however, was more concerned about his eyes than about his stomach. He was also, in keeping with his Spencerian and Shavian ideals, a vegetarian.

The family stopped briefly in England, where Georgie caught his first glimpse of what he later called London's 'red labyrinth',[1] as well as of Cambridge. They moved on to Paris (for which Borges had no great fondness[2]) – they spent a couple of weeks there visiting the great museums – and then arrived in Geneva in mid-April 1914. On the 24th, they moved into the first-floor apartment of a French-style block at 17 rue Malagnou,* in the southern, old part of the city, near the Russian Orthodox church.

We have some idea of the interior – the main room, in fact – from a photograph taken by Jorge in 1916. The room had a big fire-place and over it a mantelpiece of striped marble; on one wall hung a large mirror. As for the outside, we have only Leonor's scribbles to go by; for the rest of her life she kept a photograph of the edifice with the entrance, the two first-floor balconies and the *chambre de bonne*'s window at the top marked with crosses. Borges's room had a view onto the spire of the cathedral of Saint-Pierre.

Education for their teenage children was high on the agenda for the Borgeses. Top priority for Georgie was French, and he immediately settled down to a series of lessons with a private teacher at home. To prepare him formally for the academic year ahead, he was then sent to a summer language academy. Norah, who back in Buenos Aires had probably received only the most elementary instruction at home, may have joined him in the private lessons, and was much faster in the new tongue than her brother. She eventually went to Geneva's School of Fine Arts. Their parents, meanwhile, leaving the two in charge of Leonor Suárez, began a European tour.

---

* This was in the upper part of the street, towards the old centre, which today is rue Ferdinand Hodler, named after the Swiss painter; rue Malagnou still exists, though further to the south.

It did not last long. Having set off some time in July, they had got only as far as Munich when war broke out at the end of the month. Their being non-European made the Borges' journey back to Switzerland fractionally less fraught than it might otherwise have been. 'We were so ignorant about universal history,' Borges said in 1967.[3] The Borgeses were actually neither more nor less so than any other well-educated middle-class family of the time, though their being Argentine no doubt made them feel especially distant from the four-year conflagration that lay ahead. (Argentina declared itself neutral in 1915.)

There was no obvious reason for them to have seen the coming of world war. Their original intention had been to stay in Europe for about a year, enough time for Jorge to have his eyes dealt with, and for his children to imbibe some good teaching. When the guns began to blast in August 1914, a modest plan for an improving European sojourn inevitably turned into temporary exile.

In the autumn of 1914, Georgie became a pupil at the nearby Collège Calvin, a boys' day-school. The imposing, red-roofed buildings, creating a traditional collegiate quadrangle, were (and are still) tucked away at the end of the rue de la Vallée. Georgie was fifteen. So began his second and last period of official study. The teaching there was of a high standard and, as the college's name suggests, of a Protestant hue. It was also all in French, the one subject in which Georgie proved himself weak. He failed his first French exam.

Without telling him, his classmates signed a petition, and presented it to the headmaster; they pointed out that Georgie had passed all his other subjects in a language new to him, and that leniency should therefore be shown over this one failure. The petition worked and obviously did wonders for Georgie's self-confidence. He was soon taking deep draughts from French literature, borrowing books from a circulating library he had joined: Daudet, Zola, Maupassant, Hugo (*Les Misérables*), Rémy de Gourmont, Marcel Schwob and Flaubert were all now added to the long list of English, North American and Spanish writers he had encountered back in the safety of the Palermo library.

The schoolboys' petition is also a testimony to Georgie's popularity. School had held nothing but terrors for him, a feeling based on his experiences in Buenos Aires from 1908 on. In Geneva, the community was more multicultural – Borges observed that a 'good half' of his classmates were foreign[4] – the social climate more refined. The main subject was Latin; as long as a pupil could get by in that (Borges was more than proficient), slips in other subjects were not made too much of. Borges was liked, and not bullied for being clever. He was, in spite of comments made in later years, happy.

Yet in early maturity, he often referred to how gloomy life had been in Geneva, which was perhaps a way of dealing with what he perceived as a tricky adolescence. Adolescence is tricky whoever and wherever you are, and there is no evidence – apart from one traumatic encounter – that Borges's years of development were especially thorny. In old age, he looked back at his years in Geneva with nostalgia: 'the experiences of adolescence, all that, happened there,' he said.[5] His feelings for Geneva finally drove him back to a city he actually considered home, a place he felt it more appropriate to die in than his native town, where he very often *was* unhappy.

One remark Borges made before he died is revealing about the nature of his experience of the war years in Switzerland: he read Constance Garnett's translation of Dostoevsky's *Crime and Punishment* at the time, and told Jean-Pierre Bernès nearly seven decades later: 'This novel, with a prostitute and a murderer as its heroes, seemed to me far more fearsome than the war surrounding us'.[6]

Just as the family had cocooned itself against the coarse street-life of Palermo, so it did in Geneva: the conflict raging not so far to the north, in another francophone zone, was simply not part of the Borges' life. Georgie's life was his reading, his domain the literary imagination of the nineteenth century – Russian (although neither Tolstoy nor Turgenev was ever important to him), French, English – and in particular the works of Argentine writers.

Jorge Borges had brought to Geneva an impressive stock of volumes by people such as Sarmiento (*Facundo*), Eduardo Gutiérrez, Evaristo Carriego (whose *Misas herejes* were dedicated to Jorge), and two poets who were to recur throughout Borges's poetic life and preoccupations: Hilario Ascasubi and Leopoldo Lugones. Lugones was to become particularly important to him in the 1920s and 1930s; Ascasubi was just one amongst a group of gauchesco writers (and the most prolific) whose work had given rise in the nineteenth century to the idea of a national literature. He had served in both the navy and the army and, unlike Hernández, fought with the

Unitarians against Rosas. He passed much of his old age in exile in Paris.

Ascasubi's best-known poem was *Santos Vega*, about a gaucho troubadour. Like most gauchesco writing, it was plain, unsophisticated stuff, full of the wide, open spaces of rural Argentina, and the feats of nation-builders. For all its primitivism, it had special meaning for the adolescent Borges, who was beginning to be alert to the possibility of becoming himself, even in exile and even if he didn't yet quite know how, an 'Argentine' writer. He honoured Ascasubi by reading his verse out loud in the amphitheatre in Verona, which along with Genoa, Milan, Florence and Venice he visited with his parents in April 1915.[7]

That was the only significant foreign journey the family made in the war years. Inside Switzerland, travel was straightforward, and Georgie seems to have seen quite a lot of the country, sending a postcard in April 1916 to Norah from Montreux, for instance. In Geneva, Leonor had piano and singing lessons. Jorge took to translating Edward Fitzgerald's English version of *The Rubáiyát of Omar Khayyám*. For Georgie, the war constituted above all a period of restless literary discovery. By anyone's standards, his range of reading was astonishing. Before the end of 1914, he had come across Thomas Carlyle and G. K. Chesterton; the first, whose *Sartor Resartus* (1833–4) 'dazzled and also bewildered' him,[8] led to his first encounters with German thought and poetry. (Carlyle was the great British Germanist of the nineteenth century.)

The second, the inventor of Father Brown, was simply to become one of his favourite English writers, whom he read and re-read well into his thirties. Chesterton's compact, witty short-story style was to have a lasting influence on the way Borges structured his own stories over twenty years later. Throughout his life, Borges classed Chesterton with Stevenson and Kipling as the authors who meant most to him in English.

To this list, he soon added Thomas de Quincey and Heinrich Heine. De Quincey was attractive to Borges as an English prose stylist (he eventually deplored Carlyle's style) who often made of dreams and memory a starting-point for diffuse and suggestive texts, *Confessions of an English Opium Eater* being the most famous. Like Borges's, De Quincey's learning was eclectic, even chaotic; but his mind was, in Rodríguez Monegal's neat phrase, 'hospitable and penetrating' – exactly as was Borges's in his literary maturity.[9]

De Quincey also wrote an essay on Immanuel Kant, whom Borges tried to read at this time, unsuccessfully, confessing that, like most Germans, he was defeated by Kant's *Critique of Pure Reason*. So he turned instead to Heine's *Lyrisches Intermezzo*, one of the key texts of German Romanticism, written in 1822. With a German-English dictionary to hand, he found Heine's 'simple vocabulary' beguiled him into this, his fourth language.[10] It was an important step: Romanticism meant little to Borges (it is interesting to note that he paid scant attention to the English Romantics of De Quincey's generation, apart from Coleridge, and absolutely none to Byron[11]) but the *music* of the language of Heine offered Borges a new dimension in poetry. After reading Heine, his determination to be a poet in his own language became more pronounced.

The first book of prose Borges read in German was the Viennese Gustav Meyrink's *Der Golem* (*The Golem*), published in 1915; Georgie pounced on it. This was a wild, fantastic, Kabbalistic farrago, the tale of a Prague rabbi who, like Dr Frankenstein in Mary Shelley's novel, invents a monster – the Golem: the creature, made from mud, is then instructed to follow his master's commands.

The Golem was to loom over some of Borges's later work, being the conceit behind, notably, his creation-myth story, 'The Circular Ruins'. There was also his eponymously entitled poem (one of his longest) of the 1950s, and an entry in *The Book of Imaginary Beings*. In 1936, Borges said that Meyrink's book is full of 'mythology, eroticism, tourism, Prague's local colour, premonitory dreams, dreams of alien or previous lives, and even reality'.[12] He might have been describing the Buenos Aires of his 1940s imagination.

Heine and Meyrink tempted Borges further into German. Rainer Maria Rilke and Hugo von Hofmannsthal were amongst poets he admired but never loved; he dipped into the early-Romantic writer Jean-Paul Richter, the mid-nineteenth-century anarchist Max Stirner, and the Czech Fritz Mauthner, whose aesthetic philosophy Borges enjoyed, though not his novels. Far more important than any of these, however, were Artur Schopenhauer and Friedrich Nietzsche.

Nietzsche was a writer Borges seemed to repudiate in maturity. When he began to give long interviews in the 1960s, in which questions about his early influences inevitably arose, he was always quick to praise Schopenhauer's *Die Welt als Wille und Vorstellung* (*The World as Will and Idea*), a seminal philosophical work from 1819, and veer away from Nietzsche, who of course had a far more visceral and direct influence on literary Modernism. Borges was evasive partly because attacks on his right-wing politics in the 1960s had begun to strike home; Nietzsche's latter-day association with German fascism was unlikely to help the Argentine's cause in a climate of siege (which, as far as politics were concerned, was what Borges faced in the 1970s).

Schopenhauer's positing of an absence of human personality in favour of a world perceived in illusory time and space, which man is asked to tame through abstemious self-control, must have had a seductively modern ring for Georgie.* This was Kant without the stylistic impenetrability. It was anti-Romantic, and anti-historical; uprooted in neutral Switzerland from the vital, environmental, everyday pulse of a native city, and cut off from the immediate consequences of history then being carved out of the collapse of empires in Flanders, Borges found in Schopenhauer a non-deterministic reading of the world, a postulation of it as a kind of brilliant mental invention – imaginative nourishment of a high order for a deracinated young man trying to shape his own identity.

Nietzsche's ideas were altogether more controversial, more fluid. He had once been a follower of Schopenhauer's, but rejected his ultra-rational pessimism in favour of a creed of amorality. At its core, God was defeated, and man's will – a stoked-up, self-centered will, patently individualist where Schopenhauer's had been stoic – was the measure of reality. It was a Dionysian vision, which aimed to undermine the nineteenth-century bourgeois world order; and in that, of course, it failed. But Nietzsche's radicalism ignited the minds of many an artist and thinker at the turn of the century. His shadow fell hard across the first half of the twentieth; and Borges, however far he was from

---

* We have jumped ahead a little; Borges didn't embark on Schopenhauer until 1917, about a year and a half after reading *The Golem*. I believe it none the less makes better sense at this point to outline Borges's eclectic range of reading by language and nation, rather than by strict chronology.

the centres of European artistic life at the time, stood right under it.

An even bigger shadow, and actually predating Borges's first brush with the philosophers, was Walt Whitman's. The unlikeliest of encounters with the great American lyric poet took place when Borges read *Leaves of Grass* in German – in an Expressionist annual according to Rodríguez Monegal, and in 1915, according to Jean-Pierre Bernès.[13] Both things are possible, though Borges probably hadn't come across the Expressionists until well into 1916, after he had read *The Golem*. In his own mind, years later, all this untutored reading clearly became conflated; it is likely he did not start on Whitman until after he had come across the German poet Johannes Becher, and possibly before he had read De Quincey. However the sequence went, Georgie ordered from London an English edition of *Leaves of Grass*, bound in green, and thereafter never put it down, nor left the poet behind.

The impact of Whitman on Georgie was overwhelming. 'His power is so dominating and so clear that a mere glimpse shows us how powerful he is,' Borges wrote in 1929.[14] Whitman's restless, head-strong, pantheistic verse had the effect of a conversion on him. This *was* literature, literature in action – the concepts of Berkeleyan solipsism which he had heard about from his father, and soon found in Schopenhauer's theories of control and perception, and in Nietzsche's Dionysianism, all pulsed through Whitman's incantatory lines.

The poems of *Leaves of Grass*, Whitman had said, exemplified 'the vehemence of pride and audacity of freedom necessary to loosen the mind of still-to-be-form'd America from the folds, the superstitions, and all the long, tenacious and stifling anti-democratic authorities of Asiatic and European past'.

These must have been magical words for Georgie, stuck as he was in the midst of a European paralysis. Here was a poet who leapt out of time, at one with all he saw, felt and hoped for. Whitman's America, moreover – a country readily associated with the freedom the poet celebrated and which hadn't yet joined the war – was somewhere Borges could happily imagine:

> I am enamour'd of growing out-doors,
> Of men that live among cattle or taste of the ocean or woods

Of the builders and steerers of ships and the wielders
   of axes and mauls, and the drivers of horses . . .[15]

Whitman's was a releasing idiom; as in all adolescent literary
encounters with a new voice (and Borges deliberately used the word
'met'[16] about Whitman), Georgie believed the poet was speaking
directly to him. He elevated him beyond the status of mere hero:
Whitman became a household god, something to dream about and
worship beyond the genteel confines of non-literary Geneva. Even
when the spell had worn off, Whitman remained a prominent part
of Borges's mental furniture.

If Whitman taught him inner rebellion, German Expressionism
finally triggered off the poet in him. The Trenches produced the
quiet, late-Edwardian protest poetry of Wilfred Owen and Siegfried
Sassoon; the carnage also led – on the other side – to the angular,
angry, metaphor-rich outbursts of poets such as Becher, Wilhelm
Klemm, Ernst Stadler, and August Stamm.

Becher and Klemm survived the war, the first as a communist in
Hitler's Germany, forced into exile in the Soviet Union, the second
as a Nazi (who survived until 1968). Stadler and Stamm were both
killed, on the Western and Eastern Fronts respectively: the former
was less Expressionist than humanist; the latter was one of a group
which had established its Expressionist credentials before the war
by publishing in a Berlin magazine called *Die Sturm*. Stamm left
behind him an impressive body of war and love poetry, published
posthumously in 1919.

Expressionist work such as this reached Borges in Geneva through
magazines and journals, including *Die Sturm* and another called *Die
Aktion*. However, he did not, contrary to the impression perhaps
given so far, pursue his poetic interests in complete solitude. He
had two close friends, Maurice Abramowicz and Simon Jichlinski.
Both were of Polish-Jewish origin. The first became a lawyer, and
had aspirations to being a poet; the second became a doctor, whose
son treated Borges in his final days in Geneva in 1986.

Borges says little about either, other than that he taught them the
Argentine card-game *truco* and that they quickly beat him. Jichlinski
remembered perambulations through the streets and bars of Geneva,
accompanied by literary conversation, during which they discussed
'everything and nothing'.[17] Abramowicz was clearly the real literary

confidant; he introduced Borges to Rimbaud's *Le bateau ivre*, a poem that would be of some importance to him in the years ahead – as would Abramowicz himself, both as a correspondent and as a sort of literary entrepreneur.

Schooling, reading and, tentatively, writing continued in Geneva until 1918. It is almost certain Borges penned his first poems there. He also wrote, in April 1915, his first known attempt at a 'foreword'. This was for a book of handwritten poems by Norah, with the title *Notas lejanas* (Faraway Notes). In his maturity he produced such introductory pieces with as great a regularity as his poetry.

Georgie's sexual awakening, meanwhile, coincided with overt erotic references and imagery in Whitman and the Expressionists. Before he was eighteen – some time in 1917, it is fair to assume – Jorge Borges realised he had to do the right paternal thing, and introduce his son to a prostitute.

The problem was that Jorge was himself a covert frequenter of brothels. This of course made his son's induction into coitus less of a practical problem; but, like insisting that Georgie be sent to school in Buenos Aires in Etonian attire, he believed the lesson his son had to learn was a matter of form, of ritual, and that there was no need to help with his individual needs by parental advice and encouragement – an anachronistic thought, perhaps, in these sexually frank times. Then, masturbation was still viewed with horror; if there were proof that his parents were seriously worried about Georgie's over-indulgence in that activity, then a visit to the brothel could be seen as an appropriate cure.

Jorge may simply have been concerned about Georgie's natural reticence. He asked him one day whether he had ever been with a woman. With an answer innocently given in the negative, Jorge decided to act. He handed his son an address, at which he should report at such and such an hour, and there he would be looked after.

In the event, Georgie found the whole thing humiliating. A veiled reference to his initiation in Borges's 1975 story 'The Other' gives us some clue as to where it might have happened. We must imagine him walking to the small, pretty, triangular place Bourg du Four,[18] where in a second-floor apartment he finds himself in the hands of 'one of those complaisant Geneva girls who catered to foreigners, loners, and young men in distress', in Rodríguez Monegal's avuncular periphrasis.[19] What happened is a matter for speculation. It seems probable that Georgie's virginity ended with the predictable fumbling and rush of any inexperienced teenage male, though he was especially horrified at the loss of physical self-possession at the moment of climax. Worse, there was every probability that the 'complaisant Geneva girl' was also his father's mistress.*

Rodríguez Monegal reported that enough of Borges's friends had repeated the story over the years for it to have acquired a certain respectability. Many of those friends have died in the interim, but a number I spoke to in Buenos Aires confirmed the rumour, suggesting that Borges did confide in one or two intimates over the years – including Estela Canto – in order to relieve himself of a trauma that pursued him long into adulthood. The story was then told from friend to friend, and stuck.

The psycho-sexual effects of this error of Jorge's are examined in Chapter Six, so need not detain us here. It is worth noting that it occurred in a vacuum for Georgie: he had few friends, was cut off from his native language and customs, and had only fleeting contact with the opposite sex. Norah was a close friend at the time, and was to become closer, though propriety restrained her brother from divulging to her the details either of their father's extra-marital behaviour, or of his own terrible sexual failure. Shame prevented him, too, from sharing the same with Abramowicz and Jichlinksi, so Georgie must have felt – in matters of the flesh – very alone. From now on, it would be simply easier to avoid sex altogether. Astonishingly, another thirty years were to pass before Borges could face the implications of this self-denial.

Both Georgie and Norah were delighted by the arrival in Geneva of Fanny Haslam in 1917, some time after the April entry of the

---

* Rumours about Jorge's womanising are well supported by a story I have now encountered twice. It concerns Jorge's seeing a woman of great beauty in a Geneva street one day; he ran up behind her, whispered in her ear, only to discover when she turned round that he had propositioned his own wife.[20]

United States into the war. Braving the perils of an ocean which had already swallowed several liners caught by German torpedoes, Fanny brought with her memories of their old life, and helped relieve them of some of the loneliness of their new one. They gained a grandmother, however, only to lose the other; early in 1918, Leonor Suárez died, aged eighty-one. She was buried in Geneva, where she remains to this day.[21]

This bleak event precipitated the family's move in April of 1918 to Lugano, two hundred kilometres to the east of Geneva, on the Swiss–Italian border. There they installed themselves, well before the end of the war, in the Hôtel du Lac. Jorge's visits to his Geneva eye specialist had proved moderately successful, and he still had money enough to keep the family in some comfort in Europe for at least another year.

On his nineteenth birthday, on 24 August, Georgie asked for a German encyclopaedia. He had gained his *baccalauréat*, completed in Lugano, at the end of the school year, and was now looking for wider intellectual stimulation. With the Armistice signed two and a half months after his birthday, his interest in things German, poetry in particular, was now fed by a significant increase in accessibility to Expressionist work. The encyclopaedia also inaugurated a lifelong reliance on information catalogued rather than researched. Borges's approach to knowledge was never scholarly; in that, he remained an unreconstructed improviser.

His first literary experiments were in English and French: sonnets.* None survives, and it is safe to assume they were dreamy and derivative: 'poor imitations of Wordsworth', as he described the English, and the French, 'in their own watery way, were imitative of symbolist poetry'.[22] Georgie showed some of his work to his father, who recommended he find his own way and not seek advice. Georgie's conclusion by the end of the family's stay in Lugano was that he should press forward in his own language: 'Spanish would be my unavoidable destiny.'[23]

Lugano was a pleasant, if inconsequential interlude. Georgie and Norah were thrown together in a manner they had not been in Geneva, a city they both missed – Georgie his poetic ally Abramowicz above all. It was a time of fantasy and reflection,

---

* See Chapter Seven, pp.182–3.

Georgie cultivating his favourite writers and planning his own writing career – not discouraged, it should be stressed, by his parents – and reciting Rimbaud and Verlaine as he rowed his sister on the lake. Appropriately, one major watery poem he discovered for the first time in Lugano was Coleridge's *The Rime of the Ancient Mariner*. If much of Borges's life so far had been occupied by learning how to read, Lugano's landlocked, misty beauty taught him deep lessons in an activity Borges forever considered second only to reading: dreaming.

A decision was finally taken, some time towards the end of 1918, to return to Argentina. However, street riots in Buenos Aires in January 1919 probably suggested to the Borges parents that they could do worse than stay in Europe until things quietened down, so in the early spring of that year they moved to Spain: a natural destination for a cultivated Argentine tribe that still had only limited experience of Europe, and who would perhaps have felt short-changed had they not visited the territory of their racial ancestors. Also, Georgie's eyesight precluded him from national service. Jorge's coffers were still well-stocked, and there was little prospect of new work for him back in Buenos Aires. Europe was at peace. Why not take the chance to educate himself, and above all his children, in the values of the old country?

They travelled by train to Barcelona, a city about which Borges recorded nothing. From there they took a ferry to Mallorca. They stayed on the island for about ten months – from March to December – in Palma, in the Hotel Continental (also called 'Universal' in some accounts – the hotel disappeared in the 1940s) in calle San Miguel, opposite a church of the same name. Palma was cheap, and free of tourists. In the chatty environs of this ancient port city, particularly at its Café de los Artistas, Borges quickly made friends with other young aspiring poets, such as Juan Alomar, Miguel Angel Colomar, and José Luis Moll, who went by the pseudonym Fortunio Bonanova. Georgie was hungry for literary exchange, and the short history of Borges's bohemian life effectively begins here.

Among his new acquaintances was a Mallorcan named Jacobo Sureda, two years younger than Borges, whose family had property in the village of Valldemosa, twenty kilometres away up in the hills. Valldemosa was an ancient village where in the winter of 1838 Frédéric Chopin and George Sand had stayed together in the

Carthusian monastery. Sureda eventually published, in Germany, one book of poems, *El prestidigitador de los cinco sentidos* (1926),* and died young, of TB, in 1935. During Borges's time in Mallorca, Sureda frequently invited him to stay, for weeks at a time. Borges went willingly, happy to escape the tight family circle, and to leave his father in peace, now at work on a novel – another reason why Jorge may have decided to settle on the island. Later, in the early 1920s, Sureda and Borges corresponded; eight of Borges's letters to his friend were first made available in Spanish in 1987, in a small volume edited by the Peruvian Carlos Meneses, and will appear for the first time in French in 1997.†

Georgie also found a priest, possibly from Valldemosa, or from Palma Cathedral, indifferent to novels but quite prepared to read Virgil – in Latin – with this surprising young Argentine enthusiast. Borges was grateful for the new intellectual space and stimulation, much missed since his regular bouts with Abramowicz.

He swam a lot, a curious sight for tranquil Mallorcans who thought the best thing about the sea was the fish which came out of it; he went horse-riding, which along with swimming was a pastime he had picked up as a boy during the summers spent in Uruguay. He also submitted his first story for publication, to a Madrid magazine, *La Esfera*. It was about a werewolf, and was summarily rejected. It has never resurfaced, and Borges claimed he destroyed it[24] – as he did most things he wrote before his return to Buenos Aires.

His first article, on the other hand, was printed – not in *La Esfera*, nor even in Spanish. He sent a text, in French, to Abramowicz: 'Chroniques des lettres espagnoles: trois nouveaux livres' (Chronicles of Spanish Letters: Three New Books). Abramowicz corrected and edited it, and passed it on to the literary supplement of the Geneva paper *La Feuille*, where it was published on 20 August 1919.

The three books reviewed were *Momentum catastrophicum* by Pío Baroja, *Entre España y Francia* by Azorín, and a now forgotten work on fundamentalist Christianity by Ruiz Amado. Borges was

---

* The Magician of the Five Senses. Sureda left Mallorca in 1921 to seek a cure for his condition in the fresher climes of Lake Geneva first and then of Germany's Black Forest.
† To be included in Jean-Pierre Bernès's second Pléiade volume of the *Oeuvres complètes* (see A Note on Texts Used, pp.277–8).

particularly enthused by Baroja, a non-conformist Basque who took traditionalist Spain to task over its defeat in the Spanish-American war of 1898, when Cuba and Puerto Rico won their independence.

The article was no great argumentative triumph, but it was notable for Borges's appreciation of an anti-establishment, one might say anti-Spanish, line. He had learnt the values of scepticism and dissent. His father's anarchism had encouraged him to tow no determinist line. Whitman sang of an individual's emotional freedom from tyranny; Nietzsche preached the power of the individual will to reign over the old morality. Borges was now ready, in his own mind, to claim an intellectual stake in the war of words against conventional and political wisdom. Where else could this be more suitably carried out than in the environs of a country which, for the New World, represented all that was culturally respectable and historically continuous? While Borges's Bohemian life began in the cafés of Palma, his stance against the inflexibilities of a deference to nationhood took root – aged twenty – in a lively disrespect for Spain.

By Christmas 1919, the family had moved to Seville. Their stay, in the Hotel Cesil, was short, no more than three or four months, enough time to experience *semana santa* in the week leading up to Easter (an epic spectacle in Seville) and for Georgie to develop further his taste for café life, life in the open. He started being a poet.

He fell in with a crowd of literati whose point of focus was a magazine called *Grecia* and who met at the Cesil for their get-togethers. In this journal, on the last day of 1919, he had his first poem published, 'Himno del Mar' (Hymn of the Sea). It was fifty-eight lines long, Whitmanesque, breathy and unfocussed: 'third-rate grandiose', as Borges described it in 1970.[25] It was inscribed to another Spanish poet, Adriano del Valle, who seems to have been in love with Norah: a series of his poems in the same issue of *Grecia* carried a dedication to her, with the words 'imperious and divine star who prints the shape of her sandal on the Mediterranean of my heart'.[26]

Very little detailed information remains about the Borges' time in Seville. Borges's own memories of it revolve around *Grecia*, the fact that he was first published there, and his contact, through the magazine, with the first in a line of 'masters' – minor literary men he was to cultivate throughout his twenties and revere, learning if not the facts of life, then certainly the business of literature and literary right-thinking.

The principal Master in Spain was Rafael Cansinos-Assens. He was born in Seville in 1882, and studied for the priesthood. Finding the name Cansinos – by which he was generally known amongst his peers – in the files of the Inquisition, he was convinced he was a Jew. 'This led him,' says Borges (in one of the driest statements in the 'Essay'), 'to the study of Hebrew, and later on he even had himself circumcised.'[27] He published a book called *El candelabro* in 1914 and, when Borges knew him, three in succession, on Jewish themes, between 1920 and 1921. He was a versatile linguist, eventually mastering a dozen tongues, and as well as writing poems and stories expended a great deal of energy in praising and promoting young unknowns, while ignoring the big names of the day – such as Pío Baroja, Azorín and the philosopher José Ortega y Gasset.

One young unknown who caught his attention was Jorge Luis Borges:

he came amongst us like a new Grimm, full of discreet, smiling serenity. Refined, equable, with the ardour of a poet restrained by a fortunate intellectual coolness, carrying a classical culture of Greek philosophers and oriental troubadours which attached him to the past, causing in him a love of notebooks and folios, unimpaired by modern marvels, Jorge Luis Borges observed, argued politely with his young comrades and took from the new lyricism ... the new lesson of fugue and counterpoint with which eternal themes are rejuvenated across the ages.[28]

It is a curious and arcane statement, typical of Cansinos's mannered style,* but also one of the first portraits we have of Borges in his early years as a poet. Indeed, Cansinos's essay in the third of his four-volume account of new Spanish literature is a pioneering critical appraisal of Borges as a writer – published when Georgie was twenty-seven and back in Buenos Aires: in its

---

* Borges said he began to ape it, imitating Cansinos's 'long and flowing sentences with an un-Spanish and strongly Hebrew flavour to them'.[29]

way, quite an accolade, and to date ignored, as far as I know, in most accounts of Borges's life and work. Cansinos based his portrait of Borges on the twenty-year-old poet-apprentice he first met in Madrid, whose untutored work he began to read in the middle of 1920, and on further acquaintance with a maturer, published poet in 1923–4. The family moved there in the summer of that year, and took up residence at the Pensión Americana, on the Puerta del Sol, right in the heart of the capital.

It was a great change from provincial Seville. Cansinos had already left for Madrid by the time the Borgeses arrived in Andalusia, and lived in a flat opposite the Retiro park until his death in 1964; Georgie's introduction to the Master was long-anticipated.

> Every Saturday I would go to the Café Colonial, where we met at midnight, and the conversation lasted until daybreak. Sometimes there were as many as twenty or thirty of us. The group despised all Spanish local colour – *cante jondo* and bullfights. They admired American jazz, and were more interested in being Europeans than Spaniards. Cansinos would propose a subject – The Metaphor, Free Verse, The Traditional Forms of Poetry, Narrative Poetry, The Adjective, The Verb. In his own quiet way, he was a dictator, allowing no unfriendly allusions to contemporary writers and trying to keep the talk on a high plane.[30]

Borges is here describing a movement, named Ultraism. In the 'Essay', he uses 'ultraist' for the first time when mentioning his Sevillian counterparts; Cansinos had invented the word in 1918, and produced a manifesto in January 1919, when Borges was still in Lugano, in a Madrid magazine the Spaniard ran called *Cervantes*.

> Our literature must renew itself, reach its ultra today exactly as our scientific and political thought hopes to. Our motto will be *Ultra* and all tendencies, without exception, will have their place in our credo, on condition that they express a desire for newness . . . For the moment we believe it is enough to throw forth this cry for renewal and announce the publication of a review that will have as its title *Ultra*, and in which only what is new will find asylum.

Cansinos was an iconoclast, far more gifted in rousing his disciples to arms than he was at producing work of lasting value. In 1920, he happened to stumble upon a genuinely gifted and enthusiastic pupil in Borges.

Had it not been for Borges, Ultraism would have barely made its way to the Spanish border, let alone across the Atlantic. Cansinos was an invigorating figure, though he alone was not responsible for the advent of Ultraism. The Chilean poet Vicente Huidobro arrived in Madrid in the summer of 1918, having spent two years in Paris. Soon finding himself in the company of the anti-establishment writers of Cansinos's circle, he injected into it a taste of the French poetic avant-garde – Guillaume Apollinaire, Max Jacob, Pierre Reverdy, with all of whom Huidobro had been closely associated – and gave Cansinos's cause further credibility. Huidobro's name was to crop up, often unfavourably, in Borges's Ultraist writings in Buenos Aires; it seems the two never met.

Meanwhile, a rival of Cansinos's, who held court at another Madrid café, El Pombo, in calle Carretas (the Colonial was on the Puerta de Sol), impressed himself upon Georgie with perhaps greater literary weight than the Andalusian. Ramón Gómez de la Serna, a *madrileño*, was also a curious avant-gardist, whose singular invention was the '*greguería*'. This was a form of aphorism – 'Humour + metaphor = *greguerías*' was the formula he gave – which emerged from the particular atmosphere in Madrid at the time.

Hispanist and travel writer Michael Jacobs, evoking 1920s Madrid, explains: 'Gómez de la Serna was one of the presiding gods in Madrid's cafés . . . [and] he evolved a literary style that could have grown only out of these establishments, a style unsuited to lengthy and carefully structured compositions, but one that was dependent instead on hasty improvisations at the café table, on sudden moments of inspiration between the smoke, the coffee and the banter.'[31]

Borges later fulsomely acknowledged Gómez de la Serna in his first book of essays, *Inquisiciones* (1925), though he had only rather acerbic comments to make about him in the 'Essay'. While it seems he much preferred Cansinos's company, the trenchant, sometimes tragic, Castilian wit of Gómez de la Serna's thought and writing was, finally, more pervasive in Borges's literary memories of Madrid.

As Jacobs's depiction of Gómez de la Serna suggests, Ultraism, often defined – like Futurism – by manifestos, was as much about attitude, sheer talk, as about aesthetics. One of the last 'acts' of Spanish Ultraism Georgie witnessed took place on 28 January 1921 in a large Madrid salon, La Parisiana, where he and other poets noisily recited their verses more in provocation than with an intention to be understood; it was one of the very few occasions in his life when Borges was able to conquer his shyness and 'read' in public – before, that is, he sought professional help in the mid-1940s, when he was obliged, out of financial necessity, to give lectures.

Ultraism was a Hispanic version of Futurism, and has not weathered at all well internationally since its demise – which was arguably in the mid-1920s, when Borges in Buenos Aires ceased to be engaged in the formulaic issues which he himself had done much to lay down. In the cultural rush to be 'new' after the First World War, far more consequential movements were taking shape in Europe's other capitals.

Expressionism was already well established by the end of the war (and in his knowledge of that, Borges was far in advance of the Spanish poets he began to mix with in 1919), while Dadaism was shaking the clubs and artistic haunts of post-Armistice Berlin. Further east in St Petersburg and Moscow, history itself was overturned in 1917 – and Georgie would not be immune from the fashionable proletarian stances many European writers struck in their work, and often in their beliefs, after the Russian Revolution. In Paris, Dada would turn into Surrealism (for a few years its leader, André Breton, was a communist, in Russian revolutionary mode), which in its brief period of intellectual cogency in the mid- to late-1920s at least had an international flavour. James Joyce also published *Ulysses* there.

In Austria, at exactly the same time, the composers of the Second Viennese School were overturning centuries of rules and received wisdom governing the sound and shape of music. Picasso and Braque's Cubism had revolutionised painting, while in London Vorticism had drawn in Ezra Pound, with whom, in his promotional zeal and readiness to help young writers, Cansinos had something in common. While the young Borges was dallying with Ultraism before returning to South America, Pound was playing a part in the most fundamental shift in poetics since Romanticism; as we now know, his contribution to the making of T. S. Eliot's *The Waste Land* (1922) was central. Eliot was to be a far more significant figure for Borges

– as indeed was Joyce – in his mature writing life back in Argentina, than any of his Ultraist comrades.

Set in context, Ultraism strikes us now as parochial, and somewhat technical. Its stated preoccupations with purity of metaphor and rhythm, and a concerted avoidance of abstraction, remind us perhaps of Imagism, a school of loosely connected English and American poets – T. E. Hulme, William Carlos Williams, Amy Lowell, Ford Madox Ford, even D. H. Lawrence – which flourished during the First World War, and was eclipsed by Eliot. The Ultraists also admired the Italian Futurists, whose leader Filippo Tommaso Marinetti far exceeded Cansinos in iconoclasm. Marinetti's glorification of a mechanised future, his espousal of speed and dynamism, certainly corresponded with the Ultraist creed of the new.

Though Ultraism was fertile ground for a later wave of Spanish poets – García Lorca, Rafael Alberti, and the 'Generation of 27' – few of the poets and writers associated with Ultraism are read or remembered today; as a school, or an idea, it remains far more important for Borges's contribution to its vaguely defined literary agendas than for any appreciable achievements. Under its banner, Borges continued to publish throughout his time in Spain. After 'Himno del Mar', seven further poems followed, published in journals such as *Grecia* and *Ultra* between February 1920 and March 1921, when the Borgeses finally left for Buenos Aires. Curt, image-laden exercises in linguistic aggression, these joined five other poems, published in Spanish journals after Borges was back in Buenos Aires, to make up a volume he had planned in Mallorca called *Ritmos rojos*, what he refers to in the 'Essay' as *The Red Rhythms* or *The Red Psalms*.* There may have been as many as twenty poems intended for the book: however, on the eve of his departure to Argentina, he destroyed the original manuscript. The only remaining evidence for what would have been Borges's first book is thus traceable to a series of obscure 1920s Spanish literary magazines.

Another book he planned was to be entitled *Los naipes del tahur* (translated in the 'Essay' as 'The Sharper's Cards'). Throughout 1920 and 1921, Georgie was very industrious, penning along with his

---

* See Bernès's French translations in the Pléiade, pp. 33–40.

poems various essays and manifestos, hatched in Ultraist heat after *tertulias* – those all-night sessions in the cafés Colonial and Pombo – with Cansinos and Gómez de la Serna. 'Al margen de la moderna estética' (On the Margin of the Modern Aesthetic) and 'Anatomía de mi ultra' (Anatomy of My Ultra) were two idiosyncratic Madrid articles in which Georgie can clearly be seen exercising his right to broadcast professions of artistic faith, and which remain uncollected. It is likely he would have included them in his projected volume of prose pieces had he found a publisher; however, on his return to Buenos Aires he was unsuccessful in his search for one, so like *Ritmos rojos*, the manuscript was destroyed.

In Madrid, no one quite replaced Georgie's friendships with Abramowicz in Geneva or Sureda in Mallorca. One young man, a Spaniard and an out-and-out Ultraist, did become inextricably entwined with Borges, though it would be an exaggeration to describe him as an intimate: Guillermo de Torre was a diligent chronicler of the movement, and produced the first account of Ultraism in his book, *Literaturas europeas de vanguardia*, published in Madrid in 1925. A year younger than Borges, he enjoyed the iconoclasm of Ultraism, even co-writing some texts with Georgie, and producing at the end of 1920 something called 'Vertical Manifesto', praised by Georgie in another Ultraist organ, *Reflector* – edited by Guillermo de Torre.

De Torre was tireless in his promotion of the cause, but was himself no poet and, in Rodríguez Monegal's uncharitable assessment, 'as a leader he lacked charisma'.[32] He became close to Norah, whose woodcuts now began to appear regularly in Ultraist journals, and would continue to do so in equivalent publications in Buenos Aires. De Torre called her femininity 'dynamic and futuristic'. By the end of the 1920s, she had married de Torre, whereafter he was far more significant in Borges's life as a brother-in-law than as a fellow-writer.

The family returned to Mallorca for an extended summer break in August of 1920; Georgie stayed with Jacobo Sureda. Together, they planned an Ultraist manifesto for yet another journal, *Baleares*, in which a number of the above-mentioned poems appeared in 1921, as well as the manifesto – in February of that year. Georgie also was reunited with the Mallorcan poets Alomar, Colomar and Bonanova, and the young Ultraists often ended up at a certain Casa Elena, near

Palma's main theatre, talking and plotting until dawn. The house was evidently one of ill repute, but the prostitutes seem not to have interested the poets; the place was comfortable and had the advantage that they could talk all night without being moved on. (Borges published a curious piece about 'Spanish brothels' in *Ultra* in 1921.)

Georgie wasn't the only Borges to be published in Spain. I've mentioned Norah's woodcuts, but there was also Jorge's novel, written in 1919 in Mallorca. During that summer break in August 1920, Jorge had gone back to Buenos Aires for a brief visit that has never been properly explained. Most likely, it was to see how the land lay in the family's home city for their imminent, planned return; but Jorge may also have needed to raise funds, perhaps organise a loan, in order to publish his novel privately with a press in Mallorca.

Early in 1921, keen to keep the Ultraist spirit high with Sureda (now planning his stay in Switzerland and Germany – he did not return until the end of the 1920s) and his other friends, Georgie left Madrid to go back to Mallorca yet again, and almost certainly undertook at the same time to oversee the printing of his father's manuscript; it appeared in Mallorca in an edition of 500, paid for by Jorge, in the early spring of 1921.

The private imprint was named after its owner, Juan Guasp Reines. The novel was called *El caudillo*. Set in the 1860s in the Argentine province of Entre Ríos, where Jorge came from, it tells the story of an émigré from France, Carlos Dubois, who leaves Buenos Aires for a ranch his sick father can no longer run. There, he comes up against Andrés Tavares, a local *caudillo*, or chieftain, who throws his weight behind the Unitarian cause in the approaching civil war. Tavares also has a daughter, Marisabel, to whose charms Dubois eventually succumbs, which enrages her father. He has Dubois killed, and disowns Marisabel.

It is a short, somewhat melodramatic story, full of an understanding of the turbulent times Jorge's father lived and fought in, but short on credibility. Seventeen years after it appeared, just before he died, Jorge expressed a wish that it should be rewritten by his son, something Borges never did, but wished he had. Jorge had to be content with seeing his novella (which is what it is) in print, and distributing it amongst his friends back in Buenos Aires. Even if his son could not oblige his father with improvements during Jorge's lifetime, it was perhaps as an unconscious tribute that Georgie did eventually set some of his own much shorter, more genuinely brutal and provocative tales in the same landscape, period and martial ambience as *El caudillo*'s.

For Jorge, Europe was a successful experiment; for Leonor, a great filip to her meagre education. For their children, Europe, and Spain in particular, established working patterns and circumstances in their young lives which they carried back to Buenos Aires and which lasted for years to come: Georgie had mapped out his future terrain – poetry and magazines – in an encouragingly open if at times bombastic literary environment; this would intensify in Buenos Aires. Norah meanwhile had found her vocation as a painter, and her future husband.

The family set sail from Barcelona at the end of March 1921. Georgie knew that he was going to be a writer, but had no idea how he would put his aspirations into practice in a city he hardly knew: the land that lay on the other side of the Atlantic was one of rotten presidents, geometrical cities and, most challengingly of all, 'poets who had not yet welcomed into their hangers the strange-shaped aeroplane of the Ultra', as he wrote to Sureda in his last letter from Spain.[33] Borges prayed that the bond that united their hearts as writers would not break on the ocean.

Georgie felt the rift from Europe keenly. There, his mind had been formed and his first close friends made. One might have expected him to remain European, to be a 'European writer', a fish out of water wherever he was, or a hybrid at least in his own land. Eventually, he would rise above both categories. Leaving Spain aged twenty-one, with precocious but undisciplined gifts, Georgie Borges was yet to become an almost militant Argentine, a stage necessary in the identity of a man whose creative work seemed finally to belong to no land, and at the same time to all the world.

Chapter Three

1921–1930

Poetry and the Pamphleteer

Buenos Aires: a city founded twice, named not for its so-called 'good airs', but after a fashionable sixteenth-century saint. First to land was Don Pedro de Mendoza in 1535, repulsed by Indians and starvation; then in 1580 Juan de Garay, who scratched the grid-plan of the city onto a piece of cow hide. Mendoza died of syphilis on his way back to Spain. Garay was killed by Indians.

A century later, this obscure settlement by the vast River Plate had just 5,000 inhabitants, and one brick house. Throughout the eighteenth century, *porteños* enriched themselves by smuggling and through trade considered illegal by the Spanish crown. The break with Spain came in 1810 when Napoleon completed his invasion of the Iberian peninsula, and the Spanish government fell. The British, who had previously launched two unsuccessful invasions of Buenos Aires, understood they could not claim Argentina as a new colony; but they determined none the less to have a share in what they saw as the immense wealth to be found in this land the size of Europe, particularly that which might lie in the giant plains, the pampas, behind the port city. Argentina became a significant constituent in Britain's burgeoning commercial empire.

The first half of the nineteenth century was wracked by internal strife. Following official independence in 1816, the country was polarised by the bloody conflict between Federalists and Unitarians, and Buenos Aires was often a place of terror. The city finally consolidated political and economic supremacy, and was declared the capital in 1880. Within thirty years, the population had soared from 200,000 to a million and a half. Argentines put behind them years of frontier and civil wars, and concentrated on exploiting their country's agricultural potential. Argentina grew richer and richer until, by the beginning of the twentieth century, it had one of the world's most buoyant economies, with Buenos Aires as its nerve centre.

With wealth potential comes employment: in the 1890s and early 1900s, huge waves of immigrants – 125,000 in 1901 alone – mainly Spanish and Italian, most of them peasants, were a major cause of Buenos Aires's explosive growth. By 1910, it had become the second largest city in the Americas after New York. An enlarged and modernised port had been built in the 1890s, and soon after an urban transport system was added to the nation-wide railways, with Buenos Aires as its focal point – a network constructed by the British to ensure the safe and fast carriage of the country's goods for direct export from the River Plate.

As the populace got richer, a demand for representative government became insistent. The ruling classes – landowners, *estancieros*, the military – managed to maintain a feudal system in the country at large until at least the 1890s, and conservatives in Buenos Aires delayed universal suffrage for as long possible. Change was inevitable, and in 1911 the vote became available and compulsory to all male natives over eighteen. A figure central to political reforms of all kinds throughout the era was a curious, unglamorous but popular man called Hipólito Irigoyen, leader of the Radicals. Elected president in 1916, he was coming to the end of his first, six-year term of office when the Borgeses returned from Europe.

With the calle Serrano house comfortably let, the family made their new address at calle Bulnes 2216, nearer the centre of Buenos Aires than Palermo. Dominated by an enormous penitentiary, the area was full of beer factories, butchers and sleepy bars. The Borgeses stayed here until 1923. Jorge and Leonor were not over-concerned about their son's career; he was plainly set on being a writer, and Jorge would support him in that enterprise for as long as he could afford it – he would certainly see to it that Georgie, if he so chose, didn't have to get a job.

Thus began the liveliest decade in Borges's life, at least until his years of fame in the 1960s. There were some odd aspects to his situation in 1921. He had no university education, though he was evidently more than capable of passing through any such institution with flying colours. His parents were a bourgeois, quiet pair, proud of their inheritance, and it seems of their children. Knowing that Norah was likely to get married before long, they might perhaps also have been expected to try and push Georgie towards a stable profession as soon as they returned to their native city. Not a bit of it; contrary to the experience of those young artists whose first thoughts are of rebellion and escape, Borges received complete tolerance and active encouragement from his parents. Domestically, he was not practical – he was hopeless at cooking, and had all his clothes bought for him by Leonor – and at this stage showed no ambition whatsoever to cope by himself. Jorge and Leonor were his keepers and, in effect, his pay-masters.

Back from Europe, Georgie had struck luckier than he knew. In letters to Jacobo Sureda in 1921, he complained about Argentina's insipidity, about the boredom he felt in the quarter around calle Bulnes, and expressed a wish to be back on the old continent; in 'this America', he said, everything was tired and lifeless.[1]

He was wrong, at least in so far as his misgivings referred to Buenos Aires. The freeing-up of the political status quo in the previous two decades, and the simple fact that the country was now immensely rich, lent a remarkable self-confidence to the capital: it had grown into 'a very large, sprawling, and almost endless city of low buildings with flat roofs, stretching west toward what geographers and literary hands call the pampa', as Borges wrote in 1970.[2]

That description ignores two things: first, that one of the 'literary hands' disparagingly referred to was his younger self – in the 1920s Borges was fascinated by the idea and imagery of the pampa as an expression of national character; second, the fact that Buenos Aires, or at least the downtown zone, was also very smart, with wide, jacaranda-lined boulevards, glossy shops, endless restaurants and bars, and high, elegant façades in the fashionable *style français*:

in other words, a city – its population then close on two million – bursting with a sense of its own importance. This was all evident before the Borgeses left for Switzerland, but Georgie hadn't really seen it. Now, it was there for the taking.

Literature in 1921, according to Borges's first French translator Néstor Ibarra, was in a less robust condition:

> What can I say about the state of poetry then? Nothing could be more neutral and sluggish, nothing could be closer to decadence and death. The great [Leopoldo] Lugones had already given, twelve years earlier, of his best. Enrique Banchs in 1911 had offered almost his final word in *La urna*, which contains some of the strongest sonnets in our language: innovatory in its themes and eternal in its sensibility. Carriego was copied and diluted many times; the most famous name was that of the prolific and minor *sencillista* [literally 'simplicist', describing a school which drew on colloquial language and the everyday world] poet Fernández Moreno. But these values were either accepted or ignored, they were almost never discussed; poetry, and in general literature and art, was the most boring and incidental aspect of the life of the country.[3]

Borges was poised to inject new energy into this moribund scene. In the 'Autobiographical Essay', Borges played down the epoch, calling much of what he did 'reckless and even pointless'.[4] In fact, it was quite the opposite. In these nine years, he consolidated his vocation, and discovered most importantly the kind of writer he did *not* want to be; this, paradoxically, does not diminish his early achievements, or turn them into mere curiosities. His involvement in the Argentine literary culture of the time was not flirtation, it was deep and probing; in some senses he was its leader. He was certainly in the front line, a campaigner at full throttle, and looked up to by co-writers, many of them his seniors. So busy was he, indeed, that he ignored his emotional needs, something that was to cause him disastrous embarrassment even as late as the 1940s and beyond.

Through seven books, he more than justified his choice of profession: the poetry and essays he wrote between 1921 and 1930 were expressions of a topographical literary consciousness absolutely integral to his character: uncovering layers, some real, some imagined, of his home city, he found aspects of himself that might have remained buried had the family stayed in Europe. Georgie looked into the mirror, and, at least as far as his foreseeable future was concerned, did not flinch. The stare that came back suggested a mission; should he, could he, become Argentina's new modern poet?

The reason he did not can be found in the many decisions, successes and mistakes he made through a crowded and inchoate decade. Its experiments and byways could be pursued through several hundred pages of a separate volume, and one day almost certainly will be.[5] Here, I want to look at the salient preoccupations of Borges's 1920s, and not get too bogged down in textual or circumstantial detail; friends and achievements of these years will appear and reappear in this chapter (and some later in the book), but not all. There are indivduals he mixed with at this time who were of vital importance to him in later years, and, equally, many who fell away, perhaps fitting into the jigsaw of Buenos Aires literary life but not really into Borges's. It was the same with his influences; they were multitudinous in the 1920s, but by the late 1930s, when he began to write what the world remains fascinated in, many had been discarded.

Georgie had had teachers – his father, Rafael Cansinos-Assens – but no professors as such. He was now of graduate age, and the next master in his curious, self-made, self-teaching university coincided with his 'rediscovery' of Buenos Aires. In the annals of Latin American literature, the name of Macedonio Fernández does not leap into bright focus. If he does so today, it is largely because of Borges's association with and promotion of him.

The best part of the 'Autobiographical Essay' is, in my view, Borges's brilliant recollection of this eccentric man. Here is how he starts:

Of all the people I have met in my life – and I have met some quite remarkable men – no one has ever made so deep and so lasting an impression on me as Macedonio. A tiny figure in a black bowler hat, he was waiting for us on the Dársena Norte when we landed, and I came to inherit his friendship from my father. Both men had been born in 1874. Paradoxically, Macedonio was an outstanding conversationalist and at the same time a man of long silences and few words. We met on Saturday evenings at a café – the Perla, in the Plaza del Once.* There we would talk till daybreak, Macedonio presiding. As in Madrid Cansinos had stood for all learning, Macedonio now stood for pure thinking. At the time, I was a great reader and went out very seldom (almost every night after dinner, I used to go to bed and read), but my whole week was lit up with the expectation that on Saturday I'd be seeing and hearing Macedonio. He lived quite near us and I could have seen him whenever I wanted, but I somehow felt that I had no right to that privilege and that in order to give Macedonio's Saturday its full value I had to forego him throughout the week. At these meetings, Macedonio would speak perhaps three or four times, risking only a few quiet observations, which were addressed – seemingly – to his neighbour alone. These remarks were never affirmative. Macedonio was very courteous and soft-spoken and would say, for example, 'Well, I suppose you've noticed . . . ?' And thereupon he would let loose some striking, highly original thought. But, invariably, he attributed his remark to the hearer.

He was a frail, grey man with the kind of ash-coloured hair and moustache that made him look like Mark Twain. The resemblance pleased him, but when he was reminded that he also looked like Paul Valéry, he resented it, since he had little use for Frenchmen. He always wore that black bowler, and for all I know he may have slept in it. He never undressed to go to bed, and, at night, to fend off drafts that he thought might cause him toothache, he draped a towel around his head. This made him look like an Arab. Among his other eccentricities were his nationalism (he admired one Argentine president after another for the sufficient reason that the Argentine electorate could not be wrong), his fear of dentistry (this led him to tugging at his teeth, in public, behind a hand, so as to stave off the dentist's pliers), and a habit of falling sentimentally in love with streetwalkers.[6]

* The café is still there, modernised, but bearing more or less the same shape and some of the atmosphere of the original.

No biographer can improve on this. Borges continues for a further two pages, the most he gives to any subject in the 'Essay': he mentions Macedonio's moving from one boarding-house to the next (which prompted Leonor to think the older man was quite unsuitable as an example to her son), teaching Georgie how to read 'sceptically', lying out in solitude on the pampa and finding 'truth', but being unable to express it. Moreover, Macedonio had anarchist leanings, which must have appealed to his young acolyte; in 1899, he had founded a community of anarchists in Paraguay, and believed he could make himself president of Argentina by a subtle 'insinuation of his name' amongst the populace.[7] The very same was the subject of a fantasy novel Borges and Macedonio planned to write in collaboration with another poet of Georgie's acquaintance, who was ten years older than him and also kept horses at the Palermo race-track, Santiago Dabove.*

Provisionally entitled 'The Man Who Will Be President', the book was to feature subversive acts by a group called 'the maximalists' galvanising the *porteño* public out of their complacency: piano-rolls always stopping half-way through a piece, the city becoming full of useless objects such as barometers, and so on. Mercifully, the book was never written.

Macedonio was not all frivolity. He had read widely, including David Hume and Schopenhauer, and corresponded with the North American pragmatist philosopher William James (Henry's brother). In the early 1900s he had married Elena de Obieta, whose premature death caused in him a deep sadness. His elegy commemorating her, 'Elena Bellamuerte' (literally 'Elena Beautiful Death'), is considered one of the finest of Argentine poems. On the other hand, Macedonio also averred to an incredulous Georgie that the absurdly named Quica González Acha de Tomkinson Alvear, a 'lovable lady' of their acquaintance, had the answer to Being: by not even understanding Macedonio's question – what is Being? – her genius was proved because '"she cannot even grasp the fact that we are puzzled"'.[8]

Macedonio's utterly unstratified manner of thinking was a source

---

* They met at the Saturday *tertulias* at La Perla, along with Santiago's brother, Julio César. Other writers who were present included Leopoldo Marechal, author of a famous 1948 Buenos Aires *roman à clef*, *Adán Buenosayres*, and Raúl Scalabrini Ortiz.

of wonder to Georgie, as was his marked inability to commit himself to the page. Accustomed to the loud pretentions of Madrid Ultraists, Georgie was inspired by his new master's literary parsimony. 'Macedonio is without any doubt the only definitive man, the only thinker of the first order, to live fully without believing that his moments of life are less important just because he doesn't impinge on those of others with sprinklings of quotation or famous books.'[9]

It is significant that Borges gives so much attention to Macedonio Fernández in his memoir, and a mere page and a half to his own main activity in 1921–3, the founding and editing of magazines. Ultraism meant little to him in old age; it was none the less the guiding force behind the production of two posters, in November 1921 and March 1922, called *Prisma*.

This was the result of the combined energies of a small coterie of writers – Eduardo González Lanuza, originally from Santander in northern Spain, Francisco Piñero, Georgie's cousin Guillermo Juan Borges, then at naval college, and Guillermo's (maternal) cousin, a beautiful poetess, three-quarters Norwegian, called Norah Lange* – who were galvanised by Georgie's Ultraist discoveries in to spreading a new message to the Buenos Aires citizenry. Their two issues of *Prisma* featured laconic verses, proselytising on behalf of Ultraism, and woodcuts by Norah Borges. For the first edition, the men walked the streets over two nights in late November, pasting *Prisma* onto walls: to no great effect, by all accounts, other than bafflement. Most of the flyposters were torn down within a few days.

Modern art is often characterised by a striking gesture. Gesture, aspiration, is what *Prisma* was all about. Today, the most valuable thing about the two issues is the amount an original of either would fetch on the open market: something in the region of $10,000. *Prisma*'s real significance, however, is to show us how quick Georgie was off the mark. With restless intellectual energy, he threw himself into making an environment in which he could freely pursue his imported enthusiasms – and there was a certain genius in his ability to find enough supporters for them.

---

* Norah had a sister called Haydée, born in 1902 and her elder by four years, who was to become important to Borges in the late 1930s. Both sisters, from a large family, were prominent in literary circles throughout the two decades before Perón. Norah and Haydée's mother was Berta Erfjord, the sister of Francisco Borges's wife, Estela.

One such was Alfredo Bianchi, editor of *Nosotros* (We), a staid literary magazine founded in 1907. Having seen one of the posters, he asked Georgie to write an article explaining Ultraism. Borges obliged, and the piece was published in December 1921. It was a controlled paean to the primacy of the metaphor, highlighting the need to eliminate all ornament and vagueness from poetry – a punchy piece of youthful literary theory, illustrated by brief examples. Georgie was learning how to compress ideas. To have landed a prominent spot in so established an outlet was also a coup for Ultraism, Buenos Aires-style, and perhaps even more so for Jorge Luis Borges. From this date until the 1950s, his byline in a multiplicity of Argentine (and some Spanish*) publications was ubiquitous.

In February of 1922, Georgie saw a little more of his home country; the family went for their summer break to Comodoro Rivadavia in the far south of Argentina, to stay with Jorge's brother Francisco, now a naval captain and military boss of the area. Shortly after, Georgie went to Rosario, capital of the province of Santa Fe, where he took part in a university 'conference' on Ultraism with González Lanuza, Piñero and Guillermo Juan: their signal achievement on this occasion was to declare the movement 'dead'.

Again, there was more gesture in this than substance. It was a minor performance to bring to an end in a provincial city a movement barely heard of in Buenos Aires, a cheeky act of Modernist irony. If it had any importance, it was in just that: Borges was aware of the aesthetic sophistication in mocking one's self-proclaimed earnestness. He was to become a master of it in his maturity.

Far more important was a new magazine Georgie and his co-Ultraists were now planning. Once the second issue of *Prisma* had come and gone in March 1922, energies were turned to an even more ambitious publication: González Lanuza wanted to call it *Antena*, Norah Lange *Horizonte*, Georgie *Inquisición* – which the others found absurd – and Guillermo Juan *Norte*, or *Proa*. *Proa* (Prow) stuck. Macedonio Fernández's help was sought editorially, and he was a lively contributor. Three editions, of six pages each

---

* From Buenos Aires, Georgie continued to send Ultraist articles to the Madrid-based *Ultra*, *Tableros* and *Cosmópolis*.

– that is to say, a double-sided printed sheet folded twice – were published between August 1922 and July 1923.

This was known as *Proa*'s 'first period'. Borges did most of the editing, maintaining the intellectual and visual spirit of *Prisma*; he kept his journalistic turnover healthy with literary pieces in *Nosotros* and a more adventurous magazine, *Inicial*. Musing over the destiny of their new school of poetry with his *Proa* colleagues, meanwhile, Borges soon came to the conclusion that Buenos Aires Ultraism had an identity distinct from its Iberian counterpart:

> Ultraism in Seville and Madrid was a desire for renewal, it was a desire to surround that moment in art with a new cycle; a poetry written as if in big red letters on the leaves of a calendar and whose proudest emblems – aeroplanes, antennae and propellers – speak eloquently of a chronological contemporaneity. Ultraism in Buenos Aires was the longing to reach an absolute art which did not depend on the unfaithful prestige of mere utterance, and whose linguistic staying-power would equal that of the certainty of beauty.[10]

Many of Borges's 1920s pronouncements had this heady, campaigning flavour to them: in the febrile texture of his prose and poetry of this time, his genuine enthusiasm at the prospect of becoming a major force in modern Argentine letters is almost tangible.

His own 'certainty of beauty' would have been bolstered by a girl he was in love with. Her name was Concepción Guerrero, she was sixteen, and lived in a remote suburb. She and Georgie met some time in early 1922 at the Lange family villa, at calle Tronador 1746, in the Belgrano quarter to the north of Palermo. The house was the centre of many Ultraist gatherings, where poems were read and music played, including tangos on the *bandoneón* by Norah Lange, who wanted to encourage young men to dance with her. When he wasn't with Concepción, Georgie played chess with Norah's mother Berta.

By mid-1922 he had become besotted with Concepción's beautiful hair and great dark eyes. She came from a poor family of Andalusian origin, and Georgie's fascination in her was partly chivalrous. They became engaged, sealing their bond in the mean streets of a Buenos Aires *arrabal*, in homage to Borges's favourite landscape, and continued their courtship in the evenings at calle Tronador. There, left alone either in the villa's garden or in a dilapidated drawing-room, they kissed and consorted, and talked only a little.

It was ideal material for literature. Georgie was writing furiously, and the muse behind the poems that made up his first published volume, *Fervor de Buenos Aires*,* was Concepción or, perhaps more correctly, Buenos Aires as reflected, through Georgie's imagination, in his beloved. Of the forty-six poems in the book, many more are about forgotten corners of the city than about her; the opulent Buenos Aires of the downtown area did not interest him. Suburbs, quiet patios, modest streets in outlying districts – Palermo (actually less down-at-heel in 1922 than in 1914), the colonial façades of San Telmo, the immigrant roughness of La Boca on the Southside – did. Since 1921, he had walked everywhere in the city, and the presiding sensation recorded in these poems is that of solitude about to be relieved by some undisclosed but intimate companionship.

Fervor de Buenos Aires appeared in early 1923 in a run of 300 copies, printed privately at Jorges's expense – a peso a copy – at a printing press called Imprenta Serantes. The cover showed a woodcut by Norah, an illustration of a typical Buenos Aires house-front and patio. The pages were unnumbered, and Borges claimed the book had never been proof-read.[11] Alfredo Bianchi's services were called upon to help distribute it, but in a novel way: Georgie knew there was not the slightest chance of the book selling – that wasn't the point – but Bianchi had some influential figures, did he not, passing through the *Nosotros* office? Could he not have someone place in the pockets of his guests' coats hanging in the office lobby the odd copy of the book?

That was how it happened: Bianchi agreed to take about fifty. Illustrating Georgie's modesty, it is a very charming story, told by Borges in the 'Essay' (and elsewhere) partly against himself, but also to explain how he came to have a reputation of sorts within half a year of *Fervor*'s appearance. The *porteño* literati were conscious of his name, and of that of his book. The pockets ruse had worked. And now, to his greatest possible advantage, Borges's reputation

* Translated variously as 'Adoration of Buenos Aires', 'Passion for Buenos Aires', 'Buenos Aires Fervour'; they all sound inept in English, so here the title remains in its Spanish form.

grew on the back of *Fervor* not as an Ultraist, but as a Buenos Aires poet-dreamer. Ultraism was remote and elitist, and largely because of the contradictory bombast of its instigators never really got off the ground in Argentina; the young Jorge Luis was intellectual, shy, certainly, but not especially aloof. His natural wish was to be friendly rather than standoffish in manner.

As *Prisma* and *Proa* proved, he revelled in collaboration. The poems, moreover, in *Fervor* were a far cry from his early Expressionist experiments: portentous, self-conscious and descriptively mannered perhaps, but lyrical, free in form (genuine *vers libre*), accessible, even nostalgic in tone. It was an enthusiastic debut and has remained one of Borges's most famous books.

Satisfaction at its appearance was shortlived. The Borges family was on the move once more. Georgie had been writing to Sureda, now in Germany, about how much he was looking forward to coming back to Europe – Germany in particular. There, due to the frailty of the mark against the might of the peso, he would see to a printing of *Fervor de Buenos Aires*; and in August 1922 he stated that his father needed to return to see a Swiss eye specialist again. They would be travelling in the middle of the following year.[12] By this time, Georgie's liaison with Concepción had become a formal engagement, and he also rhapsodised about her charms to Sureda. As the day of departure drew near, however, Georgie must have regretted his father's decision, as it meant leaving his fiancée behind. Could he not have remained too? That would have entailed finding a job; and at the back of his mind was the possibility of continuing his studies in Europe, to gain some formal higher qualifications – and then on the basis of that he could marry Concepción.

Neither studies nor marriage ensued. The family travelled across the Atlantic in late spring of 1923 to Southampton. Brief stops in London, Paris, Nîmes, Montpellier and Perpignan followed; in Geneva, leaving his wife and children at the Pension des Tranchées, Jorge went to Zurich to have his cataracts operated on. They all returned to Spain in the summer, revisiting Seville and then Madrid, where they found an apartment in calle Alcalá, not far from the Retiro gardens.

It was a ramshackle trip, details of which remain scarce. In Madrid, Georgie arrived with a well-honed Ultraist persona – waving the flag for the 'new' poetics of his home city. He seems, according to what he told Sureda in a letter, to have had a lively social life, flirting with '*señoritas*' and strutting dandily about town – one of the few times in his life Borges made a reference to enjoying himself away from his manuscripts and reading.[13] He renewed his friendships with Cansinos-Assens (to whom he had written regularly from Buenos Aires*) and Guillermo de Torre, who in turn pressed his suit with Norah. Her brother abjured true romance, however, in favour of authors: he read the Basque writer and thinker Miguel de Unamuno in depth, and the seventeenth-century Castilian satirist Francisco de Quevedo also joined his pantheon of literary heroes.

In the heart of Castile, a new magazine had been launched, the *Revista de Occidente*, a Hispanic equivalent of T. S. Eliot's *Criterion*. The editor was the forty-year-old José Ortega y Gasset, a forbiddingly versatile intellectual from Madrid, where he was a professor. He was responsible for introducing Joyce and Proust to Spanish readers, and a German education gave him a lead in nineteenth- and twentieth-century thought amongst his co-intellectuals. In 1923, he was engaged in *Tema de nuestro tiempo* (A Subject for Our Time), a book that examined philosophy as the cultural touchstone of any given era.

Ramón Gómez de la Serna had read *Fervor de Buenos Aires* and reviewed it for Ortega's magazine. His notice appeared in the *Revista de Occidente* in April 1924, at around the time the Borgeses were leaving for Argentina. He was positive about the volume, less so about Borges himself, who struck him as diffident to the point of unapproachability. Still, it was more important for Georgie to have his writing taken seriously than his ego massaged; when another critic, Enrique Diez-Canedo, reviewed *Fervor* equally well in the newspaper *España*, Georgie had every reason to believe he had arrived as a writer in the old country.

He kept himself busy with articles, including one on Quevedo which was published in the *Revista de Occidente* in late 1924, his only contribution to the magazine; it was one of a number of pieces Borges worked on while in Spain, later to emerge in his first

---

* Marcos-Ricardo Barnatán reproduces five of these letters, the only ones that survive, on pp.131–9 of his book, *Borges: biografía total* (1995); they mainly record news of Borges's work on magazines, and offer glimpses of the writings and activities of the *Prisma* and *Proa* groups.

collection of essays. His Iberian sabbatical was useful for storing up textual ammunition for the next stage in his career.

There was no doubt in Georgie's mind as the family sailed back across the Atlantic from Lisbon in the spring of 1924 that his destiny as a writer lay in Argentina, and somehow in interpreting Argentina. His credentials as a poet were now inextricably linked with Buenos Aires, a city he had palpably imagined as much as he had seen and observed it in the flesh. He could have tried to be a European writer; he could very easily have remained a Spanish writer, pursuing his poetic ends through the prism of Ultraism. That he followed neither the Iberian nor Ultraist paths is an indicator of the immense impact Buenos Aires had had on him in 1921. Now, in the mid-1920s, contact with a new set of friends and literati, and certain peculiarities governing the city's literary disposition, influenced him to become a writer both of individualistic taste and site-specific preoccupation.

Almost as soon as he had landed, Borges was back in the fray, making contacts and contributing to magazines. Parts of his first Buenos Aires era had already vanished: Francisco Piñero had died tragically young, aged twenty-two, in 1923, and Concepción Guerrero was no longer the object of his attentions. According to Leonor's account, 'her celebrated tresses had been cut';[14] and it seems likely anyway that Leonor had not approved of the liaison between Georgie and this lowly girl from the outskirts. Borges made no further mention of her.

The family put up for a few months in the Garden Hotel, and then settled in a two-storey house at avenida Quintana 222, a stylish street (and street rather than avenue it is, a short one for Buenos Aires) near the Recoleta cemetery. There was a garden at the back, with a fountain and the statue of a nymph. It was the closest to the city centre the Borgeses had ever been.

The most significant cultural event in Buenos Aires in 1924 was the founding in February of the magazine *Martín Fierro*. A publication of the same name had had a brief life in 1919. Under the editorship of a man named Evar Méndez, an enthusiastic poet who worked more on behalf of others than on his own writing, the new *Martín Fierro* (so titled after Hernández's gaucho hero) became a forum for literary Argentina's anti-establishment tendencies. It was conceived not least of all as an avant-garde antidote to the eclectic conservatism of *Nosotros*. The first issues attacked Catholics, the Pope, and older poets such as Jacinto Benavente and the great Nicaraguan Rubén Darío (who had lived in Buenos Aires between 1892 and 1898). Maturing after four issues, it became more exclusively cultural, and by the end of the year Borges was contributing to it steadily.

It was the year in which *porteño* writing became polarised. A novelist called Roberto Mariani, proud of his so-called proletarian realism, took it upon himself to announce that two literary sets existed in Buenos Aires: the Boedo group (to which Mariani belonged), and the Florida group. Their ideological meeting point, and battle ground, was *Martín Fierro*. The former, named after a down-at-heel working-class district south of the plaza del Once where some of its writers lived and where their publishing house, Claridad, was based, was to represent rough and honest social concern, and was openly influenced by communism; the latter, named after the fashionable shopping street running between the plaza San Martín and the plaza de Mayo, stood for the modish literary avant-garde, for preoccupations looking more readily outwards (to Paris and Europe) than inwards (to Argentina).

Borges, who was acquainted with both sets of writers – the Floridan Ernesto Palacio and the Boedan Roberto Arlt, amongst others – never took sides himself, although he was designated a member of the Florida group. The division boiled down to class: Arlt, for instance, was thought of as 'proletarian', Borges as 'patrician'. Ultimately, the Boedo–Florida divide had little enough to do with aesthetics, and much more to do with perceived social standing. As far as Georgie was concerned, 'I'd have preferred to be in the Boedo group, since I was writing about the old Northside and slums, sadness and sunsets'.[15] In the end, he did not really care (even if the members of either faction did), mainly because he was far too busy launching a new *Proa*.

To help him in this, he introduced to the *Proa* group a new literary magus, Ricardo Güiraldes. Born in 1886, Güiraldes was an unaffected, rather charming man who had been attracted to the French literary avant-garde in the 1910s, and had spent a lot of time in Paris. He was rich, the son of an *estanciero*, and patriotic. His first works were lyrical; his prose writings then dealt with Symbolism, and turned towards singing the praises of nature and the good life in Argentina. He could find no fault with the gauchos, in marked contrast to Macedonio Fernández, who could only joke about them.

Borges recalled that on first meeting Güiraldes, the older poet told him of his envy of Georgie's English, as that meant he could read Kipling's *Kim* in the original.[16] Güiraldes already had in mind the book that was to make him famous, *Don Segundo Sombra*, reminiscent in its theme of an orphan making good of Kipling's story, and of Twain's *Huckleberry Finn*. Indeed, *Don Segundo Sombra*, with its idealised vision of rural derring-do, full of sentimental love for pre-urban society and gaucho simplicity, became the most popular Argentine novel of the century's first half. It was a fruitful time for Güiraldes, and a fortuitous moment for Georgie to have met and known him; Güiraldes had only three years to live. A measure of Güiraldes's regard for the younger man was shown by what he wrote in the copy of the first edition of *Don Segundo Sombra* that he presented to him: 'a poet, with all his soul and all his pen'.

Güiraldes joined forces with Borges and two other writers, novelist Pablo Rojas Paz and diminutive poet Alfredo Brandán Caraffa, to create a new magazine as a showcase for the literature of the new generation. Each man contributed fifty pesos to its production, and *Proa*'s second period began. The first issue appeared in August 1924, with three poems by Borges, an account of *Prisma* by González Lanuza, an essay by a writer called Luis Emilio Soto on that very same new generation and – a typically recondite Borgesian touch – a note on the director of Berlin's Expressionist journal, *Der Sturm*. '*Proa*', claimed Borges, almost as if the first one had not happened, 'emerges in the midst of an unusual flowering. Never has our country lived so intimately the life of the spirit than today.'[17]

It is impossible in just one chapter to do justice to the ferment of ideas and enthusiasms brewing in Buenos Aires which that comment reflects. The Boedo–Florida debate alone could be the subject of a long study, bringing into focus the many writers it sucked in, and oddly Borges would still remain somewhat marginal. Paris and Berlin, even London and Prague, produced much more art that lasted than Buenos Aires did, and many more writers still read the world over. As far as Spanish letters went, the arrival of the *Revista de Occidente* in 1923 was without doubt the event of greatest consequence in the decade, perhaps only to be trumped by Victoria Ocampo's *Sur* in the 1930s. Madrid's role in cultural matters was always a touchy subject for Argentines; when Guillermo de Torre announced in 1927 in a new magazine* that the 'literary meridian' of Spanish America passed through Madrid, *Martinfierristas* of all persuasions took immediate offence, and proudly reiterated their true allegiances to Paris and London. Borges was briefly contemptuous, too, confirming his now well-established distance from Spain and things Spanish – though ironically de Torre became his brother-in-law the following year.

Just as it is hard to encapsulate the literary aspirations of this over-busy Buenos Aires, so it would be easy to suggest that Borges threw himself into creating magazines purely for his own purposes. That would be unfair. He was strikingly free of airs and graces, and now, amongst his own kind, exhibited a trait that would last his lifetime: a passion for intellectual companionship with his elders. Rafael Cansinos-Assens, Macedonio Fernández and Ricardo Güiraldes all come under that heading. Joining the parade in the mid- to late-1920s were Pedro Henríquez Ureña, a Dominican professor then teaching in La Plata, the Mexican writer and soon-to-be ambassador in Buenos Aires Alfonso Reyes, and the poet Carlos Mastronardi (who was in fact two years younger than Borges).

In his friendships, as in his reading, Borges followed his enthusiasms. It was the same when it came to magazines and newspapers; he was more a zealot than a professional, keener – as a journalist – to espouse a cause than to earn a crust. There is little resembling design or calculation in Georgie's 1920s. He was simply lucky to be in the midst of a kind of literary uproar, which insisted on conducting its debates across the pages of journals, drawing a large slice of its energy from the freedom of the times, and the economic confidence in Argentina which then underpinned so much of *porteño* life. Indeed, for a writer like Borges who did not have to do anything except write, the climate could not have been more propitious.

Between 1925 and 1928, Borges published four books. *Proa* survived

---

* *La Gaceta Literaria*, published in Madrid; de Torre was its assistant editor. The Argentine reply to de Torre's claim came in the June-July issue of *Martín Fierro*.

throughout 1925, and in fifteen issues (the last appearing in January 1926) carried much of the work that constitutes the first three volumes: his second book of verse, *Luna de enfrente* (Moon Across the Way), published in March 1926, and two essay collections, *Inquisiciones* (literally, 'Inquisitions' – as usual the Spanish is preferable), and *El tamaño de mi esperanza*. Each book was published by an imprint set up on the back of the magazine, called, not unnaturally, Proa. Apart from Borges's books, the other major name to appear on the list was Güiraldes: Proa published *Don Segundo Sombra* in 1926.

Proa was owned by Güiraldes. Due to the time taken up by his novel and the onset of the cancer that was to kill him in 1927, he resigned from the magazine's editorial board in August 1925, but continued to advise and most importantly help fund both the imprint and the journal. He was well enough to enjoy the success of his book the following year, but eventually returned to Paris, where he had spent much of his youth, to die.

A poet conversant in Buenos Aires Ultraism, Francisco Luis Bernárdez, took Güiraldes's place on the magazine. For Borges, Ultraism was now something to be commemorated rather than practised. *Inquisiciones* is an almanac of his preoccupations of the first half of the 1920s, with essays on imagery and metaphor, on Cansinos-Assens and Gómez de la Serna, as well as with portraits of his Ultraist fellow-travellers, Norah Lange and Eduardo González Lanuza. The book also announces a theme that was to run through all Borges's writings until *Evaristo Carriego* (1930). In an essay entitled 'Queja de todo Criollo' (Every Argentine's Complaint), he explored the burning issue of national character:

> The native Argentine, in my understanding, is sardonic, suspicious, over and above everything without illusions, and so utterly lacking in verbal grandiosity that in few can it be forgiven and in none extolled. Silence allied with fatalism finds efficacious incarnation in the two major *caudillos* who embrace the soul of Buenos Aires: in Rosas and Irigoyen.[18]

Rosas we know about (he was the subject of a poem in *Fervor*) and Irigoyen we will come to. Both men were representative of forms of Argentine nationalism that were of persistent fascination to the *Martín Fierro* generation. And the word 'Creole'? Borges understood it in the manner in which it has been translated: native Argentine. Here is the first part of an English dictionary's definition: '1. (in the West Indies and Latin America) a. a native-born person of European, esp. Spanish ancestry. b. a native-born person of mixed European and Negro ancestry who speaks a French or Spanish creole. c. a native-born Negro as distinguished from one brought from Africa.'[19] As the context is Argentina, the French and Negro elements of this equation can be dismissed, but the ambiguity is still plain: how can a nation founded by the Spanish, one in which the Indian element was and still is slight, distinguish between what kept it native, and what made it European? Can there *be* such a thing as Argentine nativism?

For Borges, as far anyone of his class and education, the answer was clear: the native Argentine, the 'Creole', was a breed apart from the Italian and Spanish immigrants of the late nineteenth century. '*Gallegos*', the type of peasant immigrant from Spain (named after natives of the north-western province of Galicia), were to be despised. The 'Creole' was the 'real' thing. The surly, laconic aspect of the native Argentine personality had a certain power for the young Borges: distinct, uncluttered, and non-European. The theme that impelled his literary explorations up to 1930 was that of how, as a writer, he should divest himself of overbearing European influences, and, above all, of his Spanish heritage (arguably he had already done this by trumpeting his version of Buenos Aires Ultraism). This was the source of his excitement over Buenos Aires in 1921, and his continuing and determined fondness throughout the decade for the writers of the gauchesco tradition: Almafuerte, Ascasubi, Estanislao del Campo, José Hernández.

Amongst his peers, Borges took a lead in reaching back through the Latin American Modernism of Leopoldo Lugones and Rubén Darío; it was an act of poetic and literary-critical recuperation, a reclaiming of a more instinctual Argentine consciousness than Modernism, in thrall to Paris, had permitted. Borges and some of the *Martinfierristas* wanted to define a national aesthetic that would lend identity to their avant-garde. That is why Borges evoked even so reviled a figure (as far as his own family was concerned) as Juan Manuel de Rosas.

In *El tamaño de mi esperanza*, he was to go even further: 'Our first man continues to be Juan Manuel: a great example of the strength of the individual, of a great certainty over how to live, but incapable of building anything spiritual, and in the end tyrannised more than anyone by his own tyranny and bureaucracy.'[20] There was more than a touch of provocation in this kind of statement, which portrayed Rosas as a political thug, but also recognised in him a vivid individuality, a stubborn Argentineness, a material creativity, even a sort of Nietzschean will to power.

Naturally, Borges had to move beyond such primitive nativism. *Criollismo* – 'creolism' – might seem a remote and even irrelevant preoccupation to us now; and possibly it appears remarkable that the Borges the world knows – the master storyteller, the metaphysician, the literary-critical hoaxer – did so thoroughly embroil himself in issues of detailed and local, and sometimes merely fashionable, concern for so long. His fascinations and obsessions with all aspects of *criollismo* came to a head between 1925 and 1928, in the above-mentioned books and, most articulately, in his third essay collection, *El idioma de los argentinos* (The Language of the Argentines).

An arc draws itself naturally from Borges's Ultraism to his *criollismo*, his species of nationalism. They are all part of the same embrace: the need to find himself. His *criollismo* took in the native speech and orthography of Argentina, in 1925 emblazoned as it was across the title page of *Luna de enfrente*, with Jorge spelt 'Jorje'; the poems' titles were printed in a fashionable lower-case; the words for city and duality – *ciudad* and *dualidad* – lost their final 'd'. But what perhaps interested Borges most was to unite the urban and the unreconstructed, the mid-town and the liminal. *Criollismo* was disclosed, for this writer, not in the over-poeticised imagery of Argentina's open country, an infinite and unvarying space, but in the more cramped environs and speech patterns of the *orilla*, the *arrabal* – the Argentine outskirts, the slums – found of course, in its purest form, only in Buenos Aires.

The impression from *Luna de enfrente* is of a city discovered, of an articulated attitude to it having taken root. *El tamaño de mi esperanza* is a continued, and somewhat fussy, examination of the young man's relationship with his traditions and aspirations. *El idioma de los argentinos*, like the other two prose books of the 1920s a compilation of different pieces published in magazines and newspapers, is Borges's last act of nativist flagwaving.

The title reflects the longest piece in the book, which was first read to an audience in a Buenos Aires theatre in mid-1927 by a friend, Manuel Rojas Silveyra, and then published in the newspaper, *La Prensa*. Borges had begun contributing to the paper in 1926, and continued to do so regularly until 1929. The move from small magazines to a national daily marked the start of a long side-career in newspaper journalism, at its most intense in the 1930s and 1940s. A number of his *Prensa* pieces were collected in *El tamaño de mi esperanza*, too, as well as into *El idioma de los argentinos*, which again signals a pattern that was to lie behind all his mature books: first version in a Buenos Aires publication, second (though not necessarily definitive) version in a collection.

The essay, 'The Language of the Argentines', was a summation of Borges's fascination with the way his compatriots spoke Spanish, which he never considered a debasement of Castilian, but a renewal of it: it was an issue of consciousness, of identity, and a reflection of a new reality. 'Pampa', '*orilla*', '*arrabal*', the intricacies of *lunfardo* as spoken by those who knew it and those who pretended to: these were the natural if strange constituents of the country Borges had got to know since 1921. This was a lexicon and an idiom that did nothing for Spaniards. Their etymology and everyday use gave Borges, after his itinerant European adolescence, an exact sense of where and who he was.

In *El idioma* we also meet Góngora and Quevedo, Almafuerte and a fellow-Ultraist Ricardo E. Molinari, the Argentine milonga, tango and the *truco* – all favourite Argentine leitmotifs for Georgie – as well as something quite new. There was a short section called 'Dos esquinas' (Two Corners). One 'corner' – really just a few descriptive paragraphs – found its way into Borges's most famous essay, 'New Refutation of Time' (see Chapter Six, pp.166–7), and was here entitled 'Sentirse en la muerte' (Feeling in Death): a snapshot of an existential vision Georgie had one night while wandering through the Barracas district. The other part, or 'corner', was called 'Hombres pelearon' (Men Fought), which had appeared in *Martín Fierro* in February 1927 under a different name: 'Leyenda policial' (Police Tale). It concerned a knife fight between two *compadritos*, El Chileno and El Mentao, and is a working plan of the first real story Borges wrote, and published, in the early 1930s: 'Hombre de la esquina rosada' ('Streetcorner Man').

If we take 'Leyenda policial' as a prototype text, 1927 is the year in which Borges perceptibly began to move away from pure poetry. He had already shown his skills in prose, even if in later life he found his style from this period unpalatable: 'I was baroque when I was a young man. I did my best to be Sir Thomas Browne, to be Lugones, to be Quevedo, to be somebody else,' he told New York PEN in 1980.[21]

A young writer, particularly one like Borges who had no other qualifications, must explore every literary possibility. He had no intention at this stage of being a storyteller, but the little sketch in *Martín Fierro* was indicative of a new attitude towards the raw material of his home city: Buenos Aires contained its own mythology, which could perhaps be better treated in prose – prose fiction rather than prose fact or reportage (which is what a lot of Borges's writings in the first four books of prose actually are), or a species of breathless, often over-rhetorical versifying. He was beginning to find, tentatively, that there was some satisfaction to be had from make-believe.

After the closure of *Proa* in early 1926, Borges had turned his attentions to *La Prensa*, and continued to be closely involved with *Martín Fierro*. That magazine then closed at the end of 1927, by which time Borges was under a new influence: in September of that year, the Mexican writer Alfonso Reyes arrived in Buenos Aires as ambassador. He held the post until 1930. Borges, who had heard about Reyes from Pedro Henríquez Ureña, greatly admired his work, and was familiar with his first book of essays, on aesthetics, published in 1911. By the time Reyes arrived in Buenos Aires, aged thirty-eight, he had spent many years in Spain and had both produced a scholarly edition of Góngora's *Fábula de Polifemo y Galatea* and written a book about the Cordoban poet, *Cuestiones gongorinas* (Gongoran Questions). He had also translated into Spanish Mallarmé, Stevenson and Chesterton. All of this made him intellectually extremely attractive to Borges, exactly ten years his junior.

Reyes was welcomed with a banquet given by the *Martinfierristas* at which Borges apparently read out a 'Dadaist speech' with Leopoldo Marechal.[22] Thereafter, Borges visited Reyes at the

Mexican embassy in calle Posadas for lunch every Sunday, and they embarked on a literary friendship that was to last until Reyes's death in 1959.

Reyes was formidably intelligent, and one of the great men of letters of twentieth-century Latin America. Victoria Ocampo, whom Borges had met two years before his encounter with Reyes, called him 'the Aztec flower'. He was short – 'like a dumpling, a meatball', says fellow Mexican Carlos Fuentes, who knew Reyes in the post-war years.[23] The ambassador was humorous, and an energetic lover of women. His wife, Manuela, later kept photos in a scrapbook of all his lovers and showing them to guests would say how proud she was of Alfonso. She was much taller than her husband, and Reyes quipped that he had married her so she could reach the higher shelves of his library.

Fuentes's assessment of Reyes as a writer recalls, strikingly, the manner in which readers of Spanish have come to admire Borges:

> His prose was perfect: the most transparent, beautifully wrought Spanish you can read. He really made Spanish universal, he made it available. Through that transparent prose, he gave the culture of the West to Latin America, *translated* Western culture from Greece down. He did a wonderful job of essay-writing, explaining European culture to Latin Americans in terms we could understand. It was a great lesson.[24]

Borges's chosen lesson with Reyes was in style, which he openly acknowledged in the 'Essay': 'in my writing I learned a great deal about simplicity and directness from him'.[25] Along with Paul Groussac, a Frenchman who had made Argentina his home in 1866 and was now eighty, Reyes was always cited by Borges as having had the most decisive effect on his baroque tendencies as a stylist; the late 1920s saw him attempting to discard the youthful mannerisms of *Inquisiciones* and *El tamaño* once and for all.

Pedro Henríquez Ureña was the same generation as Reyes, and they had got to know each other in Mexico. Henríquez Ureña had taken refuge there from Trujillo's regime in the Dominican Republic, sailing across the Gulf of Mexico with his beautiful Mexican wife – who had unfortunately attracted the dictator's unwanted attentions – and they never returned. A mulatto, he became a highly respected figure in Argentine letters, and was considered the most eminent teacher and critic of his day. Borges became very fond of him, and on several literary occasions it was the Dominican who read speeches and lectures for him. Together, in the 1940s, they collaborated on a substantial collection of Argentine writings, called *Antología clásica de la literatura argentina*.

It was through Henríquez Ureña that Borges met the woman who forty years later would become his first wife. The full account of that bizarre marriage is given in Chapter Eight. Details of this early encounter are scarce. Elsa Astete Millán was a seventeen-year-old who lived in La Plata with her family. With her sister Alicia, she often visited Henríquez Ureña, who taught at the city's renowned university to the south of Buenos Aires. Georgie used to take the train out to La Plata, perhaps accompanied by a new writer friend, Manuel Peyrou, to visit Henríquez Ureña as well. Peyrou was three years younger than Borges; his love for Chesterton and reserved temperament made him an obvious confidant for the nervous Georgie. Borges was introduced to Elsa, and quickly found her to his fancy. Henríquez Ureña had no cause to discourage his protégé's attentions and, as with Concepción Guerrero five years before, Georgie began to think, if not talk, of marriage.

His visits to La Plata became frequent, as did his phone calls from Buenos Aires. Soon, however, it was Elsa's mother who picked up the receiver, not Elsa.

To any moderately experienced young man, the message should have been plain. Georgie, however, was not put off. He persisted, to the point one day of asking Elsa's mother, 'Why is it you who keeps answering the phone, and not Elsa?' 'Georgie, I'm sorry,' came the reply, 'Elsa is engaged to be married to someone else.' '*Caramba, caramba*,' said Georgie as he put down the phone. He did not see Elsa again for another seventeen years.

Along with Manuel Peyrou, another writer whom Borges knew from this period and who became a lifelong friend was Carlos Mastronardi. He was two years younger than Borges, and like Peyrou he shared a keen interest in things Chestertonian and detective fiction. Mastronardi's love for Paul Valéry's work, on the other hand, was not something Georgie could easily share, but that was more than offset by high mutual admiration for Evaristo Carriego.

Mastronardi was a great walker, a man of the night, and was Borges's constant companion on those nocturnal perambulations through revered *orillas* of the forgotten Buenos Aires. 'Few men protected his solitude with such care as Mastronardi,' Borges said ten years after his friend's death in 1975. 'He was an inseparable friend of the night, he knew how to take advantage of it ... To live, he chose the avenida de Mayo, perhaps one of the saddest places in Buenos Aires.'[26]

Adolfo Bioy Casares, Borges's closest friend from the early 1930s, described Mastronardi as very 'byzantine, which Borges enjoyed a lot'. In later years, when Bioy Casares's famous dinners with his wife, Silvina Ocampo (Victoria's younger sister), Borges and guests – such as Peyrou and Mastronardi – were a regular event, Mastronardi revelled in a special kind of perversity:

'He had this thing about being late. We'd be waiting at 9.15, and Mastronardi would be taking a walk round the house to arrrive at ten or later, to keep up his fame for being late.'[27] His *magnum opus*, largely unread except by a few Argentine specialists, was a long poem called *Luz de provincia*, based on his home province of Entre Ríos. He spent the best part of his life working on it.

Most of Borges's male peers and mentors from this period were, apart from Reyes and Henríquez Ureña, eccentric Argentines who as friends far outlasted Georgie's Ultraist associates: Macedonio Fernández, Manuel Peyrou and Carlos Mastronardi were talented individuals who none the less remain somewhat shadowy. Their work today receives little attention outside Buenos Aires partly because Borges has for so long claimed the world's attention, and partly because their work is, in the end, far less interesting than his. But along with his mother, father and Bioy Casares, Borges considered them amongst his closest personal friends and allies, and he cherished them deep in his memory after their deaths. (Bioy, of course, is still alive; Leonor, Mastronardi and Peyrou died within a year of each other, a decade before Borges.)

Macedonio excepted, Borges struck up friendships with the writers mentioned so far around about 1925. Someone else he met soon after his family's second return from Europe, and who wasn't a writer, was the strangest of all. Alejandro Schulz Solari, a painter, was half-Lithuanian and half-Italian. Born in 1887, he set out on a voyage to the Orient while still an adolescent, but got only as far as the Mediterranean. He spent the First World War in Paris; for over a decade he lived in various parts of Europe, and returned to Argentina in 1924.

By this time he had acquired a pseudonym, Xul Solar. He joined the *Martín Fierro* group, and in 1926 exhibited with Norah Borges in Buenos Aires; Marinetti visited the show and gave a lecture on modern art. Like Norah, Xul Solar also illustrated two of Georgie's books from this period – *El tamaño de mi esperanza* and *El idioma de los argentinos*. That collaboration was in itself evidence of a close, fast and unusually symbiotic artistic meeting of minds.

They were never intimates, in the way Georgie was with Peyrou or later with Bioy Casares. But aesthetically, Borges shared with Xul Solar a kind of meditative, visionary originality which, in his mid-twenties, the writer may not have been conscious of in himself; the space the painter had built was perhaps, as Borges frequently said of his own stories, waiting to be discovered by him.

Xul Solar's work has often been likened to Paul Klee's. Magical and brilliantly detailed, each of his pictures presents a parade of astrological figures inhabiting otherworldly landscapes. They look symbolic, but what they symbolise is purposely elusive. The painter's intention seems to be to defy the normal limitations of space, to break dimensions, yet to give every object or creature some rational definition: within the apparently limitless boundaries of his pictures, just a line, a colour, a shape, can luminously connect everything with everything else. Ultimately, the meaning the connection might suggest remains mysterious.[28]

Xul Solar was a dreamer, an inventor of imaginary worlds and – famously, as we know from Borges's 'Autobiographical Essay' – of belief systems: 'I remember asking him on one particularly sultry afternoon about what he had done that stifling day. His answer was "Nothing whatever, except for founding twelve religions after lunch".'[29] He also invented a game based on chess, called 'Pan Juego', and was fascinated by mathematics, astrology and the Kabbalah.

From this he promulgated, through his paintings and pronouncements, a form of mystical pantheism. Borges thought of him as a William Blake or Emanuel Swedenborg of Buenos Aires. Another of Xul Solar's preoccupations was language; he invented tongues, including 'Neo-Creole', a mixture of Spanish and neologisms based on English, which, Borges claimed, Xul Solar spoke to *orilleros* in a bar in the rough quarter of Chacarita.[30]

Borges claimed in the same conversation that after the statesman Domingo Sarmiento and the poet Almafuerte, Xul Solar was Argentina's third great man of genius. That is an exaggeration; as a thinker, a philosopher, Xul Solar was a dilettante, though Borges adored his completely original way of seeing the world, just as he did Macedonio's. Yet, more lastingly influential than even Macedonio's 'thought-speeches', it was Xul Solar's genuine strangeness of mind, his vividly coloured and imaginatively relentless logic, which encouraged Borges to examine the possibilities of dimensionless worlds.

Rodríguez Monegal poses this challenge in his biography: 'The influence of Xul Solar on Borges's work has never been studied, although it is considerable.'[31] That study will no doubt one day appear, and the likely focus will not be on the work Borges was engaged in when he first knew Xul Solar, but on the great stories of *Ficciones*.

The creative work that kept Georgie busy until the end of the decade comprised two further books: one of poetry, and a biography. Articles and reviews for *La Prensa* and a new magazine, *Síntesis*, continued apace. Ultraism was over and so, at least in Borges's essayistic writings, was his breed of nationalism. However, for the first and last time in his life, Borges allied himself to a political campaign which would end in the election of a government that was Argentina's last chance to stay free.

The campaign was that of Hipólito Irigoyen. He was now seventy-seven, but still enormously popular. Though he was from an old landowning family and did not openly court mass support, the masses were on his side; as a Radical, he believed in Argentina's economic independence, and in social justice. After 1916, he had up to a point been able to deliver, and quickly came to be seen as a major threat to the hegemony of the *estanciero* elite. In a way, he was a prototype Perón, though without the demagoguery, and without Perón's fatal attraction to fascism; Irigoyen was also quieter, and certainly higher-class.

Shortly after the publication by a Buenos Aires Jew, Manuel Gleizer, of *El idioma de los argentinos*, Irigoyen was returned on 1 April 1928 to the presidency: it was his second term. His first had ended in 1922, when a man appointed by Irigoyen, Marcelo T. Alvear, took office. Throughout Alvear's term, Irigoyen pulled the strings, and everyone knew it. However, what was also known – at least to politically informed liberals – was that those opposed to Irigoyen, the landowners and the military, would attempt to keep him from winning the 1928 general election by all possible means, including ballot-rigging.

Thus, in December 1927, Borges had hosted at his house in avenida Quintana a meeting of young radicals, writers and poets who pledged their support to getting Irigoyen re-elected. It was effectively a committee that he and others of Irigoyen's followers had been planning for some time. Amongst them were Francisco Luis Bernárdez, Leopoldo Marechal, Ulyses Petit de Murat and Francisco López Merino.

All had been part of Buenos Aires Ultraism, or associated with *Martín Fierro*. Not all the *Martinfierristas*, by contrast, had been so taken with the idea of a committee like the one Borges proposed, and the magazine's last issue in November 1927 contained an editorial saying as much. It was partly *Martín Fierro*'s apolitical stance which had persuaded Borges and Ulyses Petit de Murat, in particular, to make concrete their idea.

Their worst fears were not realised. Irigoyen's election victory was unexpectedly impressive. But for Georgie, public triumph would soon have been undermined by private gloom when news of Francisco López Merino's death was received on 22 May, Leonor's birthday; the 24-year-old poet had committed suicide in his home town of La Plata. The reason was not known. Borges suspected difficulties in love, and included a poem about López Merino in *Cuaderno San Martín* (San Martín Copybook), published a year and a half later, and then, over forty years later, another in *Elogio de la Sombra** (*In Praise of Darkness*).

Just six years later, Borges too toyed with the idea of suicide, and quite likely in a similar state of erotic disaffection. López Merino's death would have symbolic connotations for Borges long after the

---

* 'May 20, 1928'; it seems the news took two days to reach Buenos Aires. In his fifth conversation with Fernando Sorrentino (pp.87–8), Borges suggests that his friend took his own life because of a profound depression at being diagnosed a consumptive.

shock of seeing so close an associate vanish in the flush of youth – and also when Buenos Aires literary life was at its most adventurous, the country at its most hopeful, and Borges's optimism as a writer apparently unshakeable.

Georgie lost another friend in 1928: his sister Norah, far from dying, married Guillermo de Torre, and the couple left Buenos Aires to live in Spain. Throughout the 1920s, Norah had played more than just a marginal part in Ultraism, *Prisma* and the activities of the *Martinfierristas*. Her reputation as an artist was substantial, and she contributed to the visual impact of Georgie's published work, particularly his poetry. For his third volume, however, it was not Norah but a friend of hers, Silvina Ocampo, who provided the visual imagery; published in August 1929, *Cuaderno San Martín* carried on its frontispiece a pencil drawing of the author by Silvina.

Cuaderno San Martín was named not after Argentina's great liberator but after a type of notebook available at the time and into which Georgie scribbled his new verses. It was by far Borges's shortest book to date, containing only eleven poems. In later years, he was particularly pleased with three of them: 'La noche que en el Sur lo velaron' (translated in Penguin's 1972 *Selected Poems* as 'Deathwatch on the Southside') and two longish poems about Buenos Aires's two main cemeteries, La Chacarita and La Recoleta. There is also a poem about his grandfather Isidoro Acevedo, who died when Georgie was five; there is another about Palermo. Perhaps the most famous poem Borges ever wrote opened the volume.

As an old man, Borges professed he felt indifferent about 'La fundación mitológica de Buenos Aires' ('The Mythic Foundation of Buenos Aires', as it is translated in the Penguin volume). It has lasted the passage of time. Evocative, skilful, and certainly not as ponderous as the title might suggest, it relocates the founding of Georgie's city to Palermo and a more recent past, populated by *compadres*, *truco* players, and coloured by pink shops and graffiti on walls: Irigoyen's name looms large in the seventh stanza. Unlike the other poems in the book (bar one – a portrait of the calle Serrano garden), it is metrically and stanzaically formal, and purposefully direct. Above all, it is Georgie's last powerfully rhetorical statement about his early and subjective relationship with his home city. It is because it is really about him, and not about Buenos Aires, that Borges was compelled to belittle its importance in later life. For him it was a little embarrassing. For us, it remains a limpid snapshot of the greatest obsession of his youth: his birthplace.

The volume as a whole is technically accomplished, if somewhat sepulchral in tone. Borges did away with the typographical tics that peppered *Luna de enfrente*, and the poet's engagement with his material is richer, less self-conscious than in the effusions of *Fervor*. Much of *San Martín*, however, concerns death, forces that lie round every corner to overwhelm one's sense of locale, time and identity:

> . . . and in the mirror we are Argentine, apathetic,
> and the shared maté measures out useless hours.[32]

In early or late 1929, Borges won a prize, though as no current account tallies on this, we can only say that it was either for *El idioma de los argentinos* or *Cuaderno San Martín* – or, possibly, he won one prize for each book, about six months apart.[33] The prize was municipal, and it made Georgie Borges suddenly 3,000 pesos richer. With the money, he bought a second-hand edition of the *Encyclopaedia Britannica* (Eleventh Edition), a publication he had only had access to in the National Library. It became one of Borges's principal sources of information for the rest of his life.

The money also bought him time. With the family now reduced to four (Fanny Haslam still lived with them), the clan moved from their house on avenida Quintana to the corner of avenidas Las Heras and Pueyrredón, a fifth-floor flat with seven balconies – Pueyrredón 2190 was the exact address.

Georgie now settled down to something he had long wanted to try, an extended piece of prose on a purely Argentine theme, a biography perhaps. His parents recommended one of the great nineteenth-century poets, Almafuerte or Ascasubi. Georgie's literary instincts throughout the 1920s had manifestly veered towards the hidden, the unsung, the marginal. His choice of subject for his new book flew in the face of the obvious; somewhat to Jorge and Leonor's chagrin, their son lighted upon the life of a man they had all known in their Palermo days: the poet-*compadre* Evaristo Carriego.

The book that resulted, *Evaristo Carriego*, was the only work of prose from this era that Borges permitted to stay in print during his lifetime. It is a strange, flawed, and today virtually unreadable tome, hastily researched, and cobbled together – literally – from preoccupations its writer pursued through his twenties usually to better effect in his poetry. The best part of it is the description of Palermo in the first chapter; the 'biography' of Carriego that follows in the second chapter is a brief sketch, and perhaps good practice for the type of 'potted life' of writers Borges would produce on a regular basis, and in a very much more professional and economical form, in the pages of *El Hogar* in the late 1930s.

Much of the rest of *Evaristo Carriego* hesitates between journalism, criticism and evocations of the urban picturesque. The book became even stranger in 1955 when Borges added to it various pieces, articles mainly, written in the quarter-century between the appearance of the first edition and the publication of the fourth volume of his *Obras completas*.

One of these pieces was a celebrated history of the tango, which, unless endowed with a specialised knowledge of *porteño* Spanish, and the nuances and low-class rituals of old-time Buenos Aires, a modern reader will find indecipherable. Borges, who always preferred the tango's predecessor, the milonga, was a wretched historian, as he proved in this, the first of his 'histories', and then later confirmed in numerous statements to the effect that for him fiction was always truer than fact.

In *Evaristo Carriego*, Borges did not have posterity in mind. It was meant for a local audience, and though it found some fans among his friends, the book was a flop. It was typical of the self-irony of his maturity that he allowed it alone to represent his youthful prose. The earlier books of essays are much better.

Far from opening his career as a major writer, *Evaristo Carriego* closed, on a dying note, Borges's first experimental decade – one which, contrary to being deathly, saw him create work and a self-image that were energetically original and alive. The next decade would be spent discarding the efforts of the previous one utterly. As a writer, Borges would embrace something yet stranger: a deracinated frame of mind that challenged and undermined not just his own literary, Argentine aesthetic, but that of literature itself.

Part Two

The Book

In the course of a life dedicated to literature and, sometimes, to metaphysical perplexity, I have glimpsed or sensed the refutation of time. I don't myself believe in it, but still it often comes to me during the night or in the lassitude of dusk, with the illusory force of a primary truth.

Borges in 1946
('New Refutation of Time', *Other Inquisitions*)

Chapter Four

1931–1938

Sur, Essays and First Fictions

Borges's most important professional association throughout the 1930s was with Victoria Ocampo. They had first met in 1925, when Borges was editing *Proa* with Ricardo Güiraldes, who had taken Ocampo to visit the Borges family in the avenida Quintana. Ocampo described Jorge Luis as 'a young man' (she was nine years older) 'with a certain shyness apparent in the way he walked, in his voice, in his handshake and his eyes of *voyant*'.[1]

Victoria Ocampo, by contrast, was imperious and extroverted. An *éminence grise* to many writers, she remained a figure of towering importance in Buenos Aires's cultural life for many decades. Moreover, being published by her turned Borges from an experimental iconoclast into a professional writer.

She was one of six sisters brought up in an aristocratic tradition, which valued French and Frenchness far more than anything Hispanic, including the language. Indeed, her first language was French: 'I wasn't able to free myself from it when settling down to write,' she later said.[2] She was tall, good-looking, unconventional, bossy, and torn between the repressive expectations of her class – marriage, domesticity – and the stimulus of literature.

The latter became her life, luckily for Argentina, but entailed the sacrifice of one she could truly call her own. Literature was a form of public duty for her; friends and companions invited to her home in the leafy suburb of San Isidro included international figures such as Gandhi and Aldous Huxley. Her role models were writers such as Virginia Woolf and José Ortega y Gasset. From 1923, Ocampo had been closely associated with Ortega's Madrid journal, the *Revista de Occidente*.

Ortega was central to her life, intellectually; Borges, contrary to what is often thought, was not. As an individual he was peripheral to her classy gatherings at San Isidro. As a 'young man', and indeed throughout Victoria's life (she died in 1979), Borges was rather overawed by her, as she utterly defeated his Victorian and arguably undeveloped notions of what a woman was and did. As a writer, however, he was simply the most significant contributor to her journal *Sur* for years after its foundation in 1931.

Victoria Ocampo was a voracious reader and expert linguist, and irrepressibly European in vision. Before the age of forty, she was also very rich, being the inheritor of a vast family fortune (the Ocampos were one of the oldest families in Argentina). These attributes were ideal for the founding of a literary magazine, but she needed some persuading, perhaps some intellectual bullying, to get it up and running.

This came from two writers, the Argentine Eduardo Mallea and the American Waldo Frank. Mallea was a rather serious figure, who achieved national and even international standing long before Borges did. They got to know each other in the 1920s, and Mallea's book, *Cuentos para una inglesa desesperada* (1926) (Stories for a Despairing Englishwoman), was illustrated by Norah Borges. He was a protégé of Ocampo's and, as literary editor of *La Nación*, wielded considerable influence; books by him such as *Historia de una pasión argentina* (1935) treated themes of national regeneration, and he was – until his death four years before Borges's – a saintly presence in literary Buenos Aires.

Frank, by contrast, was a Greenwich Village literary traveller with a concern for something he called 'integral communism': he hoped for a return to pan-American values of nature, pre-industrialism, mystic union. His books *Our America* (1919) and *Virgin Spain* (1926) evinced a genuine understanding of the Hispanic world, receiving its fullest exposition in his influential *The Rediscovery of America* (1929). He was a popular public speaker in Argentina, and was supported by an Argentine publisher called Samuel Glusberg – who himself came to be a not insignificant influence on the founding of *Sur*, although he eventually fell out with the headstrong Ocampo.

Victoria wanted her own magazine, which reflected her European tastes and was not in awe of Americana. As the paymistress, she also wanted full editorial control, and got it. The magazine's logo was a simple south-pointing arrow, but its internationalist ethic was clear from the start. 'Turning one's back on Europe? Don't you see the infinite ridiculousness of this phrase?' she wrote in the first issue of *Sur*.[3]

It was launched as a quarterly in early 1931. Borges was in at the beginning, and Ocampo was keen to stress his part; she 'counted on [him] as the chief contributor to the journal and adviser to the whole enterprise', she said in 1964.[4] She couldn't pay him, but then for the first decade of *Sur*'s existence, she couldn't pay anyone. The magazine thrived on a combination of intellectual zeal and benevolent single ownership: it was Victoria's toy, to do with exactly as she pleased, and she happened to harness the most important writing talents of the day. *Sur* was a turning-point in Argentine culture.

Borges had had some experience of literary journals, and much, much more than Ocampo. He was initially bewildered by the proprietress's editorial policy: long articles by famous writers, and photos of Argentina (not Buenos Aires) and Brazil (the Iguaçu Falls) giving the first issue the look of a 'geography manual'.[5] Borges knew that a journal survives on a lively combination of serious pieces along with reviews, chitchat, light sketches, and not just a series of 'forty-page articles signed Homer'.[6]

Sur number one was still a beautiful production: it ran to 199 pages, was printed on special paper, and included illustrations of the work of Picasso. Writers who appeared included Frank, Alfonso Reyes, Ricardo Güiraldes, and Borges – on Ascasubi and Hernández. Soon, he would be contributing more idiosyncratic material: reviews of movies, translations of poems by a black North American poet, Langston Hughes, and in issue 4, a withering attack on the character of the *porteño*: he was depicted as small-minded, racist, driven by sexual machismo and trickery.* In such critiques, Borges was really

* See Chapter Six, p.143

de-nationalising himself, dancing to the Europeanist tone set by Ocampo from the start of *Sur*'s long life.

For Borges, *Sur* was a crucible: Ocampo, trusting implicitly in his literary expertise, allowed him to pursue themes that were really a working-out of his identity as a writer. Throughout the 1930s, Borges would leave behind his preoccupations of the 1920s – Ultraism, *criollismo*, how best to 'be a poet' in Argentina – and set in place the platforms for his future as a prose-writer: *Sur* internationalised him, made him see how parochial his 1920s work had been – to the extent that he began to disavow much of it – and, most important of all, published his first major short stories.

It was in *Sur* (issue 5) that he was able to pen what was perhaps the most resonant statement of literary faith in his pre-war, and one might say pre-fame, phase: distinguishing in a 1932 essay called 'Narrative Art and Magic' between two types of fictional process, he identified 'the natural, which is the incessant result of uncontrollable and infinite operations' and 'the magical, clear and defined, where every detail is an omen and a cause. In the novel, I think the only possible integrity is in the second.'[7]

Borges was not, of course, laying down his cards here as some kind of prototypical Magic Realist, but beginning his quest into a new fiction which abjured realism. It would take him half a dozen years to put the idea fully into practice; in a literary environment, such as Argentina's in the early 1930s, which favoured laboured realism, turgid explorations of the national character, it was none the less a daring position to take, especially for so young and relatively unknown a writer. Borges probably had no idea at this stage that he would never write a novel; but *not* writing one was in fact to be an integral part of his fictional revolution, almost an inverse fulfilment of this 1932 pronouncement.

Borges's 1930s were not easy. They were years of important meetings – that with Adolfo Bioy Casares in 1932 was, as we shall see, the most productive – and disappointments in love. It was the decade in which he published his first critically discussed books, in which he got – at the ridiculously late age of thirty-seven – his first proper job, in which the English strain in his family was finally extinguished (Fanny Haslam and Jorge both died); but it was also that in which he shifted from poetry to prose, and thus became the true writer he had announced at the age of six he would one day be. But he was far from happy, as he freely admitted in a 1954 preface to the book that put him on the map, at least in Buenos Aires, in the middle of the decade: *Historia universal de la infamia (A Universal History of Infamy)*.[8]

Borges's literary maturity would be characterised by a profound scepticism towards traditional modes of representation. If he was a post-Modernist *avant la lettre*, it was because he was one of the first writers to abandon, in an act that was purely imaginative, the tenets of Modernism which had sunk so deep throughout Europe and the Americas.

Borges came to occupy this position in a decade that did few nations any favours. Argentina, though geographically distant from the forces then poisoning Germany, Italy and Spain, was unable to avoid its own political tilt towards a long, dark, fascist night. Enormously successful as a trading nation between the end of the nineteenth century and the 1920s, brimful of political and electoral reforms, Argentina in 1930 saw the ousting of a now isolated Irigoyen by a right-wing coup and the installation of a government under President Uriburu which eroded gradually most democratic advances made in the first two decades of the century. It would end in a full-scale Argentine version of fascism.

Borges reacted to this, but didn't come to any specific state of political consciousness in what is known in Argentina as the 'Infamous Decade'. Intellectually he was part of a circle which looked to Europe and the United States for its ideas, promoting and feeding off a liberal internationalism of which *Sur* was the most confident embodiment. Borges was unusual amidst the pool of *Sur* contributors in that he had behind him youthful preoccupations with specifically Argentine culture, and which in the 1920s had led him to spin his own offbeat nationalism, his '*criollismo urbano*'.

As he developed through the 1930s, Borges began to shrug off his fascination for *arrabales* and *orillas* and *lunfardo*; his writings became imbued with a more tantalising metaphysics. Equally, as Europe headed for war, Borges drew on his instinctive distrust of tyranny, and was almost alone in Argentina for his denunciations of Nazism and anti-Semitism. It was only with the arrival of Perón in 1946 that Borges, using language even stronger than that with which he had condemned Hitler, finally identified his true domestic political bent. He remained out of step with his country for the rest of his life.

In 1928, Borges met Néstor Ibarra. This young Basque, with an Argentine father, had moved to Buenos Aires from France in the mid-1920s to complete his studies at the university's Faculty of Philosophy and Letters. He had discovered Borges's poetry, and become fascinated. The two men first met when seated next to each other at a dinner, after which, Ibarra later recalled, 'we walked out together and [Borges] made me go fifteen kilometres in two hours'.[9] There followed what might be called an ambulatory friendship. Borges had had an insatiable appetite for the streets of Buenos Aires, particularly at night, and particularly with Mastronardi, for a decade; now Ibarra joined him.

There was in Ibarra a touch of Boswell to Borges's Johnson. They developed a sparring verbal partnership, coining new words such as 'phanerogamic' (swimmers who swim scantily clad) and 'hypogeous' (the Buenos Aires underground, or *subte*); Ibarra remembered Borges's humour and sense of the ridiculous – such as his invention of a new French school, Identism, parodying Surrealism (for which Borges had little time*), in which things were compared to themselves, or his suggestion for a new up-to-the-mark journal, called 'Papers for the Suppression of Reality'. (The latter was to reappear in item 'p' of Pierre Menard's files in 'Pierre Menard, Author of the *Quixote*'.)

But Ibarra's Boswellian role went deeper than jokes; Borges's global future really began with him. Friendship aside, Ibarra's translating of Borges into French in the early 1940s provided the essential conduit for the Argentine's renown outside his own country. Without Ibarra's dedication over the years, Borges's work might have stayed in Spanish for much longer than it did.

Then, in May of 1932, he met Adolfo Bioy Casares, at one of Victoria Ocampo's at-homes. Adolfito or Bioy, as he is still known, was seventeen years old, and extremely precocious. Borges asked

---

* He preferred the word 'superrealism': 'The form *surrealism* is absurd; it would be like saying *surnatural* instead of *supernatural*, *surman* instead of *superman* . . .'; and then unfortunately Borges's Spanish doesn't work in English. He continues: '*survivir* por *sobrevivir* . . .' (i.e. survive).[10]

him which twentieth-century authors he admired. Bioy replied: Gabriel Miró, Azorín, James Joyce. Borges said that it was only in those authors who delighted in the charm of words that young writers could find 'enough literature to satisfy them'. It was a high-octane start.[11]

Bioy was already set on a literary career, though he hadn't yet finished his university studies; he never would, finding law a bore, and literary studies too circumscribing. He had, however, published two books, one privately and another under a pseudonym: neither did well, and he still had a long way to go before he could justify in any practical sense his early choice of *métier*. Like Borges, he would later suppress his early efforts.

He was the son of *estanciero* parents. His father's family, the Bioys, ran an estate at Pardo, his mother's, the Casares, a dairy farm at Cañuelas – they owned over a hundred milk bars in Buenos Aires, called La Martona, after Bioy's mother, Marta. His father was the son of French parents; much of Bioy's early reading and education were in French – the family library was entirely in that language.

Bioy was already aware of Borges as 'the most intelligent writer in the country' – and this as early as 1932. What Bioy meant by this comment (made in 1994)[12] was that Borges had a lively reputation, mainly through his contributions to magazines, within the Buenos Aires literary circuit and amongst those who gathered round Victoria Ocampo: an idea of such 'intelligence' would have been gleaned from only a very thin body of work.

Bioy shared with Borges a love of English writers: James, Conrad, De Quincey, among others. Their friendship lasted Borges's lifetime. If he tramped the streets with Ibarra, with Bioy Borges had a more crucial, sedentary relationship: they dined together for years, and established a writing collaboration stronger in Borges's career than any other (and there were many).

The two men were very different: Bioy was young, elegant, sporty (he loved tennis), and a burgeoning ladies' man (he had started early, falling in love with female cousins at Cañuelas, and being shown the 'topography of the female body' by a daughter of one of the estate's tenant farmers[13]); Borges was prematurely middle-aged, awkward, physically inept, indifferent to fashion and timid in company. He was, not to put too fine a point on it, turning in on himself. The bohemian days of his experimental twenties were long gone. Bioy was attracted to Borges for his conversational abilities – indeed, it was Borges who did most of the talking over the years: Bioy listened and laughed a lot. But it was conversation mainly about reading.

Borges didn't drink or smoke, though he was a big eater – if not a sophisticated one: steak, *tortilla*, *dulce de leche* (a caramel-like fudge) remained staple fare throughout his life. He ate, said Bioy, with a certain 'velocity', and drank black coffee with 'plenty of sugar'.[14] One sees in photos from this period a chubby man, unaesthetic, crumpled. He was 'comfortably wide,' as Ibarra described him. 'The skin is very white . . . The hair is very dark. Pushed back, always a bit too long. From indifference, of course, not to look like an artist.'[15] Borges took no interest in clothes, as we know letting Leonor sort out his suits at the tailor. He was sociable, remembered Bioy, but shy. He preferred people to come to him, and was always best in one-to-one exchanges.

Borges was, for most of this time, working. There were many writers in 1930s Buenos Aires busy 'being writers', but Borges considered most of them, according to Bioy, 'stupid. Work, reflection, imagination – in the house – these were the important things. Borges didn't participate in literary life; he only did so, for short bursts, to meet *señoras*. He simply could not believe this type of "literary life" would produce interesting books.'[16]

Sur and other journalism aside, Borges was now doing just that: producing books. The first since *Evaristo Carriego* was *Discusión*, a selection of essays, some of them drawn from *Sur*, including the vilification of the *porteño*, later dropped from the edition of his complete works, and the essay on narrative art and magic. Published by Manuel Gleizer, the book is a compendium of Borges's tastes and reading up until this point. Essays on Walt Whitman and Paul Groussac sit alongside chatty exegeses on the Kabbalah, Zeno's Paradox, the nature of space and time, and hell. The tone is not scholarly, but speculative and self-consciously subjective. 'I've never let a sense of duty interfere with so personal a habit as buying books,' he announces at the opening of the Groussac piece.[17] Rodríguez Monegal observes usefully that Borges's criticism belongs to the 'category [T. S.] Eliot had named criticism of the practicants; that is, the criticism practised by those who are paving the way for their own creative writing'.[18]

Borges was warming up. He had written no publishable fiction thus far, though he had imbibed vast quantities of that of other writers. *Discusión* was not so much a statement of intent as an exploration of possibilities – hence the title. It was a less ambitious book than *Evaristo Carriego*, and less purposefully Argentine than the collections of the 1920s. It was in fact his best so far and proof that Borges's critical talents, nurtured in the solitude of his reading and sharpened under the editorial deadline, were here to stay.

The book inspired an edition of the magazine *Megáfono* to devote a single issue in August 1933 to Borges's work. It was the first of many such homages over the years, and important in so far as it acknowledged that Borges's work was beginning to appeal to the taste of a wider public than just that of the esoteric literary *Sur* crowd.

Amongst the contributors were the Spaniard Amado Alonso, who noticed that *Discusión* was evidence that Borges had indeed learnt plenty of lessons from Groussac: the baroque effects of style had diminished, neatness and clarity were pushing through. Meanwhile, the writer Pierre Drieu La Rochelle, another of those French literary travellers who, like Néstor Ibarra, worked their way into pre-war Buenos Aires literary circles – and was Victoria Ocampo's lover – wrote in a short piece as he travelled back to Paris: '*Borges vaut le voyage*' – 'Borges is worth the trip'.[19] It was a prescient formula of what would drive all such travellers, not just French, to visit Borges decades later.

Drieu La Rochelle joined Ibarra and Borges on their tours round Buenos Aires. They went everywhere – Chacarita, Barracas, to the suburbs, to outlying districts such as Puente Alsina, where Drieu, feeling the closeness of the pampas to the city, came up with another apothegm, which Borges reported years later: 'horizontal vertigo'.

This descriptive oxymoron must have tickled Borges, as he remembered it in 1967, praising it as a '*très beau mot*'.[20] Moreover, it must have stuck and connected in his memory with a visit he made to the pampas the following year, 1934. There, he witnessed a scene (on the Brazilian border and which we will come to) that came to be multiply absorbed in his fictions, which – 'horizontally vertiginous' as indeed so many of Borges's were – Drieu had somehow already brilliantly defined.

In the month the honorary *Megáfono* issue appeared, the popular newspaper *Crítica* started a Saturday colour supplement. Called

'Revista multicolor de los sábados', it was edited by Natalio Botana, and presented an immediate market challenge to *La Nación*'s Sunday literary supplement, edited by Eduardo Mallea. Botana hired Borges to edit the tabloid competitor's new supplement.

It did not really amount to a job. The pay was negligible, but the inky work worthwhile. Borges recalled in 1982: 'I was in the same room as the designers, felt myself to be closely in touch with them. I liked being with the studio-workers, the linotypists. I learnt to read the linotypes, as if looking into a mirror. I also learnt how to set a page . . . The atmosphere at a printer's is very pleasant. Setting pages, correcting proofs . . .'.[21]

Borges needed outlets; there had always been a certain irresponsibility about the 1920s *Prisma* and *Proa* days, a sense of reputations being forged amongst friends, peers, co-Ultraists. It had been about writing to impress, and done very much on the spur of the moment. With the mild public success of *Discusión* behind him, Borges now needed real consolidation: *Sur* had got him off to a good start, but he had no editorial control there. With the *Crítica*'s Saturday colour supplement, he could pick and choose, and find a wider public. To help him he had Ulyses Petit de Murat, his Ultraist friend from *Martín Fierro* days, who was now a film critic for Natalio Botana.

Borges brought to the generally sensationalist *Crítica* an unlikely cocktail of names: Chesterton, Wells and Kipling all made it in translation into its pages, along with work by Ibarra, Xul Solar, Guillermo Juan Borges and Uruguayan novelist Enrique Amorim, who had married Borges's other Uruguayan cousin, Esther Haedo. But most importantly, in that same month of 1933, Borges published his first story: 'Hombre de la esquina rosada', which translates literally as 'Man of the Rose-Coloured Corner'; since di Giovanni's 1970 English translation, it has been 'Streetcorner Man'.

The story actually began life as 'Leyenda policial' (Police Tale) and was first published in *Martín Fierro* in 1927; it was collected in *El idioma de los argentinos* a year later under the title 'Hombres pelearon' (Men Fought). The transformed story finally appeared as 'Hombres de las orillas' (Men from the Edge of Town) in *Crítica* bylined 'Francisco Bustos', named after a great-great-grandfather.

Borges was playing; he was hiding; he still was not quite committing himself, or his name, to fiction. But the publication of this piece in *Crítica*, whatever he thought of it in later years –

and it was not much – heralded the career of Jorge Luis Borges, storyteller: or more accurately, anti-storyteller.

One reason he suggests for disguising his authorship is parental opprobrium. 'I knew my mother would heartily disapprove of the subject matter,' he said in 1970, and so he composed it 'in secret over a period of several months' in Adrogué. The subject is violence, knife-fighting in Buenos Aires's Northside; the inspiration is Nicolás Paredes, the Palermo mafioso whom his family had known before the First World War, and whom Borges had come across in his discovery days after their return from Europe. Paredes 'had died, and I wanted to record something of his voice, his anecdotes, and his particular way of telling them'.[22]

Borges's disguise was not so much deep as tongue-in-cheek: if he genuinely wanted his family not to identify him, he would not have used the pseudonym of an ancestor. It was probably his way of lessening the emphasis, at least, that Jorge Luis was once again evoking disreputable *compadritos*. *Evaristo Carriego* had attracted enough parental frowns.

Between August 1933 and January 1934, *Crítica* published six more of the eight pieces that comprise *A Universal History of Infamy* (the eighth, on Billy the Kid, was written specially for the book). They were all a blend of the real and imagined, stories about known figures of notoriety, such as the New York hood Monk Eastman, and the Tichborne Claimant, the facts of whose lives Borges deliberately distorted: the idea being to suggest that fiction was more real, more authoritative, than fact.

Borges described them as 'pointedly picturesque', 'narrative exercises', and in that same 1954 preface (see p.87) neatly summed up his relation to them: 'the irresponsible game of a shy young man who dared not write stories and so amused himself by falsifying and distorting (without any aesthetic justification whatever) the tales of others.'[23]

That 'dared not' is revealing: Borges's resistance to conventional fiction has about it a spirit of teasing paranoia, as if to go down the road of full-blooded storytelling were to sin, to tell crass lies. Once he had decided that all fiction was a lie, a woeful distortion of truth, he could move beyond *Infamy* and actually write about the problem: the problem of fiction as infinite deception. In admitting to the problem, Borges was to find, in the great stories (all written *by* 1954, significantly), that *that* was the fictional cud he would repeatedly chew on.

In the original preface to *Infamy*, published as a mass-market paperback by Editorial Tor (*Megáfono*'s publishing outlet), Borges had pointed up the influences behind the tales: Stevenson and Chesterton, the early films of Joseph von Sternberg, his own biography of Evaristo Carriego. He doesn't mention the Eleventh Edition of the *Encyclopaedia Britannica*, which was used for 'Tom Castro, the Implausible Impostor', nor does he admit that Marcel Schwob's *Imaginary Lives* was an important book for him at the time (though he mentions in 1970 that he tried *not* to imitate it). Rodríguez Monegal suggests Agatha Christie's *The Murder of Roger Ackroyd*, too, as an influence behind 'Streetcorner Man', with its famous narrative twist at the end:[24] indeed, from here on, Borges was to excel at such twists, and twists within twists.

Written explicitly as entertainment, the stories of *Infamy* are blueprint Borges: playful, lightly erudite, heavily parodic. They are also violent: '. . . I shot him through the back of the head. I ripped open his belly and took out his entrails, and sunk [*sic*] him in the creek.'[25] This, from the first story, is almost cartoon-like; Borges's violence was to thicken and become more sinister as the philosophical content of his work deepened. In many of his later stories, it was a way of ending, often a destiny sought within the dense structures of coincidence that entrapped his characters. In the stories of *Infamy*, violence was still an ingredient of the 'narrative exercise'.

Borges had had no experience of violence to speak of. His fascination for knife-fighting was wrapped up in a self-made mythology. The stories of *Infamy*, curiously, just predate his witnessing of a significant act of violence, in Uruguay in early 1934. He was staying with Enrique Amorim during the summer, on the Amorim family ranch out in Salto, in the north-west of Uruguay. The ranch was actually run by one of Enrique's brothers, but the writer took a close interest in gaucho life; it fed into some of his novels, such as *El paisano Aguilar*.

Borges found himself in the Brazilian city of Santa Anna do Livramento, a border-town thick with easy smuggling. There, he saw something to which, at the back of *The Aleph and Other Stories*, he alluded almost in passing: 'A ten days' stay on the Uruguay-Brazil border seems to have impressed me far more than the kingdoms of

Francisco Borges
Lafinur, who died in
battle in 1874.

Francisco Borges's
English wife, Fanny
Haslam: she outlived
her husband by
61 years.

Leonor Suárez Haedo de Acevedo, Georgie's maternal grandmother.

Isidoro de Acevedo Laprida, Leonor Suárez's husband, about whom their grandson wrote a famous poem.

Georgie's father, Jorge Guillermo, graduated in law in 1895; sitting fourth from the right and sporting an abundant moustache, he was a good friend of one of his son's early heroes, Macedonio Fernández, here standing second from the right.

Jorge Francisco
Isidoro Luis Borges
Acevedo, aged 3.

Norah Borges,
Georgie's sister, in
1910.

Leonor Borges in 1911: one of her friends said many years later that Georgie's mother was a 'nineteenth-century beauty, an absolute belle of the *belle époque*'.

The Borges family on their arrival in Switzerland in 1914. Jorge Borges had come in search of a cure for his deteriorating eyesight; his children needed a stiffer education. The start of the First World War was but months away. 'We were so ignorant about universal history,' said Jorge Luis 53 years later.

The changing face of the Ultraist poet: the first portrait, from 1921, recalls Rimbaud; in the second, from 1923, Jorge Luis has developed the slightly chubbier features he was to retain until the 1960s.

Jorge Luis Borges in 1924, shortly before his second return from Europe to Buenos Aires.

Four years later: Borges, standing on the left, with (from left to right) Sergio Piñero, Carlos Mastronardi and his future brother-in-law, Guillermo de Torre.

the world, since in my imagination I keep going back to that one not very notable experience. (At the time, I thought of it as boring, though on one of those days I did see a man shot down before my very eyes.)'[26]

This was a muted version of the event. In 1964, Borges had been much more precise. It is worth quoting this interview extract in full:

[In Santa Anna do Livramento] I had the chance to see a man killed. We were in a bar with Amorim, and at the next table sat the bodyguard of a very important person, a *capanga*. A drunkard came too close to him and the *capanga* shot him twice. Next morning, the said *capanga* was in the same bar, having a drink. All that had happened at the table next to us, but I'm telling you what I was told later, and that memory is clearer than reality. I only saw a man who stopped, and the noise of the shots.[27]

Borges was apparently agog during his Uruguayan visit, hoping for big scenes. In this bar, he got one, and it manifested itself most vividly in 'El Sur' ('The South'), not written until 1953. This, his favourite story, concerns a man named Juan Dahlmann who travels south of Buenos Aires to recover from an accident. At a train station, he encounters a group of drunk gauchos who mob him while he is eating. One of them oversteps the mark, and challenges Dahlmann to fight. They do so, to the death, with knives. (The incident and memories of Uruguay also lie behind 'The Dead Man' and 'Funes the Memorious'.)

Borges's own encounters in 1934 were happily less fatal. He got to know Silvina Ocampo properly. She was a shy, pretty woman, four years Borges's junior, a great friend of Norah's, and a marked contrast to her bossy sister. Both Norah and Silvina were painters, Silvina having studied with Giorgio de Chirico and Ferdinand Léger in Paris.

Silvina had in fact had contact with Borges earlier than this 1934 meeting, when she had provided sketches based on some of his poems for a mid-1927 issue of *Martín Fierro*; in 1929, she had, as already mentioned, drawn his portrait for the frontispiece of the *Cuaderno San Martín*. Now, with his sister far away, and still living at home with a blind father, a domineering mother and an agèd grandmother, she could see that Borges was a lonely man – somewhat adrift. He was sporting a moustache he had grown during his holiday with the Amorims. 'Borges has an artichoke heart,' she said thirty years later. 'He loves beautiful women. Especially if they are ugly, because then he can invent their faces more freely.'[28]

This was typical Silvina-speak, suggesting how unreal and myopic Borges was in his *amours*. She would not get to know him properly for another seven years, when she was married to Bioy Casares; thereafter, the three of them would remain fast friends for life, Silvina being the third permanent member of those chatty dinners that took place night after night for so many years. Both she and Adolfo were essential in sustaining Borges's confidence as a writer, right through until the years of fame, as well as becoming – in so far as anyone was – his confessors.

Bioy always thought of Borges as happy on the outside, with what he called a *fondo de tristeza*, a base of sadness, on the inside. Bioy was a flirt, and enjoyed many affairs. (Silvina, who was much older than Bioy, was to express a more intense sexual interest in women; it has even been suggested that she was a lover of Bioy's mother, Marta.) By contrast, Borges was painstaking in his attentions to women – mainly well-connected, married and Catholic – which sadly got him nowhere.

Beatriz Bibiloni Webster de Bullrich was married to a barrister, Hector Bullrich – like the Ocampos he was from an old and distinguished Argentine family, and rich with it. (He was actually enamoured of a Canadian gallery-owner.) Beatriz, or Bia as she was known, was attractive – blonde and frail – and caught Borges's attention at around this time. Later, when he published the *Obras Completas* in 1974, he dedicated one poem to her: he had written two in English in 1934, without titles. The poems did not see the light of day until 1943, in his first collected volume published by Losada.

Originally, both poems were inscribed to 'I. J.', as was the first edition of *A Universal History of Infamy*. In 1953, these initials in the book of stories were replaced by 'S. D.', for no apparent reason. 'I offer her that kernel of myself that I have saved, somehow – the central heart that deals not in words, traffics not with dreams and is untouched by time, by joy, by adversities.' These are words from the second English poem, and sum it up: stiff, unidiomatic, and pretty meaningless. The sincerity of the epigraph is also suspect: 'I. J.' has never been satisfactorily identified, though the woman he may have meant the poems for was Pipina Moreno Hueyo.

She was a lively woman, related to Adam Diehl, a poet who had been responsible for Ricardo Güiraldes's interest in the Orient. She herself was a writer of sorts, and married to a rigidly Catholic magistrate keen on giving her children and not over-fond of her artistic interests. Hector Bullrich was more indulgent towards his wife's poetic acquaintances; Moreno Hueyo, on the other hand, would not have been amused at love poems being directed publicly to his wife, so Borges – always discreet – dedicated them to the less intelligent and less compromised Bia.

If he made overtures to Pipina, Borges would have been rejected: invariably, he was. He was not famous, and he was odd – clumsy, shy, still poor. The women he mixed with were often pretty, flighty, rich, and drunk on society. Amorously and socially too, Borges was out of his depth. His inscription was an adornment, not a plea. The poems themselves show considerable erotic pressure, but amount more to adolescent *Angst* than true love verse: at best, they are a form of elaborate word-play, which Borges reputedly enjoyed sharing with Pipina. The changing initials in *Infamy* also suggest more an epigraphic prank than an amorous fixation.

In most recent accounts of Borges's life – those by Rodríguez Monegal and Marcos-Ricardo Barnatán, in particular – it has been speculated that Georgie now decided to take his own life. Barnatán provides compelling textual evidence that just before his thirty-fifth birthday, on 24 August 1934, he went so far as to plan to carry out his suicide in the Hotel Las Delicias in Adrogué. Borges never wrote about such a plan in *fact*, though suicide – more the idea of it than the act – runs through all his work. In his late poem on Francisco López Merino's suicide in 1928, Borges is significantly still haunted by the poet's death decades later; the details of it – particularly the fact that López Merino was unhappy in love – were clearly far more acute in 1934, when Borges was unquestionably at a low ebb.

In an even later story, '23 August 1983' (the date being one day before Borges's eighty-fourth birthday), the planning of suicide is more explicit. However, I do not myself believe that either of these texts, or indeed a reference to suicide in his story from the early

1970s, 'The Other', prove that Georgie wanted to carry it out. His cast of mind was to contemplate all possibilities: suicide is one way out of unhappiness, but then so is writing. The frenetic rate at which Borges worked at his desk through the 1930s is concrete evidence that he found considerable solace in the act of writing; through it, bit by bit, the unhappiness burrowed its way out.

In 1934, two major poets were in Buenos Aires: Federico García Lorca and Pablo Neruda. Neruda and Borges had already met briefly in the late 1920s, and the Argentine appeared to the Chilean to be 'worried about problems of culture and society',[29] which was Neruda's way of saying that he could not find much in common with Borges; Neruda was a man of earthly brilliance, a sensual poet far removed in his interests from Borges's rather abstract approach to verse.

They remained distant, and politically incompatible (Neruda was soon to be a member of the Communist Party), for the rest of their lives: in various interviews in later years both men grudgingly acknowledged each other's literature, but had nothing warmer to say about mutual friendship. Neruda got on far better with Lorca, whom Borges dubbed, slightingly, 'a professional Andalusian'.[30] Lorca was a lyric poet and playwright at the height of his fame, and one year older than Borges; Borges was an unknown poet, critic and pamphleteer. He was unimpressed, for example, at Lorca's citing of Mickey Mouse as the embodiment of America, and clearly considered him a show-off – which he was.

Lorca was also Spanish. Borges was not the first or last Argentine to find Spaniards slick and superficial. In his case, the prejudice stemmed from a family pride in the English strain in the Borges genealogy, and a sense that it lacked class to admit to immigrant forebears from Spain. Much as he loved his sister Norah, Borges never quite found it in him to accept she had a married a man, a Spaniard, worthy of her. Bioy scathingly called Guillermo de Torre 'a complete idiot'. Borges always referred to him as 'el cuñadísimo', 'the brother-in-lawette'.*[31]

A more auspicious meeting took place at Victoria Ocampo's house

---

* Borges later said of de Torre that he was 'the man who came to dinner and overstayed for coffee'.[32]

in 1935, with José Bianco. He was a writer ten years younger than Borges, and openly homosexual. In 1938 he would become the editor of *Sur*. When he met Borges, the older Argentine was imploring Victoria to make the journal less dry, even to the extent of suggesting they invent a pseudonymous contributor to express a composite of all their personal views. The idea was naturally rejected by Ocampo; seven years later, Borges resurrected the joke with Bioy Casares. The result was their first authorial collaboration under the name Bustos Domecq.

Bianco remembered Borges as 'unkempt', cheerfully indifferent to the impression he made, but attentive to the conversation of others, offering opinions to be disputed, and putting an end to boring talk by a joke, usually a paradox. Bianco also noted that Borges had done a review of a book by the Spanish historian Américo Castro, pronouncing that Spaniards didn't obviously speak 'better than us' but '*louder*, it is true, with the confidence of those who ignore doubt'.[33] Spaniards would always remain targets for Borges's wit.

Not long after this meeting, Fanny Haslam died aged ninety-three. She had been ill for some time, and rarely went out of the family apartment on Pueyrredón and Las Heras. Borges reported that she summoned the family to her bedside as she was failing and said, in English: 'I am only an old woman dying very, very slowly. There is nothing remarkable or interesting about this.'[34]

She had outlived her husband, the colonel, by sixty-one years – and now, 'apologised' for taking so long to die. A large slice of Borges's early life went with her, and this undoubtedly contributed to a mounting sense of loss and emotional dispossession at this time.

His father was ill with heart trouble, and completely blind. Bianco used to go with Borges to the Hotel Las Delicias in Adrogué, and remembered how silent Jorge had become – a silence no doubt compounded by his adored mother's death. More significantly, Bianco saw how much his new friend, 'so alien to life's realities', relied on *his* mother.[35] He was writing a great deal, and indeed produced 'The Approach to al-Mu'tasim' this year, a story collected in the successor volume to *Infamy*, *Historia de la eternidad* (History of Eternity), a book of essays on time and metaphysics, published in 1936.

'The Approach to al-Mu'tasim' was the first major Borgesian

fictional hoax: a story dressed up as a book review, complete with title, author, publisher (Victor Gollancz in London), and preface writer (Dorothy Sayers). So successful was the hoax that Bioy ordered a copy from Gollancz. The fifteen-year-old Emir Rodríguez Monegal, who had become a fan of Borges's by the end of the year, 'dutifully made an entry in [his] notebooks under the name of the imagined author'.[36]

In fact, no one had a neater summary of the story's status as a work of fiction than Rodríguez Monegal: 'By pretending that a story has already been told in a published book, Borges could offer, instead of a retelling of the story, a critique of it.'[37] Borges said that 'The Approach to al-Mu'tasim' seemed to 'foreshadow and even to set the pattern for those tales that were somehow awaiting me'.[38] The fraudulent learning and misleading allusiveness underlying many of Borges's central fictions had their prototype here; it was typical of him to suggest that those great tales somehow already existed, waiting for the humble scribe – Borges – to discover them, like a librarian uncovering some dusty but priceless first edition in a back room.

The big achievements lay ahead. Borges was still living at home, Leonor looking after his every practical need, though he was sleeping badly. While his intellectual life was taking ever more surprising turns, his emotional life lay buried, unattended to, childlike. You could say his lack of real affective engagement freed him to prepare for the creation of new worlds, disciplines and religions, like the ones he so admired in Xul Solar (the artist's influence was never far from the early fictions). In the writers Borges most revered – Quevedo, James, Kipling – there was a history of creative repression of which he must have been aware. The awkward writer with the artichoke heart was steeling himself to make sense of his disaffection, both with the material world and with women with whom he dared venture nothing beyond old-fashioned courtesy.

Borges also continued to need a real job. His editing for *Crítica* came to an end in mid-1935. His father's earning power was long over, and it was now not easy to survive on Jorge's pension: Argentina was not immune from the inflation of the Depression. It has been assumed, inside Argentina above all, that because he had such wealthy friends and associated with such cultural luminaries, Borges was well-off. He was not. Money dribbled in from his articles, but he had no income to speak of.

His books were not exactly sellers either. *Historia de la eternidad*, published in 1936 by a small, specialist firm, Viau y Zona, sold by the end of the year precisely thirty-seven copies – as Borges would always claim. He spoke of this feat in a 1966 interview, and explained that he wanted to apologise to and thank all thirty-seven readers, because he was ashamed (as usual) of the book, while at least thirty-seven was an imaginable figure of buyers. Selling 2,000 was too much to imagine – it was like selling nothing at all. Seventeen, or seven, might have been even better. Borges could afford to be humorous with his level of fame in 1966; not so in 1936.[39]

He got another editing post at *El Hogar* (The Hearth), an illustrated magazine, in October 1936. He looked after a foreign books page, to which he contributed articles on writers as diverse as Virgina Woolf, T. E. Lawrence, Benedetto Croce and Spengler. He continued to contribute to *Sur* too, including in December a poem on, for him, a raw subject, entitled 'Insomnia'.

> I believe this night in horrendous immortality: through time no man or woman has died; no one has died, because this inevitable reality of steel and mud has to overcome the indifference of those asleep or dead – hidden though they be in corruption and centuries past – and to condemn them to appalling wakefulness.[40]

Borges's insomnia, to plague him for years to come, was leading him towards engulfing visions of eternity. He had mapped out aesthetic interpretations of eternity in his 1936 history of it; in this poem, we see an attempt to picture eternity in physical terms. It would take the finding of his fictional voice, and a reading of Dante, in the near future – the two things were fortuitously simultaneous – for Borges to fashion a revolutionary image of eternity with both powerfully physical and philosophical dimensions.

As the 1930s dragged towards war in the western world, things got politically gloomier in Argentina. Uriburu's regime had been forced out of office by General Agustín Justo in late 1931, with the backing of the army. Nationalism came to the fore in the mid-1930s, fuelled by a commercial agreement, known as the Roca-Runciman Treaty, which maintained the strongest possible export links (in meat above all) between Argentina and Britain, to the exclusion of lively trade with other big nations, notably the United States. This aggravated Argentina's nascent anti-imperialism.

Still, Argentina did not suffer as badly as some countries during the Depression, though there was inflation. Justo, who managed to avoid full-scale dictatorship, was able to stay in office for seven years partly because Argentine manufacturing was steady, partly because radical oppostion had been stamped out in the early 1930s, and – within the same agenda – partly because of ballot-rigging.

The bogeyman for nationalist agitators came to be Britain, whose imperial management of Argentina for a century and a half was put under violent scrutiny in the late 1930s. The Roca-Runciman Treaty was seen as anti-Argentine. Little changed when a new president, Roberto Ortiz, came to power in 1938; by the time war broke out in Europe, Argentina, nominally neutral, had nurtured a sufficient strain of anti-Britishness, along with its own brand of provincial, inward-looking nationalism, to give up on democracy altogether. The generals did not declare against the Axis until the last months of the war.

After an initial ideological wobble, *Sur* came out for the Allies. From the mid-1930s on, the journal developed as a monthly, and had an almost unique role in Argentina in opposing fascism. This became abundantly clear on the outbreak of civil war in Spain in mid-1936. The magazine welcomed many Republican refugee writers, such as the Andalusian poet Rafael Alberti, and published poems expressing horror at the murder of García Lorca by Granada fascists a month after the war began. The Spaniard had left many friends behind him from his 1934 visit to Buenos Aires, even if Borges was not one of them.

In the same month as he started at *El Hogar*, Borges published a magazine called *Destiempo* with Bioy Casares, financed by Bioy. It was an eccentric affair; the editorial chief was 'Ernesto Pissavini', whom nobody had heard of, because that was the name of Bioy's concierge in the avenida Quintana. It was six pages long, tabloid in size, and only two issues (October and November 1936) out of a total of three survive, collectors' items like *Prisma*. Contributors included Alfonso Reyes and Macedonio Fernández; newer names,

Mastronardi and Peyrou, were rising writer friends of Borges and Bioy.

For Borges, *Destiempo* was light relief. His work for *Sur* and *El Hogar* took up most of his serious writing time from late 1936 through to the end of 1938. His journalistic output at this time was vast; while he wrote literary pieces on Eugene O'Neill, the Huxleys, Unamuno, Kipling and Lugones for *El Hogar*, for *Sur* he did a lot of film reviewing: Chaplin's *City Lights* (back in 1929, he had written a piece for *La Prensa* on *The Gold Rush*), von Sternberg's *Morocco*, and films by John Ford, King Vidor and Alfred Hitchcock amongst others.

Borges had long been a film-goer. It was a medium that fascinated him. 'Cinema', he said, 'has answered, probably without meaning to, two eternal needs of the soul: melodrama and epic.'[41] These were cinema's early days. For a writer with an interest in the dynamics of time, it was clearly bewitching to experience a form which could do things literature could not: move a story through physical time, with the possibility of endless return.

If movies partly inspired some of the thinking in *Historia de la eternidad*, their temporal sleights of hand were a guiding force behind the stories that lay ahead. The stories' seamlessness of plotting, finessing of surface connections and their avoidance of psychological depth link them formally to the twentieth century's popular new art: Borges comfortably embraced it.

Film was, in effect, Borges's music. He had very little interest in the latter art; other than milongas and some old tangos, and a bit of Brahms, Borges's musical culture was non-existent. Even when he went blind, he preferred conversation to tunes. His memory was a vault of quotation, not of melodies. But he still went to the movies, because he enjoyed listening to the dialogue.

Having said which, there was music in Virginia Woolf, whose *A Room of One's Own* and *Orlando* he now translated. He attributed 'euphonic virtues' to the latter, and to Leonor much of the credit for the translations of both books.[42] She probably helped him, as the idea of Leonor putting Woolf's English into Spanish alone is preposterous; but Borges felt no special ownership over this work. It was done for *Sur*, at Victoria Ocampo's behest. Borges later claimed that Woolf was much more to her taste than to his.[43] It was typical of his filial deference, coupled with a touch of facetiousness, that he should suggest such intellectual labour was not his own, but that of the woman who ran his life.

The son was soon to replace the father. By 1937, Jorge was failing. He was blind, and had been for years; but his heart condition had now undermined his health and well-being. Aged sixty-four, he was a sad, unfulfilled figure, who sat for hours in silence, staring into nothingness. Leonor's time was taken up by him almost to the exclusion of anything else – except her son's abstemious needs – and her husband's eventual passing would only be welcome relief, for Jorge, above all. He said, and his son would always remember it, '*Quiero morir enteramente*' – 'I want to die intact' – in other words, of sound mind.[44]

Borges was, as he put it, 'long past the age when I should have begun contributing to our household upkeep'.[45] Through the good offices of the Bioys, he got a job at a municipal library. It was his first full-time employment. The library was named after a popular nineteenth-century writer, Miguel Cané. It was located in the Boedo district, on calle Carlos Calvo, near avenida La Plata. It was a long tram ride from the Borges home, and even after he had alighted Borges had to walk ten blocks.

In 1937, the library had been up and running for ten years. It had been inaugurated in November 1927 in the presence of Miguel Cané's descendants. It was only the second such municipal (that is to say publicly funded) library in Buenos Aires; the first was the Manuel Gálvez library (named after another nineteenth-century author) in calle San Nicolás, opened in 1926. Miguel Cané had a collection of 6,500 books to start with, which by 1940 had risen to around 40,000. Its director was the former Ultraist poet and collaborator on *Proa*, Francisco Luis Bernárdez. Borges was taken on as first assistant.

Today, the library's façade is obscured by a tree. The stonework is attractive, but crumbly. Next to it was once the 'Hemeroteca', the magazine and newspaper archive; now, it is a well-appointed restaurant.

The library is still municipal, but in a state of shocking neglect. Inside, there is a main downstairs reading room, which amazingly contains approximately five of Borges's books – not even an *Obras completas* amongst them. A set of stairs to the left of the entrance leads to a small, wooden-floored gallery, then to a further flight of stairs which opens out on to another long reading room. Annexed to this is a series of smaller reading rooms, lined with shelves of books gathering dust. At the end of the reading room is a door opening on to another flight of stairs which leads to the roof.

Borges worked here from mid-1937 to August 1946. No one has better described his first experience of librarianship than the employee himself.

I was paid two hundred and ten pesos a month and later went up to two hundred and forty. These were sums roughly equivalent to seventy or eighty American dollars.

At the library, we did very little work. There were some fifty of us producing what fifteen could easily have done. My particular job, shared with fifteen or twenty colleagues, was classifying and cataloguing the library's holdings, which until that time were uncatalogued. The collection, however, was so small that we knew where to find the books without the system, so the system, though laboriously carried out, was never needed or used. The first day, I worked honestly. On the next, some of my fellows took me aside to say that I couldn't do this sort of thing because it showed them up. 'Besides,' they argued, 'as this cataloguing has been planned to give us some semblance of work, you'll put us out of our jobs.' I told them I had classified four hundred titles instead of their one hundred. 'Well, if you keep that up,' they said, 'the boss will be angry and won't know what to do with us.' For the sake of realism, I was told that from then on I should do eighty-three books one day, ninety another, and one hundred and four the third.

I stuck out the library for about nine years. They were nine years of solid unhappiness. At work, the other men were interested in nothing but horse racing, soccer matches, and smutty stories. Once, a woman, one of the readers, was raped on her way to the ladies' room. Everybody said such things were bound to happen, since the men's and ladies' rooms were adjoining. One day, two rather posh and well-meaning friends – society ladies – came to see me at work. They phoned me a day or two later to say, 'You may think it amusing to work in a place like that, but promise us you will find at least a nine-hundred-peso job before the month is out.' I gave them my word that I would. Ironically, at the time I was quite a well-known writer – except at the library. I remember a fellow employee's once noting in an encyclopaedia the name of a certain Jorge Luis Borges – a fact that set him wondering at the coincidence of our identical names and birth dates. Now and then during these years, we municipal workers were rewarded with gifts of a two-pound package of maté, to take home. Sometimes, in the evening, as I walked the ten blocks to the tramline, my eyes would be filled with tears. These small gifts from above always underlined my menial and dismal existence.[46]

It is a telling, hurt portrait. It reminds one of a boy arriving in a strange school, instantly to be bullied and humiliated – just as Georgie was twenty years before, in the calle Thames school in Palermo. The disparity between literary and real life, once pronounced enough in the calle Serrano, had never been more acute.

It is possible that one of those 'posh' friends was Elena Udaondo de Pereyra Iraola, another Elvira de Alvear. Both were well-known society names, their faces regularly appearing in the fashion magazines of the day. Borges would have tea with them from time to time in one of the downtown *confiterías* designed for genteel chat, and gentle beverages. Elvira, eight years younger than Borges, actually came on occasion to meet him after work at the library.

They had known each other for some years; she was a writer for whose volume of poems Borges had written a short preface in 1934. She had lived in Paris in the late 1920s, and had been acquainted with Joyce and Valéry, which must have added literary piquancy for Borges. She eventually lost her mind, and died in 1959.

Borges wrote a touching poem about her shortly after her death, remembering her smile.[47] Borges's interest in her in the late 1930s may have been romantic, he may have been 'in love' with her, or pretended to have been. More likely, this kind of gentlemanly flirtation was a way of pleasing his parents' – particularly Leonor's – social ambitions. The likes of Elvira were, at the time, the safest female company available to Borges.

The ladies were unsuccessful in their mission to elevate Georgie's status, as Borges stayed on at the library. The above account shows he felt overqualified, from a different universe to that of his colleagues, and moreover shunned. And he was horrified when one of his male co-workers displayed to him his scar-covered chest in the men's room, macho mementos from knife-fights.

The women at the library ignored him, though this changed when they discovered Borges's connections to 'posh' society ladies, Elvira de Alvear above all. They began to natter about how they could match these ladies' fashions at the races. Borges must have thought he had arrived in a hell worse than any he could imagine. In one interview, which gives a more detailed picture of these years than the essay, he put it perhaps all too mildly:

'Many people believed I was a good writer. I contributed to *Sur* and other journals, foreign writers came to Buenos Aires to see me as if I were a famous person. But my everyday life did not agree with that assumed fame: it was a curiously anonymous, annoying life.'[48] Borges was always adept at making a parody out of understatement.

His father died within a few months of his starting the job, on 24 February 1938: 'He had undergone a long agony and was very impatient for his death,' remarked Borges with similar lack of emotion.[49] Yet losing his father, whom he had adored – and who had placed such high expectations in the future of a son who could apparently do little other than write – clearly added to Borges's depression.

But the Miguel Cané library was not without its advantages. The go-slow on classification meant Borges could skive off, and read and write. He did, with an evident sense of rebellion: 'Though my colleagues thought of me as a traitor for not sharing their boisterous fun, I went on with work of my own in the basement, or, when the weather was warm, up on the flat roof.'[50] 'Boisterous fun' probably also included the rape that took place one day near the toilets, though it is not clear from the 'Essay' whether the rapist was one of the library's male employees.

Ancillary to this distasteful existence was some impressive reading. On the tram, he got through *The Divine Comedy* – 'Purgatory' in English translation and 'the rest of the way' in the original.[51] Gibbon, a huge history of Argentina, Léon Bloy, Paul Claudel, Bernard Shaw, Ariosto's *Orlando Furioso*, and above all Kafka, whom he had begun to translate, were covered in this period too.

In many ways, the library years were intellectually extraordinarily fertile for Borges. He continued his contributions to *El Hogar* – to twenty-six issues in 1938 alone – though he took a break from *Sur*; his last piece there for five months in 1938 was on Leopoldo Lugones, who had committed suicide shortly before his father's death.

This was a chance finally to pin down and negate Ultraism, and praise a new kind of formal Spanish poetry, which he had come to admire in Lugones. 'The essence of Lugones was form. His reasons were almost never right; his adjectives and metaphors, almost always,' he wrote. The piece was expanded for *Nosotros* in the middle of the year: 'To say that the leading Argentine writer has died, to say that the leading Spanish-speaking writer has died, is to say the mere truth and is to say very little.'[52]

Lugones's reactionary Catholicism and fascist opinions were not now ducked in the *Nosotros* piece; but as so often with Borges, who was very close to Samuel Johnson in this respect, the end of a poet's mortal life was an opportunity to elegise the immortal good of his work. Lugones remained important for him for ever after.

Borges's life continued much as he described it. Then, on Christmas Eve 1938, something very odd happened. He was running up the stairs towards the apartment in the Las Heras/Pueyrredón building. It seems the lift wasn't working. As he ran, he bumped into a window; it had just been repainted, and was open – the hinges clearly bringing it inwards over the stairs – in order to dry. Borges didn't see it. That in itself says a lot about the state of his eyesight.

He says in the 'Essay': 'I felt something brush my scalp.'[53] He hit the window, but so violently that it shattered and bits of glass got lodged in his head. (The use of the word 'brush' is yet another Borgesian understatement.) The collision was enough to lay him low for a while, once Leonor, one presumes, had administered first aid: badly, it seems. The wound was poisoned; Borges couldn't sleep, he caught a high fever and hallucinated.

According to his own account, he was then rushed to hospital when he lost the power of speech. An operation had to be carried out to deal with septicemia, and he hovered, he said, for a month between life and death.

The 'Autobiographical Essay' at this point is selective. In 1964 Leonor was clearer about the circumstances: Georgie had gone out to fetch a girl, a Chilean friend of his – possibly Susana Bombal, a young woman he had entertained some tender hopes and feelings for in the mid-1920s – who was coming to lunch. But 'Georgie didn't come back!' Leonor exclaimed. The police called. Georgie, so far as we can tell, had been taken to hospital. As Leonor said: 'Because the wound had not been properly disinfected before it was sutured, he had a fever of 105 degrees the next day' (Christmas Day).[54]

Her use of the passive makes it *sound* as though the disinfecting were the responsibility of a third party. In neither her nor Borges's accounts do we get a sense of exactly where he was between the collision and the outbreak of high fever. Did the accident happen with immediate transportation to hospital, without Leonor knowing – hence the call from the police – or did she take Georgie in straightaway, only to find that *her* attempts to patch him up were to end in fever, and a subsequent stay for Borges in hospital?

There is another oddity. According to them *both*, the accident seems to have occurred as Borges was running *up* the stairs: yet no mention of the girl is made during this ascent. Had Borges failed to pick her up? Why is she absent from Leonor's account at this moment?

We need to turn to Borges's 1967 interview with Jean de Milleret. Here, he says that 'a beautiful young Chilean girl' had been invited to *dinner*, and that she was already at the flat.[55] Indeed, it was she who opened the door. She had a strange look on her face, and Borges remembers this was because there was blood on his forehead; he knew because when he wiped it, perhaps in response to what he thought was perspiration from the climb, his hand was red. This, more or less, is how the incident is stitched into the 1953 story, 'The South'.

There, details end. Questions are asked not to cast doubt on the fact of the accident: it happened. Neither Borges nor Leonor could possibly have made it up. What is perplexing is the inconsistency of their accounts, and Borges's decision – within three years – to suppress the memory of the Chilean girl. Moreover, he and his mother were the only two who knew anything about it at the time. It has since become one of the most famous incidents in Borges's life, but the facts remain uncorroborated.

It is famous for what it did to Borges. It made him convalesce for a few weeks, during which time he came to doubt his sanity. His mother read to him from C. S. Lewis's *Out of the Silent Planet*. He cried, and when she asked him why, he replied 'because

I understand'. And he also understood something to do with what he should do next, something to do with his next step as a writer. He was full of doubts about that step, but knew he should, somehow, prepare for the 'final revelation'. He should write a story.

Amidst such circumstantial confusion, and yet with so simple a formula, a mid-century revolution in the art of fiction was about to begin.

Chapter Five

1939–1946

Great Fictions and Perón

'If I begin to write, if I dare to write an article on some book or another and I cannot do it, I'm finished, I don't exist any more. To make this discovery a little less dreadful, I'm going to try and do something I've never done. If I don't succeed, it'll be less dreadful for me. That at least will prepare me for accepting a non-literary destiny. Therefore I shall do something I've never done before: I shall write a story.'[1]

These were Borges's words to Georges Charbonnier in 1964, remembering his thoughts on recovering from his accident. Soon after it, in early 1939, he and his mother moved to a house at calle Anchorena 1672. It was an Andalusian-style building, with an inner patio and a garden at the back, pleasant, modest, quiet. By a quirk of fate, María Kodama's Borges Foundation has ended up next door to it.

At the time, Borges was very close to Haydée Lange, the sister of Norah and the tall, elegantly attired woman we see standing next to a bearded Georgie in a photograph taken on 1 April 1939. He picked her up most days at the bank where she worked and they then went to a restaurant in the centre of town for dinner, and took in a film at weekends. Their 'relationship' did not last long, though it seems marriage was discussed, and soon discarded.

Norah and Guillermo de Torre finally returned in mid-1938 from Paris, where they had been living since the bloody failure of Republican Spain in 1936 had forced their retreat from the Peninsula. The lived – by all accounts somewhat fractiously – with Borges and Leonor until 1943, when the family decamped to separate apartments. Leonor and Borges found another flat at the avenida Quintana 263 (the street where the Borgeses had lived *en famille* after their second return from Europe, in 1924), until, finally, mother and son made a flat in calle Maipú their permanent home.

As Europe headed for war, Argentina effectively battened down its hatches. Fascism had become increasingly fashionable in the late 1930s; the autocratic, Catholic strain in Argentine society, finding some of its extremer representatives in government, was to take even firmer hold throughout the war. President Ortiz's attempts at some liberal reform failed in 1940, and he was replaced by his corrupt sidekick, Ramón S. Castillo.

Castillo was quickly coerced by the military, who were keen for power, and for open rapprochement with the Axis. Castillo wavered, though was probably more inclined to side with the British. But he was quite unable to resist threats of American trade embargos and campaigns in the United States depicting the Argentine government as fascist and pro-Axis. In 1943, the army took over for good. Franco's victory in Spain in mid-1939 had meanwhile been something to admire; there was something attractive, too, for disillusioned Argentines in the excesses of Hitler and Mussolini.

Not, however, for Borges. As early as 1937, in *Sur*, he had pointed out how fascism was only poisoning Germany, whose culture he knew so well: 'I do not know if the world can do without German civilisation. It is shameful that it is being corrupted by teachings of hate,' he wrote, speaking of racism in current German school textbooks.[2] In October 1939, in a special *Sur* issue, against the war, he explicitly condemned Hitler and the Nazis. 'It is unarguable that a [German] victory would see the ruin and debasement of the world.'[3]

The nearest the war actually came to Argentina was in a naval battle in late 1939 off the Uruguayan resort of Punta del Este; three British cruisers tried to sink a German battleship, the *Graf Spee*, which took refuge in Montevideo harbour, only to be ejected by the Uruguayans who backed the Allies at the time. A reinforced British fleet awaited the battleship, which the German crew itself sank just out of Montevideo. The Germans then escaped into Argentina – a minor foretaste of the country's open-door policy for a much more odious breed of German escaping justice after the end of the war.

Borges stopped editing his pages for *El Hogar* in early 1939, and the literary section had disappeared by July. It seems his taste and views were simply too highbrow. But his contributions to the paper were given new life in 1986, in the first posthumous Borges volume, *Textos cautivos*. He continued now to write for *Sur*, getting into its stride as Buenos Aires's most persistently anti-war publication, and would also contribute another mocking, anti-Nazi broadside, called 'Definition of the Germanophile', to *El Hogar* in late 1940 – his last piece for the paper.

But the major publishing event of Borges's life so far was the appearance, exactly one year apart, of two stories that were to announce him as the most original and challenging voice in Argentina: 'Pierre Menard, Author of the *Quixote*' and 'Tlön, Uqbar, Orbis Tertius'.

'Pierre Menard' was written in the period immediately following Borges's accident, 'Tlön' shortly after. They were both published in *Sur*, 'Pierre Menard' in May 1939, and 'Tlön' in May 1940. They formed the core texts (along with an essay version of 'The Library of Babel', 'The Total Library', published in *Sur* in August 1939) of what came to be *El jardín de senderos que se bifurcan*, published less than three years after that watershed brush with the window.

Like 'The Approach to al-Mu'tasim', 'Pierre Menard' posed as a critical investigation. Borges wrote it as an *attempt* at a story, without being sure he wanted to commit himself wholeheartedly to fiction; it was more important at this stage after his disorientating illness to test his powers, on paper, of concentration and lucidity.

A critic, the narrator, has examined some papers belonging to an obscure French post-Symbolist poet, Pierre Menard. The critic is conceited, a snob, and anti-Semitic. Menard himself remains a mystery. He has just died. Amongst his papers are fragments of an attempt to rewrite Cervantes's *Don Quixote*, but in such a way as to reproduce the exact text: the story is thus a description of impossible authorial hubris – the desire to become

Cervantes, the hope that a new text can be a precise mirror of an old one.

The joke, which comes down to reproducing two identical paragraphs of Cervantes which excite exclamations of glee on the part of the critic as if they were different, is a brilliant one. It is the climax to a narrative which is an exposition of why, in the twentieth century, it is impossible to be an original writer.

Through the portentous voice of his critic, Borges produced his first fictional statement about the inefficacy of the written word to do anything other than imitate, and the stark dubiety of the writer's role. His narrator hails the technique of obfuscation, 'of the deliberate anachronism and the erroneous attribution'. In short, 'Pierre Menard' wittily carries out a razor-sharp act of literary deconstruction long before any 1960s toiling campus critic promoted the cause for actual academic use.

The improvement on 'al-Mu'tasim' in 'Pierre Menard' was in the confidence of Borges's scepticism: 'There is no exercise of the intellect which is not, in the final analysis, useless.' Knowing that he probably had stories to tell, Borges hereafter underlined his every act of writing with this bleak Schopenhauerian maxim; as such, 'Pierre Menard' was the harbinger of all the great future stories, where beguiling universes, almost palpably built in the course of the text, are doubted, questioned, worried over, until threatened with demolition. The starting point, as Menard states, is now always to be 'the imprecise and prior image of a book not yet written'.*

The illusion of fiction is never lost. Borges never fails to honour his reader, keep him or her enthralled, as well as endlessly amused. 'In his [Menard's] work there are no gipsy flourishes or conquistadors or mystics or Philip the Seconds or *autos da fé*. He neglects or eliminates local colour. This disdain points to a new conception of the historical novel.'[4] Borges revels in the fraud. The note he hit very precisely in 'Pierre Menard' he would go on to multiply, distort and amplify over the next ten to fifteen years. And then he would never do it, in quite the same way, again.

If 'Pierre Menard' perplexed *Sur*'s readers on its publication in May 1939, 'Tlön, Uqbar, Orbis Tertius' a year later must have had them wondering whether its author were of the same planet.

---

* See Chapter Seven, pp.189–90.

It was an even bigger experiment, 'perhaps the most ambitious of my stories', Borges said in 1982.[5] The discovery of another planet (which is the main event in 'Tlön') in science fiction is generally a cue for extravagant fantasy; for Borges in this story it was a way of reviewing the world, of offering a critique of reality. Even if the science, along with the maths, geography and language, of Tlön are indeed fictional, the story has the structural neatness and tonal formality of a fable by Aesop.

In narrative terms, nothing actually happens in 'Tlön' until the 'Postscript', 'added in 1947'. In part one, the first of the story's two bookish 'discoveries' is made: this is of an uncharted part of Asia Minor, a country called Uqbar, described in a rogue American encyclopaedia from 1917; the second, complementary discovery – of the planet 'Tlön' – is made from a similarly unlikely encyclopaedia sent to a certain Herbert Ashe in 'the hotel at Adrogué' (i.e. Las Delicias) from Brazil. It is near Brazil that the principal action takes place, towards the very end of the story: the death of a man who might or might not be from the planet which has been described in such detail in the previous pages.

It is in the detail of Tlön, an elaborate hoax we are teased into believing, in which – as with the fraudulence of Menard's enterprise – Borges takes such delight. A new world system is created, with geometry, maths, philosophy and entire structures of thought and existence to back it up; and in a masterly stroke, Borges then entrusts his readers – that is, the 'known' world outside the text – with acceptance, or not, of Tlön's veracity. He uses an image that was to become a trademark for his aesthetic of moral paralysis: 'Tlön is surely a labyrinth, but it is a labyrinth devised by men, a labyrinth destined to be deciphered by men.'[6]

By the end of the story, whether we have deciphered the labyrinth or not, we are in no doubt that Borges intends the illusion of the reality of Tlön to signify more than just a hoax. Two months after the first publication of the story, he suggested in *Sur* that throughout 1940, 'each morning, reality resembles more and more a nightmare'.[7] The civilised world was indeed collasping – the fall of Paris in May was a terrible moment for liberal intellectuals in Buenos Aires, as elsewhere in the free world. In 'Tlön', Borges was at one level pursuing a way of depicting the dizzying rift between fact and imagination, truth and its opposite – perhaps indefinable; at another, he was offering a metaphor for global catastrophe.

John King has put it well: 'In a world going mad, the intellectual response could only be a radical form of askesis, enjoying the plots of literature, but denying order to anything other than the autonomous sphere of literature.'[8]

One peculiarity in 'Tlön' was the use of real friends and co-writers as commentators on the veracity of Tlön: Bioy, Néstor Ibarra, Ezequiel Martínez Estrada, Pierre Drieu La Rochelle and Alfonso Reyes are all named in this capacity. The Princesse Faucigny-Lucinge, another Buenos Aires society *madame* of the era,[9] is actually the first to receive evidence of the physical existence of Tlön, in the form of a compass, which 'vibrated mysteriously', in her 'silverware from Poitiers'.

This documentary-like intrusion of the real happens again and again in Borges. Friends and acquaintances are introduced, as if the fictions they inhabit are just so much Buenos Aires table-talk. The blurring of the borders between real time and fictional space is to become almost a literary point of order for Borges.

He, too, is always somehow there, behind the tale – in this and in others – modest but manipulative; and yet he is not. He teases a reader into believing he or she will glide along in one form, one genre, only to subvert that expectation within a page or paragraph. This radical procedure, familiar as we are with it now, was further radicalised by Borges in the bare and uncompromising description he gave to the texts which embodied it: 'fictions', nothing more, nothing less.*

'Tlön' actually begins with a 'conversation' with Bioy Casares. It is Bioy who checks in the rogue encyclopaedia a statement he believes originated in Uqbar: 'that copulation and mirrors are abominable, because they increase the number of men'. His detail is not quite right; the Uqbar gnostic had actually said, 'the visible universe was an illusion or (more precisely) a sophism. Mirrors and fatherhood are abominable because they multiply and disseminate that universe.'

The second statement is more philosophically defiant. In it, the story's paradoxical theme is announced and, I would contest – for the purposes of this book – the overall theme of Borges's work: if

---

* Though see below, pp.130–31.

what we see is unreal, how can anything that brings that unreality into existence, be it by biological or illusory reproduction (which are anyway arguably one and the same), be trusted? Perhaps the only thing we can rely on is fiction, untruth, a strange space where time is obliterated and the constructs of empirical reality are made ghostly by the visionary but 'truer' tools of a tale.

In 'Tlön', Borges deployed astonishing narrative forces: an elaborate intellectual conceit, existential fear, and numerous, teasing autobiographical reference points. The sad protagonist, Herbert Ashe, owner of the encyclopaedia on Tlön, is a friend of the storyteller's father; Ashe himself bears a striking resemblance to Jorge, so in some ways the story was Borges's memorial to his own dead father.

Bioy, too, was on Borges's mind in 1940. Their friendship meant much to him. In 'Tlön', the narrator describes his father and Ashe's relationship as one of those 'close (the adjective is excessive) English friendships that begin by excluding confidences and very soon dispense with dialogue'.[10] It was of course the diametrical opposite of his friendship with Bioy: Borges being Borges, presenting its opposite was code for the truth.

This was the year in which his closest friend got married, to Silvina. A quiet ceremony took place on 15 January in Las Flores, a small town two hundred kilometres to the south-west of Buenos Aires. Thereafter, a routine of Friday gatherings at the Bioys' apartment in the avenida Quintana was established. Xul Solar and Pedro Henríquez Ureña would come, as would Eduardo Mallea and Manuel Peyrou. Younger writers – Ernesto Sábato, Adolfo de Obieta (Macedonio Fernández's son), María Luisa Bombal – also joined in, as well as close friends of Borges's such as Carlos Mastronardi and the Dabove brothers, Santiago and Julio César.

For Borges, these gatherings were supplemented by visits to various cafés downtown, particularly the Richmond, where the same said writers would entertain each other with literary and journalistic chitchat: both La Nación and La Prensa were (and are still) nearby. The Richmond on calle Florida remains much as it was: dark, cavernous, a cross between Manhattan speak-easy and Continental coffeehouse, today offering the same courteous service that Borges enjoyed for years, an oasis amidst this brash and polluted commercial heart of Buenos Aires.

Borges's participation in café life was always tentative. As has been said, whether at the Bioys or in cafés, he preferred one-to-one exchanges. He was in no sense a regular or a fixture at these meetings. The others, far from hanging on his every word, talked of their own work, while Borges either politely listened or suggested literary topics that had nothing to do with his writing. If he got bored, he went to a film – most of Buenos Aires's cinemas being in the same area – or on a long walk in the south of the city, through Barracas or La Boca.

Otherwise, he was at work: in the municipal library or at home, where Leonor ruled the roost, and sometimes at Adrogué. Through 1940 to the following year he wrote the rest of the stories that became *El jardín de senderos que se bifurcan*.

In between 'Pierre Menard' and 'Tlön', he had written 'La biblioteca total' ('The Total Library'), which became 'La Biblioteca de Babel' ('The Library of Babel') in 1941 – composed in Mar del Plata, a resort six hundred kilometres to the south of Buenos Aires where Victoria Ocampo had a house, and where Borges took regular holidays with Bioy.

'The Library of Babel' was clearly based on his experiences of the Miguel Cané library, though books and classification are only a starting-point: the nightmarish vision of infinity it evokes, its echoing corridors of all knowledge in every language, amount to one of Borges's most despairing statements about reality.

Again, as in 'Tlön', a world system is created, hermetically sealed. Made up of hexagonal galleries, *'The Library is a sphere whose exact centre is any one of its hexagons and whose circumference is inaccessible'*.* Humans come and go; what survives is infinity, and codes within the library that sustain infinity – Babel's version of it: 'in other words, all that it is given to express, in all languages'. In the context of Borges's own position as a librarian, the story is thus a delirious reversal of what a library is meant for – accessibility to knowledge.

'The Library of Babel' is an elaborate skit on a public service that had ceased to have any meaning to its writer. In it, books have taken a paranoiac revenge on the humanity which purports to use

---

* Italics as in original.

them for understanding the universe they, the books, are meant to explicate:

> There are official searchers, *inquisitors*. I have seen them in the performance of their function: they always arrive extremely tired from their journeys; they speak of a broken stairway which almost killed them; they talk with the librarian of galleries and stairs; sometimes they pick up the nearest volume and leaf through it, looking for infamous words. Obviously, no one expects to discover anything.

As with the two earlier stories, Borges is mapping out a topology of impossibility: 'In adventures such as these, I have squandered and wasted my years', says the narrator towards the story's end.[11] In the briefest and wittiest of fictions, Borges suggests once again that the form is best put to use in proving that nothing a fiction pretends is true can ever be so.

In a different vein, in 1940, he also wrote a foreword to Adolfo Bioy Casares's most famous novel, *La invención de Morel (The Invention of Morel)*, whose plot he compared to Kafka's *The Trial* and James's *The Turn of the Screw*. Borges's tribute to his friend was tantamount to a declaration of artistic faith. There was, he said, nothing wrong with a tightly plotted tale, nor with a detective story; the twentieth century's handling of psychological realism, of psychological time, was doing the cause of fiction no good. Stevenson, De Quincey and Wells had much to offer in areas where Proust and the Russians had nothing.

Bioy had his own say on the matter in another foreword to a book published a month after *The Invention of Morel*. This was his, Silvina's and Borges's collaborative *Antología de literatura fantástica*, published in December 1940 by a company founded by exiles from the Spanish Civil War: Editorial Sudamericana. Describing the genre being anthologised, Bioy talks of something which is both 'essay and fiction . . . exercises of unceasing intelligence and imagination [lacking] all languor, all *human elements*, emotional or sentimental'.[12] He obviously had Borges's own writings in mind; between them he and Borges were disputatiously flying in the face of conventional wisdom about how fiction should be written, and enjoying it.

Sur published Borges's 'Las ruinas circulares' ('The Circular

Ruins') in the same month, followed by 'La lotería en Babilonia' ('The Lottery in Babylon') in January 1941. In the first, the dreamer, in a Stygian parody of the Creation, is famously the dreamed. It opens with one of the most resonant (and oft-quoted) phrases in Borges: '*Nadie lo vio desembarcar en la unánime noche*', 'No one saw him disembark in the unanimous night', as the translation in *Labyrinths* has it.[13]

In only a few of Borges's stories is there a sense of physical creation: here, the 'grey man' makes an enormous, one might say superhuman effort, effectively to reproduce himself, only to be consumed by images he himself has made. Not quite cannibalism, not quite magic, and not quite real – though the tone of the story is almost scientific, anthropological – 'The Circular Ruins' remains Borges's strangest inquiry into the mysteries of ontology.

'The Lottery in Babylon', meanwhile, is a depiction, somewhat after Kafka (or 'Qaphqa', as a 'sacred latrine' in the story is punningly called), of totalitarianism. A sinister body called the Company has the power to run the lives of the Babylonians according to their success and daring, or lack of either, in a state lottery. The parallel with various political systems that had begun in Europe throughout the 1930s, and taken root in Argentina at the end of that decade, is unmistakable. The infinite game of chance is this story's universal code; a harmless form of leisure is turned into a merciless system of survival, or defeat, for those unavoidably trapped within it.

The last of the *Jardín* stories to appear in *Sur* before the volume itself was 'Examen de la obra de Herbert Quain' ('Examination of the Work of Herbert Quain'), in April 1941. This was a variant on 'Pierre Menard', though much more of a skit, an algebraic one at that, on a Johnsonian Life.

'The Garden of Forking Paths', finally, was the only story not to have pre-book life. Superficially, it follows a detective-story plot structure, with a confession at its heart; the plotting is in truth multi-layered, with each move made to push the narrative forward met with a counter-move, as in chess (a central image in the story); Sinology, the philosophy of labyrinths and gardens, espionage and premonition are all added in to build a seamlessly interwoven discourse on time – how essentially fictitious it is, and yet how inescapable.

It is the densest, and perhaps philosophically most nihilistic, story

Borges ever wrote. It was placed last out of eight ('Tlön' was first, 'al-Mu'tasim' second) in the slim, sky-blue volume published by the Sur imprint at the end of 1941.

Rodríguez Monegal called it the 'single most important book of prose fiction written in Spanish in this century' – that was in 1978,[14] when Borges's experiments had, wittingly or unwittingly to any writer who dealt in narrative, reshaped post-war fiction. But thirty-seven years before, *El jardín* must have seemed a very strange beast indeed.

The Bioy-Borges partnership was still in its mutual-admiration stage; that is to say, erudite jokes and chitchat based on a love of detective fiction had not yet quite led to 'literature' – reviews of each other's work, certainly, including a laudatory and impressively analytical one by Bioy of *El jardín* in *Sur* in May 1942. He wanted to persuade readers that Borges's writing was groundbreaking in its preoccupation with metaphysics, with – in effect – literature being about itself.

But that idea, along with the book and the review, were still far too remote for a 1940s South American audience fed on a not over-nutritious diet of nationalist or social realism. The fact that Borges's work was exhibiting something quintessential about the art of storytelling went more or less unnoticed. Moreover, his reputation was still cocooned within the *Sur* circuit (though the magazine was read all over Latin America), his daily life circumscribed by the boundaries of library and home. His new book didn't change that.

Composing at Adrogué or in Mar del Plata, it was easier for Borges to keep things hidden from Leonor's critical gaze. She had already objected to 'Streetcorner Man'; *El jardín de senderos que se bifurcan* was even stranger to her, with its multiple ironies, labyrinths, illusions, murders and cul-de-sacs. Her son's imagination was taking a dark turn: there was much wit in these stories, but little joy.

For Borges, writing was now about spareness, a singleness of tone, lexical clarity. The lynchpin in this was Bioy. A revealing confession came in the 'Autobiographical Essay': 'Opposing my taste for the pathetic, the sententious, and the baroque, Bioy made me feel that quietness and restraint are more desirable. If I may be allowed a sweeping statement, Bioy led me gradually toward classicism.'[15]

A clarification Bioy made of this statement underlines just how literary their friendship was:

> When he was young, Borges always wanted to conclude his sentences with an effect; in that sense he was a romantic writer. In his first fictions, *A Universal History of Infamy* for instance, he was an author who wanted continually to amaze.
>
> For me, classicism was all about getting through to the reader without anything being noticed. In his maturity, Borges wrote in a more harmonious way, each phrase joining neatly with the next. He became simpler and simpler through the years.[16]

Their collaborative ventures were soon under way. A month after the publication of *El jardín*, their *Antología poética argentina* appeared with Sudamericana, a ragbag of work by generally minor figures written between 1900 and 1941; it was not a success. Borges chose not to include himself, and the book might have been better had he done so. Still, it was a symbolic omission. Bioy's unswerving confidence in fiction had focussed Borges's mind on how to apply his thinking to narrative. *El jardín* was the immediate result. He had all but stopped writing poetry, and was fashioning himself into a very different kind of writer from the one he had first thought he would be.

He didn't want to write novels, unlike Bioy, whose *The Invention of Morel* had proved him more than adept in the form. But together, activating each other's instincts for writerly subversion, the two men could create something resembling an anti-novel. This was the path they set out on in early 1942: at Bioy's home, they would discuss possible story-lines, particularly in a detective mode, and conclude that classical methods of ending such a tale – discovery, denouement, melodramatic twist – left them dissatisfied, just as did sentimental ones of conventional romantic fiction.[17]

Their jokes were cues for texts. The texts could have a beginning and an end, which could be turned on their heads, shuffled like a deck of cards. They then found that somebody else was in fact 'writing' these texts, a third party who was given the baroque name of Honorio Bustos Domecq – a cross between one of Borges's great-grandfathers (Bustos) and one of Bioy's (Domecq). The strangest joke of all was for Bustos Domecq to put his detective, Don Isidro Parodi, in a jail cell. From there, he has to work out the solutions to a variety of conundrums: a man visits him in jail, to seek his help over a murder he has committed; a murdered man plots his own self-sacrifice – is it suicide?; a man cuckolded by his wife avenges the dishonour by attacking her illegitimate child.

When *Seis problemas para don Isidro Parodi* (*Six Problems for Don Isidro Parodi*) came out in mid-1942, readers were, as they so often would be by the products of Borges's pen alone, baffled. The jokes were recondite, the plots unfathomable, the author's status and identity questionable. Some readers felt insulted when they found out that Bustos Domecq was not real; others got tired of the jokes very quickly. Few appreciated the genuinely subversive spirit of the book, its parodying of, and attacks on, the complacencies of empirical narrative.

Even fewer understood that it was offered by two writers revelling in a frivolous, anti-establishment, anti-literary prank. Borges never took Bustos Domecq seriously; nor did Bioy, who claimed that little by way of hard work went into the stories. They spent most of the time laughing over the typewriter.[18]

If *Six Problems* was given short shrift, an even greater act of critical negligence occurred just before the publication of the spoof detective stories. The 1941–2 National Literary Prize, awarded by a Buenos Aires body called the National Commission for Culture, went to Eduardo Acevedo Díaz, son of a popular Uruguayan historical novelist. In second and third places were César Carrizo and Pablo Rojas Paz; Borges, who had entered the competition with *El jardín de senderos que se bifurcan*, was ignominiously overlooked – out of a jury of six, Eduardo Mallea alone had voted for him to be placed second.

There was little consolation to be had from an anonymous notice about that year's prize published in the July issue of *Nosotros*:

If the jury felt it could not offer the Argentine people, at this time in the world, with the highest national award, an exotic and decadent work which oscillates, in response to certain oblique tendencies in contemporary English literature, between the fantastic tale, boastful and recondite erudition, and the detective story – obscure to the point of darkness for whoever reads it, even the most cultivated (excluding those who might be initiated in the new magic) – then we judge that it has decided correctly.[19]

The statement was as sinister as it was convoluted. Outside the *Sur* crowd, nationalism, which Borges had come to abhor, was culturally rampant. England had fought for three years the powers Argentina now favoured, and to say that a literary work with English 'tendencies' could not be awarded a national prize reeked of open political bias. For the commission to suggest that it could intercede between the writing community and the 'Argentine people' was also fundamentally stupid.

José Bianco organised a tribute issue of *Sur* to Borges, entitled 'Desagravio a Borges' (Amends to Borges), containing notes by twenty-one writers expressing their admiration for him. Bioy opined: 'Posterity will be shown that Argentina is not just a desert peopled by members of the National Commission for Culture.'[20] Solidarity for Borges was further expressed at a dinner at a restaurant called La Pagoda, convened on 18 July in honour of *El jardín* by his friends, including many of those who had contributed to the *Sur* issue. Bianco recalled that when copies of the magazine – specially bound in bull's blood red ('because I know he does not like green') – arrived at calle Anchorena, Borges joked about the homage, and couldn't understand why so many fellow writers had seen fit to support him.[21]

The mood in Buenos Aires at this time was divisive and unstable. Throughout the early 1940s, the army had begun to make its intentions plain. From 1943 on, puppet presidents ruled in Buenos Aires in a democratic vacuum, allowing one officer in particular to consolidate his position and influence in various ministries: Juan Domingo Perón was on the march.

His time, and Borges's quarrel with him, were still some way ahead. The significance of the 1942 rally-round for Borges was its spontaneity and decisiveness, representing a ranging of the forces of liberal culture against those of bigoted philistinism. The philistines probably took no notice; a strange book which the public at large patently did not understand was no threat to the greater destiny of Argentina. But the homage by friends to Borges, the first in a series in these years, marks the moment – far more than the publication of *A Universal History of Infamy* – when his work as a writer put down firm roots into Argentine literary history. Only in retrospect can we see that Borges had far outrun his Argentine peers in sophistication, scope and intellectual ambition. Though no one knew it, least of all Borges, he was already an international writer.

The French critic-sociologist Roger Caillois had arrived in Buenos Aires in 1939. He was one of Victoria Ocampo's Paris favourites; twenty-six, youthful, handsome. 'Being unable to bring you all of the rue Gay-Lussac [where the Paris College of Sociology was based],' she wrote in *Sur*, 'I have decided to transport Roger Caillois here.'[22]

He was completely unknown in Buenos Aires, but Ocampo was unstinting in the promotion of her refined and energetic protégé. Soon, he was playing an active part in *Sur*, collaborating editorially with José Bianco, and running a publication under the magazine's aegis and patronage, *Lettres françaises*. It first appeared in mid-1941, and continued to appear until 1945, when Caillois returned to France. The magazine was famous for two things: first, for supposedly being dropped by the British over occupied France; second, for publishing Borges in French, the first foreign language into which he was translated.

That was in October 1944, when two texts, 'The Lottery in Babylon' and 'The Library of Babel', appeared under the combined title of 'Assyriennes', translated by Néstor Ibarra. Ibarra remained close to Borges well into old age, but towards Caillois Borges was less than warm.

It stemmed from a dispute they had in issues of *Sur*, in April and May 1942: Caillois had provided a sociological reading of the detective novel, and argued that the genre had begun with the formation of a Paris police force by Joseph Fouché; averring that it was in Poe's stories that the first detective fiction was foreshadowed, Borges dismissed the argument and Caillois's entire approach in biting terms. 'Caillois's conjecture is not erroneous; I just think it is inept, unverifiable.'[23] Caillois seemed not to mind; long after he left Buenos Aires in 1945, he continued to promote Borges in Europe, to such an extent that Borges later often acknowledged that it was Caillois who had really 'made him' abroad.

Caillois's wartime presence in Buenos Aires was symptomatic of the city's cultural status: a place where writers in Nazi-occupied Europe could publish and be read, French writers in particular, given the well-established ties between the two cultures. Ibarra and Caillois were the advance guard of the French tendency; and as early as 1936, at a farcical meeting of International PEN in Buenos Aires, novelist Jules Romains, philosopher Jacques Maritain and Belgian poet Henri Michaux had made considerable Francophone impact. Michaux became a regular visitor to Buenos Aires, enjoying the company of Borges, who always admired the enigmatic Belgian, translating his book *Un barbare en Asie* into Spanish in 1941.

As ubiquitous as the French were refugees from the Spanish Civil War. Borges's Ultraist sparring partner from Madrid days, Ramón Gómez de la Serna, arrived in Buenos Aires in 1936, and stayed there until his death in 1963. His last book, *Total de greguerías*, was published in 1955.

The Argentine publishing scene began to feel the effects of that war too, from 1937 on: Sudamericana has already been mentioned. The Madrid-based Espasa Calpe launched a list called Colección Austral in Buenos Aires; and going out on his own from Espasa Calpe, editor Gonzalo Losada set up a house which in 1943 published Borges's first collection of poetry since 1929, *Poemas [1922–1943]*.

He had written little poetry in the 1930s. The new volume contained concertina'd versions of the three 1920s collections – *Fervor de Buenos Aires*, *Luna de enfrente* and *Cuaderno San Martín*, revised, added to, excised – and six new poems: the two English ones written in 1934, 'Insomnia', written in Adrogué in 1936, 'La noche cíclica' ('Cyclical Night', 1940), 'Del cielo y del infierno' ('On Heaven and Hell', 1942) and 'Poema conjetural' ('Conjectural Poem', 1943).* The last three are dark, apocalyptic visions of experience outside time – the first a piece of strophic self-referentiality, the second a Dantesque meditation, the third a dramatic monologue.

The last is one of Borges's best poems, and one of his most famous. His distant ancestor Francisco Narciso Laprida recounts the last minutes of his life before being murdered by a gang of gauchos. In a powerful picture of chaos and violence, Borges does two things. He transfers his own immediate awareness of mortality into the mind of a historical personage, so that the imagining of his

---

* He had also contributed a poem, as yet uncollected, to an illustrated magazine, *Saber Vivir*, in 1940, entitled 'Para la noche del 24 de Diciembre de 1940 en Inglaterra': see p. 132.

– Borges's – annihilation remains both real, and yet distant; he can both tell and be intimately part of the same story – and Borges was always fascinated by the actual moment, the sensation, of physical extinction.

He also uses the poem as a means of political commentary. President Castillo was deposed in a bloodless coup on 4 June 1943, and General Pedro Ramírez installed as the new premier. He was dismissed in January 1944, when after persistent pressure from the United States, he agreed to confirm Argentina's neutrality by cutting all diplomatic ties with the Axis. Another general, Edelmiro Farrell, was put in charge, and was effectively run by the army. Under its command, Farrell carried on as if nothing had changed.

All political parties were abolished. Press restrictions reached a symbolic low when *La Prensa* was closed down for five days in April 1944. The country was awash with military propaganda, and fascist-like, torch-lit processions marched through Buenos Aires. Perón, now a colonel, became vice-president, as well as secretary for labour and welfare, a post created specifically for him. Not yet in the full political limelight, he was successfully wooing the broad mass of Argentines, the trade unions above all, into accepting autocracy. With obvious relish, and perfect timing, Perón was playing on the political weaknesses of his leader, and capitalising on the complete failure of democracy in Argentina since 1930.

Borges, well-educated in the methods of fascism, the European versions of which he had often denounced in print throughout the 1930s, found this power-hungry, militaristic, spruced-up 47-year-old intolerable. He was a provincial upstart, a gaucho.

In 'Conjectural Poem', 'The gauchos have won:/ victory is theirs, the barbarians''. Against the background of Perón's rise, precipitated by the 1943 coup, this was hardly a veiled a message. The poem was published exactly a month after the coup. When Borges has Laprida say, 'I see at last that I am face to face/with my South American destiny',[24] the poet-turned-fabulist was reflecting not just on an imminent, inevitable violent death, but an imminent, inevitable end to the values he understood and held dear.

Work at the library continued at its demeaning pace. Borges and Leonor moved to the avenida Quintana in mid-1943; Borges was writing at full tilt. Between May 1942 and February 1943, he published four new stories, 'Funes el memorioso' ('Funes the

Memorious') and 'La forma de la espada' ('The Shape of the Sword') in *La Nación*, and 'La muerte y la brújula' ('Death and the Compass') and 'El milagro secreto' ('The Secret Miracle') in *Sur*. Bustos Domecq was also busy with a couple of stories published in *Sur*, 'El testigo' (The Witness) and 'El signo' (The Sign), as anarchic as ever. These appeared in 1946 in a short book published privately by a fake publisher, Oportet & Haereses (a play on the Iberian towns after which two wines are named, Porto and Jerez), entitled *Dos fantasías memorables*. Another strange name then emerged after 1943, 'B. Suárez Lynch', a 'follower' of Bustos Domecq's, who published, also in 1946 and with the same punning company, a small book called *Un modelo para la muerte*. Carlos Mastronardi said of it: 'the charming and light plot, whose tracing is not easy at all, gets lost . . .'.[25]

Borges commented in 1964 that he and Bioy had probably gone too far with their jokes – 'jokes squared, jokes cubed'[26] – and for the time being they put an end to their two hybrid authors. But from one reading of these rackety tales a clear critique of a nightmare Argentina can be detected: the characters are slobs, speak in slang, and stand in mad opposition to public authority – and the reader is asked to like them. The subversive code is not instantly graspable, and for some is buried beneath too thick a layer of literary facetiousness. It had long been a favourite tool of Borges's, and the two writers encouraged it in each other. But the fun had tough edges. Borges was himself unequivocal in the 'Essay': 'The book [*Don Isidro*] was . . . a satire on the Argentine.'[27]

An important relationship for Borges began this same year with a small publisher. Emecé had been up and running in Buenos Aires since 1939. From 1951, they would publish all of Borges's prose and poetry, and become his main house in the Spanish-speaking world, until his death.

Like Sudamericana and Losada, the firm was formed by an exile from Spain, Mariano Medina del Río, who linked up with Alvaro de las Casas in Buenos Aires, a literary man, and Carlos Braun Menéndez, who had studied with Medina del Río in Spain. 'Emecé' was an amalgam of their names.

Borges began at Emecé with an editorial input into a series of small pamphlets of short stories, including his own translations – James, Melville, Kafka, Faulkner. With Bioy he put together a volume of 'best detective stories', which led in 1945 to the editing of a series of detective novels published by Emecé under the title El Séptimo Circulo (The Seventh Circle – named after Dante). One of the books they put into that series was Graham Greene's *The Ministry of Fear* – Borges claimed it was one of the finest novels to come out of the war.

And the war in Europe was nearly over. On the liberation of Paris in August 1944, Borges wrote in *Sur* of a feeling of '*physical happiness*'; the end of Nazism was in sight. Yet in Buenos Aires, the nightmare was about to begin, and this was no better illustrated than in the reaction of the police to a demonstration in the plaza Francia: a crowd gathered to hail the liberation of Paris was brutally dispersed, with injuries and fatalities. If Borges sensed relief at events unfolding in Europe, he felt only grave concern about what was in store at home. His problems would begin when it was plain that once Perón had acceded to the presidency, few had openly shared or would come to share that concern: Borges would remain something of a lone voice, on the political as well as the fictional fronts.

His new stories had become more topographical. They took place in identifiable locales. 'Funes the Memorious', about a man who remembers everything he has perceived, is set in Uruguay, the landscape that of his Haedo cousins' farm. Indeed, the narrator's 'father' has taken him to spend the summer at Fray Bentos, and cousin 'Bernardo Haedo' has just been visited. Borges has the narrator's meeting with Ireneo Funes occur in 1884, fifty years before his own memorable stay in Uruguay, when he witnessed a shooting. Indeed, it was a measure of the impact that Uruguayan stay had had on him that Borges was still writing it out of his system two decades later.

'Death and the Compass' is also about violence, but of a more constructed, meticulously planned kind. Four killings take place within the pattern of a rhombus; Buenos Aires is for the first time in Borges's fiction the precise setting for this coldly geometric tale, a detective story which turns in on itself, like 'The Garden of Forking Paths', but which also, like 'Conjectural Poem', concerns the moment of death. Likewise 'The Secret Miracle', which takes us to wartime Prague, and the execution by the Nazis of a Jewish playwright, Jaromir Hladik: God intervenes just as the bullets are about to be fired, and suspending time allows him one year to finish a tragedy he has been writing.

Given that this was published in February 1943, Borges's reactions to brutalities in the European war were extraordinarily swift. Many such stories and scenarios in books and films would take years to emerge; Borges's ability to imagine so fast and so far away is what so often bolsters the illusion that he, too, somehow worked outside time, in a manner to catch an essential moment of it.

Either side of 'The Secret Miracle' appeared 'The Shape of the Sword' and 'Tema del traidor y el héroe' ('Theme of the Traitor and the Hero') – the latter a year after 'The Secret Miracle', in *Sur*, in February 1944. Both are unexpectedly set in Ireland, the first in 1922, the second in 1824: Borges enjoyed the useless symmetry of anniversary – 'The Sword' tells of an event occurring exactly twenty years previous to its being written, 'The Traitor' exactly a hundred. Both concern political uprisings, against the British, and both play with role reversal, with the startling alterations of expected reality a willed fiction can inflict on its reader.

Both represent Borges at his devious best, and both are cruel: in 'The Sword', Vincent Moon, the narrator-betrayer posing as the victim, condemns himself to eternal infamy for his duplicity as a storyteller; in 'The Traitor', the so-called traitor Kilpatrick's death is mercilessly planned by an executioner – another breed of story-maker – for the purposes of political expediency. Both are miniaturist distillations of the more complex patterns of 'Forking Paths' and 'Death and the Compass'.

The last story of this period was 'Tres versiones de Judas' ('Three Versions of Judas'), which Borges called a 'Christological fantasy'. Published in *Sur* in August 1944, this was a return to his well-trodden terrain of an obscure scholar's epistemological research – what was the nature of Christ's sacrifice? – leading to a wonderful upset (God had inhabited not Jesus but Judas). It was the last but one story Borges wrote in this vein – 'La secta del Fénix' ('The Sect of the Phoenix') came nine years later, by which time Borges's energies had been magnificently engaged in the more 'realistic' stories that comprise *El Aleph*. (Thereafter, except for one brief story, there would be no more fiction until 1970.)

Ficciones was published by Sur in December 1944. Borges had first used the word *ficciones* in 1936, in a pamphlet celebrating the four hundredth anniversary of the founding of Buenos Aires; there, he had referred to '*ficciones porteñas*', 'Buenos Aires fictions',[28] as a way of describing an overblown picture of the city in gauchesco writing. Using it now for his new book, which constituted *El jardín de senderos que se bifurcan* and the six stories above, gathered under the title *Artificios*, Borges was close to self-mockery. Towards the end of his life, he said that *Ficciones* was nothing other than a rhyme of *Inquisiciones* (his 1925 volume of essays).[29] This rather flies in the face of the acres of print devoted to the metaphysical radicalism of the title. At least it means what it says.

The book went down better than *El jardín*. Enrique Amorim was instrumental in getting the Sociedad Argentina de Escritores, (Argentine Society for Writers), or SADE, to create for Borges a special Grand Honorary Prize for it. It was satisfactory compensation for the ill treatment given to *El jardín* by the city of Buenos Aires, but Borges was still a long way from being a seller. For that he would need a full-time commercial publisher, which Sur was not.

He continued to supplement his income from the library with work for Emecé. This included prefacing works in translation by Thomas Carlyle and Henry James. At the beginning of 1945, he edited an anthology for Emecé called *El compadrito*, containing dialogues, poems, sociological and historical reports about the urban hoodlum, the figure which had exerted so strong a fascination on him in the 1920s. It was a small affair, and remains a curiosity in the Borges bibliography; what was significant about it was his chosen collaborator, Silvina Bullrich.

She was a talented writer who alone amongst all the *Sur* literary set was to make a good living from her work, and become quite famous. She was extremely good-looking, and one of three sisters. The other two had married into money. Silvina by contrast had been tricked into a marriage with a man named Palenque Tarreras, from Rosario; he had led her to believe that he was a practising lawyer – in fact he was only just starting out. She became pregnant, which forced marriage on them; she had a son and Palenque, who decided he was gay, eventually went off to France as an envoyé for Perón.

Silvina Bullrich at this stage of her career was making a precarious living from translating from French. When Borges met her in the early 1940s, her first responsibility was to her small son; Leonor, when introduced to her by Borges, took pity on her, and the two women became good friends, their relationship being closer than that between her and Borges. In later years Silvina tended to be disparaging about his worldwide success, and cruel about him behind his back – a reflection of her popular rather than literary acclaim. *El compadrito* was her only collaboration with Borges, but significant in that she was the first in a long line of literary women who teamed up with Borges throughout the 1950s, 1960s and 1970s to produce anthologies and little books of essays.

This form of collaboration was to become almost an emblem of his sentimental life, his way for decades of expressing his interest in members of the opposite sex whom he could best reach through literature. Friendship it was, even if only for the duration of the collaboration; Borges always claimed that an ability to forge friendships was the singular talent of the Argentine.

From friendship, Argentina and hoodlums to another subject that impassioned Borges: England. With peace in Europe, Borges reaffirmed his belief in the civilised values of this 'arrogant and marginal island', as he wrote in *Sur* in July 1945. He had written a sonnet (not one of his best) lamenting the fate of the country in its darkest hours of 1940: 'England. Oh that the climes of God restore to you/Unbloodied snow, as pure as forgetfulness,/The great shadow of Dickens, the thunder of happiness.'[30]

Now, he defined the war victor as the only country not to be 'ecstatic about itself, the only one not to take itself for a utopia or paradise'.[31] In other words (the patriotic VE 1945 jamboree aside), that lethal, self-regarding nationalism which had led to Nazism and seemed now to be sweeping through Argentina was, for Borges, absent from England even in its most euphoric moment. He was continuing to pin his colours to the enshrined freedoms of a democracy his own country's authorities tacitly considered a foe. His gesture may have seemed innocent enough at the time. Within a year, Borges's Anglophilia – just one of many manifestations of his anti-Peronism – would lead to humiliation.

Argentina declared war on the Axis on 27 March 1945. The United States recognised the Farrell administration forthwith, which simply led to further confusion in Argentina. Perón's harnessing of the unions through his various ministerial posts and expert handling of the media came under intense criticism from the regime's opponents, the Fuerzas Vivas, representing employer-power.

After Germany fell on 7 May, Britain's diplomatic activities in Latin America were much reduced; against a rising tide of anti-government fervour in Argentina, the Americans insisted on elections in return for a lifting of trade sanctions. Leftist factions rounded on Perón as the principal impediment to democracy. Through them, a massive demonstration in Buenos Aires calling for an end to the old politics was organised on 19 September; many of Borges's writer friends joined it, but not Borges himself. He had been struck down by chicken-pox.[32]

In the confusing weeks ahead, Perón was first imprisoned on the island of Martín García off Uruguay, then hailed, on 17 October, by another massive crowd gathered in the plaza de Mayo in front of the governmental house, the Casa Rosada, as Argentina's next leader. He was voted into office on 24 February 1946.

What in essence happened was that Farrell's tottering regime failed to comprehend the depths to which Peronism had burrowed throughout the 1940s; in Perón's temporary absence, the reactionary feebleness of the old politics brought into sharp focus his hybrid creed's espousal of workers' rights, anti-imperialism, economic centralism and military security. In the face of this, leftist opposition evaporated; liberals and intellectuals were left without any representative to pursue a case for the middle way within government.

By contrast, with his big smile, his radio-friendly voice, his slicked-back black hair, and not least of all his blonde mistress, Eva Duarte, whom he married on 22 October 1945, Perón stood for something every Argentine politician since 1930 had manifestly failed to offer: the charismatic possibility of achieving a new order without bloodshed or corruption. That Perón was able to unite, amongst his voters, a combination of old Argentine nationalism with new ideas of worker emancipation was adroit enough. That he could do it dressed up in the clothing of fascism, and make the entire package more than acceptable – devoutly to be desired, if the homilies of his millions of supporters were anything to go by – was little short of genius. As one contemporary account, describing the 17 October rally, put it, the Argentine people experienced 'collective orgasm' in welcoming back Perón.[33]

Borges was appalled: '. . . a great number of Argentines are becoming Nazis without being aware of it,' he wrote in a Montevideo paper after Perón's release.[34] He would not stop there. His attacks on Perón, his creed and his regime in the years to come would be vocal, and continuous. Indeed, he would denounce Perón for the rest of his life.

In 1946, Borges's worst nightmare about the fate of Argentina became fact. It didn't stop him writing creatively; indeed, the apogee of his inventive powers, both in fiction and criticism, arguably still lay before him. But his life, which had not been easy until Perón, was now going to become even more difficult.

Chapter Six

1946–1955

Rising Fame

Borges's feeling of '*physical* happiness' at the liberation of Paris in August 1944 almost certainly reflected a new sexual interest. Just before that liberation, he had a met a woman of twenty-eight, Estela Canto. She was from an old Uruguayan, land-owning family whose fortunes had dwindled.

When Borges met her, Estela had already been making her living since she was twenty – as a secretary, working in advertising and stockbroking offices – but, with radio and film studies behind her, she had also branched into journalism. She thought she could be a writer, but wanted to be an actress even more. Only her mother prevented her in the latter ambition; she considered acting undignified.*

Estela was a woman of independent means, and as such a significant departure from Borges's usual choice of well-connected, well-kept society *señoras*. Dark, slim, with large brown, knowing

---

* In 1993, Estela Canto put it like this: 'I regret very much not becoming an actress, because I would have had a much more interesting life. My life *was* interesting, but not as a writer, more as a woman.' (See footnote over.)

eyes, she was street-wise and politically motivated – leftwards.* (They both despised Perón.) Borges's physical attraction to her was instantaneous: 'The smile of La Gioconda and the movements of a chess knight!' he told her on their first outing together some weeks later.[1] She was flattered, but unable, then or at any point during their association, to return a comparable compliment.

They had met at the Bioys, then living in a triplex on the corner of the avenida Santa Fe and calle Ecuador. Estela's brother Patricio, a writer and part of the Bioys' literary circle, had introduced her some months before to Silvina, with whom he was particularly friendly. Patricio then left on a scholarship to Oxford, and Estela filled his shoes. Borges and Bioy were busy with Bustos Domecq in another part of the house, so the two women learnt new dance steps together; the males of the Bioy circle – Mallea, Peyrou, Bianco, Borges inevitably – were either unable or disinclined to dance with them.

At their first meeting, it was Bioy who introduced Borges and Estela. Borges appeared distracted, and immediately averted what Estela called his 'large, celestial eyes' so as not to fix on her directly.[2] Estela, accustomed to more courteous male attentions, was taken aback. To her, he was chubby, tall, with pallid, fatty skin, small feet, and a hand that when stretched out looked as though it were boneless. His voice was tremulous, questioning, as if he were seeking permission to say or do something. Estela was not over-impressed – she had heard that this Borges, so admired by the Bioy bunch, was no great looker – but she was at least pleased to meet the man generally regarded as Buenos Aires's leading literary intellectual.

One night towards summer, the two of them happened to be leaving the Bioys at around twelve. Borges asked Estela which way she was going, and she said to the *subte* at Santa Fé and Pueyrredón, a block away, where she would catch the train home. He too had to take the *subte* home, so he walked her to the station. Once there, Borges suggested they continue walking a few blocks; the night was pleasant – the jacarandas were in full bloom and a light breeze blew from the river. Estela accepted.

---

* In the same interview, she said that the only Argentine man she had ever admired was Che Guevara.[3]

Like Borges, Estela was a tireless walker. They ended up walking all the way to the southern half of the city, where Estela lived with her mother. Borges was delighted; the Southside was the bit of Buenos Aires that always excited him most. Then, as now, it would have been more an expedition than a late-night wander, something over seven kilometres – it seems they noticed neither the stations still open on the way nor the time passing.*

They talked of the current political situation, which to both was ominous, but with a difference for both: Peronism for Borges (according to Estela) was a nightmare from which they were about to awaken, a ghastly totalitarian construct which he himself might have invented as a form of purgatory in one of his stories – but it would end. It had to.

For Estela, Peronism was all too real, and lay just 'around the next corner'. It was coming, and there was no escaping it. Canto's political antennae were arguably better attuned than Borges's, but then so, arguably, were most people's. What was vile about Perón for Borges was his affront to the imagination. For Canto, as for most liberals, Perón was a political reality that had to be accepted, challenged, and out-manoeuvered.

The couple moved on to talk about mutual friends, and other writers. In a bar on the avenida de Mayo, where Estela ordered coffee and he a glass of milk, Borges remarked not only on her smile and manner of moving, but also stated that she was the first woman he had ever met who liked Bernard Shaw. 'How strange!' he added.[5]

The comment was not a winning one, not at least for Estela. Borges had very fixed views about the writers he admired, and very fixed tastes. As we know, his views about reading and readership were equally firm, if unorthodox. With the exception of Victoria Ocampo, of whom he was always in awe anyway, he was unaccustomed to women of like literary mind. He certainly would not have expected this pretty young *señorita* to enjoy the brisk satires and provocative dramas of one of the most opinionated men then writing in English.

---

* Bioy gave an amusing (possibly apocryphal) picture of the two on their nocturnal forays throughout the following year: 'There was Estela Canto, who was practically blind, and Borges, who was practically blind – and she was drunk most of the time. After dinner with us, on the few evenings she came to our house, out they went into the street, these two blind people. . .'.[4]

But that is precisely what she did enjoy – the Irishman's rebelliousness. Rebellion was in her make-up, and Borges was not used to this, not at least in women. Estela in no way felt herself to be Borges's intellectual equal – what woman or man would? – but she had a quick independence of spirit, and was well-read. From the outset, she found herself quite unable to share Borges's enthusiasm for the likes of Chesterton and Stevenson, for instance, or for other such 'virile' writers, as she put it[6] – Conrad, Wells, Melville – for whom Borges had a somewhat obsessive affection. And she said so.

She also felt fully Borges's contempt of writing meant 'for women'[7] – romances, nineteenth-century realism, the novels of female writers of the English tradition: Jane Austen, Charlotte Brontë, George Eliot, none of whom featured in Borges's inner library (the North American poet Emily Dickinson was the only woman writer who did).

As for Henry James, whom Borges of course loved, Estela consigned the master of Rye to that very same category; his stories were the stuff of women's magazines, she said, which was bound to infuriate Borges. It did. On the other hand, there was nothing she could do to change Borges's negative view of Thomas Mann, whom she admired, nor his indifference to the Russians – Tolstoy, Dostoevsky and Chekhov (Borges seems barely to have counted drama as literature). Apparently for Borges, the best Russia had come up with was Pushkin's *The Queen of Spades*.

But the friendship Borges hoped for with Estela was not of the sort on which he based the one he had with Bioy, with Silvina, or indeed any of the other more respectable types with whom he had visited *confiterías* in the 1930s. He saw a woman – in so far as he could see much at this time – and what he saw pleased him. Estela was by no means the first to have done so. But her intelligence must have stimulated him more than usual – more, certainly, than the unavailable ladies he had attempted intimacy with before.

As far as Estela was concerned, there were the not mutually exclusive attractions of this odd, gentle man's flattery, and high intellectual stimulation. But her view of the situation – no doubt made more piquant for her by responding to Borges's flattery with a measure of coquetry (Canto admitted she was like that[8]) – was that they should become good friends, differences in reading habits aside.

They spoke English together, especially when they found enough common ground to enthuse about literature in that language. Estela also noticed that Borges would fall into English when anxious or under emotional pressure – pressure that, through his mounting desire for her in the months ahead, would become as intense as any he had experienced.

They ended their first night out in the Parque Lezama, an oasis between San Telmo and Barracas. In Estela's childhood, and therefore in Borges's a few years before, the park had been (as she described it) a 'secret, exuberant and romantic' place, with 'railings covered with jasmine, fences of irises, a perfumed rosebed in summer, a pond full of tadpoles, arbours roofed with honeysuckle, and gullies and rock gardens'.[9]

Now, it was neglected – plain from where they sat talking, on the steps of a dilapidated amphitheatre which had remained incomplete after the firm building it had gone bankrupt. Opposite them was the blue, onion-shaped dome of the Russian Orthodox church, there today, gleaming and optimistic next to the sad and still neglected park.

Estela and Borges commented on the passing of time.

Everything Borges said had a magical quality. Like a conjuror, he pulled unexpected objects out of an inexhaustible hat. I believe these were his signals. And they were magical because they suggested the man he really was, the man hidden behind the Georgie whom we knew, a man who, in his shyness, was struggling to emerge, to be recognised.[10]

Estela's portrait of the 45-year-old writer is one of the frankest we have of Borges at any point in his life. At times, it is coloured, perhaps, by a slightly prurient (if the word can be used of a woman writing in her late seventies) excitement at being able to reveal hitherto unknown facets of Borges's love life – or lack of it; the tentative, nervous, emotionally incompetent individual 'falling in love' with this sassy, sexually active, politically determined woman is a story Borges would much rather had been left untold, though aspects of his experiences with Estela did creep in – perhaps by way of revenge – to some of his own stories in *El Aleph*. But there is no need to suspect Canto of much exaggeration.[11]

It was *El Aleph*, not yet envisaged as a new volume, upon which Borges would soon be embarked. Fourteen stories in total were to be published in Buenos Aires journals before 1950, many of them written while Borges was courting Estela Canto. The stories constitute the very best of Borges the writer; yet his love for Estela was one of his low points as a man, and epitomised how ill at ease he still was with reality.

His two worlds were as schismatic as ever. From the 1950s on, his life would present him with one challenge after another to solve the division. And in a way, it was real, or adult, life for Borges thereafter that would come to dominate creative literature.

It would be easy to assign glib causes to Borges's sexual problems: a castrating mother; complexes about his sexually successful father; silly Victorian attitudes about female propriety; a closed Argentine male conservatism about the 'use' of women; and so on.

Naturally, it cannot be as simple as that. No one single cause paralysed Borges sexually – though paralysed he was. A combination of influences, some malign, brought about what was essentially a deep fear of a woman's physical self.

He was equally fearful of his own sexuality, and of the potential for intellectual dispossession, a kind of abandonment to the infinite – brain-death even – that orgasm might induce: he never lost the memory of sexual misery brought on by that encounter with his father's whore in Geneva.

Emir Rodríguez Monegal refers to a revealing text Borges wrote in the mid-1920s. Entitled 'Boletín de una noche' (Despatch from a Night), one strange passage from it points up Borges's sense of alienation from his own body. He has returned home late, and undresses in the dark: 'I am a palpable man (I tell myself) but with black skin, black skeleton, black gums, black blood that flows through intimate black flesh ... I undress, I am (an instant) that shameful, furtive beast, now inhuman and somehow estranged from itself that is a naked being.'

Rodríguez Monegal comments: 'That naked being was carefully kept in the dark by Borges. None of his close friends ever saw it.'[12]

And that is all. Rodríguez Monegal quotes these words to underline how isolated Borges was in the 1930s and early 1940s. Both these figures, the 'inhuman beast' and the potential taker of his own life, were more likely projections. Borges was always experimenting with permutations in his own identity to explore fictional possibilities. Here were two prototypes of human strangeness and alienation, examples of which were later to run in abundance through all his mature fiction.

Yet what Rodríguez Monegal misses, about the 1920s text in particular, is the young man's, the 'palpable man's', real *Angst* about sex; however intellectualised, or 'imaged' – 'black skin, black skeleton, black gums, black blood' and so on – Borges had to find a way of expressing his horror of physical life, his own not least of all. Black is the colour of death and denial. The colour symbolically consigned bodily needs to the cesspit. It was, of course, the mind that counted. It was the duty of a nascent philosopher-poet to suggest as much, even if only experimentally.

Many, many years later, in answer to a question about when, in time, he felt he existed, Borges replied either only at moments of extreme physical pain, or of extreme physical pleasure: the rest was indeterminate, perhaps dreamt.[13]

It was the answer of a sage who had effectively philosophised himself out of time, and yet who had found love, it appeared, with a much younger woman. He knew about pain, and he knew about pleasure, though neither in any particularly extreme form existed in Borges's life. But he had lived a long time, and just as he could happily take a position – sometimes at random – about politics, so he could about existence. Such statements were expected of him, and he rarely disappointed.

The older Borges, with a Japanese woman at his side, was the serenest nihilist there was. The younger man, the 'palpable man', whose overtures Estela Canto had to deal with, was far less sure of his incorporeality; he had sexual urges, like any other male in his mid-forties, but unlike most, who may generally be said to know what to do with them, Borges did not know where to start.

Though they were not really to blame, he had not been served well by his parents in this area. As 'Georgie', still living with his mother, Borges had wittingly allowed himself to avoid decisions about relationships with the opposite sex. Had Leonor come from a more emancipated climate, and been of a more enlightened intellectual outlook, she would have helped or even pushed her son into establishing a clear sexual definition for himself. But this was never a priority, least of all for Borges himself – until, that is, he met Estela Canto.

There is no reason to believe that Leonor either encouraged or discouraged Georgie in his seeking of a suitable partner. A good Catholic girl of solid Argentine stock – preferably with money – capable of running him domestically, and of dealing with his increasingly bad eyesight, would have done nicely; but Georgie didn't mix with the right class of person for that. The likes of Elvira de Alvear were fads, incidentals designed in part to please his mother, and in part to avoid the complications of real sexual relations.

Yet it would be wrong to suggest that Leonor had an impeding effect on Borges's sex life. She simply didn't know how to let him go. It was clear he could not properly look after himself, and she may have been more determined to see him succeed as a writer than as a happily married son: better to have him close at hand to fulfil that particular hope than propel him towards anything as socially conventional as matrimony, for which he was plainly unsuited.

At the back of Leonor's mind lurked Jorge. Her husband's disappointments in life and early death gave her extra reason to live for their son. And both she and Borges must have had their own memories of Jorge's weaknesses – especially for other women. Georgie's induction into sex at his father's behest in Geneva, mixed with Jorge's peccadilloes, did nothing for Borges's sexual confidence in maturity. From that day in Geneva he knew he would never live up to traditional expectations of virility, and throughout his early adulthood was simply confused by the issue. By the time he reached his forties, he was still asking himself what on earth he should do about it, but making only vain attempts at an answer. The flesh was strong, but the spirit all at sea.

There was something else. Borges emerged from a culture wholly unsympathetic to sexual hesitancy. The macho was an emotive figure, and had been, let it not be forgotten, a salient motif in Borges's early work: it abounds in gauchos, *compadritos*, *tangueros*.

Borges, no obvious species of Argentine male, was ambiguous on the matter; he had written a whole book about a type of macho, Evaristo Carriego, which contained an investigation into that most seductive image of Argentine macho, the tango. Equally, he could pour contempt on the typical *porteño*, as he had in *Sur* in 1931.

There, he had touched on a notorious Argentine sexual predilection: sodomy. Elsewhere in the world, condemnation rains down on 'the two executants of this unimaginable contact', he wrote. 'Not so for the pimps of Buenos Aires, who claim some kind of profound respect for the active perpetrator ...'.[14] Estela Canto, recounting her own sparky history of Argentine sexual history, illustrated this attitude in a suggestively fecal anecdote. A brother-in-law of an economics minister was asked by the *madame* of a brothel he frequented why he never uttered a word when in bed with whores. He replied: 'I never speak when I'm on the loo.'[15]

V. S. Naipaul was altogether more explicit:

The act of straight sex, easily bought, is of no great moment to the macho. His conquest of a woman is complete only when he has buggered her. This is what the woman has it in her power to deny; this is what the brothel game is about, the passionless Latin adventure that begins with talk of *amor*. *La tuve en el culo*, I've had her in the arse: this is how the macho reports victory to his circle, or dismisses a desertion.

What comes next would have been music, ugly as it is, to Borges's ears:

... the buggering of women is of special significance in Argentina and other Latin American countries. The Church considers it a heavy sin, and prostitutes hold it in horror. By imposing on her what prostitutes reject, and what he knows to be a kind of black mass, the Argentine macho, in the main of *Spanish or Italian peasant ancestry* [my italics], consciously dishonours his victim.[16]

This was an image of a degenerate Argentina, one created by those despised Latin immigrants, that the Anglophile Borges of the 1940s already deplored.* The ancestral heritage in his work from this period emerged, as we shall see, in a much more sinister, violent form than it had before. The ultimate macho was, of course, Perón – the humiliator, the sodomiser indeed, of Argentina. And to get the theme rolling, Naipaul in his book had made an earlier and now famous reference to his wife Eva's sexual attributes: 'She was the macho's ideal victim-woman – don't those red lips still speak to the Argentine macho of her reputed skill in fellatio?'[18]

Publicly, Borges no longer fitted his fly-postered city. Buenos Aires seemed to be in the hands of machos and pimps, otherwise dressed in the glossy garb of Perón's military. Privately, Borges felt himself at a debilitating distance from what this new order might require him to be: a true Argentine man.

The mythical sexual mores of his compatriots, which he had long known about, which in Estela Canto's account were elided into the words '*hombría*' and '*bestialidad*' ('manliness' and 'bestiality')[19] and which thirty years later Naipaul highlighted so gruesomely, were just another form of South American barbarity – or perhaps, as Borges's poem put it, 'South American destiny' . . .

Perón's election to office was over a year away when Borges met Estela Canto. Through the summer of 1944–5, he called on her most days, leaving a book for her, whether she was there or not. He phoned before these visits; if Estela was out, he might stay and chat with her mother. In the evenings, they went to the cinema, or to dine in one of the many restaurants or hotels around Constitución station. Borges always ate the same: rice soup, a well-done steak, cheese and quince jam. She drank wine, he water – 'large quantities' of it.[20]

They walked everywhere: to the twilight area west of Constitución, Barracas, La Boca, and sometimes as far north as Palermo, meeting on the street where Estela was born, a sentimental touch on Borges's part, not hers. Moving from place to place as the nights wore on, Borges would phone his mother several times, to explain where he was, reassuring her about his return.

Estela enjoyed his conversation, but his conventional manner

---

* Naipaul reports something Borges said to him: 'The country was enriched by men thinking essentially of Europe and the United States. Only the civilised people. The gauchos were very simple-minded. Barbarians.'[17]

oppressed her. 'His kisses, awkward, brusque, always ill-timed, were accepted condescendingly.'[21] When he took her in his arms, she could feel his 'his virility', as she euphemistically put it, 'the excitement of any normal man',[22] but things never got further than a few kisses. 'Sexual realisation was terrifying for him,' she said.[23]

One night at the end of summer 1945 – in April or May – they went to dine at the Hotel Las Delicias in Adrogué. The hotel had already lost its pre-war colour: the stained-glass red and blue rhombi in the windows had been replaced by colourless glass; pot-plants, ferns and palms, had gone too. The badly lit dining-room was almost empty, the food terrible.

After dinner, they walked to Mármol, the next station beyond Adrogué. Borges seemed agitated. He quoted stanzas from Dante extolling Beatrice; he guided Estela, holding her arm tightly, as if towards a specific point. In Mármol, he suggested they walk back to Adrogué instead of taking the train.

They went past a cement bench. Borges sat at one end, Estela at the other. It was dark, and only a lamp at the end of the street shed light on this uncomfortable-looking couple. Peering towards Estela through the obscurity of his weak vision and in the poor illumination, Borges asked her to marry him. Estela was surprised by the question, put to her as if from a Victorian novel. She hadn't really suspected Borges was thinking of marriage.

Estela's reply was as witty as it was swift.

'I would do it, Georgie, but you mustn't forget I'm a disciple of Bernard Shaw. We can't get married if we haven't already slept together.'[24]

Borges was instantly confused. They continued walking, kissing and hugging; though aroused, Borges had never had any intention of going that far. What should he do? Estela said she didn't love him enough to marry him; but they could be friends and, if he wanted, something more. She doubted her own sincerity, but made the suggestion only because she knew Borges would not take up the offer.

He, in his turn, was in love with her, but quite unable to reconcile the fact with any of the physical promptings which helped confirm it. Estela was clear in what she wanted, and more precisely what she didn't want. Borges thought he knew what he wanted, but had no idea how to achieve it, or if it were proper to want it.

None the less, from that evening on, Estela became Borges's 'novia', his girlfriend, though the Spanish gives more a sense of 'intended'.[25] Estela wasn't overwhelmed by the idea, but tried to live with it to keep the peace. She soon found herself up against Leonor, which didn't incline her to ally herself any closer to this strangely old-fashioned duo. If Estela came to see Borges of a morning, Leonor would be present at their meetings. She would hold forth on her illustrious ancestors, discourse idly in a manner which irritated Estela, but which Borges later reported to her was, as far as Leonor was concerned, 'for the protection of [Estela's] "honour"'.[26]

Leonor's presence in Borges's life caused friction between him and Estela – certainly from Estela's point of view. She made her dislike of Leonor overt, which must have hurt Borges. They argued. He thought about suicide. On a fifth-floor balcony at a friend's, he had contemplated throwing himself into the void. Yet it is likely that suicide was as much beyond his practical scope as sex: the attractions of suicide were, as we have seen, philosophical. But then he would insist: he loved Estela madly, and wanted to have children with her, create a family. He knew he would go blind one day, but that mattered little if she was to be at his side.

Estela was touched by his beseechings. She might have agreed to make him happy – but there was Leonor. For the younger woman, Leonor became a *bête noire*, and there is every reason to believe that Estela misjudged her character; or if not her character exactly, then the circumstances – much reduced, after all, since Jorge's death – in which mother and son *had* to live.

Whatever her problems with Leonor herself, Estela felt deeply uncomfortable about the idea of agreeing to marry a man who would have to ask his mother permission to do so.

It never got that far, of course. Curious incidents abounded in their relationship, such as an occasion when they were arrested in the Parque Lezama one night for being without their papers – this was towards the end of 1945, when police vigilance over proof of identity was getting tighter. The police accused them of 'indecorousness' (their arms had probably been linked). They were released without charge at 3.30 in the morning: 'the second time,' said Estela, 'that we'd been out at night until such an hour. There wasn't going to be a third.'[27]

Borges was apparently humiliated; he would instinctively have bridled at being manhandled by men in uniform. Estela merely saw the incident as comic and absurd.

Thereafter, their nightly outings got shorter. As the height of summer approached, Estela planned to leave Buenos Aires. Borges had been busy at work on a story inspired by a children's toy he had found back in March and enthused over to Estela: a kaleidoscope.

He called it 'an Aleph'. Through it you could see images duplicated, triplicated – worlds reflecting each other, tiny universes of coloured chips suggesting infinity. 'Aleph' is the first letter of the Hebrew alphabet, and a symbol of the Judaic godhead; the story that unfolded, one of Borges's greatest and also one of his longest, therefore had a title carrying Kabbalistic connotations – Borges's 'Aleph' was to be an emblem of the mysteries of all knowledge.

The story gains its peculiar power from a combination of urban banality and timeless wonderment. Much of it concerns the type of literary debate and gossip that Borges himself kept up with his friends. There were plenty of Buenos Aires's literati on whom the mediocre poet, Carlos Argentino Daneri, who alerts the narrator to the existence of the Aleph, could be based. And in the 1943 'postscript' to the story, Daneri's recognition in the national literary prize and Borges's lack of it recalls a similar débâcle over *El jardín de senderos que se bifurcan* in 1941.

The emotional matrix for the tale, Borges's love for Beatriz Viterbo (Borges uses his own name for the narrator), is in the past; she is a kind of anti-muse. The topographical context is contemporary Buenos Aires, modern life – 'telephones, telegraphs, phonographs, wireless sets, motion-picture screens, slide projectors, glossaries, timetables, handbooks, bulletins', as Daneri puts it.[28]

Across this mid-twentieth-century blandness, Daneri's list of the mod-cons of communication, Borges throws the hallucinatory light of the Aleph. The device is in the basement of Beatriz Viterbo's old house, due to be demolished. Borges visits it at Daneri's behest, lies down in the darkness, and experiences a kind of rapture. Buenos Aires for an instant is nowhere, while the visionary sum of experience and knowledge is all around. Beyond technology lies the possibility of eternal illumination – which can lead also to eternal despair.

Modern parlance would call what Borges sees in the Aleph an out-of-body experience, akin to the moment of orgasm and to the moment of death. Both, in Borges's life at the time, were something to be contemplated, perhaps tasted, and certainly feared. He was in love with Estela, they had embraced, but he dared not take the final step with her.

'I was afraid I would never again be free of all I had seen,' says the narrator at the end of the story. However, after the abnormal, generally a measure of reality in Borges's stories, human frailty takes over. 'Happily, after a few sleepless nights, I was visited once more by oblivion.'[29]

Not since 'Death and the Compass' had Borges written a story with such site-specificity to Buenos Aires. In its naming of streets, buildings and squares, its identification of an area Borges knew well – the part of town Estela Canto lived in – 'The Aleph' marked a huge leap in the imaginative borders of Borges's fictional universe.

'The Aleph' was also the first time he had attempted to focus on erotic love. Beatriz Viterbo is of course dead, and has been since 1929 – the story opens on the day of her death, and takes place a dozen years later; but the phrase 'I knew at times my fruitless devotion had annoyed her'[30] in the first paragraph is clear reflection of Borges's attentions to Estela. Women, sex and love were now preying on his mind with more than usual intensity.

Beatriz is not modelled on Estela; it was enough for Borges to dedicate the story to her, and later give her the manuscript. A more plausible model is Elvira de Alvear, and society women like her. The Belgrano villa of Elvira's mother, Mariana Cambaceres de Alvear, is mentioned in the text as one of the places 'dispatched' in Daneri's dreadful global poem.[31]

Estela also describes a generous little ritual Borges used to perform every New Year's Eve, which was to visit the lonely and increasingly deranged Elvira; she would tinkle her desk bell, and complain that servants never came when called. The gesture's absurdity touched Borges. In 'The Aleph', this becomes transformed into the homage he pays Beatriz by visiting her house every 30 April, the date of her birthday.

The story was published in *Sur* in September 1945. A month later Borges was in Montevideo, lecturing on gauchesco literature. It was his first engagement as a public speaker, though because of his stammer and timidity, and of his horror of displaying himself publicly, someone else actually delivered the words for him, with promptings from Borges behind. It was, according to Rodríguez Monegal, who was there, a strange but edifying performance, and significant for what it anticipated about Borges's future career.[32] Borges didn't think then that he would ever have to become a lecturer – the idea would have been anathema to him. But things were happening in Buenos Aires, even as Borges's lecture proceeded.

Perón had been heralded in on 17 October by his supporters. In February 1946, he was elected president. In the same month, Borges published in *Sur* the third of the stories to go into *El Aleph*, 'Deutsches Requiem' (the first, 'Biografía de Tadeo Isidoro Cruz' ('The Life of Tadeo Isidoro Cruz'), a gloss on *Martín Fierro*, had been published in *Sur* in December 1944). A month later, he took on extra work: as editor of a newly founded journal, *Anales de Buenos Aires*, published by a literary association similar to Paris's Société des Annales.

It was as well the new job came when it did. Within two months of Perón's inauguration in June 1946, Borges had lost his post at the Miguel Cané library.

He always claimed that it was Perón himself who personally arranged his 'promotion' to inspector of poultry and rabbits in the calle Córdoba market, but this was an unlikely fantasy. A bureaucrat at City Hall informed him of the new post, and it had probably been dreamed up by a committee.*

Borges, as he recounts in the 'Autobiographical Essay', asked why he had been deemed 'worthy' of this new position.[33] He had been on the side of the Allies during the war, was the answer, so what did he expect? He tendered his resignation the next day. Because both the clerkship and poultry-inspectorship were municipal posts, Borges's

---

* Rodríguez Monegal makes a more localised observation about the regime's intentions: 'Perón and his friends were masters in the art of the *cachada* (to grab, to take somebody unawares). To promote one of the leading Argentine intellectuals to [such a post] implied a linguistic pun. Chickens and rabbits are in Spanish, as in English, synonymous with cowardice.'[34]

Estela Canto has her own version: 'It's certain that Perón never had anything to do with this. It is quite possible that Borges's name, as with any other Argentine or foreign writer, was unknown to him. Borges was named chicken inspector by an intellectual, one of the small men of the Peronist movement, one of Evita's men, who had considerable power at the Municipality. This man wanted to make a heavy joke at the expense of a political enemy.'[35]

resignation from the latter was effective resignation from Perón's civil service – there was no way he could return in any capacity to the Miguel Cané or any other public library. He therefore had before him only his activities for *Anales de Buenos Aires*, his occasional contributions to *Sur* and other publications – and his stories. They were something, but materially it was an invidious position for a 47 year old to be in.

Perón was not going to silence Borges: 'dictatorships foster oppression', he wrote in *Sur*, 'dictatorships foster servitude, dictatorships foster cruelty: more abominable is the fact that they foster idiocy . . .'. To fight the stupidities of such regimes 'is among the writer's many duties', he added.[36] This text was read out by Pedro Henríquez Ureña at a dinner given on 8 August for Borges, just days after the chickens débâcle, another 'Amends to Borges' reminiscent of José Bianco's 1941 tribute to *El jardín*. Amongst the speakers on Borges's behalf was the president of SADE, Leonidas Barletta; and here, at the very moment of Borges's public politicisation as a writer, was hidden an irony prefiguring his four decades as Argentina's apparently most annoying literary controversialist.

Barletta was a communist; extolling Borges's courage in defying the new fascist leader was the order of those 'magnificent and terrible days', the duty of the left, and an honest one. In 1973, however, on Perón's return to power, SADE condemned Borges as a 'fascist' because he refused to support Perón – as SADE and other public bodies and figures then did, Barletta amongst them.

Peronism was a mercurial beast, and according to political expediency took institutions with it, left and right, when in the ascendant. Whatever else Borges was – and by 1973 he was an institution in his own right – he never wavered in his long and personalised hatred for Perón. But from the moment he spoke openly against him, the stammering, timid writer confronted, without knowing it, many more political forces than an eloquent denunciation of dictatorships could possibly have suggested at the time. Borges was playing with fire.

Nineteen forty-six was a crossroads year for Borges. First, he was in love with a woman who didn't want to marry him; then he lost his job. He needed help.

A degree of solace came in the form of a certain Doctor Miguel

Kohan Miller, a psychiatric doctor who worked for the medical arm of the Tribunales, the Justice Department where Jorge Borges had once worked. Kohan Miller would have some influence on both aspects of Borges's strange, late-forties crisis, which was largely sexual in origin, though the man himself remains somewhat obscure.

He was a Jewish doctor with a practice near the plaza de Mayo. Manuel Peyrou had been treated by him, and Peyrou urged Borges to visit him, the pretext being to seek assistance in conquering his timidity. Kohan Miller's training in psychoanalysis seems to have been superficial; he had gained what knowledge he had, at around the age of eighteen, from reading supervised by a professional, who was corresponding with Sigmund Freud. Kohan Miller was intelligent, efficient, direct and admired Borges's standing in Buenos Aires's intellectual circles. What he discovered was a man whose deep-rooted inhibitions, over coitus in particular, needed removing not just for the sake of his psychological health, but also for the good of Argentine literature.[37]

The only evidence that Kohan Miller was right about the latter is in Borges's intense productivity the year following his visits to the doctor: in 1947, he published in *Anales de Buenos Aires* and *Sur* five of the great stories that make up *El Aleph*, including 'El inmortal' ('The Immortal'); this is as long as the volume's title story, beginning with a Roman tribune's quest to join the City of the Immortals in desert sands – a parable full of labyrinths and hopes for endless life, for eternal escape from self.

'I am god, I am hero, I am philosopher, I am demon and I am world, which is a tedious way of saying I do not exist.'[38] In abnegating his earthly self and embracing multiple identities, this narrator is also disclaiming, in 'a tedious way', responsibility for writing the text we are reading.

Borges had never taken quite so radical a position about authorship, albeit guarded in a phrase of downbeat irony. But it is also an expression of release, or the desire for it; Kohan Miller's counselling had played a part. The four other stories of 1947 are 'Les teólogos' ('The Theologians'), 'La casa de Asterión' ('The House of Asterion'), 'La busca de Averroës' ('Averroës's Search') and 'El Zahir' ('The Zahir'), all published before six months of that year were up.

His most inventive storytelling yet was his answer to the acutest adversity.

Changed daily circumstances, too, helped this rush of creativity. Firstly, by the end of 1946, Borges and Leonor had moved to a fifth-floor flat on the calle Maipú, close to the leafy plaza San Martín and right on the edge of Buenos Aires's commercial heart. Mother and son would both live out their final days there.[39]

Secondly, Borges became a teacher. Through the offices of friends of the Bioys, he got a job teaching English literature at the Asociación Argentina de Cultura Inglesa (Argentine Association for English Culture); simultaneously, he was asked by the Colegio Libre de Estudios Superiores (Free College for Higher Studies) to give a series of lectures on American writers. Both openings came to him 'three months before classes opened',[40] at around the time, therefore, of his dismissal from the library in July 1946. (Classes for the second semester of the academic year began in September.)

For both, therefore, he had plenty of time to prepare. But lecturing, in particular, filled him with dread. 'As the time grew near . . . I grew sicker and sicker,' he wrote in the 'Autobiographical Essay'. 'Thinking of the first lecture as Doomsday, I felt that only eternity could come after.'[41] In fact, the first one, on Nathaniel Hawthorne, passed off well. He wrote the entire thing out by hand, and later collected it in *Otras inquisiciones* (*Other Inquisitions*): it is the longest essay in the book.*

Preparing lectures in this manner was too labour-intensive. So he began to write notes, in tiny, upright handwriting – a minuscule, hieroglyphic script, extraordinary for eyes so bad – and committed them to memory; he thus had the outline of the lecture in his head which, when he spoke, emerged fully formed. Eventually he hardly had to look at the notes.

To steady his nerves beforehand, he would either rehearse it out loud with his mother – for the second lecture, on Poe, he took her for a long walk in Adrogué – or, immediately before the talk, would stroll with a friend around the block where he was due to speak, usually in the Sociedad Científica Argentina (Argentine Scientific Society) in the avenida Santa Fe. He would also fortify himself with alcohol,

---

* Just longer than 'New Refutation of Time' (see p. 166), first published separately in 1947; all the others are a few pages long.

taking a nip of peach liqueur or of grappa.[42] (Generally, Borges had no taste for alcohol.)

Borges's sessions with Kohan Miller were in part to help him with his new employment. Overcoming his sexual anxieties was linked to his professional future, and Estela Canto was asked, at Kohan Miller's suggestion, to help Borges in his treatment; would she, pleaded Borges, go and see Kohan Miller herself, and talk with him about Borges's difficulties? She agreed.

She hadn't counted on the path Borges had already laid down with the doctor, even if inadvertently. Kohan Miller believed that Estela *was* Borges's intended. If the writer's fear that he was impotent could be conquered, then she would, said Kohan Miller, 'have her man for years to come';[43] if they could get Borges to speak successfully in public, then he could lead a normal sex life. 'It would not surprise me,' added Kohan Miller, 'if he did not end up being more capable in this area than many men.'[44]

The doctor had missed the point where Estela was concerned. But she did emphasise that in her view, he had got to the root of Borges's sexual confusion:

Borges, superficially a conventional man, lived under the dead weight of a command. His father had ordered him to be a *man*. Equally, he had to get married to win society's approval; as a married man it was going to be much easier for him to free himself from his feelings of guilt. Did I understand the point? Why not get married at once, leaving aside the earlier evidence? I answered that I was inclined to help Georgie and to go a great distance at that, but marriage, at least for the time being, was another thing. I could not see him as a husband.[45]

Estela had her own life to lead, and began to see less of Borges. In later years, he admitted to her that he did succeed finally in having sexual relations, with a dancer.

He knew one such at around this time, who became the dedicatee of 'The Immortal'. She was called Cecilia Ingenieros, and was the daughter of José Ingenieros, a well-known historian and sociologist; it was Cecilia who suggested to Borges the plot of his 1948 story (the only one published in that year, in *Sur*), 'Emma Zunz'. Significantly, it is the one story from this period which deals with the sexual act, albeit a calculated and violent one, carried out by the female protagonist.

Borges was often seen in Cecilia's company in the early 1940s, as he was with a number of pretty, eligible young women – starting, most notably, with Haydée Lange in the early months of 1939, when he was recovering from his accident. It seems he was very much 'in love' with Cecilia, and wooed her intensively over at least three years, from around 1941 to 1944. As with Haydée, Borges got as far as suggesting marriage to Cecilia; as the war in Europe came to a close, they even planned to cross the Atlantic together and seal the oath there, but Cecilia backed out as the travel plans took shape. It may be that her so-called fiancé's new and obvious interest in another woman – Estela Canto – put her off, not unnaturally.

Still, Cecilia remained a friend of Borges's and went on to marry a scholar, gave up dancing and devoted herself for the rest of her life to Egyptology. It was probably with a friend of Cecilia's that Borges had the only sexually intimate relations of his adult life.

It is impossible to identify her now.[46] It is reasonable to assume that she offered Borges precisely what Estela Canto had, but from which, with her, he had recoiled; with the help sought both from Kohan Miller and Estela, he was able to submit, with Cecilia's friend, to the desires he had so frustratingly dammed up with Estela.

That Borges wrote a story featuring sex is no evidence, circa 1946–7, of coitus; however, in previous texts of his, copulation had always been a notional act, a system for reproducing mankind, which inhabiting Babels and suffering eternity as it does, was not necessarily a 'good thing'. In 'Tlön, Uqbar, Orbis Tertius', of course, it had been, along with mirrors, 'abominable', a collective dissolution of identity: 'All men, in the vertiginous moment of coitus, are the same man.'[47] In 'Emma Zunz', for the first time in Borges, a sentient individual undergoes a carnal experience, though it has to be said that Emma's vengeful submission takes place, typically, 'outside of time' and is 'a perplexing disorder of disconnected and atrocious sensations'.[48]

Sex had happened to Borges; the chances are it had not greatly appealed to him, but at least he knew what it entailed – just as Emma knows, from the beginning of the tale, what terrible deed her calculations will lead to.

*　　*　　*

Borges's new work introduced him to new landscapes.

> I travelled up and down Argentina and Uruguay, lecturing
> on Swedenborg, Blake, the Persian and Chinese mystics,
> Buddhism, gauchesco poetry, Martin Buber, the Kabbalah,
> the Arabian Nights, T. E. Lawrence, medieval Germanic
> poetry, the Icelandic sagas, Heine, Dante, expressionism and
> Cervantes. I went from town to town, staying overnight in
> hotels I'd never see again. Sometimes my mother or a friend
> accompanied me. Not only did I end up making far more
> money than at the library but I enjoyed the work and felt that
> it justified me.[49]

It was a professional release, and good training for how he would
earn his living for the rest of his life. Rodríguez Monegal observed
Borges's methods closely:

> Borges sat very quietly, never looking directly at the audience
> and focusing his half-blind eyes on a distant spot. While
> lecturing, he would join his hands in small, precise movements
> of prayer or discreetly move them around; he would deliver
> his speech in a rather monotonous, low voice as if he were
> a priest or a rabbi ... His stillness, his precise gestures, the
> monotone of his voice created an almost incantatory space ...
> The immobility, the low tone, the almost fanatical concentration
> on the spoken words – all that was the lecture and not the usual
> histrionics of the orator.[50]

Rodríguez Monegal got to know Borges well in these years. Following their first encounter in Montevideo in 1945, the two men visited
each others' countries regularly. Borges enjoyed Uruguay because
of his family connections; Rodríguez Monegal enjoyed Buenos Aires
because of Borges.

His future biographer was one of the first camp followers. There
were many to come, but not all of them had Rodríguez Monegal's
literary-critical intelligence. In that way, his work, his efforts to
understand something about Borges, served two important purposes:
to give a literary shape to Borges's life, which Borges almost certainly

hadn't detected himself, and to provide a context in which to make sense of Borges for the first time in English.

Rodríguez Monegal was also one of the few such camp followers not to consign his knowledge of Borges to a mere question-answer formula. In his biography, written in English, he was rarely inspiring in his depiction of the writer. He was blinded by two things: hero-worship for his subject, and a psychological construct he needed his subject to fit. But in one particular area, he was indispensable. He was a first-hand witness of Borges's crisis years – the crises he faced under Perón and in a period of major professional transformation.

No one has bettered the picture Rodríguez Monegal gave of Borges at this time:

> He was then in his late forties, and he still had partial eyesight. He didn't use a cane. His step was nervous, almost brusque. Only when crossing a street would a natural prudence make him hold his companion by the sleeve, rather than the arm, with an imperious gesture that requested but did not beg help. With the same sudden brusqueness, he'd let go on the other side. But verbal communication never stopped.
>
> Borges dimly saw (or guessed) the slogans of the regime, the infinite repetition of Perón's and Evita's names, the calculated humiliation of patrician Buenos Aires. He'd point to each enormous letter, underline each slogan, talk and talk furiously. Gone was the Buenos Aires of his poems and dreams, the suburban neighbourhood with its general store and pink corners and local hoodlums wearing white, soft-brimmed hats, its twilight streets open to the invading pampas. Nothing was left of that mythical Buenos Aires of his tales ... he hated the demagoguery of this leader who aired social grudges, petty fascist lessons, in a colossal display of mediocrity.[51]

Rodríguez Monegal made only passing reference to Estela Canto. If he knew more about Borges's sentimental state of mind he chose to ignore it. It would have been the one thing Borges would not have talked about outside Doctor Kohan Miller's office. But Rodríguez Monegal, perhaps unwittingly, gave some hint of the sexual tension that probably underlay Borges's political concerns:

He was like a man skinned alive. Here and there the real Buenos Aires was visible to him. But from his talk a different, more ominous city emerged. It was a city of unrelieved horror, the one that was transcribed phantasmagorically and under European names in 'Death and the Compass' . . .

Listening to Borges, I found it impossible not to feel a sense of rejection mixed with quiet impatience. I did not care if somebody heard us . . . it was not that Borges's words seemed wrong to me; it was that I felt the shame of a person who spies on someone else's nightmares, who involuntarily listens to the cries and private words of a sleeper. Brutally, the passion with which Borges denounced Perón's Buenos Aires brought me into his own labyrinth.[52]

To escape the labyrinth, the two men went walking. From Rodríguez Monegal's evocative description of their expeditions, a clear idea of Borges's real passion, the unknown, unsung Buenos Aires, rolls into view:

As soon as we left the downtown streets and reached Buenos Aires's Southside, Borges's mood would change. The Southside seems (or seemed in the years between 1946 and 1949) like the setting of a Borges tale. He would drag me to see some surviving pink streetcorner; we would step on to patios whose stone pavements recalled another tyrant's times: the Juan Manuel Rosas who reappeared obsessively in his verses. We would cross squares which still held the dampness that had chilled his grandparents. Sometimes, in the evening, we would land in some café such as the Richmond del Sur, where a small band played old-time tangos above the incessant clacking of billiard balls at the back. Then, for a while, Borges would forget Perón and would even laugh. He would tap the table with his hand (somewhat short, with fat fingers) to the rhythms of the tango . . . Through that tango ritual, Borges managed to escape for a moment from Perón's moral prison, from the loud walls of his own nightmare. The Buenos Aires he loved was still alive in the music of the tango.

We often walked the streets of the Southside and also some quarters of the poorer Northside, which had nothing in common with the fashionable boutiques of Florida Street. I still remember one night when we walked through half of Buenos Aires (he walked to enjoy the quietness of suburban nights) to see a friend who lived in a Jewish neighbourhood of sad and dusty streets. On that occasion Perón disappeared from the conversation, which branched off into the labyrinths of English literature that Borges loved so much. Stevenson, Kipling, Chesterton, and James filled the solitary streets with their inventions, brought to life by Borges's words. 'Don't you agree?' he never tired of asking with his flawless courtesy. Quoting texts and commenting on them, developing precious hints and pursuing allusions, Borges managed to create, on the borders of the Peronist-made reality, an entire world. From those heady conversations we returned, half dazed, to sinister reality.[53]

Rodríguez Monegal remained a loyal supporter of Borges's. From 1945 on, he was the writer's most vigorous promoter in Uruguay. He did notice that Borges's anti-Peronism sometimes bordered on hysteria, and wanted to point out that Perón meant something, for example, to the workers whose cause (amongst others) he had so successfully espoused:* 'But how can one establish a dialogue with a dreamer?' Rodríguez Monegal asked, giving up.[54]

He did, however, keep tabs on a subversive 1947 text Borges and Bioy put together, called 'La fiesta del monstruo' (The Monster's Party). It was an unveiled satire on Peronism, and included an episode demonstrating the nature of the regime's tacit support of Nazi-like anti-Semitism. It circulated amongst the Bioy set in samizdat, and remained unpublishable while Perón was in power. Only when Perón fell in 1955 did it finally appear, in the literary pages of the left-wing Uruguayan weekly paper, *Marcha*, edited by Rodríguez Monegal.

Anales de Buenos Aires closed at the beginning of 1948. The last story by Borges published in it was 'The Zahir', in July 1947. He also ran some of his essays, on Wells, Wilde, Whitman and Chesterton, later

---

* See pp.174–5 below, for similar problems Ezequiel Martínez Estrada and Ernesto Sábato had with Borges on this issue.

collected in *Other Inquisitions*. Julio Cortázar, still unknown, made it into print for the first time under Borges's aegis, in late 1947. Borges then lost interest, mainly because the proprietress, a literary patron in the Victoria Ocampo mould, found it hard to enjoy his eclectic tastes. He was a top name but not necessarily a top editor; circulation had not held up, and Borges now had a busy lecturing schedule. He and the magazine's owner parted company.

In fact, Borges's declining editorial enthusiasms had already been noted by Victoria Ocampo. For a period from 1946 to early 1947, Borges edited *Sur* while José Bianco was in Paris. Victoria implored Bianco to return, because though she admired Borges as a writer, she did not consider him up to the job as editor. 'Borges has none of the qualities I appreciate for the work that needs to be done at *Sur*, in choosing the material and revising the translations,' she wrote. 'He is a writer of talent but lacks criteria other than his arbitrariness and fantasy.'[55] Bianco did not return, so the young Ernesto Sábato, the only person available, was put in place, his editing carefully watched by Ocampo.

Nineteen forty-eight was a quieter year for Borges. Most of the stories to be collected in *El Aleph* had been written. His income had stabilised and his career as a public speaker was definitively launched. He was installed with Leonor in permanent lodgings. He had his friends, his family – he was becoming particularly fond of his nephews, Luis and Miguel de Torre – and his writing. His fury against the regime went unabated, but that in itself became a kind of constant.

Later that year, his loathing found added fuel. On 8 September, Leonor, Norah and a friend of theirs, Adela Grondona, were walking down calle Florida. They came across a group of women chanting slogans, probably against Perón and Evita, which turned into a rendition of the national anthem. A crowd gathered round; police arrived, and in dispersing the crowd arrested some of the women. Amongst them were Leonor, Adela and Norah.

For disturbing the public peace, the 72-year-old Leonor was put under house arrest for a month. Norah and Adela were sent to jail for the same period, the Buen Pastor prison for women, where they were put in a block for prostitutes. Norah spent her time drawing hookers and thieves, all of them resembling Guillermo de Torre, according to Estela Canto.

Norah was apparently quite happy, and able to smuggle letters out to her mother and brother, saying that prison was in fact quite restful – it was better than having to go to cocktail parties all the time, and there was a beautiful chessboard-like patio. Always religious, she sang and prayed to keep her spirits up.

Norah's indefatigable whimsy did little to mollify Borges. He never forgot the insult perpetrated on his family, whose ancestors – his mother's above all – had fought for freedom against Rosas, for Argentina. He called Perón's period in power 'drab and hopeless', telling Richard Burgin (in the context of the arrests) that his first dismal thought on awaking for ten years was: 'Perón is in power'.[56] Borges remembered that he too had a detective on his heels, almost certainly the one employed by the Peronist police to keep watch on Leonor during her brief sequestration.

Just two further stories, 'La escritura del Dios' ('The God's Script') and 'Historia del guerrero y la cautiva ('The Story of the Warrior and the Captive'), appeared in *Sur* before their incorporation in *El Aleph*, published by Losada on 26 June 1949.

It was an astonishing volume, thirteen tales in which Borges deployed his wittiest skills and widest preoccupations: death, gauchos and men of war ('Tadeo Isidoro Cruz', 'The Dead Man', 'The Warrior and the Captive', 'La otra muerte' ('The Other Death')), first-person narrative relating experiences out of time, in self-created, contradictory universes ('Deutsches Requiem', 'The Immortal', 'The God's Script'), a puzzle ('The Horse of Asterion'), textual and epistemological conundrums ('The Theologians', 'Averroës's Search'), along with something new – a sterner hold on reality, an interest in place and human action: 'The Aleph', 'Emma Zunz', and 'The Zahir'.

'The Zahir' returns us to Buenos Aires. We are with 'Borges' again, as in 'The Aleph', though only just: 'I am still, however incompletely, Borges,' ends the first paragraph.[57] We understand why by the end of the story; he has become possessed by the spell of a Zahir, an ordinary coin whose two sides he can see at the same time: 'it is as though my eyesight were spherical, with the Zahir at the centre'.[58] Because the sister of a dead inamorata of his, Clementina Villar, has lost her faculties as a result of contact with the Zahir, Borges soon will not know who he is – the story has been written on the ebbing of sanity. The effect of the Zahir is to divest anyone who handles it of his identity.

That is to oversimplify grossly. Like most of the stories in *El Aleph*, 'The Zahir' exemplifies how Borges can suggest the illusion of a vast fictional canvas in miniaturist space: all the world in a grain of sand. 'The Zahir' is a perfect picture of compressed time: in it, we move from love in late-1920s Buenos Aires, through many of its streets, to Wagner, tigers, dreams, the Kabbalah, and finally to the possibility of finding God. The narrative weaves in and out of conflicting realities, taunts with its extraordinary allusiveness, cracks jokes (in love with Clementina, Borges is 'moved by that most Argentine of passions, snobbery'[59]), offers a tale within the tale, and leaves us with the impression that we have read hundreds of pages, travelled to worlds within worlds.

It would be possible to develop a critique of the whole of Borges through close textual reading of 'The Zahir'. For obvious reasons, that cannot be done here. For his contemporary readers, however – those who knew him from *Sur*, mainly – Borges had opened new doors: he had brought Buenos Aires alive without overlaying too obvious – one might say too 'realistic' – an urban reality on the multiple realities with which Borges so enjoyed playing. Here was a recognisable world, much more than the one evoked in 'Death and the Compass', with recognisable women, particularly in Clementina Villar with her addiction to Paris fashions.

From 1949 on, Borges would be referred to in newspapers and other media as 'the author of *El Aleph*', or of 'The Aleph'. Now fifty, he was the uncrowned king of Buenos Aires letters. Estela Canto, with whom he began to visit Doctor Kohan Miller again in 1949, wrote about *El Aleph* in *Sur* and interviewed him for *Nueva Gaceta*, and played no small part in painting a clear journalistic picture of the author for the wider Buenos Aires public. He had after all dedicated his most famous story to her, and she was to some extent the muse behind it and other tales in the eponymous volume. Years before she wrote her book, Canto's closeness to Borges was put to good and immediate public service.

His election to the presidency of SADE in 1950 was another form of public recognition. It was not an onerous post, nor was the society especially high profile – deliberately in these years, as it was anti-Peronist in spirit. 'We met every week,' remembered Luisa

Mercedes Levinson in 1970, 'to tell each other the latest jokes about the governing couple [Perón and Evita], and daringly singing songs of the French Resistance, even the "Marseillaise".'[60]

Borges lectured at SADE and was generally respected, but the society's agenda seems to have been more political than literary. Government officials had to attend meetings, including a policeman who attempted to make sense of Borges on Persian Sufism in one of the last lectures he gave for SADE. Borges resigned in 1953, whereafter the society imploded amidst recriminations between Peronists and communists (though it did reform again after Perón had gone). One witness remembers Borges himself trying to make sense of a rancorous SADE assembly around 1955 – the year of Perón's fall – munching a biscuit in the drizzle, and asking, 'What have we got ourselves into?'[61]

This was recalled by Elsa Rivero Haedo, in 1994. She was a journalist and writer, active in the 1940s *beau monde* of Buenos Aires. She wrote a historical novel, published in 1946, called *María de los Angeles*; set in the province of San Juan in 1824 and based on fact, it was about an Argentine woman who bought a Spanish prisoner as a husband for four hundred pesos. The novel's film rights were snapped up in the same year for sixteen thousand pesos, an enormous amount at the time.

Rivero Haedo first met Borges in 1946, at the elegant Retiro flat of Elisabeth Wrede, an Austrian artist who had known Borges for some time, and had illustrated some of his books. Wrede was a friend of Pipina Hueyo Moreno, in whom Borges had had a prolonged interest and to whom he had, quite possibly, dedicated his two English poems. Hueyo Moreno did quite a lot for Borges in these fallow years – the late 1940s, early 1950s – organising gatherings at her and Rivero Haedo's homes, where he was able to talk on literary matters that appealed both to him and these well-meaning ladies of the arts.

Hueyo Moreno gave the group a name: Pro Arte. Its purpose was to help writers and intellectuals held in abeyance by Perón's regime with modest honoraria. Borges certainly benefited from time to time from Hueyo Moreno's efforts, and enjoyed her attention, though she actually did more for Ernesto Sábato, with whom *she* was, according to Rivero Haedo, in love – not that Borges would have known anything about that.

Borges's intellectual activities immediately after the efforts of *El Aleph* took the form of collaborations, his first flurry of them with people other than Bioy Casares. Between 1951 and 1955 came five books: *Antiguas literaturas germánicas* (1951), with Delia Ingenieros, the sister of Cecilia, a book that heralded Borges's growing interest in the literature of the old European North;* *El lenguaje de Buenos Aires* (1952), Borges's essay 'El idioma de los argentinos' – suppressed by him since 1928 – together with an essay by José Edmundo Clemente, who had been instrumental in bringing out in 1951 at Emecé Borges's first collection, *La muerte y la brújula*; *El 'Martín Fierro'* (1953), a revision of some of Borges's early writings on gauchesco literature, with Margarita Guerrero (with whom he would later produce *El libro de los seres imaginarios* (*The Book of Imaginary Beings*)); *Leopoldo Lugones* (1955), again old, and some new, writings on a poet whom Borges venerated, with Betina Edelberg; and a curious book of three stories, one by Borges, one by his collaborator and one written by both, called *La hermana de Eloísa* (1955), with the aforementioned Luisa Mercedes Levinson.

None of these people, with the exception of José Edmundo Clemente, played any significant part in Borges's life. Passing acquaintance, particularly with women, would invariably lead to literary activity of some sort. Now, it was anthologising and minor criticism; later, when Borges was blind, he would have them read to him – and occasionally write with him (notably María Esther Vázquez and Alicia Jurado).

Luisa Mercedes Levinson, eventually married Wally Klappenbach, today a major shareholder in *La Nación*, was part of the Buenos Aires Bohemian set of the 1940s, on whose fringes Borges put in occasional appearances, usually at Pro Arte gatherings where he would 'lecture'. People close to Borges – Bioy and a few others – realised as the years went by that women like Levinson tended to use Borges for their own careers, perhaps unscrupulously taking advantage of his blindness; but Borges chose not to suspect baser motives, and invariably let himself be manipulated. It was better than loneliness.†

---

*It was revised with the help of Borges's friend María Esther Vázquez, and republished under a new title, with his and her names as co-authors, in 1966. (See Chapters Seven and Eight for Vázquez, and Bibliography, p. 306.)

† Significantly, Borges left his and Levinson's volume out of the Emecé 1979 *Obras completas en colaboración*, considering it too slight to be of value.

In a way, this first phase of collaboration was a form of rehearsal for Borges's future agenda: blindness, which he knew would envelop him; and the writing of surrogate fiction. Though he may not have known it yet, the great stories were done; but writing in the same vein – carrying perhaps thinner blood – would have to continue.

With Bioy, all said, there was no shortage of projects in this period. An anthology of detective stories appeared in 1951 with Emecé, as did one of fantasy tales in 1955. More gauchesco poetry was collected in two volumes published by the Fondo de Cultura Económica in Mexico, the first and not the last time Borges had his work brought out, by the same house, in the home country of his beloved Alfonso Reyes. A rather eccentric project involving two film scripts also appeared in 1955, with Losada, under a single title, *Los orilleros-El paraíso de los creyentes* (The Hoodlums-The Paradise of the Believers). Neither saw the light of day – not surprisingly, as Bioy recalled:

> We worked on them a lot, but we did not really know how to do a film script. *Los orilleros* was a film with a series of compartments, each with its own ending; but a film has to go through to one end.
>
> Borges had the idea that the characters in the films could speak sententiously, in unforgettable phrases. Can you imagine Argentine actors having to speak like that? It was ridiculous. And there were jokes as usual – it became very tiring. Now the films are rightly forgotten.*62

The two friends' attempts to transfer their farces to screen were doomed to failure, Borges's proven enthusiasms for and expertise in the form notwithstanding.

Three major publishing events between 1951 and 1955 were amongst the most momentous in Borges's writing life. First, as already mentioned, there was Emecé's *La muerte y la brújula*, Borges's first real commercial edition. It consisted of nine popular stories drawn from *Ficciones* and *El Aleph*, firmly securing him as Emecé's most

---

* A feeble version of *Los orilleros* was attempted by Ricardo Luna in 1975; Bioy clearly includes this in his statement.

important author for the next thirty years.[63] Indeed, within two years of that volume, José Edmundo Clemente was in charge of the first complete works, *Historia de la eternidad* being republished in 1953. *Historia universal de la infamia* followed a year later. Borges's only proviso in allowing this to occur was that *Inquisiciones*, *El tamaño de mi esperanza* and *El idioma de los argentinos* – 'preposterous volumes', he called them[64] – should not be included. They were not.

In France meanwhile, in 1951, Roger Caillois brought out Paul Verdevoye and Néstor Ibarra's translation of *Ficciones* in his La Croix du Sud series, under the aegis of Gallimard, with the introduction written by Ibarra. Two years later came *Labyrinthes*, a small volume containing just four stories: 'The Immortal', 'The Story of the Warrior and the Captive', 'The God's Script', and 'Averroës's Search'. Caillois wrote his own preface.

Both books formed the bedrock of Borges's world renown. Caillois and Néstor Ibarra's transatlantic scouting activities in the 1940s had rather resembled those British collectors of the nineteenth century who amassed treasures and artefacts of other cultures for display in museums and galleries back home. Caillois's exportation of Borges was one of the twentieth century's most fortuitous acts of literary plundering.

For French intellectuals and readers of 'serious' literature, Borges was the ultimate item of collectability: stark, nightmarishly rational, self-reflective, somehow French in manner but utterly foreign in subject matter. Over the next decade, indeed, before he began his globetrotting, Borges was to be more consistently admired in France than anywhere in the world – including Argentina. The path towards global Borges was dug by the nation that, in its post-war intellectual restlessness, seemed to be waiting for him. Argentina was not yet mature enough.

The third big publishing event for Borges before the end of Perón was the appearance, with Sur, of *Otras inquisiciones*.

This was a book of essays in the style of *Discusión*, published exactly twenty years before. José Bianco helped Borges choose the thirty-nine pieces that make up the volume, drawn from fifteen years' worth of critical writing, the bulk of them published in the newspaper *La Nación*.

In no sense a conventional critical volume, it is a broad miscellany of Borges's tastes and preoccupations: poets of the Spanish and

English classical traditions – Coleridge, Quevedo, Keats – favourite writers – Hawthorne, Whitman, Valéry, Chesterton, Wells, Shaw, Kafka ('Kafka y sus precursores' ('Kafka and his Precursors') is one of Borges's most renowned essays about another author) – and contains a clutch of more ruminative, abstract ponderings, some central to the Borgesian critical canon – notably 'El espejo de los enigmas' ('The Mirror of Enigmas'), above all 'Nueva refutación del tiempo' ('New Refutation of Time').

It is in fact a rather chaotic book, which in its title Borges does nothing to play down: deliberately echoing the 1925 volume, his first published prose writing in book form, he suggests a mere continuation of an idiosyncratic and wholly unacademic quest into genre, philosophical concepts, and literary interconnectedness. It offers neither unity of purpose nor grand debates. Borges had never been a scholar, which is why he so enjoyed inventing them in his fiction. *Other Inquisitions* (as the English translation is called) is far from fiction, though one of its most striking aspects is the similarity of tone in the essays to his stories: density, teasing scepticism, an almost promiscuous allusiveness.

The book shows how Borges came to be a writer of fiction. It helps explain why he chose the form of short story he made so peculiarly his own: the fictions of *Ficciones* and *El Aleph* are, technically, mirror images of the essays of *Other Inquisitions*, all of which were written during his most fertile period as a storyteller. Critical gems in their own right, they are stylistic test-runs for the brilliant inventions forged alongside them.

The laissez-faire title of the book disguises the fact that it contains the fullest declaration of faith Borges wrote in his career – typical evasion tactics. 'New Refutation of Time' is an involved, recondite text. Its citation of Berkeley, Leibnitz, Hume, amongst many others, makes it seem philosophically top-heavy. However, these masters of scepticism are there for good reason.

The essay is concerned with the fixity of identity within the fluidity, the illusion, of time. As the title suggests, Borges seeks to deny time's existence. Why? Because in much of his life, dedicated, as he admits, to 'literature . . . and metaphysical perplexity',[65] he has perceived precisely that: a refutation of time. That is to say, scanning his output and twenty-five years of intellectual inquiry, he observes that his scrupulous avoidance of any commitment to known reality amounts to a moral position in itself.

Thus, this 'new' refutation of time is a summation of his personal and literary obsession with the problem; he chooses to illustrate it, sensibly, with a personal experience, first written about in 1928. Introducing the scenario with an exposition of the principle of repetition, of endless return, he recalls a walk he took one evening in Barracas. A street he encounters seems not to have changed since the nineteenth century. He suddenly feels 'dead':

> that pure representation of homogeneous facts – clear night, limpid wall, rural scent of honeysuckle, elemental clay – is not merely identical to the scene on that corner so many years ago; it is, without similarities, the same. If we can perceive that identity, time is a delusion: the indifference and inseparability of one moment of time's apparent yesterday and another of its apparent today are enough to disintegrate it.[66]

That phrase, 'it is, without similarities, the same', gets to the heart of the Borgesian vision of reality, which is a deceptively light paradox, a conceit: all various things, as perceived by the multiple 'I's of the universe, remain in time the same. This suggests that the existence of a single 'I' at any given moment can be the only measure of reality, which of course denies history, belief, and that the passing of time makes any difference to the state of things as they are.

'New Refutation of Time' was less a message to Borges's readers than an elaborate memo to himself. That is the character of the whole of *Other Inquisitions*. As a work of criticism *per se*, the book is almost useless. As a companion volume to the books of Borges's fiction that came before it, it reads as a natural successor. As a measure of Borges's achievements as a writer to date, it is a seminal book: just as *Ficciones* and *El Aleph* were unique, *Other Inquisitions* would never be repeated.

Indeed, the major characteristic of Borges's work from now on is that it would, in its own inimitable way, endlessly repeat itself. His demons exorcised – and his fury with Perón shortly to be spent – the magical fabulist, weaver of labyrinths and inventor of fiction which played intricate tricks on itself, had nothing new to say. What Borges hoped for now was that life, his life, would simply get better.

Part Three

The Man

Although at my age almost everyone I know is dead, I prefer to live my life looking forward. The past is a subject for poems, for elegies, but I try not to think about the past. I would rather spend my time thinking of the future, although quite possibly I have little future left. But I hope to conserve my mind; I hope to continue dreaming and writing. I come from a sad country.

Borges in 1984
('A Day in the Life of Jorge Luis Borges',
Sunday Times Magazine)

Chapter Seven

1955–1964

Borges Global

By September 1955, Perón was gone. Spirited away to Paraguay, and thence to Madrid, the dictator's rule came to an end after nine years of demagoguery and, latterly, alleged mental instability. After Evita's death aged thirty-three in 1952 of cancer of the uterus, Perón had become increasingly distant from the people who had once held his wife in veneration, her beloved '*descamisados*' (shirtless ones), and let himself be dictated to by the military. There were also rumours of sex with teenage girls. That was perhaps the least of his problems. His biggest mistake, amongst many after 1948 (until when he and his wife had enjoyed an extended political honeymoon), was to interfere with the Catholic Church.

Peronism as a creed had become state policy in 1947 with the establishment of the official 'Peronist' party. By 1949, when Perón forged a new constitution ensuring presidential re-electability for an unlimited number of six-year terms, a major economic crisis could be disguised by sheer force of the personality cult surrounding Perón and his wife. Then, when Evita died, the potential for unbridled mythologising of the cult was exploited to full and dynamic effect.

However, setting up Peronism as a form of state religion was too much. Education, welfare and public morals were the Church's guarded terrain, and Perón's programme of secularisation, including the legalisation of divorce in 1954, was bound to upset the conservatives. The Church took against him, and carried the military with it. When aircraft, hoping to spark off a military coup, bombed the Casa Rosada in mid-1955 and killed several hundred during a rally for Perón, the writing was on the wall.

The transition to a new politics, or rather away from dictatorship, was called the 'Revolución Libertadora', the Freedom Revolution – 'long-hoped-for', Borges called it.[1]

But Peronism had grown deep roots. From now on, muddle was supreme in Argentine politics, not least of all because of the confrontation between Peronism and the country's new masters. From 1955 to 1958, Argentina was run by two generals, Eduardo Lonardi and Pedro Aramburu. Top of their agenda was the eradication of Perón's deeply ambivalent legacy. The economy had all but collapsed, and even after a brief period of democracy until 1966, it was the military who took control behind the scenes in an attempt to dig Argentina out of bankruptcy and decay; the generals believed, rightly or wrongly, the politicians to be ineffective. The old liberal Argentina was to all intents and purposes dead.

Borges's reaction to this was simple: anything was better than Perón. Whatever happened to Argentina after his downfall could only be an improvement on the ways of the 'Unspeakable'.[2] That there never was an improvement was a fact Borges tended to ignore, at least for another two decades, when the return of Perón galvanised him into a new round of denunciations.

In June 1956, Borges made outspoken attacks on Peronism in Montevideo. He had been invited by the Argentine Embassy to speak at conferences, and was interviewed by the press. In his replies, he poured scorn on the recently deposed regime – Borges here began his enjoyment of renown, away from his home town and venting public spleen on the thing he hated most.

He also had the writer Ezequiel Martínez Estrada in his sights, whom he accused of tacitly defending Perón. Martínez Estrada attacked back in print, referring to the depths of self-debasement writers such as Borges had had to plumb in order to vilify Perón. Borges ridiculed Martínez Estrada in another article. Ernesto Sábato, who by now had come into his own as a writer (*El túnel* – *The Tunnel* – was published in 1948), then joined the fray, coming to Martínez Estrada's defence and accusing Borges of being simplistic.

Borges at once again struck back, effectively equating Sábato's own language with Peronist slogans. He took the opportunity to make a declaration of political faith: 'Ethics', he wrote, 'do not stem from the State; something [he implies Peronism, but he means any form of populism] does not stop being atrocious just because thousands have proclaimed it, and acted it out.'[3]

The statement was important for two reasons: first, it signalled a parting of ways between Borges and Sábato, who now remained ideologically divided – rather as Borges and Neruda had been since the late 1920s. (Between the trio of Argentina's most famous post-war writers – Borges, Sábato and Cortázar – there was a kind of Roman-senatorial spirit of strife, with two of them forever cantankerously incapable of seeing eye to eye, while the third, the Parisianised Cortázar, privately ploughed his own furrow.)

Secondly, Borges's contempt for mass movements was now a matter of record. His words prefigured the position of anti-collectivism, and even antagonism to democracy itself, which was to make him so tricky a political a figure throughout the 1960s and 1970s.

Post-Perón, Borges found himself compelled to publicise strong ethical views that had developed during the rise of European fascism, and reached their venomous acme under the South American Unspeakable. Now, world politics, world ideologies, were much more complicated. For a man who, apart from lecture tours inside his own country, had not travelled away from the River Plate area since 1924, the world might indeed all too easily be seen in opposites of black and white.

The problem was that with the Cold War polarising ideologies and, in Latin America, leading to a release of anti-imperialist, economically protectionist fervour, impatience with Borges's species of old-fashioned individualism was inevitable, amongst intellectuals, at least. The political drift of much of Latin America as the 1960s approached was towards right-wing dictatorship, actively encouraged in Washington and the capitals of Western Europe to stave off a deepening of Soviet influence; inspiration for opposition and dissent was inevitably found in Marxism.

The culmination of Marxist hope for a new order eventually

appeared in the figure of a maverick rebel from Argentina (perhaps not surprisingly) – Che Guevara. Guevara represented a fresh ideal, the romantic guerrilla, to take sinister form in the early 1970s in Argentina with the Montoneros and the ERP. While Borges's own social and political ideals were rooted in a gentler anarchism – the Spencerian values of his father – these murderous Argentine groups who thought nothing of assassination had the whiff of the gaucho combatants populating Borges's later, more realistic stories. It was a dangerous sort of life reflecting a consummate fantasist's art.

In many Latin American societies, right up to the 1980s, where the capitalist status quo was not so much upheld by the vote as mercilessly imposed by a military elite, communists were seen as subversives – and that included a large community of writers. Borges was never of their number. Nor was he ever actively politically engaged, but none the less availed himself of the freedom to speak his mind – and why not? Tilting towards conservatism in his public utterances was clearly a deliberate choice Borges made once Perón had been seen off, though he remained disinclined to articulate a mature political allegiance.

The worst that can be said of Borges at this stage is that given his rising public profile, a trumpeted non-espousal of left-wing ideology, clearly associated with the cause of genuine liberation, might have been injudicious. This was to become particularly apparent in 1959, with the arrival of Fidel Castro and the Cuban Revolution; Ernesto Sábato and Ezequiel Martínez Estrada, amongst dozens of intellectuals of their generation, welcomed it. Borges, almost alone, considered it a disaster.

It would be too much to describe Borges's polemic with the above two men, and his truculent attitude towards watershed events like Cuba, as the 'politicisation' of Borges. In later years, his truculence would come to be perceived as reactionary, and used by a younger generation of highly politicised students and readers to turn away from his literature. In truth, Borges was simply out of touch, and took a literary old buffer's pleasure in being so.

As if to underline this, Borges could now see very little. Vision in the left eye had gone, while only a blur remained in the right eye: it accounted for the hooded nature of the latter, the eyelid keeping its own curious movement in time with the little Borges could register – the colour yellow, mainly.

Operations on his cataracts had started in 1927, carried out by

Doctor Amado Natale; by 1954, Borges had undergone a total of eight operations. At the end of that year, his ophthalmologist advised him against reading and writing ever again. To anyone in good health in their mid-fifties, this would have been deprivation enough. For a writer, it was a potential catastrophe. But Borges had always known it was coming. He had watched both his grandmother and his father go blind; his own eyesight had always been bad, so bad indeed that he very rarely bothered to wear spectacles after childhood. He accepted his hereditary condition with the stoicism that began to characterise his poetry.[4]

Blindness to this degree meant that he became more dependent on others than before. This was not a problem for Leonor, who had looked after him for years anyway. The couple had also had extra help from 1947, a year after they had moved to calle Maipú, in the form of a maid, Epifanía Uveda de Robledo – Fani, as she was always known.

Fani had been abandoned by her husband, and she was very much Leonor's find. She stayed with the Borgeses until Jorge Luis left Buenos Aires for good in late 1985, and some say she was not held in any special affection by him. Borges put up with her because she was in his mother's employ – she had her own room in the Maipú flat – and was there to do the rudimentary things he was incapable of, and for which Leonor had increasingly less time the more she had to occupy herself with her son's affairs.

The major factor in Borges's working life at this point was his sudden employability. For a blind writer in his mid-fifties out of tune with the political times, the irony was little short of wondrous. His first real job since his post at the Miguel Cané library was as a teacher of literature at Buenos Aires University, given to him by the caretaker government of General Eduardo Lonardi in 1955. This soon turned into a 'directorship' at the Faculty of Philosophy and Letters.

The post was not as elevated as it sounds. Meagrely remunerated, a position like that at the university was subject to the whims of government. Borges was famously anti-Peronist, but also a bit of a public menace to anyone trying to form an administration in what was rapidly proving an ungovernable country. Dissent from students and intellectuals was the last thing the new authorities needed, even if they were inclined to encourage the kind of anti-Peronism Borges was so vocal in espousing.

Educational resources were also inevitably thin; keeping university salaries as low as possible would perhaps discourage better minds from actively seeking jobs in an intellectual environment, and thus causing trouble. Borges, ever passively grateful for the chance to work without having to go through anything so complicated as an application, had stumbled on an improvement to his life as an itinerant lecturer. But one witness to his new-found employability, Elsa Rivero Haedo, recalls just how passive and overtrustful he was:

> One day I saw him in the street, as we all did in the Maipú area, wandering around about to fall into a hole – we'd rush over and help him on his way home. On this occasion, he was trembling, almost in tears.
>
> 'Do you know what's just happened to me?' he said. 'I've just come back from picking up my salary at the university, and it's *half* what I thought it would be.'
>
> Borges had been summoned to the office of Gino Germani, a senior official in the university, also an educational theorist, and asked: 'How much interest *is* there, Borges, in these German and English things [referring to the literature Borges taught]? You know that we have to watch our budget, and that if there isn't enough interest we simply can't keep the department going.'
>
> Borges was deeply offended. He had a colleague in the Romance languages department, and answered, stuttering: '*Caramba, caramba*, I'm sure if my colleague agrees to accept a cut in case we are being paid too much . . .'
>
> And Germani had taken Borges at his word. Borges was always doing this, accepting just enough money to buy one shoe out of a pair . . .[5]

In 1956, he became a professor of English and American Literature in the same faculty – Philosophy and Letters – and it was a post he held on to until 1968. He never filled it with any true academic distinction – he was far too wayward for that; what students enjoyed for over a decade was his inimitable chitchat. And there was his status. In a sense, the mere presence of 'Jorge Luis Borges, author of *Ficciones* and *El Aleph*', was distinction enough.

His appointment as Director of the National Library in 1955, however, had the greatest symbolism, and it lasted longer than his university job. It was the most prominent redress offered to him for the indignities endured under Perón, and probably the biggest honour he ever received from his own country in his life.

Of course, Borges didn't seek the post. In the opening days of the 'Libertadora', a friend of his, Esther Zemboraín de Torres Duggan,[6] came up with the idea that the name of a new director of the library, untainted by Peronism, should be put forward to the authorities. That meant, ultimately, to the transitional military regime, then headed by General Eduardo Lonardi. Initially, the recommendation was turned down. The outgoing director, a Peronist, was not exactly sympathetic. So Esther Zemboraín solicited the support of Victoria Ocampo and three or four other associates in the Ocampo-Bioy crowd to lobby the authorities on Borges's behalf.

Borges suggested, facetiously, that he might take a job in a provincial library; why, he asked Victoria, did they not seek a post for him in Lomas de Zamora (a town to the south of Buenos Aires, a notorious hoodlum zone)? 'Don't be an idiot,' Victoria replied. Thus it was that in October 1955, Borges found himself in the Casa Rosada in front of the acting President of Argentina.

'How odd,' he thought. 'The dictator is no longer in the Casa Rosada and, for the first time, I shall shake the hand of the President of the Republic. It all seems like a dream.'

With him was the writer Manuel Mujica Láinez, who apparently thanked Lonardi grovellingly for at least enunciating (rather than proclaiming) the name of Jorge Luis Borges as the library's new director. Back at Maipú, Leonor had heard news of his appointment on the radio. That night, they walked together to calle México, where the library was situated, and Leonor asked him, Why not go in, now that you're the director? Borges, understandably superstitious given the joke played on him by the Peronists in 1946, refused to enter.[7] However, within days, the Ministry of Education confirmed Borges's appointment; he took up office.

The National Library, located in a building of 1901, had originally been marked for housing the national lottery.[8] An imposing façade in a narrow street, it has nothing in particular to mark it out as bibliographically venerable. Inside, on the marble staircase that twisted to the first-floor offices, were the sculpted symbols of fortune which identified (and still identify) the building's first intended use. Through the lobby pillars, however, was an impressive reading room, full of desks, the high walls lined from top to bottom with books.

Between shelves, walls were carved with the names of history's great writers – Dante, Shakespeare, Calderón.

The multiple appropriateness of a librarian, sacked by one government, reinstated by another, responsible for dizzying stories first about a lottery, then a library, must have appealed to the new incumbent. Even more serendipitous was the fact that a previous director, Paul Groussac, was a literary hero of Borges's and had been blind.[9] Blindness and the national librarianship were a Buenos Aires speciality. The writer José Mármol, a National Library director until 1871, also went blind.

The coincidence was celebrated in a poem Borges wrote once well-installed at the library, and his disability was deemed permanent. In 'Poem of the Gifts', he salutes God, no less,

> . . . who with such splendid irony
> Granted me books and blindness at one touch . . .
>
> Groussac or Borges, now I look upon
> This dear world losing shape, fading away
> Into a pale uncertain ashy-grey
> That feels like sleep, or else oblivion.*[10]

In a high office tucked away on the first floor, Borges enthroned himself. It abutted on to a bare outer office, where part-time secretaries worked at a desk under one window. In Borges's office, the wallpaper was green, decorated with bamboo-like fronds; the panelling was of polished mahogany.[12] Many accounts have him sitting behind Paul Groussac's U-shaped desk, one that the former director had had specially made for him. In fact, Borges never used it, preferring a large mahogany table. Nearby were some revolving bookshelves and a tall chest of drawers, containing drafts of poems that Borges would dictate over the years to any number of secretaries.

A few doors away, following the four walls of the reading room, was a balcony; from it, Borges could survey all that he was now master of – if only, that is, he could have seen it. In fact he had, when he was much younger; in the 1920s, before acquiring his own *Encyclopaedia*

---

* In the 'Autobiographical Essay', he commented on the irony of being handed 'at one time 800,000 books and darkness'.[11]

Britannica, he had come to consult the library's copy on the open shelves – though he never actually used the books, as he was too shy (so the story goes) to ask for them.

Now, seeing was of secondary importance. Borges was in charge of what he had already written about. The library, with – for Borges – kinetic, real worlds contained within the binding all round him, was simply a mirror of everything he had already imagined.

He remained there for eighteen years. One of the first people to witness him in his element was Emir Rodríguez Monegal. His first-hand account of Borges in action in 1956, leading him through the crypt of the library where the bulk of the books were stacked, is an enduring one:

> Borges took me in hand and led me around, seeing only enough to know where each book he wanted was. He can open a book to the desired page and, without bothering to read . . . quote complete passages. He roams along corridors lined with books; he quickly turns corners and gets into passages which are truly invisible, mere cracks in the walls of books; he rushes down winding staircases which abruptly end in the dark. There is almost no light in the library's corridors and staircases. I try to follow him, tripping, blinder and more handicapped than Borges because my only guides are my eyes . . . [He] drags me, makes me . . . fall exhausted into the centre of darkness. Suddenly, there is light at the end of another corridor . . . Next to Borges, who smiles like a child who has played a joke on a friend, I recover my eyesight . . .[13]

Work at the library was not taxing. The post as director was a nominal one, an honour. It was rounded off by the directorship of a magazine called *La Biblioteca*, a bibliophile journal resurrected in February 1957 from a pre-war incarnation. José Edmundo Clemente was Borges's assistant, and was effectively the main administrator and principal librarian. Borges used the library for his own work, which was now poetry.

A return to poetry was the most significant shift of literary emphasis Borges had made since sitting down to write 'Pierre Menard'. He never quite lost his sense of destiny as a poet, and preferred to think

182

of himself as one from now on, over and above his reputation as a storyteller.

Between 1964 and 1985, he produced eight further volumes of poems – excluding collected volumes, and one which was a book of song lyrics.* If one were to generalise about the work, it would be fair to call it ruminative in tone, nostalgic in subject matter, and often formal in structure. Some individual poems rise above the rest – 'Poem of the Gifts', 'Adrogué', 'In Praise of Darkness' – mainly because Borges is in them, addressing a personal dilemma, recalling a place close to his heart, speaking his mind.

More often than not, however, Borges chose literature and not the world as the subject of his verse. One only has to look at the titles of many poems written from the late 1950s over the next two decades – 'A Luis de Camoens', 'Emerson', 'Spinoza', 'Ricardo Güiraldes', 'A John Keats', and so on – to get an idea whence he drew his inspiration.

What those named poems have in common above all is their form: they are sonnets. It is a well-known fact of the Borges story that, once blind, poetry was something he could 'see' in his head: his memory being what it was, he could carry around forms, metre and rhyme, and reproduce them in exactly the shape in which his brain had moulded them, like rubbing letraset on to white paper. He was very precise, and honest, about this in the 'Autobiographical Essay':

One salient consequence of my blindness was my gradual abandonment of free verse in favour of classical metrics. In fact, blindness made me take up the writing of poetry again. Since rough drafts were denied me, I had to fall back on memory. It is obviously easier to remember verse than prose, and to remember regular verse forms rather than free ones. Regular verse is, so to speak, portable.[14]

The sonnet form is the epitomé of prosodic neatness, and has been for centuries. Its lineage through Petrarch and Dante, Shakespeare and Milton and, of course, Góngora and Quevedo had an antiquarian appeal to Borges. Its precisely patterned rhyme scheme through two quatrains and two tercets offered a structure within which Borges

* *Para las seis cuerdas* (*For the Guitar*): see p. 206.

could work comfortably. He lighted upon the sonnet as a physiological necessity.*

Settling into his new role as poet-librarian, Borges's office became a dictation centre. The first original book written in this manner, a collaboration, was with Margarita Guerrero, who had also helped Borges produce the little book about *Martín Fierro* in 1953; the new book, *Manual de zoología fantástica*, a menagerie of creatures mad and miscellaneous, was published in 1957 in Mexico. Ten years later this became much-enlarged into *El libro de los seres imaginarios*, the first of Borges's works to be translated by Norman Thomas di Giovanni – *The Book of Imaginary Beings*, as it was called (for which see pp.224–5).

At home in Maipú, it was Leonor who took notes and wrote for him. At the National Library, it would be down to anyone who happened to drop by. He had a very particular way of working:

> He dictates five or six words, which initiate a prose piece or the first verse of a poem, and immediately has them read out. As the words come, the index finger of his right hand slides down the back of his left hand, as if it were running over an invisible page. The phrase is repeated once, twice, thrice, four times until he sees how to go on, and he dictates another five or six words. Then he has the whole thing read out. As he dictates with punctuation, that has to be read out too. This fragment is reread, accompanied by hand movements, until he encounters the next phrase.
>
> I've sometimes read out a section of five lines a dozen times. Each of these repetitions is preceded by Borges's apologies – he seems somewhat tormented by the supposed inconveniences he makes his scribe suffer. The result after two or three hours of work is a half page in a notebook which needs no corrections.

The witness is a woman called María Esther Vázquez.[17]

She was born in 1941 into a family of Galician origins. Her father died when she was very small; her mother encouraged her in her

---

* Borges attributed to the sonnet something less concrete, too: 'There is something mysterious about the sonnet. Its form . . . may seem arbitrary, but throughout the centuries and across geography it has displayed a capacity for endless modulations.'[15] His first major translator was not so sure, 'wearying', he wrote two years after Borges's death, 'of those same fourteen hendecasyllabic lines, the inevitability of those seven pairs of rhymes'.[16]

literary interests. Precociously intelligent, María Esther read her mother's entire library aged eleven, and was at university by the age of sixteen.

Around this time, in 1956, she heard about Jorge Luis Borges. News of his university lectures (which were less lectures than *charlas* – chats) had travelled fast. With a small group of fellow students from the Faculty of Philosophy and Letters, she went and saw him in calle Maipú. Borges was never shy of visitors, and positively encouraged them – the younger the better, and best of all if female. María Esther, on the other hand, was so shy at this time, she couldn't even accept a cup of tea from Leonor.

She managed to overcome her shyness. By 1957, she had got a job at the National Library, helping José Edmundo Clemente. She had also caught the attention of one José Luis Ríos Patrón, a poet who had written one of the first monographs on Borges at the beginning of 1955. It seems that he and María Esther were engaged to be married, or at least Ríos Patrón came to believe they were. María Esther clearly had other ideas – she had already met her future husband, another poet, Horacio Armani – and could not possibly answer Ríos Patrón's needs.

Ríos Patrón begged her, in vain. Finally, he gave her an ultimatum: she must agree to marry him, or he would kill himself; and one day, he did just that, shooting himself in front of her on a Buenos Aires street, near the radio station where María Esther was starting a career in broadcasting. Ríos Patrón died in her arms.*

Traumatised, María Esther was sent to Europe by her mother. She returned in 1961, not as an employee at the National Library but as a freelance broadcaster at Radio Municipal. She did, however, begin a new association with Borges, taking dictation from him and helping him with secretarial duties.[18] After Leonor, María Esther Vázquez was Borges's first full-time amanuensis.

We have already seen how readily Borges collaborated with women, from the succession of volumes he produced with four of them between 1951 and 1955. With María Esther Vázquez, there was more than collaboration: she entered his life at the dawning of his

---

* This is something I have heard from two reliable sources in Buenos Aires, but I have been unable to verify it. Vázquez makes no mention of it at all in her biography, *Borges: esplendor y derrota* (Tusquets, 1996).

international success, and eventually became a travelling companion, as well as a supplementary ear to Leonor.

Vázquez's was a controversial role, as we shall see. But the degree to which Borges acknowledged her importance is reflected in his making her the dedicatee of his 1959 'Poem of the Gifts'.

How, then, did Borges suddenly become famous? The French editions of his stories were of course instrumental, but don't entirely account for the dimension (to borrow his own word) of his global renown in the early 1960s.

Two things happened after 1955 to pave the way. First was the heaping on of honours; the directorship of the National Library was one of them. More conventional recognition came in the form of a doctorate from one of Argentina's oldest universities, Cuyo, in 1956. It was the first such academic honour in an endless series until Borges's death. In the same year, he also won the National Prize for Literature, not an enormous global distinction, as Borges recognised in conversation with Jean de Milleret ten years later.[19] The military government, in power until 1958, wanted to disavow Peronism in all fields, including culture. From that point of view, Borges was the perfect carrier of the new propaganda. It also conferred on him establishment status.

With such status come critics; and this was the second strand to the manner in which Borges was 'launched' in the late 1950s. It seems hard to imagine, but apart from the odd press review and a number of in-house 'homages', critical attention to Borges was negligible in Argentina until at least the publication of *Other Inquisitions*.

His actual reputation stemmed from the devoted readership of a wide circle of friends, and the spirited efforts of a few literary entrepreneurs – women, mainly, in Buenos Aires, and Frenchmen in Europe. A couple of extended appreciations of *Other Inquisitions* by María Rosa Lida de Malkiel and Enrique Pezzoni respectively were published in *Sur* in 1952. The first proper book of criticism, *Borges y la nueva generación* by Adolfo Prieto, appeared in 1954. Then, between 1957 and 1959, came four books about Borges, including one by Ana María Barrenechea, perhaps the most perceptive and sensitive of Borges's early critics.[20]

But not all the attention was favourable. A common line of attack was that Borges was elitist. This antipathy originated amongst nationalist critics: as early as 1948, H. A. Murena had objected in *Sur* that Borges fed on Argentine national symbolism in his poetry without properly invoking his nationality. In 1951, Murena raised further objections to Borges's anti-Argentine multiculturalism, to which Borges replied in a lecture in the same year, 'El escritor argentino y la tradición' ('The Argentine Writer and Tradition', later collected in *Labyrinths*); here, he pithily outlined his vision of the writer as a receptacle of universal realities, regardless of nationality. 'I repeat that we should not be alarmed and that we should feel that our patrimony is the universe; we should essay all themes, and we cannot limit ourselves to purely Argentine subjects in order to be Argentine . . .'[21]

It was this kind of supposed bloodless evasion of '*engagé*' literature, writing which acknowledged a necessary contemporaneity and locale, which underlay the accusations levelled at Borges by Ernesto Sábato in 1956, and was to be a persistent cry for the rest of Borges's writing life. It tied in closely with objections to his political conservatism, and was often unintelligent. Ideologically aggressive critiques of his work, which identified Borges with a dandyish aristocracy, an ivory-tower aestheticism, were often ill-informed about his social background (middle-class), about his financial circumstances (unimpressive), or indeed about the intrinsic nature of his fiction. How much easier it was to lump Borges haphazardly with the pre-war so-called 'smart set' – the Bioys, Ocampo and so on – than work through the dazzling complexities of his best prose (even if it had, admittedly, been written in a fifteen-year period now over), or identify him for what he was: a toiling artificer, with an apprenticeship that went back to the 1920s, and whose principal tool was a dense, sceptical imagination.

The point is that after 1955 Borges's reading public at home increased dramatically, in large part because of the efforts made by Emecé, a prominent commercial firm. Emecé's collected works were beginning to have marked impact; at the same time, Borges was on his way to becoming an institution, not least because of his position at the National Library. His appearances in the cultural and literary pages of the Buenos Aires dailies, not just as a byline but as a subject, were increasingly common from the late 1950s on.

As if in conscious anticipation of the fame and attention that lay ahead, Borges had a new invention up his sleeve. This was the 'Borges' persona, the 'other' man who had moved on from, and now concealed, the nervous, shy, emotionally myopic one of the Ultraist years, and the even more confused one behind *Ficciones* and *El Aleph*. A composite creature who had already been evoked in some of the stories, notably 'The Zahir' ('I am still, however incompletely, Borges'), he was both elusive alter-ego and escape route.

In a way, this Borges had been evolving over many years. The writer was always experimenting with permutations of identity, questioning ontological fixity, chipping away at the tyranny of a stable tale and teller, until he came up with a scapegoat: the double, one who could both be 'talked to' and effectively take on the attributes of the real Borges, the one Jorge Luis was saddled with – a man afflicted with blindness, encroaching old age, obsessed with riddles, paradoxes, labyrinths, an unslakeable thirst for foreign (mainly English) literature – and behind which the private 'I' could be dissolved.

The lover, the Ultraist, the Argentine, the experimenter were now the province of a defeated past. Even as early as 1954, in his preface to that year's edition of *A Universal History of Infamy*, Borges gave a hint of the future abandonment of that once uncertain writer-in-the-making.

The new bardic Borges announced himself most openly in a volume Emecé published in 1960: *Dreamtigers*.* This is a compendium of short pieces, some of which went back to the days of *Crítica*. One, 'Dialogue on a Dialogue', a wry sketch about the afterlife, first appeared in Borges and Bioy's short-lived 1936 magazine *Destiempo*.

Most of the pieces were relatively new, begun at around the time Borges was going terminally blind, in 1954–5. He called them 'sketches and parables', 'odds and ends', which led to a book he said, with good reason, he 'accumulated rather than wrote'.[23] Borges's new editor at Emecé, Carlos Frías, wanted a new text to top up the 'so-called' (Borges's phrase) complete works. Some time in late 1958, therefore, Borges spent a Sunday digging out uncollected fragments from a desk drawer. He was aided by Leonor, to whom he had in recent years been dictating new pieces – and he continued to do

---

* The Spanish, *El hacedor*, meaning 'the maker', is not unnaturally the best rendition of the book's title, implying artificer, fabulist, conjuror, weaver of spells, as well as the more portentous 'artist'; the English title, *Dreamtigers*, named after one of the short, opening prose pieces, came about because the first translators in 1963 were flummoxed by '*hacedor*'; Borges always said it was simple – he had taken it from a famous poem by Dunbar.[22]

so throughout 1959. To the twenty-two prose pieces were added twenty-four poems (the first being 'Poem of the Gifts'). Frías was then charged with the task of giving order to the chaos, and the book was duly published in 1960.

Dreamtigers remains many people's favourite Borges work, as indeed it appears to have been Borges's: it 'seems to me my most personal work,' he wrote in the 'Autobiographical Essay', 'and to my taste, maybe my best'.[24]

This is slightly disingenuous. Borges was keen to realign himself in relation to his own output, and show a new face and voice to his readers. He was never overtly proud of the great stories of the 1940s and early 1950s, and expended considerable energy in distancing himself from them. In its emphasis on the oracular and poetic sides of his personality, *Dreamtigers* was indeed personal, but also amounted to an effective disavowal of the revolutionary Borges.

Dreamtigers offers a combination of the recognisable sage and more intimate touches, Borges both concealing and revealing himself: in other words, image-making. Altogether it lacks the impact, drive and angularity of the stories, mainly because the narrator is projecting not a series of enigmas but a version of himself. In a fantasy prologue, Borges presents his new book to Leopoldo Lugones; then, in piece one, he paints a picture of its creator, its maker ('*hacedor*'): a figure, with a voice that might be Homer's, who slowly accepts a condition of blindness. The mask, which had been worn by both Joyce and Milton before Borges, is here a thin one. We know this is Borges talking:

> When he knew he was going blind, he cried out; stoic fortitude had not yet been invented . . . but one morning he awoke, looked (without astonishment now) at the dim things around him, and unexplainably felt – the way one recognises a strain of music or a voice – that all this had already happened to him and that he had faced it with fear, but also with joy, hope, and curiosity.[25]

The seer is in place – and Borges immediately returns to his childhood. Piece two, 'Dreamtigers', recalls the boy's fascination with the Asian beast, how he dreamt about tigers, drew them, and how they have come to symbolise a lithe, brutal, other reality challenging the temporal everyday: he remembers that with the power of his dreams, he himself can engender that reality – '*voy a causar un tigre*', in the most felicitous phrase in the book, 'I am going to cause a tiger', though he finally admits to failure: the animal's form is indistinct, confused, elusive.

This is the essence of the book, a successive 'causing' of scenes, vignettes, literary montages, strange encounters which shimmer in and out of focus. It reads like a commentary on Borges's unconscious or submerged mental life, without a single overtone of analysis or therapeutic twinge, but with all the otherworldly, and by now familiar imagery and preoccupations, intact: mirrors, with a tyrannous life of their own; the violent weapons and deeds of gauchos; ancestors; and the ever-present Perón. It is a kind of encyclopaedia of Borges's hobby-horses, and through it, the great enumerator of arcane phenomena remains as resolutely non-realist as ever. As a poem later in the book, 'El otro tigre' ('The Other Tiger'), puts it,

> . . . the tiger addressed in my poem
> Is a shadowy beast, a tiger of symbols
> And scraps picked up at random out of books . . .[26]

Reality is fugitive. As so often in Borges, the most assertive certainties are drawn from reading – hence a predominance in *Dreamtigers* of parables relating to Dante, Cervantes, Shakespeare, *Martín Fierro*.

The most famous entry in *Dreamtigers* is the final prose piece, 'Borges y yo' ('Borges and I'). I have already mentioned how the book deals in revelation and concealment, and this little dramatic monologue encapsulates that pattern. It is, at one level, a highly autobiographical statement, but deceptively so: 'I have a taste for hourglasses, maps, eighteenth-century typography', says the writer – which in Borges's case was not so, he couldn't see such things, although he might once have enjoyed them – but he goes on:

> . . . the roots of words, the smell of coffee, and Stevenson's prose; the other man shares these likes, but in a showy way that turns them into stagy mannerisms. It would be an exaggeration to say that we are on bad terms; I live, I let myself live, so that Borges can weave his tales and poems, and those tales and poems are my justification.[27]

This was as clear an articulation as Borges ever made about the manner in which texts 'wrote him', rather than the other way round. They lived though him, not he through them. He acknowledges an animus, more or less outside his control, as being responsible for work which has made the reputation of a certain 'Borges'.

He was always modest. Here, the writer takes that virtue to a metaphysical extreme, bowing to the publicly 'visible' other – a fiction – and as ever, when in most exquisitely sceptical mood, casting doubt over the existence of a 'real' Borges. 'Which of us is writing this page I don't know', the text ends. In the most cunning and diverting move of his literary career, Borges had become his double.

Another strand to *Dreamtigers* was completely new. Three items in the book, two in prose, one a poem, were concerned with Anglo-Saxon matters.

In 1958, Borges had taken up Anglo-Saxon as an ancillary intellectual exercise to his lectures on English literature at the faculty. He had done so with some students keen to supplement their orthodox English studies with something a little out of the ordinary. As Borges put it in the 'Essay': 'We had just polished off all English literature fom Beowulf to Bernard Shaw in the span of four months . . . at home . . . I had copies of Sweet's *Anglo-Saxon Reader* and the *Anglo-Saxon Chronicles*. When the students came the next Saturday morning, we began reading these two books.'[28]

The idea was to explore literature outside the set curriculum, which was both worthwhile and pleasurable. Lighting upon Anglo-Saxon as the desired terrain is something generations of Oxford English students, forced to work their way through Sweet in their first year, will find incomprehensible. But for Borges, Anglo-Saxon was never a formal undertaking, and he certainly never gave a 'course' in the subject. It was a new hobby, a pastime; any other sixty-year-old might have taken up golf, bridge or ceramics.

Leonor thought he should take up Greek. 'Why this barbaric language?' she asked him when Sweet and the *Chronicles* had been removed from a bookshelf in Maipú, and dusted down ready for use. Georgie couldn't see enough to learn the Greek alphabet from scratch. However, many years before, he had made a study of Norse and Saxon kennings, in an essay published in *Discusión*. Also, with his knowledge of German, he at least had the rudiments of Old English inside his head.

Borges never intended to master it; rather, to enjoy it. 'I had always thought of English literature as the richest in the world; the discovery now of a secret chamber at the very threshold of that literature came to me as an additional gift.'[29] His manner of learning it was unusual, and typical of his style at this stage of his life: he collaborated with fellow enthusiasts, and turned the whole enterprise into an open-ended experiment rather than a pedagogical pursuit.

One of his first students was the writer Vlady Kociancich. In 1958, she was a pretty seventeen-year-old in her second year at the Faculty of Philosophy and Letters, and knew about Borges's reputation as a writer, although she hadn't yet read him. At the end of one of his faculty lectures, she went up to him to talk about Sutton Hoo, the Saxon burial site that had recently been discovered in East Anglia and caused great excitement on front pages round the world.

Kociancich was far more interested at the time in the actual treasure of Sutton Hoo than anything to do with Germanic languages. But Borges suggested they went for coffee, and asked her to form part of an Anglo-Saxon study group. She readily agreed.

There were three of us in the group, one a boy called Fonseca, another an engineer who was supplementing his own studies with English but who eventually disappeared from the faculty, and me.

The myth is that Borges gave seminars on Old English; this is incorrect. He was learning it himself at this period. We would consult the primer, to see how things declined, and then with the *Reader* in front of us, Borges, with a great big smile, would ask: 'Who's going to read?' No one knew how to read it, let alone pronounce the stuff. So we had to make approximations, knowing that in Shakespeare's time, for instance, 'To be or not to be' might have been, with long and open vowels, 'To bay ar nat to bay' . . . We played, hoping what we came up with would roughly correspond to what was spoken in the tenth century.

Borges's understanding of German etymology permitted him to find a solution before consulting Sweet's glossary. And because I had a good memory, I could then recite the texts back to him as we walked through the streets after classes. Months later, a Scottish acquaintance of Borges's gave him an immense Anglo-Saxon dictionary; we also discovered a book of grammar and pronunciation in French. And with that we tackled the *Chronicles*. People think that Borges, peering at his pocketwatch, could see more or less who or what was around him. But truly, he was blind. He could not read, and he had begun to dictate at this time. Learning Old English was a feat of memory for him. You might think that such a subject could only be for bored housewives whose children have left home, but not at all. It was all for Borges's memory.[30]

For a man obsessed with memory and the tricks it could play, the notion of a device – and Old English was just that – which could keep his recollective powers intact was a powerful incentive indeed. Without the ability physically to read or write, the outer reaches of etymology were an intoxicating substitute for the labours of creation.

> All praise to the inexhaustible
> Labyrinth of cause and effect
> Which, before unveiling to me the mirror
> Where I shall see no one or shall see some other self,
> Has granted me this perfect contemplation
> Of a language at its dawn.[31]

So ends the poem in *Dreamtigers* which announces Borges's voyage of linguistic discovery. These undulating lines serve as a kind of epigraph for the mood and themes which permeated so much of his work until the end of his life.

There was a psychological motive, too, in the Anglo-Saxon embrace. Borges had a romantic affiliation with England, a view of the old country that bordered on reverence. He admitted as much in the 'Essay', reiterating fondly his sense of connection with the English past through his Haslam line, from 'Northumbria and Mercia'.[32] In practically every interview he gave from this era onwards, he rarely failed to refer to his 'Englishness', and his abiding love for the literature. Forever after, few interviewers could stop him from quoting a bit of King Alfred or 'The Wanderer' – proof, if proof were needed, that Borges's lust for literary adventure remained undimmed.

Where in 1945 Borges's elation at British victory over Germany was the culmination of a decade and a half's genuine commitment to the tenets of liberal democracy, his support for England, as expressed through this literary find, was now a form of political mischief-making. Again, he alludes to this in the 'Essay', when he talks about his more 'nationalistic countrymen, who dub me an Englishman' – this, of course, was said in the heated late 1960s, when he was a celebrity and often censured for his lack of 'patriotism'.[33]

Borges had stopped being self-consciously 'Argentine' in the early 1930s. As Argentina became more unstable throughout the 1960s, more hostile to the free world and Borges more famous, the one thing which he was not going to let go of, and which had come to him unexpectedly, was a spirit of internationalism – multiculturalism, you might call it. This was a rich picking from seeds sown many years before, when Borges had grubbed around so widely in unknown writing from overseas: Kafka, Faulkner, Wells amongst some of the better-known names. As daily political and social life got increasingly darker at home, Borges's sense of his own profile in the international literary community, particularly when he wasn't writing at full tilt, kept him going.

One of the most interesting things about *Dreamtigers* was the timing of its Buenos Aires publication. In a way Borges could not have anticipated, and for which the creation of 'Borges' in that book was perhaps, even if unconsciously, the wiliest defence, life was about to take over.

Borges became famous fast because of a prize, as unknown in 1960 to the world at large as Borges himself. The prize followed *Dreamtigers* by a matter of months, though it was awarded less for *Dreamtigers* than for his earlier books of stories, *Ficciones* and *El Aleph*.

The Prix Formentor was hatched by six international publishers* to honour 'an author of any nationality whose existing body of work will, in the view of the jury, have a lasting influence on the development of modern literature'.[34] It was also designed as a kind of alternative Nobel, which many at the time believed was becoming haphazard and over-politicised. Any international prize was likely to have some political colouring, and at least two members

---

* Gallimard (France), Einaudi (Italy), Rowohlt (Germany), Seix Barral (Spain), Grove Press in New York and, in London, Weidenfeld & Nicolson.

of the publishing panel were renowned anti-fascists: Einaudi and Gallimard. Victor Seix and Carlos Barral from Spain meanwhile, operating practically underground, had to be careful not to taunt Franco.

The publishers met for five days in Mallorca in a town and hotel which gave the prize its name in spring 1961, and decided upon the award, to be granted immediately. The prize money was $10,000, a considerable sum then; the deal was that the winning author's work should subsequently be diffused to as wide an audience as possible.

There, of course, was the rub. No one had heard of 'Formentor', least of all Borges. And no one in the world at large, outside a small circle of Spanish and French readers interested in new writing, had heard of Borges.

He was dining with Bioy on a Sunday in mid-1961 when the news came to him by phone. He thought it a joke, and a very good Borgesian one it would have been. But it was for real, even if he got only half the prize money. The publishers had decided to split the award between Borges and Samuel Beckett.

That mattered little. What counted was publication in the country of each publisher – in Borges's case, of *Ficciones*, which of course had already had ten years of life in French. It took another year for the book to appear in English for the first time, under its Spanish title.[*] But word was out; the Formentor did its work.

Borges became a fêted literary personality almost overnight. For major literary cultures – the United States, Britain, France, Germany, Italy – it was as if he *alone* had altered the way people wrote and thought about writing. There was some truth in this, even if it was somewhat retrospective. After the war, European literary endeavour seemed exhausted. Joyce's *Finnegans Wake* was

---

[*] An Italian anthology of some of Borges's stories had appeared in 1955 with Einaudi, translated by Franco Lucentini. Entitled *La Bibiloteca di Babele*, it was one of the very few volumes of Borges's work, pre-Formentor, published outside Argentina other than the French editions of the early 1950s. (Another, *Labyrinthe*, appeared chez Hanser Verlag in Germany in 1959.) In Italy, this edition and Borges's subsequent renown there helped the speedy conferral on him by that country's government of the title of *Commendatore* soon after the Formentor. It was Borges's first foreign award.

the last great experimental fiction Modernism produced, and the few who read it barely understood it. The French New Novel was desperately arid, and certainly unfunny. (Borges, claimed as an important influence on the *Nouveau roman*, was horrified when it was suggested to him that its practitioners had taken his fictions as their model.)

In Britain, post-colonial fiction was hidebound by an obstinate naturalism. German writers were left to lick the wounds of their country's horrifically exposed psyche. Spain and Italy, whose languages and cultures might be said to have much in common with Borges's, not unnaturally took him on board to chart a course out of relative literary emptiness.

For literatures everywhere, Borges *was* a way out. His intellectual rigour, decorated with that twinkling veneer of comic playfulness, was both a reflection of, and an answer to, the fractured cultures of Europe. Borges's stories, moreover, were entertaining. It was a relief to find a world-class writer who did not insist on strictly representational fiction, on a primordial psychological seriousness. After Borges, it seemed, writers could return, refreshed, to a new, knockabout narrative freedom.

The acclaim for Borges that came with the announcement of the Formentor genuinely opened up the world to him. It began with the United States. A chair at the University of Texas, Austin, was endowed by something called the Edward Larocque Tinker Foundation. The post required lectures and readings, and was offered to Borges for a semester in September of 1961.

If the Formentor gave him a global profile for the first time, the appearance after 1950 of translations of individual stories in magazines had given him something of a reputation in Latin American departments on some US campuses. A North American university post was both a measure of his intellectual standing *and* a reflection of his sudden fame. Borges accepted the post with alacrity. He was to give seminars on Leopoldo Lugones and an introductory course on Argentine literature. He found when he got to his classroom on campus that the thirty-odd students were far more interested in his own work. They were also, he noticed, more enthusiastic about literature than exams.[35]

When Borges arrived in the States, it was not – despite all appearances – as a prim academic but as a literary revolutionary.

Conservative in dress, courteous in manner, of exotic origin and unfailingly witty, he cut an odd figure. He seemed to have come from nowhere, or at best out of a painting by Magritte. Having apparently turned modern fiction inside out, here was a besuited blind man delighting his audiences with runic word-play, and making metaphysical jokes about Milton.

Thus it was in the USA that Borges made his erstwhile radicalism known, for the first time, outside Argentina. He was in charge of 'Borges'; it was his show. But he was an anomalous presence. There were his extraordinary stories, their marvellous universes, and the inescapable challenge each presented to the conventions of plausible reality. For hungry readers in a literary culture fast being dominated by academe, and thus taking itself far too seriously, Borges was also an exciting writer, whose texts stretched belief, yet seemed to stand for a Joycean literary lack of compromise.

On this first trip to the States, however, he was accompanied by his mother. At the time, there was no alternative: Borges had to be looked after, his clothes prepared, his schedule organised. He could see little, and nothing in the practical life of the USA was ever going to improve his now entrenched impracticality.

One of his first North American observers and interviewers was an academic and Spanish specialist named James E. Irby. His first encounter with Borges in mid-December 1961 confirmed the Argentine's otherworldliness:

> I see a sixty-two-year-old man, of average height, whose corpulence is accentuated by the loose grey suit which hangs off him a little. His head is large compared to the rest of the body; his features seem curiously magnified, stretched. His brushed-back white hair sometimes falls round his temples and ears, giving him the look of an old-fashioned poet or American senator, as in all the best caricatures. He is nearly blind; after several operations for cataracts and detachment of the retinas, his eyes – 'eyes of that indifferent blue which the English call grey', under ample eyebrows and eyelids half-asleep – see nothing but confusion.
>
> Printed clear and large, a book's title – if he brings it very close to his face – he can see. He moves about alone in a room, but to go more than a few paces he tends to hold someone's arm.

His movements and gestures are heavy, hesitant, somewhat clumsy, and not just because of his blindness. He doesn't know exactly what either his hands or body are doing.

About Borges's voice, Irby was less conciliatory:

The voice is rather disagreeable, cavernous, thick; his intonation when he reads out somewhat melodramatic. But the tenderness with which he caresses a phrase in repeating it, his submission to the verbal enchantment of the poetry, are intimate and moving.

Leonor, of course, could not be ignored:

Those who don't know that Borges is single think, seeing him and his mother together, that they are man and wife. Doña Leonor is small, alert, energetic; she is good-looking, fine-featured, with very penetrating eyes. She's a cultivated woman, speaking both English and French . . . Sometimes she claims not to be Argentine, but Spanish . . .

She calls her son 'Georgie', looks after him constantly, and organises his life. In all aspects of daily and practical life, Borges's relation to her is one of almost complete dependency, particularly since his sight has gone; she reads him the books he can't read; she is his scribe for correspondence and writings.[36]

This then was the Borges who emerged into the gaze of the world: unseeing, nannied, professorial, vastly lettered, talkative, and perfectly comfortable with his fame. He adored the United States, and before returning to Buenos Aires in February 1962 made lecture visits to New Mexico, California, New York, Connecticut, and Massachusetts, as well as to three great East Coast universities, Harvard, Yale and Columbia.

He always spoke of the generosity and friendliness of Americans; he took to the country and travel within it with as much gusto as he had the touring schedules around Argentina in the early years of Perón. For someone who had spent a large part of his adult life praising and promoting North American literature in his home country, it was almost proof that the universe, made such a mockery of in his fables, did after all exist.

It was not all plain sailing. Borges misread the sensitivities of at least one fellow Latin American nation. Praising the achievements of the North Americans at the site of the Battle of the Alamo did not endear him to Mexico, which has always been sore about the appropriation by the United States of its former northern territories. Borges's reputation as a writer in Mexico was high at the time; but his pronouncements about the Alamo – and, equally, against Castro – were bound to foment left-wing disapproval amongst Mexican intellectuals. A proposed invitation while Borges was at Austin to have him come and talk in Mexico was withdrawn even before it was announced, though Borges seems to have been blissfully unaware of the fact.[37] He was not to make his first visit to that country for another eleven years.

The United States would have to wait a mere five years for Borges's return. In the interim, his public image somehow achieved the marketing status of a pop group. When in 1962 *Time* magazine declared him to be perhaps the 'greatest living writer in the Spanish language today', Borges as 'Borges' caught the world public imagination. At home, in August 1962, after his return from the States, he was elected to the Argentine Academy of Letters – an organisation which in fact bored him, and which over the years he rarely visited.[38] More prestigious was another foreign award in November of that year, from the French government, an equivalent of the Italian honour conferred the year before: Borges became a Commandeur de l'Ordre des Arts et Lettres.

At the beginning of 1963, he travelled to Europe for the first time since 1924. The impetus for the journey came from the British Council in Buenos Aires. The director, Neil MacKay, who had spent many years in Latin America, was an acquaintance of Borges's, having first met him in 1950, at the height of Peronism. Towards the end of 1961, he recommended to the London office that Borges be invited to Great Britain as 'a friend of the Council, and a faithful upholder of our cause down through the years'.[39]

By the end of 1962, the visit had become combined with an additional stint in Paris; an organisation called the Congrès pour la Liberté de la Culture (Congress for Cultural Freedom) was prepared to pay for Borges's passage to Europe. Things were complicated first by the necessity of Leonor's accompanying her son (MacKay stressed how helpless Borges was without her), and the question of how her costs would be covered; and then by a further invitation in mid-January 1963 from a Spanish writer, Fernando Quiñones, to visit Madrid.

In the end, Borges went first to Madrid, where he was overjoyed to meet his old master, Cansinos-Assens – now eighty-one and in the last year of his life; he then visited Geneva, briefly – a stopover to recover his adolescence and education. There, he met Maurice Abramowicz and Simon Jichlinski – incredibly, he had seen neither man since 1918, and now could see them hardly at all . . . The first had become a lawyer, and a city councillor; the second a doctor. According to Barnatán, they all went to a tavern called the Crocodile in rue du Rhône to listen to tangos.[40] Borges was in Paris for no more than a week – somewhat to the chagrin of the Congress;[41] finally, he arrived in London in mid-February 1963.

As they journeyed from capital to capital in Europe, Leonor had never seemed happier, remarkable for a woman of her years. This of course was what she had been waiting for, as far as her son was concerned, all her life. For Borges, who had not been to Geneva since 1918 or Madrid since 1924, the return to early youth was uplifting. 'I was greatly moved [on visiting Geneva],' Borges said in 1967. 'Geneva is a city I know better than Buenos Aires. Besides, Geneva can be learned because it is a normal-size city, shall we say, while Buenos Aires is such an outrageous city that nobody can ever learn it.'[42]

The impact of Britain on Borges was intense. It was, however, the worst winter there for decades. Snow covered the land. Some doubts over the wisdom of bringing over two elderly people from the midsummer of the southern hemisphere had been expressed by the Council, to say nothing of possible problems posed by adverse weather conditions.

In the event neither Borges nor Leonor was in the slightest bit perturbed. Borges was thrilled to be in *the* country of literature. 'I feel this damp air on my face,' he said on arrival (and right on cue), 'and in breathing it also feel the greatest poetry of all time: it was written by the English.'[43]

In his early youth he had seen no more than a few London streets and, even more cursorily, Cambridge. In 1963, he became the pilgrim any other book-bitten aspirant might have been in his or her teens or twenties. In his sixties, Borges was catching up:

> I made many pilgrimages: to London, so teeming with literary memories; to Lichfield and Dr Johnson; to Manchester and De Quincey; to Rye and Henry James; to the Lake Country [sic]; to Edinburgh. I visited my grandmother's birthplace in Hanley, one of the Five Towns – Arnold Bennett country.

Scotland and Yorkshire, rather surprisingly, reminded him of his own country.

> I think of [them] as among the loveliest places on earth. Somewhere in the Scottish hills and glens I recaptured a strange sense of loneliness and bleakness that I had known before; it took me some time to trace this feeling back to the far-flung wastes of Patagonia.[44]

Borges is clearly not 'remembering' from direct experience, something for which, like facts, he had little time. He could not possibly have 'seen' the hills and glens, and had visited Patagonia only once.

As in all the best moments of Borges's life, when stepping 'out of time', he imagined rather than saw space, and was little concerned as to whether what he imagined was real or even plausible. Borges's Britain was a literary conceit, much coloured at this stage by his recent forays into Anglo-Saxon. He wasn't remotely concerned with the place as it found itself in the early 1960s;[45] he was, on the other hand, everlastingly and proudly aware of his British ancestry. Part of the conceit was to link that with the country, and the culture of the Dark Ages, providing for himself an inner genealogy that fed into his writing rather than prompting any enthusiasm for reality. With Borges, it was ever thus.

The official object of the trip was to give the annual lecture at Canning House in Belgrave Square, on 19 February.* The title

---

* Canning House was, and still is, a small, private organisation dedicated to Hispanic and Luso-Brazilian culture. It has one of the best Spanish and Portuguese libraries outside Latin America and the Iberian Peninsula.

was 'The Spanish Language in South America'. The director of Canning House was warned by MacKay that Borges's voice was rather low, and that they would have to make a careful recording of the lecture if a transcript were needed. Borges spoke clearly, and the evening was in fact an enormous success – bolstered by a few dozen uninvited extras from the Argentine Embassy across the road, sent to support their national literary hero, but who had no tickets. (Canning House's director later said that everything – in those pre-Falklands days – to avoid a 'diplomatic incident' was done; the Argentines were duly squeezed in.[46])

The Council looked after Borges and Leonor well. He saw Peter Brook's production of *King Lear* with Paul Scofield at the Aldwych Theatre, lunched with the poet George Macbeth of the BBC's Third Programme, and was driven to Henry James's house in Rye (as he says in the 'Essay') and H. G. Wells's in Sandgate. After the Canning House lecture, he went everywhere: to Oxford, Bath, Birmingham, and Manchester. In the Saxon church in Deerhurst, in the Cotswolds, he fulfilled a long-held ambition to recite the Lord's Prayer in Old English. In Scotland, he visited Glasgow and Edinburgh, and managed to see Sir Walter Scott's house at Abbotsford – and should have seen more. Leonor, however, caught a chill in early March; and bad weather in the far north curtailed further Scottish wanderings.

A great many people wanted to meet Borges while he was in Britain, though MacKay had warned the Council that that wasn't Borges's first priority: 'People tire me; places don't!' was the message passed from Buenos Aires to London at the end of January 1963.[47] Stephen Spender, who had been responsible for publishing 'The Babylonian Lottery' (*sic*) in *Encounter* in June 1962, and then 'The Circular Ruins' and 'The Library of Babel' in July, was one major literary figure Borges conversed with in London. At a reception, the Spanish historian Salvador de Madariaga was also especially keen to meet him, as the two men had been amongst the first contributors to *Sur*, now in its twilight years. Other writers at the same reception included V. S. Pritchett and Al Alvarez.

This, the main branch of Borges's European tour in 1963, was a great success. He was still some way off being the lionised figure of the late 1960s and early 1970s, but he hadn't come to Britain to be lionised. He had come to be educated in the England of his brightest literary dreams, to absorb its atmosphere, and to enjoy himself. The British Council was delighted with him: Borges's modesty, said one report, amounted 'almost at times to docility'; he was a man of 'exquisite courtesy and sensibility . . . remarkably few of our many Visitors are so conscious of being "our guests"'.[48] Leonor made no less of an impact, particularly in the manner in which she made so few demands on her own behalf.

In 1964 and 1965, two voyages, one to Europe again, one to Peru, found Borges with a new companion in tow: Leonor had been replaced by María Esther Vázquez. Perhaps a blow to Leonor – although she was nearly ninety – this was a fabulous opportunity for the 23-year-old journalist. The personal consequences of this replacement for Borges, however, were more devastating than he could have imagined.

Nineteen sixty-six was a relatively quiet year amidst all this international to-ing and fro-ing.[49] Nineteen sixty-seven was to prove one of his most momentous. As his fame grew, his imagination fell into abeyance; Borges's life as a writer changed dramatically after the Formentor, to the extent that he now wrote very little. In the personal domain, perhaps for the first time ever, things suddenly counted for more than the next story, essay or poem.

Borges began to look for something to transform his condition as lone son dependent on lone mother. Against the background of an extraordinary rush of global fascination in this shy and elusive man, we need now to look at what it was Borges really wanted – and it was neither fame nor riches – and how he went about finding it.

Chapter Eight

1964–1968

Love and Marriage

Two forces, one public, one private, pulled Borges in opposing directions in the early 1960s. The first was the suddenness and totality of his fame. His first two trips out of Argentina since 1924, to America in 1961 and to Europe in 1963, were with Leonor; imprinted on the world eye was this curious image of an old man and an even older woman courting the American and European media as if they had been doing it all their lives. It was too good to be true, as became clear when Borges decided he needed a new chaperone, and perhaps a less outmoded image, from 1965 on.

In Paris, the literary *feuilleton L'Herne* published a special issue devoted to Borges in 1964, an honour previously reserved only for French writers. Leonor was a significant presence in the volume, providing her own account of Borges's early life.[1]

The second force at work in the early 1960s was real enough, and altogether closer to home. In the same year as the *L'Herne* tribute, María Esther Vázquez became publicly prominent in Borges's life, just as Leonor had been on his first two trips.

Leonor had grown tired on both the American and European tours, and according to most accounts expressed no wish to go to West

Germany in 1964. She was now eighty-eight. Borges had been invited by the Congress for Cultural Freedom to an international gathering of writers in September of that year in Berlin, and then by UNESCO in Paris to give the keynote speech on Shakespeare, in celebration of the four-hundredth anniversary of his birth. In place of Leonor, Borges asked María Esther to go with him.[2]

She had already become a close companion during post at the National Library, and Borges had become very fond of her. In his own mind, beyond mere fondness, the company of a much younger woman in his international public duties suggested the possibility of a longer-term relationship.

In fairness to María Esther, there is no reason why she should have suspected that Borges needed from her more than professional help: she was almost forty years his junior, and Horacio Armani was already in her sights. But Borges was strangely incapable of reading the human heart. In many cases with women, he seemed to use his blindness to underline the fact that *if* he did not want to see – understand – something, he just did not. The experience of thwarted passion for Estela Canto seems to have taught him little.

None the less, he was still in complete possession of his faculties. Vázquez recalled:

> In 1964, Borges seemed to me as old as the Pyramids. But he always remembered where everything was. He got around the bathroom by touching things. At night, a pile of clothes was made for him, underwear on top, main clothes underneath – there was never any problem. He preferred small rooms to big ones in which he could get lost. He was a man in full strength.[3]

Together, they had a busy and amusing time. In Berlin, Borges shared the limelight with the Brazilian writer João Guimarães Rosa, the Guatemalan Miguel Angel Asturias (later winner of the 1967 Nobel Prize), the Paraguayan Augusto Roa Bastos, and Eduardo Mallea. It was an impressive show of Latin American talent, and proof to European literary audiences at least that that continent's writing was here to stay.

At table, however, Borges was fussy about his food.

Once in Germany he asked for a *tortilla de papas*. The waiter brought him a French omelette. So I had to explain in German the difference. Borges meanwhile provided his own explanation as to how to make *tortilla* in Spanish. Eventually, an omelette with potatoes on a side plate was brought in, and Borges of course said this wasn't how it was done, it couldn't be eaten.[4]

No mention at all of Germany and France is made in the 'Autobiographical Essay'. About Copenhagen and Stockholm, however, he was rhapsodic, comparing their beauty to San Francisco's, Edinburgh's, Geneva's.[5] Invited to Stockholm by his Swedish publisher Albert Bonnier, Borges was a guest of the Argentine Embassy: from now on, embassies were to become regular places in his life, whether abroad, or back in Buenos Aires – before the end of the 1970s, he was honoured in his home city half a dozen times by foreign governments, principally the Italian.

In Paris, Borges gave his talk, 'Shakespeare and Us', in French, apparently improvised. In fact, he had originally dictated it in Spanish to Vázquez, translated it into French, then had her tape it so he could listen to and learn it by heart. They stayed with Néstor Ibarra, who had long since returned to the French capital and now shared his life with a young French woman, a scientist. The young Peruvian Mario Vargas Llosa, then working as a journalist for RTF in Paris, met Borges and asked what he thought of politics: '*Es una de las formas del tedio*,' was the lapidary answer: 'It's one of the forms of tedium.'[6]

In Britain, where Borges and Vázquez went before Sweden, the writer was once again the guest of the British Council (Borges covered Vázquez's costs). Borges was keen to see those northern parts of Scotland he had missed the year before because of Leonor's ill health. On their way north, the poet Herbert Read invited them to spend a night in his house, Stonegrave, in the Yorkshire moors. Leonor had translated some of his verse into Spanish, and the year before Read had been keen to have both mother and son to stay. Partly because of the weather, and partly because of the packed nature of Borges's itinerary, it hadn't been possible.

This time, Borges was neither lecturing nor on official public show. The Council saw the visit as a furthering of good cultural relations between Britain and Argentina, and were disinclined to turn down helping a writer who had so pleased them on his first visit. 'If Borges were a schemer,' MacKay had written from Buenos Aires, 'it would be easy to refuse but, as you will remember . . . he is a very childlike person in his ways and it is hard to disappoint him.'[7]

The stay in Yorkshire sparked off a round of poems on Anglo-Saxon and Nordic themes, including 'To a Sword in York Minster', based on an ancient Danish weapon exhibited in the museum adjoining the cathedral, which Read was keen to show the writer. Read, Borges later stated, added the 'Minster' to the poem's title.

Vázquez remembered the Reads' house as 'full of little passages, staircases leading to rooms of all sizes, where it was easy to get lost'. Apparently, this was one reason it was deemed best for the two Argentine guests to be brought breakfast by Lady Read in their separate rooms, rather than gathering formally round a table. In a muddle over the 'complications' of an English breakfast – eggs, bacon etc. – Vázquez put salt in Borges's coffee, which elicited the comment: 'English *café con leche* gets worse every day.'[8]

Scotland was once again highly appreciated, including a visit to Banff, on the far north-eastern coast. The Argentine liberator, General San Martín, was a freeman of the town, and a tree to commemorate the fact had been planted there in 1950. Inverness, Fort William and Glasgow followed, with a return to London at the end of October. Before flying back across the Atlantic, Borges and Vázquez visited Spain; in Madrid, Fernando Quiñones, a flamenco expert, entertained both with a night of *cante jondo*.

The year 1965 is left out of the 'Autobiographical Essay' altogether – with, I suspect, good reason; it concerned María Esther Vázquez, a subject which suddenly became painful for Borges.

Also left out is a major publication of the year before, a new *Obra poética*, which contained a section at the end entitled 'El otro, el mismo' (The Self and the Other). Comprising twenty-nine poems, the section was really a new book within an old one; this *Obra* was Borges's first complete book of new poems since the 1943 *Poemas*, and the fifth of his career. The volume contained the entirety of his poetic output, though heavily revised and edited – a process Borges rarely admitted to in his writings and public utterances – including the poems from *Dreamtigers*. Then in 1965, *Para las seis cuerdas* (*For the Guitar*) appeared, a small book of lyrics for milongas and tangos, to be sung to the guitar (the 'six strings' of the Spanish title).[9]

Sur prepares for launch, 1930. Back row (from left to right): Eduardo J. Bullrich, Jorge Luis Borges, Francisco Romero, Eduardo Mallea, Enrique Bullrich, Victoria Ocampo and Ramón Gómez de la Serna; seated (from left to right): Pedro Henríquez Ureña, Oliverio Girondo, Norah Borges de Torre, María Rosa Oliver, Carola Padilla, Ernest Ansermet and Guillermo de Torre. The photograph on the table on the far right is of Ricardo Güiraldes.

Borges, bearded and recovering from his accident in late 1938, standing next to Haydée Lange, whom he courted in 1939: the photo is dated 1 April 1939.

Borges with Adolfo Bioy Casares in Mar del Plata, 1942.

Borges with Estela Canto on the Costanera Sur in March 1945; Borges was at the height of his infatuation with her and was embarking on the great stories that went into *El Aleph*, published four years later.

Borges and Leonor on the balcony of their flat in calle Maipú, December 1962.

The couple arrive in Britain in February 1963

The years of fame. From the 1970s on, Borges became one of the most frequently interviewed and widely travelled writers in history. Here, he talks to the Italian writer, Alberto Moravia, in March 1981; and below, in New York in 1983, to Bianca Jagger. Fans of Nicholas Roeg's film, *Performance*, will remember the shot of Bianca's husband Mick Jagger (her ex, of course, in 1983) reading a copy of *Ficciones* in the bath.

Borges in Paris, receiving the Légion d'honneur in January 1983.

Walking along the Seine with his future wife, María Kodama.

Borges in a hotel in Palermo, Sicily, May 1984.

Jorge Luis Borges, by 1985 one of the world's legendary literary figures, nine months before he died.

Borges was also very much on the move; the first journey of the year, and his last for the time being with María Esther Vázquez, was to Peru. He lectured in Lima, and with Vázquez ascended the heights of the country's great Inca site in the Andes, Machu Picchu. He was, records Vázquez, bored. This chimes in well with his well-known aversion to pre-Columbian culture. But there may have been another reason for his apparent lack of interest.

Borges and Vázquez were working on two projects together at this time: one was a revision of the book on Germanic literature Borges had published, with Delia Ingenieros, in 1951; the other was a brief introduction for Argentine students to English literature. Borges and Vázquez's professional association had developed into a close partnership, and Borges sincerely believed that marriage was on the cards. It was a subject that preoccupied Leonor as much as it did her son. She urged him to make a decision, though was not enamoured of the idea of María Esther as her future daughter-in-law. 'She's squeezing him out like a lemon', she would say.[10]

It was generally thought that Vázquez had strung Borges along. When she announced, in November 1965, that she was getting married to Horacio Armani, Borges was crestfallen. Many of his friends have since averred that he was profoundly upset by Vázquez's decision, which he considered a kind of abandonment, a defection. It is probable that his visit with her to Peru highlighted tensions between them; certainly, her betrothal to Armani after they shared a trip back from the provincial city of Mendoza was a death knell to Borges's amorous hopes with her.

In 'El otro, el mismo', one sonnet in particular seems to allude to his feelings for Vázquez. 'Adam Cast Forth' tells of Adam's ejection from Eden: 'this now unhappy Adam' tries to recall the delights and pleasures of paradise, realises that it will exist for others and that all that is left for him is 'the unforgiving earth'. Written in 1963 or, at the latest, 1964, when Borges still had high hopes about María Esther, the poem ends on a note of optimism: 'Nevertheless, it means much to have loved,/ To have been happy, to have touched upon/ The living Garden, even for one day.'[11]

In 1966, a new collected poems appeared with the section 'El otro, el mismo' significantly expanded. Two darker sonnets, under the title '1964' and written almost certainly after the débâcle with Vázquez in 1965, were part of this expansion; the first, addressed to an anonymous 'you' – in other words, Borges – opens baldly with 'The world is no longer magical', and goes on to speak of desertion: 'Today you have only/ The faithful memory and empty days.' The second, written in the franker first person, opens equally starkly: 'Now I will not be happy.' All that awaits is death – and in what remains of life, sadness, and a vain tendency to turn 'To the South, a certain door, a certain corner', as the poem ends.[12]

Borges had already begun to attach enormous importance to the possibility of happiness. He equated it with marriage, or at least with some kind of domestic partnership with another woman who was not his mother – adore Leonor though he did. In some respects, matrimony, sentimental equilibrium, had become Borges's mission in these early years of his international success: to match all the public attention he was receiving with a private contentment, something of which he could be proud, and which he could display to the world.

His concentration on this was partly why he was writing even less than usual, or so little of the type of work that had made him famous. Poetry had become just as much a refuge for his sentimental life as it was a prosodic discipline. Indeed, the two throughout this emotionally trying period, right up until the end of the 1960s, were inextricably entwined. Borges's secret sadness, never on show to his global public, was that he was not himself entwined; nor was he getting any younger.

On learning of Vázquez's engagement, he went to the dentist, and had his teeth out. It seemed the only solution to his distress: a bit of physical discomfort to take his mind off this latest sentimental failure.[13] Throughout the rest of the year, there was plenty more to occupy him. He had been awarded a KBE at the end of 1964, and went to the British Embassy in Buenos Aires in the early part of 1965 to receive it. Victoria Ocampo accompanied him to receive a CBE. Soon after he was at the Italian Embassy for an Italian poetry prize.

In October, he was invited to lecture at universities in Chile and Colombia. It was his first time in either country. Confirming his break with María Esther, he was accompanied on both trips by an old friend of some twenty years' standing, Esther Zemboraín de Torres Duggan.

She was a frail, Anglophile woman, married to a boozy, somewhat abusive Basque. A dedicated Catholic, she was also socially well-connected and 'in love' – when she first met Borges – with the pre-Socratics.[14] She had suffered a nervous breakdown in 1949, but had subsequently been active in the arts, and was often to be seen at Pro Arte gatherings. María Esther Vázquez remembers her wearing very high heels and large hats:[15] in other words, a typical Borges *señora*.

Unbeknownst to him, a rather atypical Borges *señora* lay waiting in the wings: domestic, recently widowed, old-fashioned and, compared to most of the women Borges had consorted with, distinctly plain. A year would pass before he was re-introduced to this old flame of his youth, a year in which Argentina endured yet another change of government, this time led by a brutish, almost caricature dictator, Juan Carlos Onganía;[16] in which Borges ran into some trouble at the Faculty of Philosophy and Letters, criticising both changes made at the university by the new regime, and professors appointed to teach literature;[17] and in which he neither travelled nor wrote much, though he picked up more international awards: another Italian literary prize, and the Ingram Merrill Foundation in New York presented him with a generous literary prize, worth $5,000.

This was useful money, as he had resigned his post at the university in 1964. For the hours he still taught of his own volition – three a week – he was not paid a salary, but relied solely on his 20,000 peso state pension, which had become due to him on his official retirement in August 1964, and on his nominal pay as Director of the National Library. That was Borges's style: literature first, remuneration an incidental.

I say Borges was writing little: in fact, he wrote one story, his first substantial tale since 1953, but very different in style and preoccupation from those of the *Ficciones* and *Aleph* years. It was the result of a request from a 'Buenos Aires bibliophile Gustavo Fillol Day', who wanted to publish a work in 'one of those fine and secret editions meant for the happy few'.

Borges had been reading Kipling's *Plain Tales from the Hills*, and was keen to try his hand at straight, unteasing narrative which would reflect both his love of Kipling and something of the old, wild Argentina which had so fascinated him in the 1920s and 1930s. Indeed, its inspiration, Borges said four years later, was a comment made by his favourite hoodlum, Nicolás Paredes: 'Any man who thinks five minutes straight about a woman is no man – he's a queer.'[18]

Called 'La intrusa' ('The Intruder'), the story delves into macho

Argentina. It is a rough, bleak tale about two brothers who share a woman, sell her off to a brothel and then murder her. Borges thought it one of the best he had ever written. It is certainly a strong, unusually vindictive piece of work, written – not, I believe, coincidentally – six months or so after his break with Vázquez.

Estela Canto, to whom Borges had given some vague clues as to its contents in the 1950s, thought the subject of 'The Intruder' was homosexuality, or macho bonding, at the very least. Borges would not have objected to the latter, but vehemently denied the former.[19] For him, it was about the opposite of homosexuality; its starting point was, after all, Paredes's peculiarly unpleasant observation about male interest in the female. It was about virility, or what Borges thought of as virility, which invariably involved or led to violence. If anything, it was really a gritty celebration of misogyny; Borges's recent rejection by a young woman over whom he had come to have some mastery, which he had expected to continue, was patently not unrelated.

Borges dictated 'The Intruder' to Leonor early in 1966 and it appeared in April in an edition of fifty-two copies. First circulated among friends, it was then included in the third Emecé edition of *El Aleph*; it went largely unnoticed until it re-emerged, slightly revised, in *El informe de Brodie* in 1970 (see p. 226).

He also worked in the latter part of 1966 on an introduction to North American literature with Esther Zemboraín. Collaborating with another lady of breeding and education was a form of writing, but an indulgent one. 'The Intruder' notwithstanding, Borges could keep his mind and memory exercised, while putting his *imagination* to sleep – something some would argue he had done anyway since 1953, when he had written his last great fiction. Borges embarked on these projects as much for companionship – that is, to avoid boredom – as for their intrinsic literary value.

Much amusement would have been had from reworking his and Margarita Guerrero's 1957 *Manual de zoología fantástica* at around the same time. Ten years after the first edition, it was now expanded by thirty-four new entries, and appeared in 1967 with a small publisher called Kier.

With Esther Zemboraín, he was determined on something critically weightier. She had already said no once to Borges's suggestion that they do a book together. When he prevailed upon her again – and this could have been as early as 1965, during their travels in Chile and Colombia – she suggested a book on English literature (she loved Shakespeare and Keats); Borges had to point out his commitment to the volume he had already undertaken with María Esther Vázquez, with its publication imminent. He favoured American literature; Zemboraín agreed reluctantly.

Borges dined with her from time to time, in a flat she had overlooking the Bioys', in calle Posadas.[20] When he wasn't dining with her, he was of course with the Bioys, and could be seen from Zemboraín's dining-room windows, eating and stuck fast in conversation with his closest friends.[21]

A leading topic between Bioy and Borges at the time was Bustos Domecq; along with his collaborations with the two ladies, Esther and María Esther, Borges's revived partnership with Adolfito for the production of further silly tales by their invented author was very much a feature of the period 1966–7. Borges wrote:

> By that time, Bioy and I had invented a new way of telling gruesome and uncanny tales. It lay in understating the grimness and essential horror while playing up certain humorous aspects – a kind of graft between Alfred Hitchcock and the Marx Brothers. This not only made for more amusing and less pretentious writing, but at the same time underlined the horror.[22]

This 'new way' led to the first Bustos Domecq volume since 1946, *Crónicas de Bustos Domecq* (*Chronicles of Bustos Domecq*), published by Losada in mid-1967.

The book appeared under Borges and Bioy's names, understandably since both men were now far more famous than they had been twenty-five years before when *Don Isidro* had appeared with Sur, with no clues as to who Bustos Domecq really was. Now that it was confirmed for the public that the hack-author was a composite of Argentina's two most renowned literary friends, a joke, how could the stories be taken seriously?[23]

This time, the squibs were shorter, more facetious: 'These were articles written on imaginary, extravagantly modern artists – architects, sculptors, painters, chefs, poets, novelists, couturiers – by a devotedly modern critic. But both the author and his subjects are fools, and it is hard to tell who is taking in whom.'[24] Borges's description of *Chronicles* makes it sound witty and up-to-the-mark: divertingly post-Modern.

In truth, Bustos Domecq has not survived the passage of time. Half the effort of reading him in *Chronicles* is working out what he is writing about, and why; why read the stuff at all? Much of the book is internalised punning, self-referentiality without graspable humour, wit without much of an eye on the audience. In the 'Essay' Borges then goes on to make one of the most ridiculous statements in his career, about this book: 'I think they [the *Chronicles*] are better than anything I have published under my own name.'

Modesty was a notable feature of Borges's personality. False modesty erupted whenever he became his own critic. As with his comments on *Dreamtigers*, he was here playing up the virtues of a patently inferior work in order to get away from what had truly made him 'Borges', the great writer he was, as far as revolutionary prose was concerned, but which he really wanted to be for work *other* than *Ficciones* and *El Aleph*.

In retrospect, arguably more absurd than anything he said about himself was what he said about Bioy's part in *Chronicles*: he called them 'nearly as good as anything Bioy has written on his own'.[25] If they hadn't known each other so well, it might have been an insult. Bioy of course didn't mind. It was all part of the joke. Confusion, not clarification, was the object of Bustos Domecq's endeavours. So was praising piffle. An amusing if sometimes irritating side to Borges was his ability to pull a fast one when in apparently most serious mode.

Borges had called the twenty-one-year gap between Bustos books 'a long eclipse'.[26] Bioy was less categorical: 'Was it actually an eclipse? I don't know whether it was a stopping of the work, or people stopping to talk about Bustos Domecq.'[27] Commenting on the almost complete critical silence that greeted Bustos Domecq, Borges quipped (playing on a Spanish saying, '*Sobre gustos no hay nada escrito*' – 'There's no accounting for taste'), '*Sobre Bustos no hay nada escrito*' – 'Nothing's written about Bustos'.[28]

Esther Zemboraín was keen to finish the American literature book by mid-February of 1967, the height of the holiday season when she would have family responsibilities. She never called Borges to arrange work sessions; he always called her. But suddenly, some weeks before this deadline, he stopped calling; he seemed to have disappeared. Breaking with habit, Zemboraín rang Leonor. She was none the wiser about her son's movements.

No wonder. When Borges did return to work with Esther, he shyly announced to her: 'Something very emotional has happened. I've got engaged.'[29]

So began one of the most bizarre episodes in Borges's life. He had not communicated with Elsa Astete Millán for over twenty years. Shortly before the publication of *Ficciones* in 1944, he had written to her; two letters survive, strange, stilted, belated declarations of love, which in retrospect read like test runs for the more passionate missives sent to Estela Canto a year later.[30]

All the more surprising, then, that Borges asked Elsa to marry him in 1967, twenty-three years after he wrote those letters. Elsa was fifty-seven. The man she had married instead of Borges in 1928, Ricardo Albarracín, had died of lung cancer in 1964; he and Elsa had had about ten happily married years together before he became terminally ill. They had a son together, also called Ricardo.

Borges knew this, as his good friend and first translator Néstor Ibarra had married Elsa's sister, Alicia, though they later parted and Ibarra returned, as we know, to France. Elsa would see Alicia most Saturdays; after Albarracín's death she had become increasingly reclusive. In early 1967, Alicia rang one Thursday to check that she, Elsa, was coming that Saturday to see her, as Borges, no less, had rung to say that he would like to come along too if Elsa were going to be there.

Manuel Peyrou probably put Borges up to this. Borges then made inquiries through Peyrou and others about her well-being. He was matrimonially at his wits' end. What he wanted was simple: a home he could call his own.

To Vlady Kociancich he confided in English: 'I need a home'.[31] In English, he felt free to divulge such a confidence. Borges had much to protect from the outside world, his privacy above all: people – writers, journalists, translators – were now beating a path to his door. To them, the famous writer appeared content with his lot, wedded to circumstances and habits he neither had the power nor wanted to change. He and Leonor were, it seemed, a couple surrounded by their own unique *porteño* mythology. Was it possible for him to alter this scenario, painlessly, and before it was too late?

To his friends, Georgie was discontented, even sad; in Bioy

Casares's phrase, always with that '*fondo de tristeza*'. Borges was desperate to change things, which is why, for him, he was writing relatively little. He had decided to find not only a home but a life he could call his own – one that didn't belong to that 'other' Borges, the one to whom 'things happened': having books published, being awarded prizes and fêted wherever he went in the world.

On meeting Elsa, he was profoundly moved. They sat together the whole afternoon, chatting away, until Borges summoned up the courage to ask her when she was going. She had planned to go home that evening, but was intrigued to know why Borges had asked the question. So she replied: the following day. Borges immediately invited her out to dinner. Elsa enjoyed walking, and had rarely had such an invitation during her years with the dying Albarracín. She accepted, and they went to a restaurant called the Pedemonte, then to the cinema. Later, Elsa walked back with him to Maipú, and went on her way.[32]

So began a renewal of the couple's friendship which led to marriage, in private and at a registry office, some months later, on 4 August 1967. (A church ceremony took place on 21 September.) Leonor did not, it seems, at first approve. Elsa had no English, for a start, for Leonor a major drawback in the light of her son's upbringing and Anglophilia. Elsa also clearly lacked culture, displaying a weakness for shopping and no interest in books.

'Who are you going to marry,' Leonor mischievously asked Georgie shortly before he tied the knot, 'Margarita Guerrero or Elsa Astete?' (Margarita Guerrero was a renowned beauty, and Leonor was not the only one to have picked up a rumour that Borges might have had a romance with his collaborator on *Imaginary Beings*.) 'I think it'll suit you better to marry Elsa, because she's a widow, and already knows about life.'[33] Leonor came to believe Elsa was the safer option, if only because she was conventional and unthreatening. In truth, a liaison between her and Borges could not have been more unlikely.

Leonor seems to have softened further. Elsa lunched with her future husband and mother-in-law every Sunday, and on one of these Sundays Leonor specially invited eight women friends of hers to meet her son's fiancée. Elsa felt accepted. Leonor also finally organised all the details of the wedding.

However, others remember Elsa as a chatterbox, a thoroughly unBorgesian purveyor of small-talk, exasperating to Borges's friends and admirers who knew that his enjoyment of talk was almost purely literary. For some, Elsa was simply uncouth in her lack of education. Rodríguez Monegal reported slyly: 'If time had changed him for the better (he was now Borges), blindness prevented him from modifying his image of Elsa.'[34]

Borges was on a prolonged rebound after María Esther Vázquez. With Elsa, he could, he believed, build that home of his own which had eluded him for so long. It is possible that Elsa was in fact just a means to that end – some even believe to this day that the whole thing was 'arranged', so that the great blind writer could be properly looked after as Leonor ailed.

The general belief was that Borges was indeed 'married' to his mother. But that had not left the best of impressions in the United States. A writer of Borges's seniority and international standing required the stamp of maturity, an outward show at least of independence. With a wife, Borges could be more than just a writer; he could be, as his father had so long ago urged him to be, a man.

However the idea came into being – and the likeliest cause was an access of spontaneous sentimentality on Borges's part – it was flawed from the start. Borges was Borges. He could never retreat from his reputation. Domestication at this stage of his life was an absurdity. He wanted to graft an image on to himself which reflected a world of safe privacy; he was already deeply private, if he needed to be, and there was in reality little point in changing the shape of that privacy.

But change it he did, at least in concrete terms. He moved out of Maipú and into an apartment at avenida Belgrano 1377 with Elsa, closer to the National Library. Originally, he had wanted to live in the library, imitating Paul Groussac, who had lived and died there. But Elsa insisted on the new home. The small flat was on the fourth floor, with a living room containing a dining area in one corner. There were two bedrooms, one for Elsa, one for Borges, a tiny kitchen, and a room for the maid. It was dark and uninviting. Here it was that Borges imagined he would find married bliss.

One reason he did not was his patent unfitness for the marriage bed. If ever there was a confirmed bachelor in the history of literary masters, it was Borges. (One thinks of Doctor Johnson again.) Elsa was a mother, and had been married for nearly forty years. But she was not yet sixty. If she made physical demands on her new husband, which is unlikely (they did not, as the two separate bedrooms suggest, sleep together), she would have encountered at the very least unwillingness, and certainly incompetence. For Borges, the realisation of their essential incompatibility came all too soon.

Another reason for his not settling down with Elsa was that within a month of their marriage, he was back in the United States, invited for seven months to fill the Charles Eliot Norton poetry chair at Harvard. Elsa went with him. There, she was clearly out of her depth; her lack of English was a grave impediment, and the nature of Borges's duties intellectually bemusing for her.

Borges was to give six honorary lectures, entitled 'This Craft of Verse'. His salary from the Eliot Norton endowment was $24,000, not a sum Borges was accustomed to; but he still treated such fees with the same indifference as he did his minor remunerations from classes and lectures in Buenos Aires. (Riches from his writings were still a long way off.) For that reason, Elsa was a good thing: she handled all household, and his professional, finances.

Borges travelled, making more 'pilgrimages' in search of Hawthorne, Emerson, Melville, Emily Dickinson, Longfellow. He found new friends, and was as eager as ever to lap up the adulation. He was, apparently, happy with Elsa. A sonnet, 'Elsa', written towards the end of 1967 ends:

> Elsa, your hand's in mine. We see
> snow in the air and we love it.[35]

The upbeat final couplet, mentioning Elsa's name for the first time, is a long time coming. The rest of the sonnet describes a struggle to emerge from the familiar motifs of Borges's unhappiness: insomnia, lovelessness, fever. Lines end with harsh-sounding words: '*castigo*', '*temían*', '*atroces*', '*feroces*' – 'affliction', 'feared', 'atrocious', 'ferocious'. Only '*bendigo*', 'I bless', rhyming with '*castigo*', in the fourth line, rings a softer tone, suggesting some sort of redemption. 'Elsa' is an affirmative statement; but it is not a celebratory love poem.

Within four months of that sonnet came another: 'James Joyce'. Borges claimed no particular allegiance to the Irish writer, though he had been the first Argentine to write about him back in the 1920s. *Ulysses* he said he could never finish, but he said that about a lot of novels. What he admired in Joyce was his daring, his commitment, his flagrant anti-naturalism.

He also recognised something, metaphorically, in the structure of Joyce's masterpiece which mirrored his own condition. Joyce's Ulysses, Leopold Bloom, is the vessel of multiple experience, and multiple time, through a twenty-four-hour cycle in early twentieth-century Dublin. Borges, like Bloom an insecurely married man, wanted to pay homage to Bloom's creator, widely acknowledged as the century's greatest writer of English prose. In doing so, Borges felt impelled to depict something about his daily routine in late twentieth-century Massachusetts:

'In a man's single day are all the days/ of time . . .' the poem opens. It is poem about endurance, and ends, uncharacteristically for Borges, with a prayer:

> Grant me, O Lord, the courage and the joy
> to ascend to the summit of this day.[36]

Direct and confessional in tone, it demands an answer as to why he asks God to help him reach the day's end. He was happy in his work, and in his fame. America loved him, and Borges loved America. He felt at home there. With Elsa, however, the new hearth-keeper and travelling companion, it seems he was already in trouble.

His poem is a private, pointed appeal to powers beyond to help him face a terrible, circular reality he had made his own.

Of the many meetings that autumn and winter* of 1967, the most consequential for Borges was with a 34-year-old Italian-American: Norman Thomas di Giovanni. Small, energetic, ambitious, he was a translator living an hour north of Boston. In 1965, he had published an English anthology of the verse of the Spaniard Jorge Guillén, who had left Spain in 1938 at the height of the Civil War and did not return until after Franco's death. Guillén was a poet Borges admired.

Borges was lodging with Elsa in an apartment house on the corner of Concord and Craigie streets in Cambridge. He wanted to add to his duties as the Eliot Norton lecturer, and asked if he could do some teaching on Argentine literature. The faculty was only too delighted. Guillén's daughter Teresa, who coincidentally happened to be living in Harvard with her husband, used to come and pick Borges up to

---

* In the northern hemisphere, naturally.

take him to his office in Hiller's Library, on the Radcliffe campus where Borges gave his classes. It was to be from Teresa that Borges first heard di Giovanni's talents praised.

In 1967, di Giovanni was working on a bilingual anthology of Latin American poetry. He hadn't come across Borges before, and was immediately struck by a number of poems he had to read for the anthology. One in particular, 'Elvira de Alvear' (from *Dreamtigers*), alerted him to what he called Borges's 'humanity'.

He then read an interview with Borges, by Ronald Christ, in the 1967 *Paris Review*, which confirmed and added to what he thought he had discovered in the writing; someone 'modest and lovable and curiously self-effacing'. He bought Borges's latest *Obra poética* in Cambridge's foreign-language bookshop, Schoenhof's, and was told by the bookseller that Borges was speaking in Harvard the following week. It was November.

Having fallen for the poetry, di Giovanni now fell for the poet. He wrote to Borges, saying that he would like to do a volume of his poems in translation, rather like the one he had done of Guillén's. Borges agreed to see him, and di Giovanni duly arrived at Borges's lodgings on 3 December, at six o'clock, with his copy of the *Obra poética*.

> That visit . . . has never ended. Borges and I liked each other, we enjoyed the work, and it was the right hour to have come knocking. At the time, Borges was suffering from an unhappy private life and from the peculiar isolation it had forced him into. I happened along, all unwittingly, to help fill those long empty Sundays he so dreaded, to offer him the kind of work he could give his mind to (this in turn earned him much-needed self-justification), and to lend him the ear he desperately required. Ironically, in the short space of three weeks or a month, I had become the last American to discover Borges and the first to work with him.[37]

This recollection, written in 1971, is striking for a number of reasons. First, di Giovanni and Borges 'liked each other'. As friendships went, it was rather an extraordinary one. Di Giovanni, almost half Borges's age, was pugnacious, wily, extroverted: in personality the polar opposite in every way to Borges. On the other hand, di Giovanni was also intelligent, witty, solicitous, and above all treated Borges as a poet – one of high distinction – where before every foreign admirer knew him only as a short-story teller. Borges certainly liked di Giovanni for this. His subsequent readiness to work with a translator on his *poems* is further evidence that it was in this body of work that he identified himself as a writer: hence di Giovanni's phrase, 'much-needed self-justification'.

The second striking feature of the above is actually in the first line. The year after di Giovanni wrote it, 1971, his close association with Borges was to come to an end. Di Giovanni continued to translate him, but never lived in Buenos Aires again. He had had great plans for a complete translation of Borges. Borges, however, did not in the end fall in with them. Di Giovanni's optimism and energy were indefatigable (in 1971, he was still confident about the future with Borges), but it was this which seems finally to have exhausted the older writer.

The third matter is the reference to Borges's 'unhappy private life'. He meant of course his marriage to Elsa. Elsewhere, di Giovanni was more explicit: 'he had a lousy marriage – and I was getting divorced from my first wife.'[38] (He had been married for seven years.)

The two men chimed there, and found obvious compensation in embarking on Borges's last great period of work, as it turned out. What is remarkable is that it began when Borges was so low in his marriage, so soon after it had started.

'The problem was Borges and Elsa had nothing in common. Meeting Elsa again after so long was, for Borges, a form of destiny. I pointed out this sort of thing happens in literature, not in life. "You've fallen into the trap of literature," I told him. He said, "Yes, I suppose I have."'[39]

Borges returned to Buenos Aires in April 1968. A month later, he was back at the Italian Embassy to receive the Order of Merit. After the highs of the USA, things this year were to be quieter, as they had been in 1966 – although of course this time he had a wife. He went on a short trip with Elsa to Chile, his second visit to the country, to take part in a 'Congress of Antiracist Intellectuals'.[40] Back in Buenos Aires, Elsa took dictation, read to him, and occupied herself with household matters.

When not at home, Borges was at the library. Elsa's description of him as he came and went shows him in an ordinary, elderly marriage

– and he as the blind partner who needs to be cared for. In the morning she woke him at eight, with a bath prepared; Borges took an hour over it. He dressed, had his coffee and buttered bread, and went off to the library. He returned every day at one:

> We had lunch, then slept until four-thirty. He had coffee on waking – he didn't like tea – then went back to the library. At eight in the evening, he was home again. At around this time, nearly every day, we went to dine at Bioy Casares's house. On returning, we sat in the living room, reading until two or two-thirty in the morning.[41]

Thus he continued in this daily rhythm, one established since the early 1960s. Marriage confirmed Borges in a stabilising pattern in fact started for him by his job at the National Library back in 1955. Life with Elsa was not going to change him in that respect; sadly, he had little to give to the marriage itself.

Borges was married to his dreams, or to the library office. What he had built for himself in the late 1960s was something he had been working towards for over a decade – a structure in which he could be himself, eluding 'Borges': library, lunch, siesta, library, the Bioys, books. When he had to be 'Borges', add foreign travel. The vital things missing were emotional fulfilment, and work, real work: original literature.

The arrival in Buenos Aires of Norman Thomas di Giovanni in November 1968 interrupted nothing – though it changed a lot. The American gave Borges's life a new impetus. Di Giovanni had flown down to continue what he and Borges had started earlier that year – the production and translation of poems for an edition in English: 'that had been the pact,' di Giovanni later wrote. 'I would not come as a tourist.'[42] Di Giovanni's original idea had been to stay for about five months. But he worked so well with Borges that he saw no reason to leave. He stayed for nearly four years.

Chapter Nine

1968–1972

New Space with di Giovanni

One of the first things Borges and di Giovanni did together was visit Carlos Frías at Emecé. The state of Borges's works in English translation was complicated, to say the least. The volume that he and di Giovanni were working on in the first instance was to become *Selected Poems 1923–1967*; its publication was four years off, but the book was already 'closed' by the time di Giovanni got to Argentina. (The volume drew together a wide range of American writer-translators, including John Updike, John Hollander and Richard Wilbur, as well as di Giovanni himself.)

The English rights to other books were being fought over by at least three New York publishers: Jack Macrae at E. P. Dutton, Seymour Lawrence at Atlantic-Little, Brown (who was to publish the *Selected Poems* in 1972 under his own imprint), and James Laughlin at New Directions, publishers in 1962 of *Labyrinths* (see Introduction, pp.xxiv–v). Di Giovanni thought it imperative that Borges in English be free of anthologies. Jack Macrae agreed, and was determined to bring an integral Borges to his list; and one of Borges's first translators, Alastair Reid, was also very keen on the Borges–di Giovanni team, and lobbied on their behalf with Macrae.

Borges and di Giovanni's meeting with Frías revealed, a couple of weeks later, that eight books were available for translation, including Bustos Domecq's *Seis problemas* and *Crónicas*.[1] Di Giovanni had already been granted, by Borges, *carte blanche*[2] to handle Borges's affairs in English, a task he now pursued with considerable boldness. Contracts for the available volumes were set up with Dutton; the cut between the two men was fifty-fifty – a ratio, di Giovanni points out, first suggested by Borges as they were working on the *Poems*, and which obtains to this day.[3] (For Bustos Domecq, the split was three-way, Bioy naturally being the third party.)

Di Giovanni also came armed for the translating process with help from the Ingram Merrill Foundation, the same New York body which had awarded Borges $5,000 in 1966. This time, the Foundation entrusted Borges's new man with $4,000. There was thus no lack of infrastructure for the exacting task of rendering Borges into the language he considered second only to his mother tongue, and which he perhaps loved more than Spanish.

In the opening stages of his and di Giovanni's partnership, the unique focus of their attention was poetry. Elsa had been sending poems published in *La Nación* to di Giovanni in Boston, which under contract were then translated for and appeared in *The New Yorker*. For both men, such a contract meant money, two cheques that came to di Giovanni, one of which he then passed on to Buenos Aires; there, all the money was handled by Elsa.

After the poems that had gone into the *Selected Poems*, and after those that Borges had secreted away at the end of volumes reprinted throughout the 1960s, di Giovanni found that there were seventeen new ones. It was with these that he arrived in Buenos Aires. He felt that another thirteen would be enough for a book, and said so. Borges thought otherwise.

> 'No, no!' he protested, flying into a rage. 'I won't publish another book. I haven't published a new book in eight years, and I won't be judged by this stuff.'

Borges was, added di Giovanni, 'beside himself in a way I had never seen before'. The subject was a hot potato, and di Giovanni let it drop.

Not, however, for long; according to di Giovanni's own account, the very next night, when he had been taken by Borges for dinner in calle Posadas to meet the Bioys, Borges brought the subject up himself:

'Di Giovanni has a crazy idea. He wants me to publish a new book of poems' . . .
    'But Georgie,' Bioy immediately chimed in, chuckling his infectious little chuckle. 'That seems to me a splendid idea.'[4]

With such support from Bioy, Borges considered the project more temperately. The following week, after Borges paid an unusual visit to Emecé, Carlos Frías agreed too. For the first time since *Dreamtigers*, Borges began to plan a completely new book.

It is difficult to know what caused Borges's initial reluctance. Most probably, it had to do with a crisis of confidence brought on by his failing marriage. Life with Elsa had induced in him a certain torpor; he was content with 'Borges', but the great and strange work which had made that colossus he knew was over. And now here was a young American suggesting he take on again the tasks of the writer – that is, poet – enshrined in *Dreamtigers* but who, for the moment, seemed to have dried up. Why should he bother? He was Borges, after all. Yet the thinness of his output throughout the 1960s must only have added to a sense of inadequacy.

Di Giovanni was at close hand to witness Borges's creative depression. They went on one evening at the beginning of December 1968 to Palermo, which Borges told di Giovanni he hadn't visited for thirty years.* They ate *empanadas* at the house of Elsa's cousin Olga (who had visited them in Harvard), had some *caña quemada* – a sort of rum – at an old café-store, and went wandering:

. . . like an eager schoolboy, he showed me a narrow, cobbled alleyway, pointing out that it was untypical for running in a diagonal instead of forming the side of a square. And on the spot he began recounting the 'plot of a story that has the ghost of Juan Muraña as a protagonist'. (An entry in a pocket notebook tells me this.) But of course he at once lamented the fact that, though he might still compose some poems, he would never set

---

* Or just over twenty, if Estela Canto is to be believed. See Chapter Six, p. 144.

down this story, since there was no way he could ever manage to write prose again.[5]

To deal with his block, Borges resorted to petulant exaggeration. He may have been depressed, but di Giovanni was winning him over. That reference to Juan Muraña, an old Palermo hoodlum, was a clue to what Borges *might* have had in mind, as far as stories went. By 1970, as we shall see, they had come a very long way indeed – the tales just needed tickling out. Di Giovanni was the man for the job.

Together, they worked hard. In the mornings Borges dictated to secretaries, at least three women in rotation: in the afternoons, he and di Giovanni tackled translations. The only interruption to this first phase of writing was a visit Borges and Elsa made to Israel in the New Year of 1969. Invited by the Israeli government, the couple arrived in Tel Aviv on 20 January, and proceeded to enjoy ten days there and in Jerusalem. Borges met David Ben-Gurion, and gave a series of conferences. He was buoyed up by this visit, especially as he had been unequivocal in his support for Israel during the 1967 Arab-Israeli War.

'Since my Genevan days,' he wrote in the 'Essay', 'I had always been interested in Jewish culture, thinking of it as an integral element of our so-called Western civilisation . . .'.[6] He had a genuine feeling for the pioneering spirit of this controversial Middle Eastern state, but was unclear in his own mind about the self-evident conflict between 'Jewish culture' and Israeli belligerence.

As usual in internationally sensitive matters, Borges underestimated world intellectual opinion – or simply didn't care; the left in the United States, and in the developing nations of his own continent, naturally sympathised with the Palestinian cause. A Great World Writer publicly siding with the perceived oppressor of a now nationless people struck a discordant note; Borges's political gaffes were to get worse in the years to come.[7]

In Buenos Aires throughout February 1969, the writer and his translator worked on an English edition of *The Book of Imaginary Beings*. Borges was delighted with the result, and insisted he and di Giovanni add some new entries to the mad menagerie of Buraks, Garudas and Rukhs, in English. They came up with four, including 'An Experimental Account of What Was Known, Seen, and Met by Mrs Jane Lead in London in 1694' and 'Laudatores Temporis Acti' (worshippers of time). The manuscript was on its way to New York by the beginning of June. Borges, in a little gesture that epitomises the sweet frivolity of the book, told the letterbox where the package should go: *Norteamérica*. 'Otherwise, how would it know?'[8]

Nineteen sixty-nine was a remarkable year for work. Life outside work, outside the library, which in an ideal world for Borges would have meant a happy home and family life, all but evaporated. In a way, it was the best thing that could have happened. The effect of di Giovanni on Borges's inner world was tangible, explosive. He was like a crafty gym master getting a slothful pupil to perform somersaults the pupil thought he had forgotten. Borges the married man had to become a writer again.

At the University of Oklahoma, an Estonian intellectual in exile, Ivar Ivask, first an admirer of Guillén and now of Borges, wanted the Argentine to pay them a visit. He pushed the university's foreign-language department to invite him to come and talk about Argentine writers, and a visit was set for the beginning of December. By the time Borges and di Giovanni arrived there, the extraordinary transformation that had occurred in Borges's creative outflow was obvious.

First, he had published on his seventieth birthday in August *Elogio de la sombra* (*In Praise of Darkness*), his new book of poems, which also contained short prose texts, similar to those in *Dreamtigers* but not as numerous. He had co-translated his first book with di Giovanni. He had entered into contractual agreements to co-translate another eight volumes. And most significantly he had, as that reference to Juan Muraña suggests, started a new story.

The genesis of what became *El informe de Brodie* (*Doctor Brodie's Report*), published exactly a year after *In Praise of Darkness*, is recounted with engaging vivacity in di Giovanni's short memoir, and cannot be improved upon.[9] In essence, what di Giovanni did was to stimulate Borges's imagination, and his memory: he reminded Borges of what narrative powers he had, of what use he could put them to; he also cajoled Borges into believing he could reach back through his preoccupations with formal verse to the masterly prose inventions of the 1940s.

I do not wish to mislead. *Doctor Brodie's Report* is a very different beast from *Ficciones* and *El Aleph*. Comprising eleven short stories, the book exhibits a fascination with aspects of Argentine life that took root in Borges's imagination long before the 1940s: knives, gauchos, criminality, the literal and metaphorical outer limits of Buenos Aires. The locations are concrete, recognisable, human, either in Buenos Aires or outlying regions. This is the Buenos Aires of Borges's deep past. But the confidence and leanness of the stories as pure fiction – pure fictions – are unmistakable.

Three great stories, 'La intrusa' ('The Intruder'), 'El encuentro' ('The meeting') and 'El Evangelio según Marcos' ('The Gospel According to Mark'), ensure *Brodie*'s high position in the Borges canon. 'The Intruder', as we know, had been dictated to Leonor at the beginning of 1966. Now, Borges described it as 'the first of my new ventures into straightforward storytelling';[10] and some straightforward storytelling it was: Borges had not been so visceral or unpleasant since *A Universal History of Infamy*. Such is the spirit of *Brodie*: curt, violent, cinematic.

'The Meeting', a powerful piece involving knife-fighters at the turn of the century, was the story Borges had embarked on in early 1969. Apart from 'The Intruder', he hadn't written anything like it since the mid-1930s. 'Streetcorner Man' is the obvious precursor. 'The Meeting' announces a wilful return to the narrative territory of those years: age reinvigorating itself through the obsessions of youth. 'The Gospel According to Mark', similar in character to 'The Meeting' and 'The Intruder' – all backwatersmen and moral degeneracy, concerning a medical student who tries to teach three ranch dwellers the message of the Crucifixion – remains Borges's most perfectly shocking story: its last sentence is both one of the most suggestive, and least enigmatic, of any he wrote. 'The shed was without a roof; they had pulled down the beams to make the cross.'[11]

Yet throughout this most unadorned of Borges's books, characteristic narrative uncertainties abound: 'who knows whether the story ends here' ends 'The Meeting'. When 'Juan Muraña' opens with a clear first-person resumé of a Palermo upbringing, the writing in 1930 of a 'study of Evaristo Carriego', even mention of a classmate Roberto Godel – a real childhood friend of Borges's – we suspect that Borges is somehow misleading us.

In 'Guayaquil', the narrator pauses before the second paragraph to comment on the melodrama of the first. In four stories, 'El indigno'

('The Unworthy Friend'), 'Historia de Rosendo Juárez' ('Rosendo's Tale'), 'Juan Muraña' and 'El informe de Brodie' ('Doctor Brodie's Report'), that well-tested technique of Borges's – presenting himself as the innocent receptor of strange tidings from uncharted frontiers – is put to dynamic and entertaining use.

The story to which the volume owes its title and which ends it is vintage Borges. In ironic imitation of Jonathan Swift,[12] David Brodie D.D. has been to Africa, where he has found Ape-men and a species called 'Mlch', whom Brodie terms Yahoos, 'so that my readers will be reminded of their bestial nature and also because, given the total absence of vowels in their harsh language, an exact transliteration is virtually impossible'.

The report left dates from the 1830s, and in contrast to Lemuel Gulliver's misanthropic treatise in the fourth book of Swift's masterpiece, Brodie offers up a vision of semantic mayhem:

> The word 'nrz', for example, suggests dispersion or spots, and may stand for the starry sky, a leopard, a flock of birds, smallpox, something bespattered, the act of scattering, or the flight that follows defeat in warfare. 'Hrl', on the other hand, means something compact or dense. It may stand for the tribe, a tree trunk, a stone, a heap of stones, the act of heaping stones, the gathering of the four witch doctors, carnal conjunction, or a forest.[13]

This harks back to the enumerative, brilliantly facetious Borges, combining the astronomical ambition of 'Tlön, Uqbar, Orbis Tertius' with the faultless nonsense of *Imaginary Beings*. Brodie has stumbled on a universe where the norms of linguistic meaning have been violently subverted, the dignities of authority savagely dismantled: like Tibet's Dalai Lama, only certain signs on a certain baby boy lead to the proclamation of a new leader – in the land of the Yahoos, however, 'so that the physical world may not lead him from the paths of wisdom', he is castrated, blinded, has his limbs chopped off, is kept in a Castle called 'Qzr', and displayed on the outbreak of war, only to be killed under a hail of stones 'flung at him by the Ape-men' in their adulatory excitement.

Brodie as a whole is relatively light on this type of anarchy; indeed, stories such as 'El otro duelo' ('The End of the Duel') and

'La señora mayor' ('The Elder Lady'), one of Borges's weakest, are almost genteel.[14] In 'Doctor Brodie's Report', however, Borges reserved until last the filibustering energies that lie behind 'The Lottery in Babylon', 'Ibn Hakkan al-Bokhari, Dead in His Labyrinth',[15] and Bustos Domecq. The story bears all the traces of the Borges who had openly, magnificently disposed of the boundaries of realism so long before in *El jardín de senderos que se bifurcan* thirty years before.

Needless to say, the vision of a dehumanised leader in 'Brodie' was probably a joke at the expense of Perón, or any leader like him – even *any leader*. Borges's preface to *Brodie* is famously terse, in statements about both his fiction, and politics in old age (it needs pointing out that 'Brodie' itself was, by Borges's own admission, the only non-realistic story in the volume).

I am not, nor have I ever been, what used to be called a preacher of parables or a fabulist and is now known as a committed writer ... I am a member of the Conservative Party – that in itself is a form of scepticism – and no one has ever branded me a Communist, a nationalist, an anti-Semite, a follower of Billy the Kid or of the dictator Rosas. I believe that some day we will deserve not to have governments.[16]

This was a personal statement of idiosyncratic political taste, not a tract. However, if political foes needed ammunition for calling Borges anti-democratic – at the worst 'fascist' – in the years ahead, their arsenal was all there in this preface.

In Oklahoma, three and a half months after the publication of *In Praise of Darkness*, di Giovanni managed to persuade Borges to be even more personal. After nearly two weeks, the last of six lectures Borges gave at the university was, finally, to be about himself, something he had never done before. On the day, he fell into a fit of nervousness, like those that used to precede his lectures back in 1946. To talk about himself was a bit like having sexual relations: the prospect paralysed him.

Di Giovanni calmed him down and the talk was of course a wild success. Rodríguez Monegal, who had spent the 1960s editing an influential magazine in Paris called *Mundo Nuevo*, an important player in the Latin American boom, was also there. It was the first time the two men had met outside the River Plate, and Rodríguez

Monegal's vision, and indeed his reading, of Borges had a longer
pedigree than most. Now, a new generation of readers was eagerly
reaching a new Borges: 'They were literally spaced out by his words,
by the incantatory way in which he delivered them, by his blindness
and his almost uncanny face.'[17]

Perhaps more significant is what came of the talk: di Giovanni hit
upon the idea of using it for a written account of Borges's life. Back
in Buenos Aires, he asked Lowell Dunham, head of Oklahoma's
languages department, to send him a transcript, and wrote to Jack
Macrae in New York to say that a new volume of translated stories
he and Borges were working on would include the story of Borges's
life, along with some notes about the stories themselves.

> I knew that readers were having difficulty with Borges; worse,
> I knew that the universities kept him swathed in unnecessary
> mystery. At the same time, since his stories were really all about
> himself, his various guises, and dimensions of his thought, what
> better setting for them by way of introduction than the story of
> his life?[18]

The transcript arrived from Oklahoma in April 1970. The talk,
they realised, had to be completely reworked – it was more a ramble
than a chronology. In effect, they had to start again, and Borges was
quite willing.

Together, Borges and di Giovanni worked on this new 'story'
throughout the middle of 1970, as often as they could. Weekends
were generally kept for their non-working lives. Di Giovanni had
got married the day after the publication of *In Praise of Darkness* to a
23-year-old student he had brought with him from the States in late
1968, named Heather Booth. He also had his own circle of friends,
including the writers Manuel Puig and Humberto Constantini.*

When not at home or in the library, meanwhile – and the latter
was by now preferable to avenida Belgrano – Borges was much in
demand for lectures. He and di Giovanni had to steal hours when
they could for the memorious labour of what was shaping up as the
'Autobiographical Essay'.

In May 1970, however, Borges faltered. Work slowed to a snail's

---

* Both dead; another was the writer Isidoro Blaisten, now sixty-three, and living in
Buenos Aires.

pace. Borges appeared distraught, and couldn't go on. On the 16th of that month, trying to proceed with the 'Essay' at the library – di Giovanni recalls it was a Saturday – Borges suddenly announced: 'I've committed what seems to me now an unaccountable mistake, a huge mistake. A quite unexplainable and mysterious mistake.'[19]

The problem was Elsa. The marriage had failed, and Borges was helpless. He had to get out. Alicia Jurado, a friend of Borges's since 1954 and generally impartial, felt that Borges had to face the problem head on. He had sought Jurado's advice:

> 'Do you think it would be wrong if I were to separate?'
> 'Georgie, who's going to think it wrong? Why?'
> 'Because I have to separate.'
> 'Talk it over with her.'
> 'No, I can't. She'll make a scene, and I can't bear scenes.'
> 'If you've been living with her for three years, she should have some kind of explanation, as it'll affect her life.'[20]

He never did explain anything to Elsa; instead, he poured out his woes to di Giovanni.

Having listened to what he already knew, di Giovanni went straight into action. That very afternoon they met a close friend of di Giovanni's, Guillermo Peña Casares, who knew the law, to get some idea of how to proceed. Two days later, they took further advice from a practising lawyer, Carlos Ordóñez, a friend of Borges's from Córdoba. The situation was clear, but stark: divorce didn't exist in Argentine law, and the only option was legal separation. Moreover, because Ordóñez was based in Córdoba, he would have to appoint a Buenos Aires lawyer to take the case forward.

As the weeks ticked by, Borges worked as best and as often as he could with his amanuensis, until 7 July: that was the day set for Borges's escape from the institution he always assumed would make him happy, but which had done the opposite. He was nearly seventy-one, and as miserable as he had ever been with a woman.

He and di Giovanni had a watertight plan:

> That chill, grey winter's morning . . . I lay in wait for Borges in the doorway of the National Library, and the moment he arrived, I leapt into his taxi and off we sped for the intown

airport. Borges, a trembling leaf and utterly exhausted after a sleepless night, confessed that his greatest fear had been that he might blurt the whole thing out to Elsa at any moment.[21]

Elsa asked her husband that same morning as he was leaving for the library what he wanted for lunch: he replied '*puchero*' (stew) – one of his favourite dishes.

At one o'clock, the doorbell went; Elsa, with her *puchero* nicely prepared, thought Borges must have forgotten his keys. When the maid opened the door, five men were standing there. One was the lawyer appointed by Ordóñez, Martínez Carranza, accompanied by Carranza's son, with a legal order to remove Borges's belongings – principally his library, some five hundred books. The other three men were from the removal firm.[22] 'What pained me most,' Elsa remembered twenty-three years later, 'was that when [Borges] asked for *puchero*, he already knew he wouldn't be coming back.'

Borges and di Giovanni made their escape to Córdoba. The writer had some engagements, including a lecture on the nineteenth-century conquest of the Indians in a town called Coronel Pringles, reached after a day's drive across the pampa. Throughout the trip, Borges was exhausted. His spirits picked up when they arrived the next day for a banquet at Coronel Suárez, a town named after his great-grandfather. Next stop was Pardo, where Bioy's family had its *estancia*; Borges and di Giovanni rested for three days in more relaxing surroundings than either had been in together for weeks. They continued work on the 'Essay'.

By 29 July, they were in Tres Arroyos, a town in the south of Buenos Aires province. Borges was lecturing on Almafuerte. In a hotel, the 'Essay' was finished. Two weeks later, in Buenos Aires, Borges put the finishing touches to a long tale called 'The Congress', his first since the stories of *Brodie*.

Release from avenida Belgrano had focussed his mind: away from domestic misery, his well-tested natural inventiveness flourished again. He had not found a home; but he had refound, with a little help from di Giovanni, Borges.

Elsa was left alone: 'Until my son Ricardito died, this was the biggest shock of my life,' she said.[23] She never really forgave Borges for the manner in which he left her. She disappeared from his life.

*   *   *

Ten days after returning to Buenos Aires, Borges travelled with di Giovanni to Brazil. There, he received a major biennial Latin-American prize, called the Inter-American Prize for Literature, or the Matarazzo Sobrinho Prize, administered by the state of São Paulo. It was worth $25,000; Borges would need every penny of it. His separation from Elsa would not be cheap.

That was his only foreign trip in a dramatic year. In fact, he cut it short, excusing himself from a courtesy visit to Brazil's President Castelo Branco in the capital Brasilia: Borges found the country too hot, and felt the urgency of putting his life back into shape. He also had to return to Leonor, who was old and he was concerned about her.

Leonor had of course been the first to be informed about her son's flight from Elsa; now she had him back at Maipú. Deprived of her *raison d'être* – Georgie's welfare – her enthusiasm for life had vanished. Elsie Haedo went and saw her in Borges's absence:

> When she saw her son was married and could be looked after, she proceeded to die. I saw this woman of enormous vitality stretched out on her bed, talking about the past: everything was now over. Then the phone rang; it was Georgie. She was transformed, came alive – she was suddenly young again. And because Georgie was entirely dependent on her, he could be cruel, capricious and rude: a typical only son.[24]

Leonor's mobility was now limited due to her great age, and daily domestic matters at Maipú were dealt with largely by Fani. But there was no denying Leonor's victory: Georgie was back where he should be. Life, for her, returned to normal.

For Borges too. *Doctor Brodie's Report* had been published in early August. With di Giovanni, work on a new volume of translations had to be completed. This was *The Aleph and Other Stories*, containing the 'Autobiographical Essay', published first in *The New Yorker* on 19 September 1970. The magazine paid $9,000 for it. *The Aleph* appeared the following month.

For complex reasons to do with copyright, claimed by New Directions in New York over stories from the Spanish *El Aleph* already translated and published in *Labyrinths*, this new *Aleph* could not be an exact English version of the original. It was a cause of frustration to both di Giovanni and Borges, who was determined that his work in English should be represented only by what he was now doing with the North American.*

In the early part of 1971, globetrotting took on new dimensions. The pretext for Borges's eight-week trip from March to May, encompassing America, Europe and the Middle East, was to receive an honorary degree from Oxford, originally offered in 1970. Fatigue after his trip to the US at the end of the previous year was the reason given for not being able to travel to England then. Now, the doctorate *honoris causa* was something Borges really could not resist – academic recognition from one of the oldest universities in the world, right in the heart of his beloved England, and one where, most importantly, Anglo-Saxon was still taught. The British Council was offering to put £100 towards the trip; the Institute of Contemporary Arts, hosting a series of talks by Borges in May, after the Oxford investiture, would underwrite all his other costs.

A second impetus for the voyage was provided by the biennial Jerusalem Book Fair's awarding Borges that year's Jerusalem Prize, started in 1963. Bertrand Russell and Max Frisch had won it before him. But money for the trip had to be found. Di Giovanni wrote to a friend at Columbia University in New York, Frank McShane; he was head of the writing programme there, and had written a biography of Ford Madox Ford. He agreed to raise funds to the tune of $3,000, in return for talks by Borges.

Borges, di Giovanni and Heather flew to New York, then to Salt Lake City. *The New Yorker*'s publication of the 'Essay' – in which the writer expressed a hope 'to see Mormon Utah'[25] – had elicited an immediate invitation from the Bringham Young University, which was readily accepted. Borges was there for a week. Back in New York, he picked up another honorary doctorate, at Columbia; and it was here that things got unruly.

Borges's talks on Argentine writing proceeded in their normal, seemingly improvised manner.[26] An additional event at Columbia (for which a further $1,000 was forthcoming) was then organised at short

* The book that came out both in the States and Britain is the only means by which the extraordinary volume published in Buenos Aires in 1949 (with a second edition published in 1952 containing three additional stories – see Note 15 for this chapter, p. 228) has been accessible in English. In other words, *El Aleph* is the only major Borges work of prose fiction not yet published in its entirety in English as a single volume. That may soon change (see A Note on Texts).

notice – a gathering of other Latin American writers, intellectuals, even politicians. One of these individuals, a poet called Nicanor Parra, along with an anti-poetry claque, tackled Borges over his refusal to engage in the burning political issues of the day, particularly those which affected Latin America. Borges had his characteristic answer:

> I believe in revolution, and am waiting for it to come. In the revolution there will be no political leaders. There will be no propaganda and there will be no *banderas*, no flags . . . When they tell of some new revolution I always ask 'and do they have a flag?' and when they say 'yes', I know that it is not my revolution.[27]

If this most unbellicose of individuals had a war-cry for these restive years, this was it. There was nothing new in Borges's declaring his belief in non-politics. It was eloquent, but it was not what this audience, or some of it, wanted to hear.

A group of Puerto Rican students were angry about Columbia's apparent racism, and from the back of the hall started to attack the guests for condoning it by coming to the university. In the hubbub, one of these students called Borges '*hijo de puta*' ('son of a bitch' in English); the Spanish states that the mother of the addressee is a whore. For good measure, the student added that Borges had nothing to contribute to any discussion about Latin America, because he was already dead.

More because of the insult to his mother than for the imputation of his supposed mortal redundancy, Borges lost his temper. He thwacked his cane on the desk, and challenged the student to a duel outside the lecture-hall.

Rodríguez Monegal, who first reported this incident, was an eyewitness. 'The student must have been barely twenty. Borges . . . was frail, holding his cane in trembling hands. But he meant every word of his chivalrous invitation.' Rodríguez Monegal managed to take Borges aside, and tried to explain that it was the political atmosphere of the times that lay behind the outburst: he shouldn't take it as a personal affront. Borges wasn't listening.

> He stopped me dead and said that of course he knew the student did not intend to attack Mother, because if he had thought so, he would have taken his cane and smashed it over the student's

head. He was trembling while he said it and his cane moved uncontrollably.[28]

Rodríguez Monegal asked his old hero to visit Yale, where he was chairman of the university's Spanish and Portuguese departments. There, proceedings were quieter. On the night, there was some difficulty in finding the right hall for Borges's appearance, as the one reserved – for two hundred people – had filled with five hundred by the time the main speaker arrived, and there was no room for him.

A comical procession around the campus to relocate led to one of Yale's largest halls, and after much delay, the evening began. It was all about literature. The entire audience was on Borges's side; when, finally, he was asked whether he had ever been in love, and he replied with a sibilant 'Yes', he won the day: 'the audience roared, and the happening ended.'[29]

For the next leg of the journey, di Giovanni had a surprise for Borges – a detour to a little country that had a hold on Borges's imagination rather in the same way Britain did: Iceland. Anglo–Saxon had led Borges to Old Norse, and he had become fascinated by the Sagas.

'¿Pero cómo, cómo, cómo . . . ?' gasped Borges when di Giovanni announced the plan.[30] Di Giovanni had some friends in a Buenos Aires travel agency, and through them had made a booking on Icelandic Airways from New York to Tel Aviv via Reykjavik. In early April, Borges thus made a physical arrival in another country of his dreams – and once there was joined by a young woman, half-Argentine, half-Japanese, who was studying Old Norse with him back in Argentina. Her name was María Kodama.

From Iceland it was on to Israel (di Giovanni having to carry with him a dozen volumes of the Sagas presented to Borges in the office of a newspaper editor[31]). The party spent four days there, with the ceremony taking place on 19 April. The prize was worth $2,000.

From Israel, he flew back to London, and visited Scotland – his first trip there since 1964 with María Esther Vázquez. He wanted to rest after what, after all, had been a packed month and a bit. The party first visited Edinburgh, then stayed with Alastair Reid, near St Andrews. Borges needed to drink in more of the North Sea and asked Reid to take him to a position where he could meditate before it. Reid stood him in front of the cathedral in St Andrews, and Borges asked him to come back in ten minutes to collect him. As he walked away, Reid saw that Borges had somehow got turned round; he was staring into his yellowish nothingness, deep in meditation. Reid quietly returned to his side, and helped Borges back to where he wanted to be.[32]

In Oxford, in the last week of April, Borges was awarded his doctorate. Apart from the pomp of the ceremony in the Sheldonian Library, there was one essential duty to perform there: he had to have an Anglo-Saxon lesson.

The man he was after was named Richard Hamer. Hamer was a tutor in English at Christ Church in his mid-thirties, and in 1970 had published *A Choice of Anglo-Saxon Verse*, a volume containing twenty-two poems, both in Hamer's translations and in the original Anglo-Saxon. Someone had found the book for Borges in Buenos Aires, and he had been entranced.

After the degree ceremony, a reception took place in Broad Street, and Borges insisted on meeting Hamer. Indeed, it had been stipulated in the Buenos Aires British Council's original proposal for a visit by Borges, made in November 1970, that this 'Professor' (as the Council termed him) meet 'Professor Harmer' (*sic*).[33]

Hamer was a junior don, and the Council was surprised that Borges wanted to see him and not Oxford's senior professor of Anglo-Saxon, Alastair Campbell. One memo rather stuffily reads: 'it had not occurred to Mr di Giovanni, Borges' secretary, to do his homework on Professor Campbell as well. Being an American, he possibly did not appreciate the subjects of protocol.'[34]

At the party, Hamer was found, and Borges took him off to an alcove in the Broad Street reception room. For three-quarters of an hour, Borges quizzed Hamer over aspects of pronunciation and metre in Anglo-Saxon verse. He was courteous and, Hamer remembers, determined to get answers, rather than display his own knowledge. And he was clearly quite uninterested in the party, or the other guests. He asked to see Hamer the next day, who agreed to the meeting; but when he got there, Hamer was met by di Giovanni, who explained that Borges was too tired to work. Could he, however, help with a list of problems that Borges had drawn up? Di Giovanni handed him the list and Hamer duly obliged.[35]

The final destination was the Institute of Contemporary Arts in London, where he gave four sell-out talks between 3 and 13 May. Chaired successively by Frank Kermode, Bryan Magee, John

Spurling and Alastair Reid, these were high-profile events, in which Borges graciously and wittily explained the impulses behind his stories, and – for the first time in public – his verse. His visit was crowned by a talk at London's Royal Horticultural Hall, which many attended but few – due to Borges's weak speaking voice – could hear. At both venues, political run-ins were mercifully avoided.

The Cuban writer Guillermo Cabrera Infante, in exile in London since 1966, had first met Borges in Oxford. A week later, in London, he dined with him at Brown's Hotel, where Borges particularly delighted in staying, because Robert Louis Stevenson had always stayed there too. At dinner, Borges slopped soup down his tie (to hide his embarrassment, Cabrera Infante did the same), and was determined to prove that he and Cabrera were related. An ancestor of Borges's, Colonel Cabrera, was in the Argentine army, though Borges had no illusions about him:

> Imagine, he was the founder of Córdoba, in Argentina. Can you think of anything more stupid? He had the opportunity to found a city, a lucky strike, and he had to call it Córdoba. Didn't he know there was already a city, an illustrious one, called Córdoba, in Spain? He should have known but he was simply stupid.[36]

Borges was lionised in Britain, as he was everywhere he went; but not everyone was convinced.

Before his investiture at Oxford, the *Guardian* had published two articles about him, one above the other on the same page; the first was a portrait of his literature, the second a hostile account of his politics. 'He has fallen headlong into a position of collaboration with ultra-reaction', declared the headline over the latter, lifting a statement from the article written by Peter Fuller and Maxine Molyneux.

The piece did not shy away from associating Borges directly with a regime presided over by a recently installed dictator, Alejandro Lanusse. 'Argentinian [*sic*] students, intellectuals and revolutionaries stopped reading him a long time ago. Now they regard him with a sneering contempt, usually reserved for members of the military oligarchy who run the country.'

It was an easy generalisation, containing some truth, but little accuracy. Argentine students, let alone revolutionaries, had hardly ever read Borges at all, though they knew exactly what he stood for: great writing, reactionary politics. Those Argentines and other Latin Americans who had actually read him tolerated the true naivety of his politics, while managing not to lose sight of his importance as a writer in Spanish.

The *Guardian* piece was, not surprisingly, out to castigate Borges for his apparent naivety, his lack of engagement, something over which he had laid down his cards in the preface to *Doctor Brodie's Report*, in his confrontations with audiences in the States, and elsewhere. Those words would now pursue him wherever he went and whenever he was asked to pronounce on world, and particularly Latin American, affairs.

> I used to believe in democracy, but now I can't. I think that maybe Argentina should have elections in the next fifty or perhaps one hundred years. But now we are not ready for that kind of thing. And as Communism is creeping into all our neighbouring countries, I really don't know what will happen.[37]

He then quickly dismissed his views as those of an ageing 'pessimist'.

Argentina was indeed lurching from bad to worse. A succession of *juntas* from 1966 on had abolished elections, banned trades unions and other political bodies from participation in the nation's affairs, and sanctioned state repression through an increasingly virulent secret police force. Forever the anti-nationalist, Borges rather unhelpfully believed that the Argentine body-politic could, for the time being, come up with nothing better.

When Perón returned to the Casa Rosada in the year Pinochet took power in Chile, Borges could be forgiven a sense of amused outrage. Communism may have been crushed in Argentina's western neighbour, but in Argentina for Borges something far worse than either Communism or Pinochet had re-erupted. The Unspeakable was back.

It had been an exhausting four or five months. In Buenos Aires, finding new rhythms for work and for the patterns of his social life, with Leonor at his beck and call, Borges suddenly lost his appetite for sessions with di Giovanni. Their contract, di Giovanni reminded him, stipulated that *A Universal History of Infamy* was next in line for translation. Borges was not interested. He let di Giovanni work on it alone; their daily meetings ended.

Within six months, even thrice-weekly consultative meetings had halted. Borges could not face going back over his early work. He found it inadequate, and as di Giovanni said twenty-two years later, 'He didn't like the style of it any more.'[38] That unique, symbiotic, inter-linguistic collaboration built in late 1967 came to an abrupt end.

In June 1972, di Giovanni left Buenos Aires to live in England with Heather and their one-year-old son. He and Borges didn't see each other for another seven years. Di Giovanni believed that Borges had simply been tired, and done enough translating for the time being.

But the situation was more complex; di Giovanni was aware of it, because on his first day with Borges in Buenos Aires in 1968, Borges had introduced him to someone who – even as he and di Giovanni were doing their pioneering work from 1969 to 1970 – came to fill the writer's life in a way no one, with the exception of Leonor, had done before.

She was the young, almost invisible woman who had joined Borges in Iceland in April 1971. Unlike Borges, who eventually accepted the good di Giovanni had done for him – in English, above all – she never could reconcile herself to the North American's role in Borges's life. Today, she controls every word Borges wrote. In 1968, when di Giovanni first met her, María Kodama was just another one of Borges's students.

Chapter Ten

1972–1986

The World with Young Eyes

María Kodama first met Borges, so far as we can calculate, when she was twelve years old. A friend of her parents introduced her to him at a lecture to which her Japanese father had taken her, in 1958, three years after Borges had been appointed to the directorship of the National Library, and when he was already well-established on the lecture timetable at the University of Buenos Aires. The writer seemed to her accessible enough, though a twelve-year-old girl is naturally tongue-tied in the presence of someone apparently so famous and who (in María Esther Vázquez's phrase) must have looked 'as old as the Pyramids'.

Aged sixteen, she says, she began studying Anglo-Saxon with Borges.[1] That makes the date 1962, which is probably a little early. Vlady Kociancich doesn't remember María's participation in the study groups until well into the 1960s, when Borges had turned his attentions to Old Norse. María remembers that the group met at a *confitería* called La Fragata, on Corrientes and San Martín, which certainly corresponds with Kociancich's observation that the weekend sessions had – by the mid-1960s – moved out of the National Library.[2]

Old Norse was indeed the first, real, intellectual connection, from Borges's point of view, with Kodama; and she was a model student. In the di Giovanni days, she remained a shadowy figure, quiet, willowy, somewhat inscrutable, who then had no influence on Borges's life. Chief organiser of his daily affairs was, of course, Elsa.

Leonor, meanwhile, was ailing. After di Giovanni departed and Borges began to spend much more time back at calle Maipú, it became clear Leonor had little life left in her. Aged ninety-six, she had not gone out of the apartment for several years. By 1973 she was confined to her bed, looked after by Fani.

Very slowly, she began to die. For Borges the experience was agonising and the end could not come soon enough. But the process took two years, for though Leonor was desperately ill, she was also desperately stubborn.

He, by contrast, had found a new lease of life. Relieved of daily translation duties and in 1973 – by choice – of his job at the National Library, and having put well behind him a paralysing three years of marriage, he began at last properly to reap the benefits of his fame. Borges travelled almost non-stop for over a decade, rarely paying his way; but for his audiences, and the institutions who financed his trips, he more than justified the expense and effort to get him where he was wanted. He was an old man enjoying a prolonged, if not over-productive, Indian summer. He was also, though he claimed to find the notion puzzling, one of the most famous writers on earth.

Over a period of fourteen years, from 1972 until his final departure from Buenos Aires in November 1985, Borges's travels add up to a quasi-self-exile. The release from marriage and from di Giovanni, and finally, in 1975, from his mother – who was really his life's partner – gave Borges the impetus to seek something he had long waited for: a taste of real freedom.

But another reason for such extensive travelling, and therefore for his frequent absences from Argentina, was the need to escape a new national nightmare. The 1970s were without doubt the most brutal and the most self-destructive years in Argentina's modern history. Although Borges's politics aggravated his many admirers and inspired his detractors to heights of contempt throughout the decade, he was right in his view that the country (first under Perón and then under the generals), and Buenos Aires in particular, became an intolerable place, a 'sad country'. Also, with long-term friends and associates now dead or dying – in addition to Leonor, Norah Lange, Carlos Mastronardi, Manuel Peyrou and Victoria Ocampo all passed on in this decade – and with his attachment to María Kodama delicately turning into a romantic if curious partnership, Borges saw no reason either to witness the horrors or suffer further indignities at home.

Life, especially after 1975, was to be found abroad, where he was known and loved. At home, where he was increasingly criticised and sometimes physically threatened, life simply had to be endured. Buenos Aires was no fun at all. Having a woman half his age at his side when he might otherwise have been alone in this ambience was one of the boons – perhaps the luckiest – of Borges's last years. Unlike many writers who survive in solitude to a great age, Borges would neither be abandoned nor die alone.

The only year in which he did not travel was 1974. The other thirteen years form a continual itinerary of continent-hopping. The most exotic destinations were Egypt (1978), Japan (1979 and 1984), and Morocco (1984); the smallest countries he visited were Ecuador (1978) and Puerto Rico (1981 and 1984); the most frequently visited were the United States and Spain (eleven times each); apart from these countries, the two cities he went to most were Paris (seven times) and Geneva (five times, including his final visit). The two major European countries where he was widely translated and read but visited least were Germany (twice, in 1979 and 1982) and Britain (just once, in 1983). He never returned to the Scandinavian mainland, though he did make one further trip to Iceland, in 1979. (See Appendix One for an itinerary of his journeys from 1972.)

I have not here attempted to cover in any detail these trips, as such an account would soon become a tedious recitation of similar episodes: with María Kodama, Borges travelled, soaked up atmospheres, attended cocktail parties (which always bored him), gave talks and interviews, made jokes, and found the world was, to his great surprise, fascinated by him. Suddenly, after years of self-confinement in Buenos Aires, there was enormous human and cultural variety available to Borges.

Yet there was also a sameness in the manner in which he behaved and enjoyed himself abroad: he was, after all, 'Borges'. His itineraries were organised for him, he was led and guided – by Kodama, and by friends in every country he visited – and, in his own way, he absorbed much. But he saw nothing: his voyage through the modern world was entirely passive, and relatively uneventful.

The best record of his reactions to places is to be found in *Atlas*, a photographic album of Borges's travels from the late 1970s until 1984, first published in that year in Buenos Aires, and then in 1986, after his death, both in Barcelona and in an English edition. It consists of short texts evoking a city, a street corner, a hotel, a monument.

'María Kodama and I have shared the joy and surprise,' he wrote in the introduction, 'of finding sounds, languages, twilights, cities, gardens and people, all of them distinctly different and unique. These pages would wish to be monuments to that long adventure which still goes on.'[3]

In March 1972, Borges was back in the United States. He was accompanied by Donald Yates, one of his original North American translators who had spent some time in Buenos Aires before di Giovanni's arrival. At the University of Michigan, Borges was awarded another doctorate *honoris causa*, one year after his Oxford laurels, the second of numerous such doctorates bestowed on him by universities across the world in the decade ahead (see Appendix Two).

At the end of 1972, Perón returned for a brief visit to Argentina. In the following year, the country had three presidents: Hector Cámpora, Raúl Lastiri, and finally, winning the general election in September 1973 with sixty per cent of the vote, Juan Domingo Perón.

Throughout his eighteen years of exile, at least half of them spent in Franco's Spain, Perón had kept his political contacts in Argentina warm, and his supporters had long anticipated his 'restoration'. By the time a succession of *juntas* following that of Juan Carlos Onganía (1966–70) had led the country into almost complete anarchy, all with varying degrees of hardline military backing, Perón was thought by what remained of the government in 1973 to be the only answer.

The violent suppression in May 1969 of the *cordobazo*, a huge strike and riot in the city of Córdoba resembling the Paris student riots of 1968, had effectively brought the right-wing military to power in 1970. As that regime, under two presidents – Roberto Levingston and Alejandro Lanusse – became more and more repressive, the activities of underground terrorist groups, above all the neo-Peronist Montoneros and the non-Peronist ERP (an armed Trotskyite group operating mainly in Córdoba), grew more ruthless. The guerrillas' first spectacular assassination was that of former President Pedro Aramburu, in June of 1970.

Revenge-murder politics soon poisoned the country (though this was but a prelude to what followed after 1976). For many, the return of Perón was a godsend. His hopes and aims could be harnessed to any apparently just political cause. As one historian put it, 'Peronism, in its new polymorphous guise, was suddenly all things to all men, an almost perfect prototype of Latin American populism. Perón's name now evoked multifarious associations and expectations.'[4]

For Borges, of course, the 'new' Perón was the last straw. He resigned from the National Library a month before Perón took up office again on 17 October, twenty-eight years to the day since he had been acclaimed by thousands in the plaza de Mayo in 1945. Borges was not going to allow the revamped Perón to impinge in any way on his professional life, as Perón's municipal toadies had in 1946. He therefore ducked out of view and, by December 1973, was making his first trip to Mexico, where he had been awarded the Alfonso Reyes Prize.

On 10 December, *Newsweek* published an interview with Borges. It was one of the most outspoken he had ever given. Asked if he felt threatened by the new regime, he answered:

Not at all. I've had no contact with the government. They know that if they hurt me it would cause an international uproar. And I've helped them. I made the world more aware of Argentina, and by resigning my post as director of the National Library . . . I spared them the embarrassment of firing me. I felt resigning was the honourable thing to do.

He went on: 'Perón is a second-rater. He's nothing special, nothing substantial. When he dies it will be as if nothing had happened. He will have no effect on the country.'

In that last statement, Borges was unfortunately quite wrong. Perón's legacy from 1946 to 1955 was deep and abiding, as the popular desire in the early 1970s for his return made very evident. Today, in spite of attempts by the generals to dismantle the creed in the late 1970s and then, conversely, by the return of democracy in the mid-1980s, Peronism has not gone away.[5]

In his *Newsweek* interview, Borges reserved his sharpest insults for the dictator's new wife, María Estela Martínez de Perón, 'Isabel' as she was known. Asked what he thought of her, Borges managed also to raise the ghost of the first Señra Perón (Isabel was Perón's vice-president): 'A poor substitute for Eva. A streetwalker too. The first one died, poor thing, so they said we'll have to find a replacement. Streetwalkers are easy to replace.'[6]

This kind of attack was typical of Borges's behaviour towards the governments of the mid-1970s; he took any opportunity he was offered to attack the regime, both Perón's and that of his successor, Isabel. The immediate upshot was that he and Leonor began to receive threats. On one occasion, Leonor answered the phone, and the caller announced he was going to come and kill her. She gave him the Maipú address, and told him to hurry up, as she was an old woman of ninety-eight, and would not last long. On another occasion, a bomb was placed outside the door of the Borges' building but failed to go off. 'Look how cowardly they are,' the 74-year-old Borges told an interviewer, 'putting a bomb here. It would be easy enough to come up and attack me head-on. I always have my knife, don't I?'[7]

Two deaths directly affected Borges in 1974. Perón died on 1 July; for Borges it was thirty years too late, yet for Argentina something of a disaster. What vestiges of order Perón's position as head of state had permitted now completely disintegrated. Under Isabel, guerrilla kidnappings and assassinations became a way of life; by 1975, a Gestapo-like organisation called the 'Triple A' (Alianza Argentina Anticomunista) was murdering fifty left-wingers a week. The era of the *desaparecidos* – the 'disappeared' – had begun in earnest.

The death of a small child in this atmosphere would appear to be a minor statistic. But in November 1974, Luis de Torre's five-year-old daughter, Angélica – Borges's great-niece – drowned. Borges responded with a poem which he included in his collection of poems of the following year, *La rosa profunda* (The Unending Rose).

'How many possible lives must have gone out/ in this so modest and diminutive death?' the poem opens. Lamenting the loss of an innocent child in a touching sonnet, Borges's focus was on a family tragedy, though ironically in line twelve he calls his country 'brave'; he was of course referring to an older Argentina. The last line, however, is unwittingly closer to the mark: 'Over us looms atrocious history.'[8]

Published by Emecé in August 1975, *La rosa profunda* was Borges's third book since *Doctor Brodie's Report*. The first was a book of poems and short prose pieces, called *El oro de los tigres* (The Gold of the Tigers). The second was Emecé's one-volume *Obras completas*, published in July 1974, containing all of Borges's poetry from *Fervor de Buenos Aires* to *El oro de los tigres* – with many omissions from, and much editing of, the pre-1960s volumes – and all his prose (though no previously uncollected journalism) from *Evaristo Carriego* to *Brodie*. (The works in collaboration were kept back for a separate volume, published in 1979.)

The book was an immediate success, and quickly sold out; queues formed outside several Buenos Aires bookshops where it had gone on sale, and in a number where Borges had agreed to sign copies – by then he would sign anything, his nose right up against the frontispiece, the signature a weird scrawl. If people until now had thought Borges studiously unprolific, the 1,200-page *Obras completas* was proof that, with one or two fallow patches, the great *porteño* scribe had not stopped writing for a solid fifty years.

Sections of *El oro de los tigres* and *La rosa profunda* were translated into English by Alastair Reid and published as the second part of Allen Lane's 1979 volume of stories, *The Book of Sand*:* the stories first appeared in Buenos Aires in March 1975 as *El libro de arena*. These thirteen prose texts all dated from after 1970 – in other words they were all post-*Brodie* – and only one, the longest, called 'El Congreso' ('The Congress'), had seen the light of day, having been published in a slim volume as a collector's item in 1971. Much of 1974 would have been spent preparing the book for Emecé.

The Book of Sand was Borges's last book of fictions. Four further stories were added to the canon by the time of his death, collected in two volumes – *Rosa y azul* and *25 agosto y otros cuentos* – and read somewhat like afterthoughts. Neither book was published by Emecé; by contrast, the firm printed 40,000 copies of *The Book of Sand*, which sold out in two months. In pure sales terms, it was Borges's greatest success in his lifetime – he had come a long way from those thirty-seven copies of *Historia de la eternidad* sold in 1936.

As a book, however, *Sand* is patchy and, though I hesitate to coin the phrase, sub-Borgesian: that is, Borges well below par, keener

* The stories were translated into English by di Giovanni.

to be the Homeric fabulist the world expected him to be than determined, under his old aggressive aesthetic, to innovate and amaze. Most of the tales are more openly fantastic than any fiction he had written since the 1950s. One such is 'El otro' ('The Other'), where in 1969 the elderly Borges meets his young, Genevan self in Cambridge, Massachusetts; another is the title story, about a book whose contents are kinetic and whose pages are infinite – perhaps the most 'Borges-like' of all the stories in the volume.

In 'Undr' and 'La Secta de los Treinta' ('The Sect of the Thirty'), he used his well-tested technique of relating a mystery by means of so-called scholarly presentations of a manuscript – in the case of 'Undr', from the Bodleian Library. 'The Congress', at twenty pages long by far the most extended fiction Borges had penned since the 1940s, is a bibliophile fantasy, about a secret society that, in order to store up all knowledge, collects books from all over the world, which are then ordered to be destroyed in a conflagration. Borges thought highly of the piece, and included in it a rather breathy scene of sexual congress (the pun intended) between the narrator, Alejandro Ferri, and a woman, Beatriz Frost, he meets in London. By the standards of mid-1970s fiction, however, Borges's presentation of sex here was predictably tame.

'The Congress', while absorbing, really reads like an urbane re-rendering of 'The Library of Babel'. One feels here and throughout much of *The Book of Sand* that Borges is taking us nowhere new. In 'El espejo y la máscara' ('The Mirror and the Mask'), 'Undr' and 'El disco' ('The Disk'), he uses settings inspired by his interest in old Nordic and Anglo-Saxon culture and legends. At times in *Sand*, Borges stuck a note reminiscent of those kitsch Dark Age sagas with comic-book covers: horses in the mist framed by Celtic tracery. '"The king is no longer called Gunnlaug," he said. "His name is now another. Tell me about your travels"' (from 'Undr', meaning 'wonder').[9]

More striking in *Sand* is the one and only love story in Borges's entire output. 'Ulrike' ('Ulrica' in the original Spanish) is really a fantasy, too, set in the north of England, about a tryst between a Norwegian woman and a Colombian man, Javier Otálora. Nothing happens, other than the build-up to their union – which occurs in the story's veiled and exalted last sentence. Their love seems to echo a pattern in legend, and thus they call each other Byrnhild and Sigurd, from the Norse *Saga of the Volsungs*. The story is clearly a tribute to María Kodama.

Inevitably, much speculation has been raised over the nature of her and Borges's love life; no concrete conclusions can be arrived at – it is impossible to know if they had physical relations, other than by asking María Kodama directly. From the evidence in 'The Congress' and 'Ulrike', Borges had finally, in old age, admitted into his mind the possibility of writing about sexual experience, and the regular company of a much younger woman cannot have been a hindrance to this admission. However, given what we know of Borges's tortured amorous history, and his age when he and Kodama were together (to say nothing of hers), it is improbable that normal sexual relations existed between them. As Borges writes of the Norwegian in 'Ulrike', who has imposed certain conditions for their one night together, 'To a bachelor well along in years, the offer of love is a gift no longer expected'.[10]

It was Borges's way of saying that an old man must abide by what the younger party feels is right for her. The flowering of his love for Kodama contained a mix of tenderness, romance, companionship and dependency. The fact that he could not see her naturally led to fantastic imaginings about her, and – because his métier was telling stories – to giving her some fictional shape; Ulrike and Beatriz are versions of María Kodama. In life, however, Borges and María's relationship has to have been asexual.

Four months after the appearance of *The Book of Sand*, Leonor died, on 8 July 1975. Because she was Borges's mother, she was almost as famous as her son. The obituaries were many and detailed, and some papers tastelessly ran a two-month-old photograph taken of her in bed on her ninety-ninth birthday, enfeebled and withered, with an awkward Borges standing next to her.

Rodríguez Monegal recorded Borges's memories of Leonor's final days: 'he began telling me about her agony, how she pleaded for months with God to be spared the pain; how she addressed her long-deceased mother and father, begging them to ease her out of life; how she also called on Father [Jorge]; how finally she begged the maid to come and throw her into the garbage can. For the last two years her moaning and her cries could be overheard even over the phone. When the end came, she was reduced almost to bare bones, held together by only a film of parched skin, like a mummified image of herself.'[11]

The funeral took place in the Recoleta, and from this sombre occasion another notorious image emerged in the press: one of Borges crying.

Amongst the countless hundreds of photographs of Borges taken from the 1960s on, this is perhaps the only real glimpse we have of 'Georgie' – the genuinely vulnerable man who yet set such store by emotional self-control. In mourning his mother's passing, he was also counting the cost of the long life he had spent with her. As he wrote in a famous poem published in *La Nación* soon after the funeral, 'I have committed the worst sin/That a man can commit. I have not been happy.'[12]

Borges's final decade was spent trying to put that situation to rights. He did not give up writing, but as the safe terrain of *The Book of Sand* showed, he really felt no need to go anywhere new, either in his mind or on paper. The real world – of aeroplanes, international conferences, fees and royalties – was still relatively fresh to him. Blind and out of touch as he was, and perhaps taking up a final position of glorious contradiction, he decided to look at the world not as a labyrinth, not as an infinite representation of self-defeating perplexity, but as an object, full of people and voices and languages and countries. He was also in love. In so far as he could, he was determined to enjoy the hubbub, as well as the novelty of a woman's prolonged attentions.

After *La rosa profunda* and a book of selected forewords, both appearing in 1975, Borges published four further books of new poems, and three collections of essays.* The essays were drawn mainly from old articles and lectures, and belong strictly to the domain of literary criticism. His poetry was now a pastime, full of memories and nostalgia, and of reflective portraits of writers ancient and modern; its tone veered between philosophic serenity and fanciful mythmaking. Much of it was *about* precisely that: Borges the Blind Sage – Homer, Milton, Groussac, Joyce – making

---

* *La moneda de hierro* (The Iron Coin) (1976), *Historia de la noche* (History of the Night) (1977), *La cifra* (The Code) (1981) and *Los conjurados* (The Conspirators) (1985); the essays were *Borges, oral* (Borges, Orally) (1979), *Siete noches* (*Seven Nights* – see Bibliography for the English edition) (1980) and *Nueve ensayos dantescos* (Nine Dantesque Essays) (1982).

verses to pass the time. It was all distinctively Borgesian, and very often dull.

For Borges, the 1970s were really about one thing: how to remain intact as 'Borges', in a climate at home in which he might have been better off had he been the nervous and unknown figure of the 1930s and 1940s – though of course, like so many intellectuals under the generals after 1976, he probably would not have survived the onslaught of repression. Borges was quite right in 1973 when he said that no Argentine government would dare harm him – the most famous man in the country – for fear of worldwide repercussions.

Still, his high profile was a liability. When Isabel Perón was toppled in March 1976 by the military, Borges publicly welcomed her successors. He had lunch with the new leader, General Videla, declaring afterwards his *junta* to be gentlemen. He was vilified by the left everywhere for this open support of the new dictator and his henchman, vilification which only intensified when towards the end of the year he went to Chile to meet General Pinochet, and accepted an award from Argentina's neighbouring *generalísimo*: the Grand Cross of the Order of Bernardo O'Higgins.

It was a gross miscalculation. In Madrid – whose population was enjoying its first taste of life after fascism (Franco had died a year before) – a Borges *Festschrift* publication organised by the magazine *Cuadernos Hispanoamericanos* was immediately cancelled and held back for another *sixteen* years. In Stockholm, it seems the decision was taken not to award Borges the Nobel Prize.

Borges and the Nobel had long been a burning issue. The *Corriere della Serra* in Italy had conducted a worldwide survey in October 1970, which found that Borges won more votes for that year's prize than the eventual winner, Alexander Solzhenitsyn. In 1972, when calls for Perón's return had reached fever pitch in Argentina, Borges, in exasperation, let himself be interviewed by María Esther Vázquez for *La Nación*.[13] There, praising Europe's political enlightenment and lamenting Argentina's backwardness, he let slip his view that the country's forebears were 'wise to use the remnants of black slaves as cannon-fodder, that it was a historical achievement to have rid the country of its native Indians, and it was only to be regretted that the seeds of ignorance had survived to allow for the growth of Peronism'.[14]

His comments about Peronism were par for the course at the time, and simply encouraged those anonymous death threats noted earlier. His apparent racism was quite another matter, and has ever since been cited, along with his later gaffes, as legitimate justification for his being denied the Nobel laurels. Year after year it was asked why Borges did not win, in spite of repeated nominations; and year after year, it was assumed that it was his politics which failed him at the last post. The issue still burns today, though now, ironically, the criticism has turned on the Nobel committee for having made such a historic error in bypassing the Argentine master.

Borges eventually understood that Videla's regime was ruining the country. Thus he got himself into new trouble when he criticised Videla's plans to go to war over Chile's possession of a tiny clutch of islands in the Beagle Channel in 1978. 'How long must we put up with Borges spreading chaos and deprecating everything the people love, and now he is a convinced and confessed anti-Argentine?' roared the mass-market paper *Crónica*.[15]

Over Argentina's invasion of slightly larger islands in the South Atlantic just under four years later, Borges – who was in America at the time – despaired, of Galtieri's rashness certainly, but he wasn't inclined to condone Thatcher's Task Force either.

Still, the Falklands conflict engendered one of his great images – 'two bald old men fighting over a comb'[16] – and a poem, 'Juan López y John Ward', published in an English translation in *The Times* in September 1982. Alongside a photograph of Borges ran a short statement, which ended, '. . . it seems to me an excellent opportunity to say in England that not all of us Argentines are demented. We are not accomplices.'[17]

Borges had little else to say about the war, or indeed about Argentina's defeat. His readiness to participate in a BBC documentary on his work made later that year in Buenos Aires and Uruguay indicated that the anti-British sentiment still at large in Argentina had not swayed him. One very old friend in Buenos Aires never forgave him his 'neutrality', protesting to me in 1994 that Borges had effectively deserted his country in its hour of need. In October 1983, before the democratic elections which brought Raúl Alfonsín to power were held, he told Nicholas Shakespeare in London:

The people were so easily taken in by propaganda, by television, by loud politicians, and made into a shouting mob. Now they have other fish to fry with the elections, which will give a semblance of freedom at least. If we're lucky, we'll get the radicals instead of the Peronists. They're not too bright but they're honest and they mean well. I hate politics. I'm a mild, stay-at-home anarchist and pacifist, a harmless disciple of Herbert Spencer.[18]

To the end, after so many years of political ineptness and caprice, Borges never really changed his tune.

Apart from hours spent in the company of María Kodama and his cat Beppo, the other major pleasure for Borges throughout the 1970s was his friendship with Adolfo Bioy Casares. Their dinners together at calle Posadas continued on a regular basis, and Bustos Domecq was back to his old tricks again by the middle of the decade. Light-hearted collaboration with Bioy must have been a relief for Borges after the rounds of interviews, the ceaseless travel, and the hostility in the very air of Buenos Aires. Their last book together, *Nuevas crónicas de Bustos Domecq*, appeared in 1977.

Bioy remained loyal to Borges until his death, and after. Towards the turn of the decade, however, he found himself slowly but perceptibly distanced from Georgie. Borges's travels and María Kodama had a lot to do with this. A new band of younger, foreign acolytes – amongst them Jean-Pierre Bernès, former French cultural attaché in Buenos Aires, and Franco Maria Ricci, a wealthy Milan publisher – were increasingly prominent in the writer's life, especially as Borges had become such a central and fashionable figure in modern French and Italian letters. In the late 1970s and early 1980s, Borges was frequently in both France and Italy, being consulted by these men and others on the passage of new books as well as his complete works into each language. It was an enormously time-consuming process.

In Buenos Aires, there would be just time enough to rest before planning the next voyage with María Kodama, and probably not as much time as Silvina and Bioy would have liked to catch up with the itinerant Georgie. María was proud of her independence, and chose never to live with Borges. He would not have countenanced that anyway unless she married him, and, though he wanted to, she did not, and he respected her decision.[19] Bioy, meanwhile, no doubt felt that back from his travels Borges *could* afford to see more of him. To this day, there was and is no love lost between Borges's oldest friend and his widow.

Vlady Kociancich, who had known Borges well since the late 1950s and is an intimate friend of Bioy's, was in as good a position as anyone to observe relations between the two men. While having little to say on María Kodama's role, she noticed how jealous Georgie could be:

> Bioy and I began to meet outside the dinner hour, away from the house on calle Posadas and from the presence of Borges. For some years, I thus was accustomed to have tea with Bioy, and to dine with Borges. Borges did not greatly like this change. He was a very possessive friend. It was then, I think, that Borges stopped calling Bioy 'Adolfito' . . . To me the diminutive seemed somewhat ridiculous and above all I thought it shored up this false image of Bioy as the *simpático* dandy, the most delightful of Borges's friends. So I called him plain 'Bioy'. Borges dropped the 'Adolfito' from our conversation and asked: 'So what news of Bioy? You, of course, see him more than I do' – although they had dined together the night before.[20]

Recalling the 1960s, Kociancich was also a witness to Borges's preferred form of socialising, and remembers a famous café, the Saint James, now demolished, which he used to patronise:

> In the 1960s, the Saint James was a meeting-place for mature writers, not students. It was a big, elegant *confitería*, neutral, tranquil, with plenty of businessmen going there in the afternoons, and women taking tea. It was a meeting-place of some ceremony.
>
> Borges was very sociable. He gave the impression of being aloof, but he was always with friends. Bioy was different; he didn't like the literary life. Borges liked it, because he liked to talk. Once a month, in the *Prensa* circle, Peyrou, the Dabove brothers, and maybe one or two writers more used to meet. And to the great scandal of the others, Borges would invite me or María Esther Vázquez. The presence of a woman civilised

the conversation. Some meetings were in the Café Richmond, on calle Florida, and also at the Saint James, or the Querandí near the National Library.[21]

By the Kodama era, all of this was over, not least because so many of Borges's oldest friends were now dead. From the 1930s, only Bioy and José Bianco remained.

So how alone after 1980 was Borges? The answer seems to revolve around perceptions of María's hold on his heart. About this, Bioy is unequivocal: 'Borges used to say that when he was with her, he wished she were elsewhere; when he was without her, he wished she would come. "Without María, I wish she would come; with María, I wish she would go." It was a strange relationship – not peaceful.'[22]

Alicia Jurado remembers a tenderer episode from the early 1980s: 'One day, Borges and I were lunching in the Hotel Dora, opposite his house. I asked him, "Do you think you are in love with María?" and he blushed, and laughed like a schoolboy – he didn't say yes, and he didn't say no. He blushed – and there he was, at eighty-something . . .'.[23]

When asked about the discrepancy between their ages, María Kodama remains clear about her position during her time with Borges:

It is very important to know that we were both very independent people. I could not have supported being wrapped in him as if by an octopus, and nor he. From time to time, we must have had our possessive moments, and we had a joke: '*Octopus dixit*' [Octopus spoke]. Neither he nor I could be the octopus; there had to be a beautiful relationship, one which should exist between two people who love each other: respect for freedom, and sharing everything, and never to lie.[24]

Borges had rarely been ill throughout his life. In 1978, he underwent surgery on his prostate gland in Buenos Aires, though he insisted on only a local anaesthetic. He apparently astonished his surgeons by explaining to them the etymology of the word '*quirófano*', the Spanish for 'operating theatre'. Latterly, he was also diabetic, which might account for how much thinner he became in old age, though María Esther Vázquez says firmly this was because he ate less.[25]

On his eighty-second birthday, on 24 August 1981, he stated 'I need to live, at least, one year more'.[26] That was the year of his last published short story, 'La memoria de Shakespeare' ('Shakespeare's Memory' – as it became in di Giovanni's translation, which first appeared in *The Times*, then in a volume called *Winter's Tales 2*, published in London by Constable in 1986). Old as he was, Borges was still dreaming hard: 'Shakespeare's Memory' was based on a dream he had had, in which he bought the very same – Shakespeare's memory.

International honours continued to flood in. In 1980, Borges received the Cervantes Prize in Spain, handed to him by King Juan Carlos; in 1981, Italy's President, Sandro Pertini, delivered to Borges the Balzan Prize; in 1983, France's President Mitterrand made him a Commandeur de la Légion d'honneur. In 1984, on Borges's eighty-fifth birthday, Franco Maria Ricci presented him with eighty-five gold sovereigns, one for each year of his life.

In spite of all this adulation, by mid-1985 Borges knew there was not much life left for him. His beloved Beppo had died the year before – apart from Bioy and María, the cat was the last of his intimate friends to go. Disillusioned with Raúl Alfonsín's government, and knowing his time was near, Borges made one final contradictory decision: his family's remains lay in the Recoleta, and, too experienced in the tricks of time, he felt no fear about the inevitable: but he was not, to everyone's exasperation, going to die in Buenos Aires.

When he left the city for a tour of Italy in November 1985 with María Kodama, only she, his doctor and of course Borges himself knew he had cancer of the liver. The prognosis was bleak: the condition was incurable, and the progress of the cancer was likely to be fast. For someone of robust constitution, death might have been a few years off. For someone of Borges's frailty and age, it might come very fast.

Italy in early winter was Borges's last pleasure. By January of 1986, he was in hospital in Geneva, the city he had chosen to die in. He felt safe in Switzerland, away from the glare of media intrusion that would have been his lot in Buenos Aires. The country had an order and a history, in time and of course within his own lifetime, in which he felt comfortable.

His decision to go to Geneva was not sudden; he had visited the city many times in recent years. Ending up there in what he knew would be the year of his death was the culmination of a profound need, not a whim. For Borges it was natural to want to die in a place which, in his memory – perhaps the most compelling criterion for a man whose entire life had been lived through memory – was as much home to him as Buenos Aires. As he wrote in the short meditation that closes the last book published in his lifetime, '*Los cantones ahora son veintidos. El de Ginebra, el último, es una de mis patrias*', 'Today the cantons number twenty-two. That of Geneva, the last one, is one of my homelands'.[27]

Borges survived another six months. In his absence from Buenos Aires, mutterings in the press about María Kodama's status, and what would happen to her, and more significantly to Borges's rights, after his death, could not fail to reach the couple. They were staying at the Hôtel l'Arbalète, at 3 rue Maîtresse, not far from the Rhône on the edge of the Old City. It was a half-world existence. Friends came by, people who were not known to the writer asked constantly after his health, doctors – including Borges's old friend Simon Jichlinski's son – were in attendance, and his French editor Jean-Pierre Bernès recorded hours of conservation. (One day, Bernès's tapes will be used to tell another version of Borges's life.)

The writer and critic Jaime Alazraki visited Borges in the hotel in late May 1986:

> Borges was sitting on a chair, meticulously dressed, tie and suit, facing the door. I sat next to him, very close to his right side. His voice sounded husky and punctured with muffled blanks. It was very hard to follow his speech. At times, he had to repeat the same sentence a couple of times before I was able to understand. More disquieting still was the shape his head had taken . . . The Borges I was sitting next to in Geneva . . . was . . . a physical ruin. His head was deformed, as if the frontal bone had grown beyond proportion and was threatening to tear the skin through. It was not so much the ravages of time as the onslaught of disease, as if his mind kept growing while his body decayed.[28]

Then, on 24 April 1986, Borges got married, for the second time, to the young woman he had known for about twenty years, and who had been his constant companion for the past few.

It was a controversial affair. Divorce did not exist in Argentine law, only official separation; technically, Borges was still married to Elsa Astete Millán. Were he to marry again without legal annulment of his first contract, Borges would be committing bigamy. Application for a marriage licence was therefore made through an agency specialising in obtaining the appropriate legal sanction from Paraguay or Uruguay. In both countries, divorce was permitted, and in Paraguayan law wedlock in such circumstances would be permitted.

The licence, after some complications, was granted. It was issued in an obscure town in the Paraguayan Chaco, three hundred kilometres from the capital Asunción, called Rojas Silva. The fact that neither partner was physically present seems not to have worried the town's authorities at the time; that there was no mention of the marriage in the records at the Paraguayan Consulate in Geneva seems stranger. The legality, in the strictest sense, of the marriage has ever since been the subject of generally hostile press examination: to no effect.[29]

Jorge Luis Borges died eight weeks after his marriage, on the morning of Saturday 14 June 1986. By this date, María Kodama, with the help of Borges's Spanish publisher, had found an apartment nearby, where for a brief period the writer and his 40-year-old spouse had enjoyed some domestic privacy.

Borges had expressed no desire to be buried in Argentina and so, according to his instructions, and after some wrangling with the Swiss authorities, he was buried in the cemetery of Plainpalais, the cemetery 'des Rois' – 'of the Kings' – as it is known in Geneva. The funeral took place in the cathedral of Saint-Pierre, in the Old City of Borges's adolescence, where orations were given by both a Catholic and a Protestant priest. Though Borges had been an agnostic for all his life, according to Alazraki he had accepted absolution from the Catholic priest the night before his death.

The ceremony was attended by, amongst others, an Argentine who had appeared in early versions of films of Borges's stories and is now a writer living in Paris, Hector Bianciotti; the Belgian novelist Marguerite Yourcenar; the widow of Julio Cortázar; and Franco Maria Ricci. Borges was buried not far from the grave of John Calvin, next to a yew tree – '*if*' in French. Calvin and Kipling: Borges was in admired and – in the case of the author of Britain's perennially favourite poem – adored company.

Go to Plainpalais today, and on the map at the cemetery lodge you read the following: 'Borges Jorg-Luis 735 D/G6'. The front side of his gravestone carries the inscription '. . . AND NE FORHTEDON NĀ'; '. . . and should not be afraid'. The words are from the Anglo-Saxon poem, *The Battle of Maldon*. On the reverse side, there are two lines: 'HANN TEKR SVERTHIT GRAM/OK LEGGR I METHAL THEIRA BERT'; 'He takes the sword Gram, and lays it naked between them' – the Old Norse epigraph from *The Saga of the Volsungs* which heads the short story about María Kodama, 'Ulrike'. Beneath are the words 'DE ULRICA A JAVIER OTÁROLA', 'From Ulrike to Javier Otárola'.

The site and the tributes combined sound like an answer to Borges's last wish.

Jorge Luis Borges left behind him one of the great literary legacies of the twentieth century. In life, he was neither hero nor campaigner; he was a timid and in many ways conventional man.

In art, he produced work of a boldness that militantly refused to accept the conventions he had inherited. He embraced the Modernist habits of irony and formal self-consciousness, and yet managed in his great work of the 1940s to make a mockery of Modernism. He defied schools and categories, and in his unique prose united, usually with the lightest of touches, the literatures of centuries.

He effected a revolution in written Spanish which influenced a generation. In his profound understanding of the idiom of his Castilian ancestors – Góngora, Quevedo, Cervantes – and in his humility before masters of modern Spanish style – Reyes, Unamuno – he learnt to dignify a literature which until this century looked as though it were worn out. Borges also rediscovered the importance of the Jewish and Arab traditions in Hispanic literary culture; studies and appreciations of the Semitic strata of Borges's writings proliferate and will continue to do so.

He did not stop there. The enormous international reach of his intellectual appetite – through English, North American, French, German, Italian and Scandinavian literatures – brought a richness to the language and discourse of his continent that remains unrivalled. Borges lived for literature. He lived a life of the mind, some of whose obscurer pathways and corridors it has been possible in these pages to follow only speculatively. He was a master of concealment, and if in his stories if he had to choose between elucidation and enigma, he always settled triumphantly for the latter. He was a maker, not a doer; and of course the Spanish word he gave to his 1960 volume, '*hacedor*', meaning both maker and doer, would to the multilingual Borges have had a delightful ambiguity.

He spent the best part of his life reading, dreaming his dreams wide awake, and writing – which may be no more and no less than any writer should hope to achieve. George Steiner wrote of him in 1970: 'Had he produced no more than the "Ficciones", Borges would rank among the few fresh dreamers since Poe and Baudelaire. He has, that being the mark of a truly major artist, deepened the landscape of our memories.'[30]

If Borges can teach us anything today, a quarter of a century after that axiomatic observation was made, it is that the human imagination, that making capacity of the inner world, is still worth a lifetime's dedication.

Epilogue

Afterlife

In October 1995, María Kodama announced that fourteen biographers were at work on Borges. Of those, 'only eight have interviewed me, and I think only one is producing something that seems to me really interesting.'[1]

This biography is certainly one of the fourteen (one amongst a variety of languages); and this biographer has also interviewed the widow three times. However, my account is not the one singled out for her approval. A widow is inclined to light upon her voice of authority (Kodama has no interest in penning her own portrait), and rely on her instincts to obtain the desired result: the production of the right story.

The fruits of such an enterprise will emerge in due course, possibly before the end of the millennium. This is likely to include a major publication by Borges's French editor and literary companion in his final years in Buenos Aires, and then in Geneva, Jean-Pierre Bernès.

Bernès recorded hours of tape as Borges died in the Swiss city throughout the first six months of 1986, which may, incorporated into Bernès's book, provide new perspectives on Borges's life necessarily excluded from this account. Bernès and María Kodama are said to be close friends.

The natural timing for a definitive and authorised version of Borges's life would, then, be 1999, the centenary of his birth. Over the next few years, we can expect a flurry of biographies of this most intractable of figures, in addition to Bernès's

While I have attempted to probe as close to the heart of the matter of Borges as possible, I would never claim this book represents the whole truth – that needs at least ten years' work – nor have I sought authorisation: I would not have been granted it.

The problem with Borges, as with any writer whose fame has exceeded the frame of his mortal personality, is a problem of interpretation. In Borges's case, the problem is especially acute because of a messy situation left amongst friends and family after his death, and leading therefore to a host of conflicting claims over ownership.

Ownership at one level is straightforward. María Kodama is Borges's sole inheritor, and will control his copyrights in all languages, and in all parts of the world where Borges is published, read, adapted for film and in the media, quoted in print and so on, for the duration of her lifetime. As she is childless, the situation after Kodama's death is less clear: Borges's estate may pass for the set period of copyright – that is, until the year 2061 – into the hands of a trust. For the forseeable future, there is no question about the nature of Kodama's relationship with her late husband's works: financially, legally, textually, she is in charge.

At another level, ownership of a writer like Borges involves his readers and his critics. In a sense which would very much have met with his approval, Borges, 'first and foremost . . . a reader', is the sum of his interpretations: like Beckett, like Joyce, like Kafka, Borges has grown a multi-dimensional profile, arising from a plethora of international readings and analyses.

It was pointed out in the Foreword to this book that while Borges is known the world over, he cannot yet be understood in his entirety. In a purely textual sense, this is to deceive his readers. (See further comments on this in A Note on Texts Used and Bibliography.)

María Kodama has had a ten-year fight on her hands. Only recently has she solved the problem of the future publishing and promotion of Borges's work throughout the world, by appointing a New York literary agent noted for his toughness (see p.280). Immediately after Borges's death, she was very much alone, often attacked in the Argentine press, and surrounded, in Buenos Aires, by friends and associates of Borges's who, during the decade of his partnership with Kodama, felt cut off. She also seems to have been ill-served by earlier literary advisors.[2]

The problems began with Borges's will. He made one in 1979, in which he divided his possessions and money between Kodama and Fani, the calle Maipú servant. Just before departing for Europe in November 1985, Borges then altered the will, with the advice of a new lawyer, naming Kodama as sole inheritor, and leaving Fani something in the region of $2,000.

In late 1986 Fani contested this alteration, claiming through laywers – organised for her by her ally, María Esther Vázquez – that Borges had been subjected to undue pressure to change his mind. Kodama *'captó la voluntad'* of the writer, it was claimed:[3] literally, captured his will. In other words, it was alleged that Borges had been too infirm to oppose the recommendation that Kodama be elevated to the status of sole inheritor.

Fani lost the case, including the small amount left to her in Borges's revised will. Many have since commented that Borges was never over-fond of Fani – the least of her faults being that he disliked her cooking.[4] She was left embittered by the judgment against her, and even while the case was proceeding gave a frank interview to the Italian magazine *Oggi*, airing her grievances about the effects of Kodama on the writer's last years.[5]

Then there was Norah's family. Agèd (now ninety-three), frail, and barely able to speak when I met her in 1993, Norah's interests were represented by her elder son Luis, a lawyer. A small provision was made for Norah in the 1985 will; however, both de Torre brothers, Luis and Miguel, were dissatisfied with the manner in which their uncle had got married in April 1986 and challenged the status of Kodama as Borges's legal widow.

Like Fani's, their case was dismissed. Further claims made by direct members of Borges's surviving family on his inheritance – and by implication over his copyrights – were put paid to, once and for all. In the case of Borges's nephews, such justice seemed particularly appropriate. In 1979, Luis with Miguel's connivance took funds from a bank account of Borges's to finance a property deal; Borges found out about this only when the bank rang to check whether he had intended to empty his account. Though he continued to see Norah, and was fond of her until the last, he never met either nephew again.

The claims of ownership: the issue of who should handle Borges posthumously has cropped up over and over again in the last decade. Technically, there should never have been any doubts; Fani met her Waterloo, as did Luis and Miguel de Torre. Having secured her legal position and seen off her (if not precisely Borges's) enemies, Kodama was finally able to announce in 1989 the setting-up of the Fundación Jorge Luis Borges.

This is based in a house at calle Anchorena 1660, next to the one Borges lived in with his family in the late 1930s. Kodama lighted upon it, after some difficulty and indecision, in 1994. She bought it, renovated it, and opened it in the spring of 1995. It contains Borges's library, photographs, various ornaments and objects belonging to the writer, as well as a database for use by students and researchers.

Carping about this institution, *because* it is run by Kodama, and resentment amongst Borges's few surviving friends over Kodama herself, are unlikely to abate in the immediate future. One legitimate concern is the nature of her intellectual hold on Borges's work: her partnership with Borges took root long after he was past his literary prime. Kodama had and has no editorial experience. She does not share a deep past with Borges the *writer*. Adolfo Bioy Casares alone can claim that today.

Moreover, the loose and haphazard manner in which Borges wrote and dispatched his texts (in the days of the great fiction and essays, invariably to magazines first), and then dealt with his publishers – principally Emecé – has long had a disabling effect on access to an editorially integral output. An agent, ideally a native Spanish-speaking one, is what Borges needed from the 1970s on; when di Giovanni left Buenos Aires in 1972, a vacuum in such matters appeared, and only recently has it been filled.

Leonor was already far too old in 1972 to help her son as she had for so many decades. Emir Rodríguez Monegal's premature death in 1982 deprived Borges of someone who could at least have advised with some academic rigour on the passage of his Spanish and English texts from manuscript to volume form. Carlos Frías, who also died prematurely – in 1991 – seems to have had limited understanding of the global publishing implications of Emecé's most distinguished writer.[6]

The foundation in Buenos Aires is unlikely to overcome these shortcomings. It cannot be a satisfactory repository for an integral Borges, for the main reason that it contains no manuscripts or letters. Because Borges had physically stopped writing long before he met Kodama, such manuscript material as does exist lies in the hands of private collectors who guard their treasure closely. Even if they are prepared to lend material for special purposes or exhibitions (as many did for a show at the Pompidou Centre in Paris in 1992, called 'L'Univers de Borges'), the last thing they will do is donate, let alone sell, it to María Kodama.

This is a vexed question. My own experience of the Borgesian letter-and-manuscript quest is not necessarily typical, but I believe it throws up some lessons. A brief account of it here will illustrate the enormous difficulties facing all researchers into Borges's life and work. Some aspects of it, I fear, resemble a Borges short story.

A first clue was given to me by Norman Thomas di Giovanni. Borges and Maurice Abramowicz, Borges's close friend in Geneva during the First World War, corresponded after the Borges family left Switzerland for Spain in 1919, and di Giovanni, who persuaded Borges to talk about Abramowicz in the 'Autobiographical Essay', emphasised that the letters, if accessible, would be worth seeing. I'm sure he was right. It also seemed a fair assumption (on my part) that any of Borges's letters to Abramowicz would, should they still exist, be in Switzerland.

I found myself in Basel in October 1993. I did not have time to visit Geneva, but naturally wondered whether Abramowicz might still be alive. He was not, but his wife, Isabella, was – I had looked up the name in the phone directory.

I rang Mrs Abramowicz in Geneva and asked her about the letters. In her reply, she sounded distressed. Apparently, María Kodama had paid her a visit after Abramowicz's death a few years previously, and taken the letters from her. I found this rather surprising. So on my first visit to Buenos Aires a few weeks after that conversation, I asked María Kodama during our first meeting whether she knew anything about the Abramowicz letters. She said yes, and she would like to have photocopies of them for use in the Foundation. She did not want them for herself; they should be available to those who were curious. They were quite numerous, she believed, and interesting from a literary point of view. As far as she knew, they were still in Geneva.[7]

In November 1995, I rang Mrs Abramowicz again. She sounded more frail, more distracted than she had during our first conversation. She had changed her number. She did not want to talk about Borges, or her husband, now (for her) long since dead. I asked if she could confirm the circumstances of the Borges-Abramowicz letters' disappearance. '*C'était pénible*,' she said. 'It was dreadful. Everything went when he died.'

Over the whereabouts of the Abramowicz letters, there thus remains a mystery.

Other manuscript material is scattered the world over. Kodama believes, for instance, that Donald Yates has some valuable material. Yates, it seems, decided to write a biography of Borges, and may have taken back with him to the States manuscripts the writer gave him. When I asked Kodama whether she had been in touch with Yates, she said she did not have his phone number.

In Mexico, meanwhile, some of Borges's correspondence with Alfonso Reyes in the 1920s is accessible in the Capilla Alfonsina. In Madrid's National Library the manuscript of 'El Aleph' is to be found, sold in May 1984 at Sotheby's, New York, by Estela Canto (to whom Borges gave the original) for $25,760 to the Spanish government. Borges's letters to her are in the San Telmo Collection in Buenos Aires: Jorge Helft purchased them in December 1994 at auction at Sotheby's.

Helft's collection also includes other letters, and Borges's notes for lectures;[8] I was able to see the Canto letters (thirteen out of the fourteen reproduced in Canto's book), just before Christmas 1994 in a hotel in Paris, where Helft picked them up after the auction and allowed me a private viewing – in his presence, of course.

In his San Telmo house in Buenos Aires a week or so earlier, however, in spite of great help provided over videos, first editions and other books, I was offered a view of photocopies only of the notebooks in his collection, and given typed print-outs of Borges's two 1944 letters to Elsa Astete Millán. I did not have a sense that I would be trusted with the real thing.

Less protective was Solange Sanguinetti, daughter of Carlos Ordóñez, the lawyer who helped Borges in his legal separation from Elsa in 1970. As a gift of thanks to Ordóñez, Borges handed over a box of manuscript material after the case was concluded – probably without knowing what it contained. On Ordóñez's death, his daughter inherited it.

Mrs Sanguinetti permitted me a viewing: along with notebook material similar to that which exists in Helft's collection, all of it unpublished, there were first drafts, in Leonor's hand, of items that went into *Dreamtigers*, and most fascinating of all, a neat, handwritten draft of 'Emma Zunz'.

It was not the first time I had seen Borges's handwriting, in the flesh so to speak. Alicia Jurado had shown me notes, in tiny, spidery, extraordinarily unsophisticated calligraphy, on Buddhism and related matters, which eventually made their way into her and Borges's collaborative text, *Qué es el budismo*, published in 1976. The calligraphy in Mrs Sanguinetti's collection was exactly the same; an educated guess would suggest that the bulk of the material in Borges's hand there dated from the 1940s, some possibly from the 1930s.

There is an essay on the pampa, and on what the word means. There is also amongst many quotations from other writers one from George Bernard Shaw: 'I liked sexual intercourse because of its amazing power of producing a celestial flood of emotion & exaltation of existence which, however momentary, gave me a sample of what one day may be the normal state of being for mankind in intellectual ecstasy.' If this were copied in about 1945, then without question it serves to illuminate further some of the thinking that lay behind 'The Aleph'.

Mrs Sanguinetti now has no interest in selling her manuscripts. She did approach María Kodama, who could not afford them. Kodama declined an offer of photocopies for the Foundation.

In Britain, meanwhile, the last act in my manuscript-quest proved the least edifying.

Mrs Sanguinetti gave me the name of a London collector who, she said, had some invaluable Borges manuscripts. She handed me his card before I left Argentina in December 1994, and in January 1995 I rang him. A man with a rather prim, upper-class voice answered. I explained who I was and what I had been told in Buenos Aires. Could he help?

To cut a long story short: he confirmed that he had some manuscripts, but rather than giving an answer to my main objective – to look at his material – proceeded to quiz me on every aspect of my book: my research, whom I had seen, where I had been, who the publisher was, what stage I was at, and so on. This continued for several weeks, until he finally said – in what must have been my sixth polite request as to the possibility of consulting, in all confidentiality, his Borges papers – that what he had was all 'in Germany'.

Feeling I had been led round a veritable garden of forking paths (and I had the suspicion that he would not have caught the allusion had I said so), I gave up. But not for good. Several months later, I tried again.

Two lengthy telephone conversations, during which I was once more subjected to a barrage of queries about what I was up to, resulted in a most eccentric suggestion: the publishers of my book would pay, would they not, for my being able to consult his material? Otherwise he couldn't see what was in it for him. Once his papers had been *seen*, what would they be worth?

Exactly the same as if they hadn't been seen, I presumed. I wasn't going to contaminate them, was I? In his mind, apparently, I was. I began to feel as if I were seeking some forbidden fruit, or an object with magical powers like the Aleph, perhaps a trinket from Tlön.

I attempted to explain that my researches had a purely literary motive, that I was a *bona fide* biographer who had only an increased understanding of my subject – Borges – in mind. I was a writer of limited resources. What he had in his possession was of potentially great value to the story of this major twentieth-century author's life and work (did it need saying?). I would, of course, guarantee him the strictest confidentiality and . . .

Stressing this in a variety of permutations in our last conversation, I knew my time was up.

In the end, I fear I might as well have been talking to one of those many non-Hispanic individuals who, after they have heard three words (I hope correctly pronounced) in answer to a cordial inquiry made about my current project – 'Jorge Luis Borges' – have asked: who?

Beyond the constrictions of legal copyright, I have come to believe that this state of affairs has a more deleterious effect than I could ever have anticipated on understanding a man who was, let it be remembered, always generous in facing the world's fascination in him.

Talking recently to the literary agent Deborah Owen, whose best-selling client Ellis Peters had just died, I found myself in sympathy with her assessment of what lay ahead: 'Do I want to have just an estate,' she mused, 'the mere business – counting the pennies – of a writer's output? You live for the writer, and after they've gone, it's just money and heartache.'

In Buenos Aires, in 1994, Borges's nephew, Luis de Torre, asked me for $200 to look up addresses for the Borges family in Spain from the 1920s. It was clear, perhaps belatedly, that the values dominating the name of this most ungrasping of writers are, even in the heart of his surviving family, those one associates more readily with a designer label.

Jorge Luis Borges would have been astonished.

Appendix One

Borges's Travels, 1972–1985

1972: United States: Durham, Houston, Michigan
1973: Spain; Mexico
1975: United States: Michigan
1976: Spain; United States: Maine, Cincinatti, Washington; Mexico; Chile; Spain; Italy
1977: Paris; Geneva; Italy; Greece; Paris; Spain
1978: Paris; Geneva; Egypt; Mexico; Colombia; Ecuador
1979: Paris; Germany; Iceland; Japan
1980: United States: New York, Chicago, Boston, Indiana; Spain; Paris; Italy; United States: New York; Spain
1981: Italy; Spain; United States: Harvard, New York; Puerto Rico; Italy; Mexico
1982: United States; Ireland; Germany; Geneva; Spain
1983: Paris; Britain; United States: Austin, Madison, Carlisle; Brazil; Spain; Geneva; United States: Chicago, New York, New Orleans
1984: Italy; Japan; Greece; Turkey; United States: New York; Puerto Rico; Paris; Spain; Portugal; Italy; Morocco; Portugal
1985: Italy; United States: Santa Barbara; Italy; Spain; Geneva

Appendix Two

National and International Awards, 1961–1986

❧

1961: Prix Formentor, Mallorca, Spain
1962: Commandeur de l'Ordre des Arts et Lettres, France
1963: Gran Premio del Fondo Nacional de las Artes, Argentina
       Doctorate *honoris causa*, Universidad de los Andes, Colombia
1965: KBE, Britain
       IXth Poetry Prize, City of Florence, Italy
       Orden del Sol, Peru
1966: IXth International Madonnina Prize, Comune of Milan, Italy
       Ingram Merrill Foundation Literary Prize, New York
1968: Honorary Member, American Academy of Arts and
          Sciences, Boston
       Order of Merit of the Republic of Italy
1970: Doctorate *honoris causa*, Oxford University, Britain
       Inter–American Literary Prize (Matarazzo Sobrinho), São
          Paulo, Brazil

1971: Doctorate *honoris causa*, Columbia University, New York
Jerusalem Prize, Israel
1972: Doctorate *honoris causa*, Michigan University, East Lansing
1973: 'Illustrious Citizen', Municipality of Buenos Aires
Alfonso Reyes Prize, Mexico
1976: Doctorate *honoris causa*, Cinicinnati University
Doctorate *honoris causa*, Universidad de Santiago, Chile
Order of Bernardo O'Higgins, Chile
'Club de los XIII' Prize, Buenos Aires
1977: Doctorate *honoris causa*, Sorbonne, Paris
Doctorate, Universidad de Tucumán, Argentina
1978: Golden Keys of the City of Bogotá, Colombia
1979: Gold Medal, Académie Française, Paris
Order of Merit, Federal Republic of Germany
Falcon Cross, Iceland
Canoabo de oro Prize, Republic of Santo Domingo
1980: Honorary Prize, Argentine Poetry Foundation, Buenos Aires
Cervantes Prize, Spain
La Sila Literature Prize, Spain
Cino del Duca Prize, Paris
1981: Balzan Prize, Italy
Member of French Academy of Moral and Political Sciences,
Paris
Ollin Yolitzi Prize, Mexico
Doctorate *honoris causa*, Harvard University, USA
Doctorate *honoris causa*, Universidad de Puerto Rico
1983: Commandeur de l'Ordre de la Légion d'honneur, Paris
Doctorates *honoris causa*, Texas and Madison Universities
Grand Cross of Alfonso X 'the Wise', Spain
T. S. Eliot Prize, Ingersoll Foundation, Chicago
1984: Doctorates *honoris causa*, Palermo, Venice and Rome Universities
Doctorate *honoris causa*, Tokyo University
Doctorate *honoris causa*, Crete University
Doctorate *honoris causa*, Universidad de San Juan
Knight of the Grand Cross of the Order of Merit of the
Republic of Italy
1986: Etruria Literature Prize, Volterra, Italy

Appendix Three

Films of or Based on Borges's Stories, and on Borges

Días del odio, based on 'Emma Zunz', by Leopoldo Torre Nilsson, 1954 (Argentina)

Hombre de la esquina rosada, based on 'Streetcorner Man', by Réné Mugica, 1957 (Argentina)

Borges, documentary by Luis Angel Bellalba, 1966 (Argentina)

Invasión, based on an original idea by Borges and Bioy Casares, by Hugo Santiago, 1968 (Argentina)

The Inner World of Jorge Luis Borges, documentary by Harold Mantell, 1969 (USA)

Borges, two-part documentary by André Camp and José María Berzosa, 1969 (France)

Emma Zunz, based on the story, by Alain Magrou, 1969 (France)

La strategia de la ragna (*The Spider's Stratagem*), based on 'The Theme of the Traitor and the Hero', by Bernardo Bertolucci, 1970 (Italy)

Les autres, based on an original script by Borges and Bioy Casares, by Hugo Santiago, 1974 (France)

Los orilleros, based on an original script by Borges and Bioy Casares, by Ricardo Luna, 1975 (Argentina)

El muerto cacique Bandeira, based on 'The Dead Man', by Hector Olivera, 1975 (Argentina)

Borges sobre Borges, documentary by Carlos Gdansky and Adolfo García Videla, 1975 (Argentina)

Borges para millones, documentary by Ricardo Wulicher and Bernardo Kamin, 1978 (Argentina)

Los paseos de Borges, documentary by Adolfo García Videla, 1980 (Argentina)

La intrusa, based on 'The Intruder', by Carlos Hugo Christiensen, 1980 (Brazil)

Borges and I, BBC 'Arena' documentary by David Wheatley, 1983 (UK)

Historia del guerrero y la cautiva, based on 'The Story of the Warrior and the Captive', by Edgardo Cozarinsky, 1992 (Argentina)

A Note on Texts Used

Throughout this biography, I have where possible referred to Borges's works in English. I say 'where possible' because it simply seemed incorrect to translate everything into English when far from everything has been translated. The titles of major works, such as Historia de la eternidad, *which has no English edition, have been translated on first mention in my text, but remain in Spanish thereafter; smaller works, both early and late, also remain in Spanish. In the case of works with editions in English, their first mention in the text is in Spanish, followed in brackets by the English title – which is what is used thereafter.*

Ten years after his death, Borges can still only be read in truncated form. There is no integral Borges; the text closest to this elusive goal exists, half-completed, in French. Jean-Pierre Bernès's Pléiade edition (*Oeuvres complètes*, Volume I, Gallimard, 1993) contains pretty well everything Borges wrote, including many of his articles, up to 1952 and *Otras inquisiciones* (*Other Inquisitions*). Its one drawback is that its selections are based on the Emecé 1974 *Obras completas*, overseen by Borges and stiffly edited on his behalf. Bernès has to some extent circumvented this by, for instance, reproducing as appendices poems and essays that belong to those first six books of Borges otherwise adulterated or suppressed completely by the writer while he was alive.

The Pléiade's Volume II is destined for publication in 1997. This will include substantial texts such as *El hacedor (Dreamtigers)*, *El informe de Brodie* (*Doctor Brodie's Report*), and *El libro de arena* (*The Book of Sand*), as well as all the smaller volumes of poetry and essays Borges wrote right up until his death in 1986 – in French of course, and no doubt accompanied by as much detailed and comprehensive textual and contextual analysis as Bernès has provided in Volume I. (One illuminating aspect of it will be the appearance there of Borges's correspondence with Jacobo Sureda: see Chapter Two.)

For those who read French, these are the volumes to turn to, at least to gain a working understanding of *what* Borges wrote. Volume I contains the best of Borges: all his fiction between 1935 and 1953, considered by many, including this biographer, to be the essential Borges. Whatever problems continue to linger over *how* to translate Borges, into any language, it is appropriate that the completest version of him is to be found in the language that first got him known outside Argentina.

In Spanish, the problems multiply with each successive volume, from *Fervor de Buenos Aires* through the following sixty years. The problems really begin with Borges himself. His habit of changing texts from edition to edition, of suppressing, or excising, sometimes re-introducing in modified form, words, phrases, lines – mainly in the poetry* – has landed any potential bibliographer with a lifetime's toil. A Borgesian joke of the highest order, it might be thought, recalling James Joyce's comment that he wrote in the way he did in order to keep the professors busy for centuries.

I haven't attempted even the shadow of such a task. The Bibliography that follows the Notes opens with a list (pp.304–5) of everything Borges published with Argentine, Mexican and Spanish houses, and will at least give as full an idea of his total output – in Spanish – as is currently possible. I have tried throughout my entire text to be bibliographically consistent, though

---

* See Penguin's *Selected Poems*, pp. 333–44, for a detailed account of the printing history of Borges's poetry until 1969.

the duplication of Borges's works in Spanish may have led to some inadvertent errors.

In the absence of a definitive edition of Borges in Spanish (again, see Bibliography for further details), I have used what is presently available: the Emecé *Obras completas* editions; that imprint's individual paperback editions; the Seix Barral paperback editions of the first books of essays; and editions of various – mainly later – works brought out by houses other than Emecé. All references, whether from Spanish, French or English sources, are itemised in the Notes.

In English, unfortunately, the problems deepen. Great services were rendered by Norman Thomas di Giovanni in disseminating Borges's works in the English-speaking world in the late 1960s. It is due largely to his work with Borges in Buenos Aires that English readers could capitalise on the disparate Borges made available through the translations in *Labyrinths*, first published in 1962 in America.

Because of copyright difficulties in that volume, however (see Chapter Nine, pp. 232–3), new attempts by di Giovanni at the stories in *Ficciones* were confined to just two of the *Labyrinths* texts, 'The Circular Ruins' and 'Death and the Compass'; both appeared in Jonathan Cape's 1971 *The Aleph and Other Stories*, which contained, amongst other pieces, those stories of the original Losada *El Aleph* (1949) which had not made it into *Labyrinths*: 'The Life of Tadeo Isidoro Cruz', 'The Other Death' and 'The Aleph'.

Added to the Cape volume were a very early and very short story, 'The Two Kings and Their Two Labyrinths' (first published in *El Hogar* on 16 June 1939), 'Ibn Hakkan al-Bokhari, Dead in His Labyrinth' (first published in *Sur* 202, August 1951) and 'El hombre en el umbral' ('The Man on the Threshold') (first published in *La Nación* on 20 April 1952), all of which were included in Losada's second edition of *El Aleph* (1952). In this volume 'La espera' ('The Waiting') (first published in *La Nación* on 27 August 1950) also appeared, the only story from this edition which was also translated for *Labyrinths*. Finally, two stories from this first great period (that is, until 1953), 'Examination of the Work of Herbert Quain' (first published in *Sur* 79, April 1941) and 'The South' (first published in *La Nación* on 8 February 1953), appeared in neither *Labyrinths* nor *The Aleph and Other Stories*; they could, however, be first read in English the Grove/Weidenfeld edition of *Ficciones* (1962), a volume that has now been reissued in the new Everyman's Library, published in 1993.

Di Giovanni and Borges's first collaboratively translated volume was *The Book of Imaginary Beings* (USA 1969, UK 1970). After *The Aleph and Other Stories*, containing the 'Autobiographical Essay', came *Selected Poems*, *A Universal History of Infamy*, *Doctor Brodie's Report*, *The Book of Sand*, *In Praise of Darkness*, two Bustos Domecq volumes and finally *Evaristo Carriego*. There, in the main, di Giovanni's work came to an end.

And there, indeed, Borges in English comes more or less to an end (though see Bibliography for English volumes not mentioned here). In New York, an attempt at Viking is being made to instigate a new, total translation of Borges into English, which in the normal course of events will then appear under the Viking/Penguin imprint in London.

It is shame enough not to have had for so long a uniform edition of Borges in his own language, one to which he gave new life, and which so inspired the writers of the Latin American 'boom' of the 1960s. In October 1995, a complete and new Borges in Spanish was put out to tender: through a newly appointed agent in New York, Andrew Wylie, María Kodama sought $1 million for the Spanish rights in her late husband's works from competing publishers in Spain and Buenos Aires. That deal has now been concluded, with the hardback licence going to Emecé in Buenos Aires and the paperback licence to Alianza in Madrid. In the meantime, is it too much to ask to have Borges properly accessible in the language he respected more than his mother tongue?

In both Spanish and English, it is a matter of the utmost urgency that clear and informed decisions be taken to make Borges easily readable and available, for general readers and students alike. The mess that confronts both groups at the moment can only keep the complete Borges at a distance.

This in turn leads to a view of him as a less cohesive writer than he actually is. The constituent parts of Borges – *porteño* Ultraist, radical fiction-maker, incisive critic, ruminative poet – make up a scintillating whole, and only the whole makes sense. As Borges himself pointed out in the 'Autobiographical Essay', speaking of his first creation, *Fervor de Buenos Aires*, 'I think I have never strayed beyond that book. I feel that all my subsequent writing has only developed themes first taken up there; I feel that all during my lifetime I have been rewriting that one book.'

A complete Borges, in English as in Spanish, will show to what extent that assertion holds true. Only with responsible publishing can that happen, and a full measure of Borges's world standing as a writer be addressed and debated, as already happens with those with whom he keeps company: Kafka, Faulkner, Joyce, Gide, Hesse, Beckett.

Hispanic and Anglo-Saxon editors and translators could, perhaps, learn something from their French counterparts. It is only fair to add that the Pléiade is a unique literary institution, allowing such comprehensive editing (as in Bernès's Volume I) for commercial and academic consumption. There is, as has been mentioned, some justice in the flowering of Borges's complete *oeuvre* (a word he disliked) in the language that led directly to his world renown. It is to be hoped that before the millennium is out, justice will also have been done in the two languages that were Borges's own.

Notes

Foreword

1. 'Tlön, Uqbar, Orbis Tertius', *Labyrinths*, p.30.
2. Quoted in *Borges: biografía total*, Marcos-Ricardo Barnatán, p. 221.
3. 'There is a rather shameful book of mine called *El tamaño de mi esperanza*. I have spent part of my life burning copies of that book. I've paid very high prices for them. When I am dead someone will dig up that book and say that it is the best thing I have written.' 'The Spanish Language in South America – A Literary Problem', talk given by Borges at Canning House, London, 19.2.63, *Diamante* XV, Hispanic & Luso-Hispanic Councils, p.10.
4. Foreword, *Selected Poems*, p.xiii.

Introduction

1. *The Western Canon*, Macmillan (London), 1994, pp.463–77.
2. The term maintained its art–historical function for years afterwards.
3. 'Borges's Fiction', *A Writer's Reality*, Mario Vargas Llosa, p.10.
4. 'The Author as Librarian', John Updike, *The New Yorker*, 30.10.65.
5. '"Se ha planteado un grave problema ético para el país, tanto con el terrorismo como la represión"', J. Iglesias Rouco, *La Prensa*, 6.5.80.
6. 'World View: Argentine repression deplored by writers', Arrigo Levi, *The Times*, 5.6.80.
7. *Conversations with Jorge Luis Borges*, Richard Burgin, p.22.
8. The writer Silvina Bullrich (see p.131) famously announced on Argentine television that Borges was impotent; in Buenos Aires in October 1993, Estela Canto told me she didn't know whether he was or not, as she had never had the opportunity to find out. Canto's book is occasionally exaggerated, but I believe largely accurate, in so far as her memory allowed her to be forty years after the events it describes. She provided irrefutable evidence of Borges's passion for her in reproducing the fourteen love letters he sent her (*Borges a contraluz* pp.123–54), which makes a chatty and anecdotal book one of the most authentic memoirs of Borges

in existence. See Chapter Six of this book for an account of the affair.
9. *Paper Tigers: The Ideal Fictions of Jorge Luis Borges*, John Sturrock, p.1.

Chapter One

1. The best explanation in English for the layman about the wars with, and waged by, Rosas, and who he was, can be found in *Selected Poems*, pp.310–13.
2. 'Lugones points out that the gaucho was a *mestizo*, in other words a mixture of the Indian and of the Spaniard or Portuguese ... He lived the life of a cow-man in the plains; and the Spaniard in him loathed the Indian, and vice versa – meaning that the gaucho formed a national type, a diverse Spanish and Indian type, and this is one of the things that explains why the war of independence was conducted in the main by Argentines, Venezuelans and Colombians – that's to say, by plainsmen and gauchos, people who differed from the Indian or the Spaniard *per se*.' 'El gaucho Martín Fierro', talk given by Borges at the Department of Spanish at Bristol University in February 1963, *Diamante* XV, p.17 (author's translation).
   Bernès has this description: 'Originally, the gaucho is the peasant breeder of the plains of Argentina, Uruguay and Rio Grande do Sul. In most cases, he is a mix of Spaniard and Indian, and an excellent horseman dedicated to the rearing of transhumance. In the era of the colonies, the term *gaucho* was pejorative, signifying "thief and assassin". With the wars of independence (1810–1816), during which the gaucho distinguished himself, the word acquired an honourable connotation ...'. (Bernès – see Note 39 of this chapter – p.1437.)
3. Such poems are many. They include 'Isidoro Acevedo' from *Cuaderno San Martín*, 'Conjectural Poem', 'A Page to Commemorate ... Victor at Junín', 'Allusion to the Death of Colonel Francisco Borges', 'The Borges' and 'Junín' from 'The Self and the Other', and 'Juan Crisóstomo Lafinur' from *La moneda de hierro*.
4. 'Autobiographical Essay', in *The Aleph and Other Stories*, p.204.
5. *Selected Poems*, p.326.
6. 'Essay', p.208.
7. *Selected Poems*, p.67.
8. 'Essay', p.204.
9. Interview, Elsa Rivero Haedo, Buenos Aires, 21.10.93.
10. *Entretiens avec Jorge Luis Borges*, Jean de Milleret, p.213.
11. Interview, Vlady Kociancich, Buenos Aires, 25.10.93.
12. *Veja* (Brazil), 26.8.70 (cited by Rodríguez Monegal – see Note 18 below – pp.11–12).

13. *Megáfono*, April 1934.
14. The account of Borges's early years in Jurado's book (see Note 22 below) is based largely on Leonor's memories, which could on occasion be fanciful. The image of Georgie hanging round Miss Tink's neck is one such – courtesy of a letter to me from Jurado of 20.12.95 – but at least it has the ring of maternal veracity.
15. 'Essay', p. 212.
16. ibid., p.213.
17. ibid., p.209.
18. *Jorge Luis Borges: A Literary Biography*, Emir Rodríguez Monegal, p.72.
19. Domingo Sarmiento (1811–88) was the first civilian president of Argentina (1868–74) after the adopted constitution of 1853. He was a vigorous opponent of Rosas, and spent many years in exile for his pains. His great work is *Civilización y barbarie: Vida de Juan Facundo Quiroga* (1845, published in English as *Life in the Argentine Republic in the Days of the Tyrants*, 1868). 'Part essay, part polemical pamphlet, part poem and part novel,' says Jason Wilson, '*Facundo* explains *gaucho* customs, and violence.' (*Traveller's Literary Guide to South & Central America*, p.443).
20. 'Essay', p.210.
21. *Diálogo con Borges*, Victoria Ocampo, p.40.
22. *Genio y figura de Jorge Luis Borges*, Alicia Jurado, p.26.
23. 'Essay', p.209.
24. *Conversations with Jorge Luis Borges*, Richard Burgin, p.34.
25. Talk by Borges at Institute of Contemporary Arts, London, May 1971.
26. Quoted in *La Guía Pirelli: Buenos Aires, sus aldredores, y costas del Uruguay*, Sudamericana, 1993, p.193.
27. 'Propos de Mme Leonor Acevedo de Borges', *L'Herne*, p.11.
28. 'Essay', p.208.
29. Jurado, p.29.
30. Victoria Ocampo, p.53.
31. Letter to author, Alicia Jurado, 20.12.95.
32. Though see the opening of 'Juan Muraña', in *Doctor Brodie's Report* (1970): 'I was on the train to Morón. Trápani, who was sitting next to the window, called me by name. For some time I could not place him, so many years had passed since we'd been classmates in a school on Thames Street. Roberto Godel, another classmate, may remember him.' (Di Giovanni's translation, p.81.) On 14 June 1996, *El País* in Madrid carried a report about some letters Borges wrote to Godel from Switzerland in 1919. They had recently been published by *La Nación* in Buenos Aires, and are owned by an Argentine impresario, Alejandro Vaccaro (who is working on a three-volume biography of Borges). The letters reveal that Borges found Swiss girls hard work, was 'in love' with an ugly Czech girl, and had been 'inspired' by the Russian Revolution.
33. Letter, Jurado, 20.12.95.
34. *Evaristo Carriego*, in di Giovanni's translation, p.59.

35. Borges also referred to Paredes as '*un hombre guapo y paquete*' – for which the nearest translation might be 'neat and spry'; interview, Alicia Jurado, Buenos Aires, 29.11.94.
36. 'Essay', p.211.
37. Burgin, p.20.
38. 'Propos', *L'Herne*, p.10.
39. Chronologie, *Oeuvres complètes*, ed. Jean-Pierre Bernès, Vol. I, p.xxxvii. Bernès also mentions a three-scene tragedy written by Borges in 'around 1907', called *Bernardo del Carpio* (Bernès, p.1554). (See Chapter Ten, Epilogue and A Note on Texts Used at the end of this book for details about Jean-Pierre Bernès and his work on Borges.)
40. ibid., p.1554.
41. A rumour that has done the rounds for years. Speculations about Borges's auto-eroticism were rife even while he was alive; the source of this one in particular was Joan Evans de Alonso, widow of Amado Alonso, a poet who knew Borges well.

Chapter Two

1. 'The Kabbalah', an English translation of a lecture given by Borges in 1970 printed in Jaime Alazraki's *Borges and the Kabbalah*, pp.54–61. (For Borges's interest in Judaism, see also his 'Una vindicación de la cábala' in *Discusión*, his first essay on the subject.)
2. 'Autobiographical Essay', in *The Aleph and Other Stories*, p.214.
3. 'Harto de los laberintos', interview with César Fernández Moreno in *Mundo Nuevo* 18, December 1967.
4. 'Essay', p.214.
5. Interview with Fernández Moreno, op. cit.
6. Chronologie, *Oeuvres complètes*, ed. Jean-Pierre Bernès, Vol. I, p. xliv.
7. There is some confusion over the precise location. Most accounts, including Borges's, place it in Verona. In later years, Leonor said it happened in the amphitheatre at Nîmes, in southern France, which the family might also have visited in this same year – 1915 – though because of the war, it is more likely, if they went anywhere near the area on this first European voyage, that they dropped in on their way to Geneva in spring 1914. The alternative is that Leonor is remembering a visit to Nîmes the family made in 1921 on their way back to Switzerland and Spain.
8. 'Essay', p.216.
9. *Jorge Luis Borges: A Literary Biography*, Emir Rodríguez Monegal, p.127.
10. 'Essay', p.216.
11. He had no time for Blake. Keats and Shelley, by contrast, were idolised by Jorge, and were read by Georgie from an early age. As influences, however, they are entirely absent from Borges's poetic writings.
12. *El Hogar*, 16.10.36 (collected in *Textos cautivos*, pp.35–6).

13. Rodríguez Monegal, p.148; Chronologie, Bernès, p.xliv.
14. 'El otro Whitman', *Discusión*, *Obras completas*, p.206 (author's translation).
15. 'Song of Myself', 14.
16. 'Essay', p.217.
17. Rodríguez Monegal, p.115.
18. '"Nor have I forgotten one evening on a certain second floor of the Place Dubourg."
    '"Dufour," he corrected.
    '"Very well – Dufour."'
    'The Other', *The Book of Sand*, p.12.
    Borges has deliberately and doubly misremembered the real name of the Genevan square. Barnatán (*Borges: biografía total*, p.89), meanwhile, speculates that the assignation took place in rue General Dufour, in a building on the corner with place de la Synagogue.
19. Rodríguez Monegal, p.113.
20. Interview, Elsa Rivero Haedo, Buenos Aires, 21.10.93; Barnatán, p.88.
21. Rodríguez Monegal (p.474) reports, from a conversation he had with Borges after Leonor's death in 1975, on Leonor Suárez's colourful last words. A devout Catholic all her life, at the moment of truth she swore, said Borges, for the first time: '*Carajo*,' she said, '*basta de sufrir*'; 'Fuck, enough suffering.'
22. 'Essay', p.218.
23. ibid.
24. *Entretiens avec Jorge Luis Borges*, Jean de Milleret, p.29.
25. 'Essay', p.220 – a comment made after a few lines of the poem in English translation.
26. Bernès, p.1263.
27. 'Essay', p.221.
28. 'Jorge Luis Borges', *La nueva literatura III: evolución de la poesía 1917–1927*, Rafael Cansinos-Assens, p.281 (author's translation).
29. 'Essay', p.222.
30. ibid., pp.221–2.
31. Chapter 3, 'Comedies of Gesture', *Between Hopes and Memories: A Spanish Journey*, Picador, 1994, p.42.
32. Rodríguez Monegal, p.163.
33. Chronologie, Bernès, p.l.

Chapter Three

1. Chronologie, *Oeuvres complètes*, ed. Jean-Pierre Bernès, Vol. I, pp.l–li.
2. 'Autobiographical Essay', in *The Aleph and Other Stories*, p.224.
3. *La nueva poesía argentina*, Néstor Ibarra, Buenos Aires, 1930, pp.15–16 (cited and translated by Sarlo – see Note 5 below – p.116).
4. 'Essay', p.230.

5. For English readers, Beatriz Sarlo's *Jorge Luis Borges: A Writer on the Edge*, Chapters Seven and Eight, provide an authoritative if dry literary-critical reading of the period; for Spanish readers, see Rafael Olea Franco's *El otro Borges, el primer Borges*; for French readers, see Bernès, pp.1257–1421.

6. 'Essay', pp.227–8.

7. This eccentric desire of Macedonio's has been located in various sources.

8. 'Essay', p.230.

9. 'La lírica argentina contemporánea', *Cosmópolis* 36 (Madrid), December 1929.

10. 'E. González Lanuza', *Inquisiciones*, p.96, Proa, 1925 (author's translation).

11. 'Essay', p.224.

12. Chronologie, Bernès, p.liv.

13. *Borges: biografía total*, Marcos-Ricardo Barnatán, p.187.

14. *Jorge Luis Borges: A Literary Biography*, Emir Rodríguez Monegal, p.184, citing Alicia Jurado, p.37.

15. 'Essay', p.236.

16. Rodríguez Monegal, p.190.

17. *Proa* 1 (second period), August 1924.

18. *Inquisiciones*, p.132 (author's translation).

19. Collins English Dictionary, 1979, p.352.

20. *El tamaño de mi esperanza*, p.13, Seix Barral 1993 edition (author's translation).

21. 'I Always Thought of Paradise as a Library', *Borges at Eighty: Conversations*, ed. Willis Barnstone, p.123.

22. *Martín Fierro*, 31.8.–15.11.27. In this issue, the last, a photograph of the banquet was reproduced. The idea of Borges giving any kind of 'speech' is difficult to imagine, as he was pathologically averse to public speaking: his essay 'The Language of the Argentines', remember, had been read *for* him. This was to be his style until, in 1946, he had no choice but to overcome his terror of facing an audience (see Chapter Seven, and Chapter Nine, Note 26).

23. Interview, Carlos Fuentes, London, 28.6.95.

24. ibid.

25. 'Essay', p.237.

26. *Clarín*, Buenos Aires, 4.86.

27. Interview, Adolfo Bioy Casares, Buenos Aires, 18.11.94.

28. Today, one of Buenos Aires's finest museums is Xul Solar's former house, at calle Laprida 1214, where his magnificent watercolours and acrylics can be seen.

29. 'Essay', p.237.

30. *Conversaciones con Borges*, Roberto Alifano, Torres Agüero Editor, Buenos Aires 1994, p.51.

31. Rodríguez Monegal, p.217.

32. 'Deathwatch on the Southside', translated by Robert Fitzgerald, *Selected Poems*, p.69.

33. In the 'Essay', Borges says for *El idioma*; Rodríguez Monegal says for *Cuaderno San Martín*. Barnatán says he won second prize for *El idioma* in a municipal competition for *prose* and, a year later, in the same for *poetry*, second prize for *San Martín* – Georgie then spending the winnings on the encyclopaedia.

Chapter Four

1. 'Visión de Jorge Luis Borges', Victoria Ocampo, *L'Herne*, p.22.

2. 'Malandanzas de una autodidáctica', Victoria Ocampo, *Testimonios: quinta serie (1950–1957)*, (Buenos Aires), 1957, p.20.

3. 'Carta a Waldo Frank', Victoria Ocampo, *Sur* 1, summer 1931.

4. Victoria Ocampo, *L'Herne*, p.22.

5. 'Entretiens avec Napoléon Murat', *L'Herne*, p.377.

6. *Entretiens avec Jorge Luis Borges*, Jean de Milleret, p.61.

7. 'El arte narrativo y la magia', *Sur* 5, summer 1932.

8. *A Universal History of Infamy*, in di Giovanni's translation, pp.11–12.

9. *Borges et Borges*, Néstor Ibarra, *L'Herne*, Paris, 1969, p. 16 (revised and enlarged from *L'Herne*'s original 1964 interview – see Note 15 below).

10. 'Vindicación del 1900', *Saber Vivir*, 12.45.

11. There are various versions of how and when Borges and Bioy met – mainly because both men themselves gave variant accounts of the episode over the decades. It seems that the bulk of their first conversation took place in Bioy's car as he drove Borges back to central Buenos Aires. Borges could not drive.

12. Interview, Adolfo Bioy Casares, Buenos Aires, 18.11.94.

13. 'An Evening with Bioy', talk by Bioy Casares given at the Royal Aeronautical Society, London, 20.10.93, collected in *The Borges Tradition*, p.91.

14. Interview, Adolfo Bioy Casares, Buenos Aires, 1.12.94.

15. 'Borges et Borges', Néstor Ibarra, *L'Herne*, p.420.

16. Interview, Adolfo Bioy Casares, Buenos Aires, 8.12.94.

17. 'Paul Groussac', *Discusión*, *Obras completas*, p.233.

18. *Jorge Luis Borges: A Literary Biography*, Emir Rodríguez Monegal, p.245.

19. 'Borges vaut le voyage', Pierre Drieu La Rochelle, *Megáfono*, 1933, reprinted in extract in *L'Herne*, p.105.

20. De Milleret, p.177.

21. *Borges el memorioso*, Antonio Carrizo, p.218.

22. 'Autobiographical Essay', in *The Aleph and Other Stories*, p.238.

23. *A Universal History of Infamy*, p.12.

24. Rodríguez Monegal, p.254.

25. 'The Dread Redeemer Lazarus Morell', *A Universal History of Infamy*, p.27.
26. Commentary on 'The Dead Man', *The Aleph and Other Stories*, p.271.
27. 'L'électricité des mots', Carlos Peralta, *L'Herne*, p.413.
28. 'Images de Borges', Silvina Ocampo, *L'Herne*, p.27.
29. Letter from Neruda to Hector Eandi, 24.4.29, quoted in *Review 74* (New York, spring 1974) in monograph by Rodríguez Monegal.
30. *Conversations with Jorge Luis Borges*, Richard Burgin, p.110.
31. Interview, Adolfo Bioy Casares, Buenos Aires, 1.12.94.
32. 'My Dinners with Borges', talk given by Guillermo Cabrera Infante at the Royal Society of Arts, London, 29.9.88, collected in *The Borges Tradition*, p.19.
33. Rodríguez Monegal (p.284) strangely attributes this to part of Bianco's statement, 'Des souvenirs', in *L'Herne*; Borges's comment was actually made in the original review, collected in *Otras inquisiciones*.
34. 'Essay', p.206.
35. 'Des souvenirs', José Bianco, *L'Herne*, p.38.
36. Rodríguez Monegal, p.265.
37. ibid.
38. 'Essay', p.240.
39. 'The Art of Fiction XXXIX', Ronald Christ, *Paris Review* winter/spring 1967, p.126.
40. 'Insomnio', *Obras completas*, p.859 (author's prose translation).
41. Quoted by Hellen Ferro, 'Borges y el cine', *Cinco años después*, Buenos Aires, 1991.
42. *El Hogar*, 30.10.36 (collected in *Textos cautivos*, p.39).
43. Chronologie, *Oeuvres complètes*, ed. Jean-Pierre Bernès, Vol. I, p.lxx.
44. 'A mi padre', *La moneda de hierro*, p.81.
45. 'Essay', p.240.
46. ibid., p.240–2.
47. 'Of Elvira what I saw first, years and years
    Past, was her smile and it is now the last.' 'Elvira de Alvear', *Selected Poems*, p.137.
48. 'Entretiens avec James E. Irby', *L'Herne*, p.398.
49. 'Essay', p.242.
50. ibid., p.243.
51. ibid., p.242.
52. 'Leopoldo Lugones', *Sur* 41, February 1938; *Nosotros* 26–28, May/July 1938.
53. 'Essay', p.242.
54. 'Propos de Mme Leonor Acevedo de Borges', *L'Herne*, p.11. Leonor's memory was faulty on more than one occasion here; she referred to her and 'her husband' going to the hospital – in which case the accident would have to have happened on Christmas Eve *1937*, as Jorge died in February 1938. The 'fantastic stories' she then referred to in the 'Propos'

began to be published in *Sur* in spring 1939, 'Pierre Menard' being the first. It is inconceivable that her son had written the latter over a year before publishing it in magazine form. Leonor's curious resurrection of her husband in 1964 was an 88-year-old's wishful thinking rather than accurate recall.

55. De Milleret, p.70.
56. 'Essay', p.243.

Chapter Five

1. *Entretiens avec Jorge Luis Borges*, Georges Charbonnier, p.109.
2. 'Una pedagogía del odio', *Sur* 32, May 1937.
3. 'Ensayo de imparcialidad', *Sur* 61, October 1939.
4. 'Pierre Menard, Author of the *Quixote*', *Labyrinths*, pp.62–71.
5. *Borges el memorioso*, Antonio Carrizo, p.222.
6. 'Tlön, Uqbar, Orbis Tertius', *Labyrinths*, p.42.
7. 'Ellery Queen: *The New Adventures of Ellery Queen*', *Sur* 70, July 1940.
8. Sur: *A Study . . . 1931–1970*, John King, p.93.
9. See *Borges a contraluz* by Estela Canto, p.169, for a colourful description of the princess.
10. 'Tlön', op. cit., pp.27–43.
11. 'The Library of Babel', *Labyrinths*, pp.78–86.
12. *Antología de literatura fantástica*, p.13.
13. 'The Circular Ruins', *Labyrinths*, p.72. Di Giovanni's version reads: 'Nobody saw him come ashore in the encompassing night . . .' (*The Aleph and Other Stories*, p.55). See his comments on how he and Borges arrived at this translation in *The Return of Eva Perón*, V. S. Naipaul, pp.120–1.
14. *Jorge Luis Borges: A Literary Biography*, Emir Rodríguez Monegal, p.358.
15. 'Autobiographical Essay', in *The Aleph and Other Stories*, p.246.
16. Interview, Adolfo Bioy Casares, Buenos Aires, 18.11.94.
17. ibid.
18. ibid.
19. *Nosotros*, July 1942, (author's translation).
20. 'Desagravio a Borges', Bioy Casares, *Sur* 94, July 1942.
21. Bianco, *L'Herne*, p.43.
22. Victoria Ocampo, *Sur* 59, August 1939.
23. 'Roger Caillois: "Le roman policier"', *Lettres françaises*, 1941, printed in 'Articles non recueillis', *Oeuvres complètes*, ed. Jean-Pierre Bernès, p.955.
24. 'Conjectural Poem', *Selected Poems*, pp.95–7.
25. Carlos Mastronardi, *Sur*, December 1946.
26. 'Entretiens avec Napoléon Murat', *L'Herne*, p.378.

27. 'Essay', p.246.

28. *Homenaje a Buenos Aires en el cuarto centenario de su fundación*, Buenos Aires, 1936, p.526.

29. See Bernès, p.1542, Note 2.

30. 'Para la noche de 1940, en Inglaterra', *Saber Vivir* 4/5, November/ December 1940.

31. 'Nota sobre la paz', *Sur* 129, July 1945.

32. *Borges a contraluz*, Estela Canto, p.102.

33. Rodríguez Monegal, p.391.

34. *El Plata*, 31.10.45.

Chapter Six

1. *Borges a contraluz*, Estela Canto, p.27. (All the quotations from this book have been translated by the author.)

2. ibid., p.23.

3. Interview, Estela Canto, Buenos Aires, 26.10.93.

4. Interview, Adolfo Bioy Casares, Buenos Aires, 1.12.94.

5. Canto, p.27.

6. ibid., p.78.

7. ibid.

8. ibid., pp.98–9.

9. ibid., p.28.

10. ibid., p.29.

11. The letters (see Introduction, Note 8) sent by Borges to Canto, the first nine between December 1944 and early 1945, the next five in 1949, are vivid testimony to a fraught and erotically confused state of mind. They do not tell us much about Borges's working life (though there are allusions to journals he was contributing to, to the first phase of his collaboration with Bioy and, in three letters (Canto, p.136, p.138 and p.143), to 'The Aleph'). Their tone of melancholic urgency does two things, however: confirm what Canto says in her account about Borges's painful if bottled-up desire for her; and reflect the claustrophobic, febrile atmosphere of the stories of *El Aleph*, being written at the same time.

12. *Jorge Luis Borges: A Literary Biography*, Emir Rodríguez Monegal, p.349.

13. In conversation with Bernard Pivot, 'Apostrophes', RTF, 1980.

14. *Sur* 4, spring 1931.

15. Canto, p.42.

16. *The Return of Eva Perón*, V. S. Naipaul, p.155.

17. ibid., p.129.

18. ibid., p.107.

19. Canto, pp.40ff.
20. ibid., p.30.
21. ibid., p.82.
22. ibid., p.95.
23. ibid., p.98.
24. ibid.
25. ibid., p.99.
26. ibid., p.105.
27. ibid., p.108.
28. 'The Aleph', *The Aleph and Other Stories*, p.17.
29. ibid., pp.28–9.
30. ibid., p.15.
31. ibid., p.19.
32. Rodríguez Monegal, p.386.
33. 'Autobiographical Essay', in *The Aleph and Other Stories*, p.244.
34. Rodríguez Monegal, p.392.
35. Canto, p.118.
36. 'Palabras pronunciadas por Jorge Luis Borges en la comida que le ofrecieron los escritores', *Sur* 142, August 1946; Borges's and Barletta's texts were then reprinted in the anti-Peronist *Argentina libre* on 15 August.
37. In 1990, Kohan Miller gave a Spanish newspaper some taste of his sessions with Borges: 'Borges had treatment for nearly three years, from 1946 to 1949. He came twice a week. These sessions were very agreeable for me because not everything was psychotherapy . . . Sometimes we included the problem of the anguish he suffered as a neurotic. Borges was a man of great understanding. He had an extraordinary capacity to understand everything in a few words, and to come up with the precise and necessary questions to fill the gaps a medical explanation might leave. Above all, he was greatly inhibited. The patient who suffers from this condition doesn't only suffer from an inhibition over speaking or some other kind of inhibition. In general, he suffers from several inhibitions, and this was what was happening with him . . . I could alleviate the verbal impotence but could not finish treating him for sexual impotence, although I could help up to a point.' Interview conducted by Rita Goldaracena, *El País*, 21.12.90 (author's translation).
38. 'The Immortal', *Labyrinths*, p.145.
39. This was how Alicia Jurado, who got to know Borges in 1954, remembered calle Maipú: 'The flat was small; there was a hall and on the right-hand side a living-dining room, which is where all the books were too. There were a sofa, two armchairs, a little desk, and daguerrotypes of some of the ancestors; and then on the left, there was a little passage, then Borges's room, which was very small, and then his mother's. There was a bathroom between. A little kitchen was next to the living room, and beyond that was the servant's room. Then there was a small balcony. The furniture was

Victorian, nothing particularly distinguished. It had sentimental value for Borges, as some of the things were inherited from his ancestors.' Interview, Alicia Jurado, Buenos Aires, 29.11.94.

40. 'Essay', p.245.
41. ibid.
42. See Canto, p.118. She says that Borges soon gave this habit up.
43. ibid., p.117.
44. ibid., p.119.
45. ibid.
46. Esther Zemboraín de Torres says the dancer went on to become 'an astrologer'; interview, Buenos Aires, 27.11.94.
47. 'Tlön, Uqbar, Orbis Tertius', *Labyrinths*, p.36.
48. 'Emma Zunz', *Labyrinths*, p.167.
49. 'Essay', p.245.
50. Rodríguez Monegal, pp.395–6.
51. ibid., pp.396–7.
52. ibid., p.397.
53. ibid., p.398.
54. ibid., p.397.
55. Letter from Victoria Ocampo to José Bianco, 26.1.47, quoted in Chronologie, *Oeuvres complètes*, ed. Jean-Pierre Bernès, Vol. I, p.lxxviii.
56. 'Essay', p.248; *Conversations with Jorge Luis Borges*, Richard Burgin, p.137.
57. 'The Zahir', *Labyrinths*, p.189.
58. ibid., p.196.
59. ibid., p.191.
60. *Análisis*, Buenos Aires, 17.8.70.
61. Interview, Elsa Rivero Haedo, Buenos Aires, 13.11.94.
62. Interview, Adolfo Bioy Casares, Buenos Aires, 18.11.94.
63. The stories were: 'Streetcorner Man', 'Emma Zunz', 'The Waiting', 'Funes the Memorious', 'The Shape of the Sword', 'The Theme of the Hero and the Traitor', 'The Garden of Forking Paths', and 'Death and the Compass'.
64. 'Essay', p.230.
65. 'New Refutation of Time', *Other Inquisitions*, p.172.
66. ibid., p.180.

Chapter Seven

1. 'Autobiographical Essay', in *The Aleph and Other Stories*, p.248.
2. Borges made an excellent joke (ibid.) out of his innate sense of etiquette: instead of implying that he would simply refuse to meet Perón, he

stressed that his being unable to *shake the man's hand* made it impossible – embarrassing for Borges *and* for Perón – even to agree to such an introduction.

3. 'Un curioso método', *Ficción* 6, March-April 1957.
4. Borges's best poem on the subject was 'Poema de los dones' ('Poem of the Gifts', *Selected Poems*, p.128–31); see p.180.
5. Interview, Elsa Rivero Haedo, Buenos Aires, 21.10.93.
6. *Ficciones*, and a poem from the late 1950s, 'Una brújula' ('Compass', *Selected Poems*, pp.108–9), were dedicated to her; see pp.210–15.
7. 'Quinta conversación', *Siete conversaciones con Jorge Luis Borges*, Fernando Sorrentino, p.90.
8. Today, it has become a concert hall, with the original fittings still intact.
9. Groussac had intervened personally with the government's plans to house the lottery in the building.
10. *Selected Poems*, pp.129–31.
11. 'Essay', p.250.
12. *In Memory of Borges*, ed. Norman Thomas di Giovanni, p.18.
13. *Jorge Luis Borges: A Literary Biography*, Emir Rodríguez Monegal, pp.430–1.
14. 'Essay', p.250.
15. Foreword to a privately printed volume, *Siete poemas*, published in 1967: see *Selected Poems*, p.297.
16. *In Memory . . .* , di Giovanni, p.21.
17. *Borges: Imágenes, Memorías, Diálogos*, María Esther Vázquez, pp.28–9 (author's translation). This 1977 book provided the basis of Vázquez's later and fuller 1984 book, cited in the Bibliography.
18. In spite of frequent references to secretaries in accounts of Borges's life from this point onwards, the only people who existed for him in that official capacity were those women who were employed by, and worked for him at, the National Library. Others, such as Vázquez, di Giovanni and María Kodama, were friends who happened to help him, offering their services out of admiration, not for remuneration.
19. *Entretiens avec Jorge Luis Borges*, Jean de Milleret, p.82.
20. Her *La expresión de la irrealidad en la obra de Jorge Luis Borges* (translated as *Borges the Labyrinth Maker*, by Robert Lima, New York, 1965) was first published in Mexico in 1957.
21. *Labyrinths*, p.219.
22. Rodríguez Monegal (p.438) reports that Borges thought up the title in English first.
23. 'Essay', p.253.
24. ibid.
25. *Selected Poems*, ('The Maker'), p.278.
26. ibid., p.143.
27. ibid., p.282.
28. 'Essay', p.252.

29. ibid.
30. Interview, Vlady Kociancich, Buenos Aires, 1.12.94.
31. 'Embarking on the Study of Anglo-Saxon Grammar', *Selected Poems*, p.153.
32. 'Essay', p.253.
33. ibid., p.252.
34. Cited by Rodríguez Monegal, p.443.
35. 'Essay', p.254.
36. 'Entretiens avec James E. Irby', *L'Herne* (author's translation), pp.388ff.
37. According to Rodríguez Monegal (p.446), the editor of an important journal, *Revista de la Universidad de México*, influenced Borges's effective debarment from the country. In June 1962, the magazine published an article attacking Borges for 'McCarthyism' but admiring his work; it also published Irby's interview.
38. Interview, Alicia Jurado, Buenos Aires, 14.11.94.
39. British Council file, 1963, ARG/320/80.
40. *Borges: biografía total*, Marcos-Ricardo Barnatán, p.74.
41. British Council file, 1963. ARG/320/80.
42. 'Harto de los laberintos', interview with César Fernández Moreno in *Mundo Nuevo* 18, December 1967. See also Borges's comments on Geneva in the 'Essay', p.215.
43. Reported in *La voz de Buenos Aires*, 15.2.63.
44. 'Essay', p.256.
45. Peter Chambers in the *Daily Express* (14.2.63) rose to the occasion of Borges's visit to, and articulation of his views on, Britain:

    [JLB:] '. . . behind these dim, unseen things, I sense what I always knew was here in England. I feel a great strength. You are not a people for show. You do not need theories, ideologies, revolutions, proclamations.'

    I was overwhelmed to hear all this. Didn't Borges know about our new 'public image'? The latter-day satirists have put tarnished old Britain in a dunce's cap.

    Our historic purpose? It is expressed in bingo-parlours, wild-cat strikes, and a government of ex-public-school fumblers.

    Our heritage? It survives in Beefeater travel-posters, and Olde Englishe Tea Shoppes which sell cola.

    Our strength? President de Gaulle boots us out of Europe. President Kennedy dictates our defence programme.

    Surely Borges couldn't have been talking about Britain?

    Si, señor! He meant us.

    Perhaps we need a blind poet from Buenos Aires to see ourselves in focus.
46. British Council file, 1963, ARG/320/80.
47. ibid.
48. ibid.
49. In 1980, Borges said: 'If I stay at home I am repeating the same day over

and over again. When I travel every day is different. Every day brings a gift. So I enjoy travelling . . . But if I stay at home the whole thing is rather drab. Every day is the mirror of the day that came before it.' 'I Always Thought of Paradise as a Library', *Borges at Eighty: Conversations*, p.124.

Chapter Eight

1. The writers honoured by *L'Herne* before were Réné-Guy Cadou, Georges Bernanos and Louis-Ferdinand Céline. Many international figures have had a similar *L'Herne* volume dedicated to them since; at the time, Borges's being chosen was a remarkably enlightened move on the part of the editors, and a measure of his deep penetration into French literature. The *L'Herne* volume was the single most important literary-critical enterprise about Borges published in his lifetime.
2. Esther Zemboraín de Torres has a different version: 'The invitation to Berlin came. Leonor packed for them both; Borges asked her why she was doing so – and then explained that he was taking María Esther Vázquez'; interview, Zemboraín, Buenos Aires, 27.11.94.
3. Interview, María Esther Vázquez, Buenos Aires, 7.12.94.
4. Interview, María Esther Vázquez, Buenos Aires, 26.10.93.
5. 'Autobiographical Essay', in *The Aleph and Other Stories*, p.257.
6. Interview, Mario Vargas Llosa, Jerusalem, 15.3.95.
7. British Council file, 1964, ARG/0320/2.
8. Interview, María Esther Vázquez, Buenos Aires, 26.10.93.
9. Except in the English *Selected Poems*, the volume is normally referred to as *For the Six Strings*.
10. Interview, Alicia Jurado, Buenos Aires, 29.11.94.
11. *Selected Poems*, p.215.
12. *Obras completas*, p.920 (author's translation).
13. Interview, Vlady Kociancich, Buenos Aires, 1.12.94.
14. Interview, Esther Zemboraín de Torres, Buenos Aires, 27.11.94
15. Interview, Esther María Vázquez, Buenos Aires, 7.12.94.
16. Onganía was born in 1914, and died in June 1995; he ruled Argentina until 1970. An obituary by Andrew Graham-Yooll (*Independent*, 10.6.95) ended: 'the damage wreaked on Latin American society by the likes of Onganía will prompt the conclusion that he died five decades too late'.
17. See an article entitled 'Enérgica réplica a Borges de la Facultad de Filosofía', *El mundo*, Buenos Aires, 19.4.66.
18. Commentaries, *The Aleph and Other Stories*, p.278.
19. Borges's aversion to homosexuality was well-known. Marcos-Ricardo Barnatán, once a friend of Borges's and one of his recent biographers in Spanish, dreamed up a story in which Borges had to spend – by necessity

rather than choice – a night in Junín, sharing a bed with another man. The man passes part of it in 'some weird ritual', which Borges only later understands, by reading about it in a book, as pederasty. After the story got back to Borges, he refused ever to meet Barnatán again. (See Cabrera Infante in *The Borges Tradition*, pp.18–19.)

20. The flat – the top floor at calle Posadas 1650 – belonged to Silvina Ocampo's family; Bioy took up residence with her there in 1953.

21. Vlady Kociancich was a frequent guest at these dinners in this era, and this was how she remembered them: 'Dinner was served by a servant in white gloves. There was silver everywhere. The food was abominable, and Borges used to say we should have something to eat *before* having dinner there. Bioy was suffering from headaches at this time, so there was an enormous amount of pumpkin purée, and no salt – potatoes, and no salt; and dried meat. Dessert was fine, but there was only water to drink. Borges didn't drink, though he sometimes had a glass of wine. During dinner, Bioy ate, Silvina talked, and Borges talked the *whole* time – a monologue, as always. Bioy laughed but didn't talk much; he spoke very little during these gatherings. Borges, if necessary, would simply talk alone. There was always a "I wonder if", followed by a joke, a satire, a tale.' Interview, Vlady Kociancich, Buenos Aires, 1.12.94.

22. Commentaries, op. cit., p.279.

23. Some of the stories might also have been too close to the bone. Borges and Bioy had no qualms about ridiculing the pretensions of Buenos Aires cultural life, and doubtless made many literary and artistic *porteños* – if not named, then certainly implied – feel uncomfortable.

24. 'Essay', p.247.

25. ibid.

26. ibid.

27. Interview, Adolfo Bioy Casares, Buenos Aires, 18.11.94.

28. 'Genio y figura de una intensa amistad', *La Nación*, 3.4.83.

29. Interview, Esther Zemboraín de Torres, Buenos Aires, 27.11.94.

30. They are curious documents. Both indicate that Borges and Elsa met at this time – away from her, Borges laments in each their distance, how he cannot get out of his mind her smile, her voice, conventional effusions for a man in the 'opening' stages of courtship. Both indicate that he had held firm in his heart some of the feelings of two decades before. But the letters' formulaic nature, their very romantic *politeness*, suggests he was going through the motions, for old times' sake, rather than making a genuine or intimate appeal to a woman he really loved.

31. Interview, Vlady Kociancich, Buenos Aires, 1.12.94.

32. 'Una historia de amor y desamor', Alejandra Florit, *La Prensa*, 31.10.93. This was the first press interview Elsa Astete Millán had given since her separation from Borges in 1970.

33. 'A Borges lo arruinaron las mujeres', Néstor Montegro, *Siete Días*,

298

26.11.87. This interview was first published on 28.10.87 in the Italian magazine, *Oggi*.

34. *Jorge Luis Borges: A Literary Biography*, Emir Rodríguez Monegal, p.470.

35. *In Praise of Darkness*, p.25.

36. ibid., p.29.

37. Introduction, *Selected Poems*, p.vxii.

38. 'See how (Jorge Luis) Borges writes', *Committed Observer*, Andrew Graham-Yooll, p.138.

39. Interview, Norman Thomas di Giovanni, Lymington, 15.10.95.

40. As of writing, the author has been unable to find any further details about this strange trip but it is mentioned in more than one Spanish chronology of Borges's life.

41. Astete Millán, *La Prensa*, 31.10.93.

42. *In Memory of Borges*, ed. Norman Thomas di Giovanni, p.32.

Chapter Nine

1. The others were: *Evaristo Carriego*, *Discusión*, *Historia universal de la infamia*, *Historia de la eternidad*, a proposed second *Antología personal*, and *El libro de los seres imaginarios*.

2. Introduction, *Selected Poems*, p.xvii.

3. Borges had asked whether that was the arrangement di Giovanni had had with Guillén. Di Giovanni said it was, and for his part Borges saw no reason to change things; interview, di Giovanni, Lymington, 15.10.95.

4. *In Memory of Borges*, ed. Norman Thomas di Giovanni, p.22.

5. ibid., pp.23–4.

6. 'Autobiographical Essay', in *The Aleph and Other Stories*, p.257.

7. At Harvard in 1967, a reporter from a local newspaper had done an interview with Borges, in which Borges expressed admiration for American efforts in Vietnam. Di Giovanni was appalled; in reply, Borges explained that he was a guest in the United States, and felt it incumbent upon him to praise his host country. 'America is Emerson, Hawthorne, Melville,' Borges rhapsodised. Di Giovanni answered, 'Yes, Borges: Emerson, Hawthorne, Melville, but not Lyndon Johnson. Those guys would have been *marching* on the White House.' Di Giovanni rang the reporter to explain that Borges really did not know anything about Vietnam, and persuaded him to keep the writer's comments on the subject out of the article. (Interview, di Giovanni, Lymington, 15.10.95.)

8. *In Memory* . . . , di Giovanni, p.24.

9. ibid., pp.25–30.

10. Commentaries, *The Aleph and Other Stories*, p.279.

11. 'The Gospel According to Mark', *Doctor Brodie's Report*, p.22.
12. Book Four, *Gulliver's Travels*.
13. 'Doctor Brodie's Report', *Doctor Brodie's Report*, p.117.
14. 'The elder lady' herself was modelled on a great-aunt of Borges's; see Afterword to *Doctor Brodie's Report*, p.124.
15. Observant readers – but Borgesians above all – will notice that this great story (mentioned on p.xxiv) has not been dealt with in this book. It comes from the same period – the early 1950s – as 'The Man on the Threshold'; neither the last, nor another fine story, 'The Waiting' (1950), have made it into my text. Nor have two even shorter texts, 'The Two Kings and Their Two Labyrinths' and, finally, 'El fin' ('The End'), a gloss on *Martín Fierro*, included in later editions of *Ficciones*. Pressure of space and time is the cause, but bibliographical information about them ('The End' excepted) can be found on p.279.
16. *Doctor Brodie's Report*, p.10.
17. *Jorge Luis Borges: A Literary Biography*, Emir Rodríguez Monegal, p.452.
18. *In Memory . . .* , di Giovanni, p.32
19. ibid., p.33.
20. Interview, Alicia Jurado, Buenos Aires, 14.11.94.
21. *In Memory . . .* , di Giovanni, pp.34–5.
22. One version of the story is that Borges wanted only his copy of *The Arabian Nights* – so why the removal men?
23. Elsa Astete Millán, interview in *La Prensa*, 31.10.93.
24. Interview, Elsa Rivero Haedo, Buenos Aires, 21.10.93.
25. 'Essay', p.257.
26. Borges was always insistent that he did not 'lecture'; his predilection was for the '*charla*', literally chat, an extension of his preference for one-to-one encounters in those rare social occasions he attended. The irony is that most of what Borges spoke about in his 'lectures' was also an exercise in perfect and eloquent recall.
27. 'I ask nothing better than to be forgotten', Anna Mayo, *The Village Voice*, New York, 22.7.71.
28. Rodríguez Monegal, p.453.
29. ibid., p.454.
30. Interview, di Giovanni, Lymington, 15.10.95.
31. This was simply in reply to Borges's voicing a hope to possess one day an edition of the Sagas.
32. Interview, Alastair Reid, London, 3.7.95.
33. British Council file, 1971, ARG/2501/51.
34. ibid.
35. Interview, Richard Hamer, Oxford, 10.10.95.
36. *The Borges Tradition*, ed. Norman Thomas di Giovanni, p.28.
37. *The Guardian*, 23.4.91.
38. *Committed Observer*, Andrew Graham-Yooll, p.141.

Chapter Ten

1. María Kodama maintains, as many such a celebrated widow might, some mystique around her, including details of her age. As of writing, I calculate her to be fifty, having been born in 1946. (The date is corroborated in Barnatán's chronology.) An interview with José Manuel Fajardo in *Cambio 16* from 26 December 1989 describes her as being 'forty-five years younger than him [Borges]', which would make her fifty-two; a less flattering portrait, by Norma Morandini, in the same magazine in January 1987 describes her as just 'forty years younger', which makes her fifty-seven. María Esther Vázquez states that she was born on 10 March 1937, which makes her fifty-nine. Most reports have her – as indeed does she – appearing in Borges's classes in around 1967, when she would, according to my chosen calculation, have been twenty-one.

2. 'La intimidad de una mirada compartida', Hugo Beccacece, *La Nación*, 12.9.93. Interview, Vlady Kociancich, Buenos Aires, 1.12.94.

3. *Atlas*, p.8.

4. *Argentina: 1516–1987*, David Rock, p.359.

5. I write these words just as it is announced that the North American popstar Madonna is to play Eva Perón in Alan Parker's film version of the Andrew Lloyd Webber-Tim Rice musical, *Evita*. Graffiti have appeared all over Buenos Aires expressing outrage at the casting, and Peronists (numerous in Carlos Menem's government) are reminding the world that Evita was – is – like 'a mother' to them. Terrorism has even been threatened as a means of reprisal.

6. 'Perón Is a Second-Rater', Ann Scott, *Newsweek*, 10.12.73.

7. *Borges: biografía total*, Marcos-Ricardo Barnatán, p.395.

8. 'In Memory of Angelica', *The Book of Sand*, p.177 (in Alastair Reid's translation).

9. 'Undr', ibid., p.63.

10. 'Ulrike', ibid., p.13.

11. *Jorge Luis Borges: A Literary Biography*, Emir Rodríguez Monegal, p.473–4.

12. 'El remordimiento' (Remorse), appeared in *La moneda de hierro*, Borges's 1976 volume of poems.

13. *La Nación*, 6.8.72.

14. I am grateful to Andrew Graham-Yooll for providing me with copious press cuttings covering Borges's political views from the 1960s to the 1980s. These are Graham-Yooll's words from an article published in an Edinburgh journal, *The Literary Review*, August-September, 1980.

15. Cited by Graham-Yooll, ibid.

16. In fact, Borges heard this from someone else, though the phrase has always been attributed to him.

17. 'A Falklands epitaph, by Jorge Luis Borges', *The Times*, 18.9.82.

18. 'Dreaming tricks and paradoxes', Nicholas Shakespeare, *The Times*, 6.10.83.

19. This is how María Kodama has put it: 'Borges, who was a man of his era, with certain romantic customs and habits, said, "I am a Victorian man, and if we are to launch ourselves into the world, I would like us to be married . . ." He also wanted to die in peace. I told him, "Borges, I am an independent woman." He said, "All right, promise me that if I die before you, as will happen, that you will marry me, so that I can die in peace and happiness." I said, "I promise it. Also, you must promise me that if I die before you, we will marry so that you will be at peace and happy."' Interview, Buenos Aires, 20.11.94.

20. 'El escritor y sus amigos' (The Writer and His Friends), talk given by Vlady Kociancich at the Society of Antiquaries, London, 28 October 1992.

21. Interview, Vlady Kociancich, Buenos Aires, 1.12.94.

22. Interview, Adolfo Bioy Casares, Buenos Aires, 18.11.94.

23. Interview, Alicia Jurado, Buenos Aires, 29.11.94.

24. Interview, María Kodama, Buenos Aires, 20.11.94.

25. Interview, María Esther Vázquez, Buenos Aires, 7.12.94.

26. Barnatán, p.477.

27. 'Los conjurados', *Los conjurados*, p.97.

28. *Borges and the Kabbalah*, Jaime Alazraki, p.177.

29. An unsigned article in *Clarín*, 'Denuncian que sería nulo el matrimonio de Borges con Kodama' (Buenos Aires, 5.12.94), states that the validity of the marriage remains open to some doubt *because* of the absence of the couple from Rojas Silva, but that because it had never been legally annulled it continues to be recognised.

30. 'Tigers in the Mirror', George Steiner, *The New Yorker*, 20.6.70.

Epilogue

1. 'La "conjura" de Borges', Javier López Rejas, *Diario 16*, 17.10.95.

2. 'Kodama . . . defines herself as a woman clumsy in economic matters – "I was swindled by my previous agents" – and clarified that she did not appoint Andrew Wylie after her husband's death: "I took him on after my six previous agents did not provide, out of idleness, what I required."' 'María Kodama no regatea el precio de la obra de Borges', Amelia Castilla, *El País*, 17.10.95.

3. 'El último mito de Borges: su herencia', Norma Morandini, *Cambio 16*, 12.1.87.

4. Alicia Jurado dined with Borges from time to time in his last years, and once asked: '"Why don't we eat at your house, get her [Fani] to boil some rice or cook some eggs or something?" This was instead of going to a restaurant every time. "Oh no," he said, "she cooks very badly, let's go out." He always paid for me.' Interview, Buenos Aires, 29.11.94.

5. See Chapter 8, Note 33.

6. The posthumous fate of Borges's works in Spanish with Emecé has now been decided. Sari del Carril, daughter of the firm's long-time chairman Bonifacio del Carril, was – when I first met her in October 1993 – in full conflict with María Kodama over the future of Borges's rights. Happily, that conflict has been resolved, at some cost to Emecé: see A Note on Texts Used, p.280.

7. Interview, María Kodama, Buenos Aires, 1.11.93.

8. A large portion of Helft's material was bought from Miguel de Torre, who before selling his uncle's manuscript and photographic miscellanea reproduced it in a book – now a collector's item – called *Jorge Luis Borges: manuscritos y fotografías*, published in 1987.

Bibliography

The problems of the availability of Borges, above all in Spanish and English, have been dealt with in A Note on Texts Used. As far as criticism is concerned, there are a great many books on Borges, in many languages, most undoubtedly unknown to Borges himself. The only excuse offered for the incompleteness here is that it must needs reflect the three languages I read (Spanish and French along with English), as well as a determination not to overwhelm the reader with a surfeit of literary criticism, a lot of which is boring, sub-Borgesian, bad, or all three.

This bibliography is in five parts: first come Borges's own works in Spanish. Because of so many reissues, combinatorial volumes, changes and excisions from one book to the next, one decade to the next, I have chosen simply to list the books as published in chronological order, suffixed by the date of publication, and the first publisher.

This may not in itself be bibliographically useful, but it is at least historically correct. In Spanish, it is of course possible to read all of Borges – that is, his complete collected works – in Emecé's multiple-volume editions.

However, because these are to be superseded by a new commercial edition, and then a fully fledged scholarly edition, in the years to come (see A Note on Texts Used), it is difficult to recommend the current Emecé volumes as sources for the standard texts. Most of Borges's individual works are available in one Emecé edition or another, some in circulation, some not; his suppressed books of essays from the

1920s – in other words his first three books of prose – have now been brought out in single-edition paperbacks by Seix Barral.

Then comes a list of the books Adolfo Bioy Casares and Borges wrote together, following the same bibliographical principle as above. This is supplemented by a list of the books on which Borges collaborated with other people, and which are generally still available, or collected in the Emecé *Obras completas en colaboración* edition. Anthologies have not been included.

Part three consists of Borges's works as they were published in English. Only a few of these volumes are currently available in Britain, mainly in Penguin paperback: it seems that, if new translations of Borges in New York definitely go ahead, this situation will change over the next five years or so. Those Penguin paperbacks generally available in British bookshops are marked with an asterisk, thus*.

Part four lists as many of the best books on Borges as it seemed wise to include, while part five lists a few works of general interest.

1. Works in Spanish (unless otherwise stated, place of publication is Buenos Aires):

Fervor de Buenos Aires (poems), privately printed, 1923
Luna de enfrente (poems), Proa, 1925
Inquisiciones (essays), Proa, 1925
El tamaño de mi esperanza (essays), Proa, 1926
El idioma de los argentinos (essays), Manuel Gleizer, 1928
Cuaderno San Martín (poems), Proa, 1929
Evaristo Carriego (biography), Manuel Gleizer, 1930
Discusión (essays), Manuel Gleizer, 1932
Historia universal de la infamia (stories), Tor, 1935
Historia de la eternidad (essays), Viau y Zona, 1936
El jardín de senderos que se bifurcan (stories), Sur, 1941
Poemas [1922–1943], Losada, 1943
Ficciones (stories), Sur, 1944
El Aleph (stories), Losada, 1949
La muerte y la brújula (stories), Emecé, 1951

Otras inquisiciones (essays), Sur, 1952
Poemas, Emecé, 1958
El hacedor (poems and short prose pieces), Emecé, 1960
Antología personal, Sur, 1961
Obra poética, Emecé, 1964
Para las seis cuerdas (lyrics for songs), Emecé, 1965
Elogio de la sombra (poems and short prose pieces), Emecé, 1969
El otro, el mismo (poems), Emecé, 1969
El informe de Brodie (stories), Emecé, 1970
El oro de los tigres (poems and prose poems), Emecé, 1972
Obras completas: 1923–72, Emecé, 1974
El libro de arena (stories), Emecé, 1975
La rosa profunda (poems), Emecé, 1975
Prólogos (essays), Torres Agüero Editor, 1975
La moneda de hierro (poems), Emecé, 1976
Rosa y azul (two stories), Sedmay Ediciones (Madrid), 1977
Historia de la noche (poems), Emecé, 1977
Obras completas en colaboración (works in collaboration), Emecé, 1979
Borges, oral (essays), Emecé/Editorial de Belgrano, 1979
Siete noches (essays), Fondo de Cultura Económica, 1980
La cifra (poems), Alianza (Madrid), 1981
Nueve ensayos dantescos (essays), Espasa-Calpe (Madrid), 1982
25 agosto 1983 y otros cuentos (four stories and interview), Siruela (Madrid), 1983
Los conjurados (poems and short prose texts), Alianza (Madrid), 1985
Textos cautivos (articles from *El Hogar*), Tusquets (Barcelona), 1986
Obras completas (in four volumes), Emecé, 1989

2. Works in collaboration:

With Adolfo Bioy Casares:
Seis problemas para don Isidro Parodi (stories), Sur, 1942
Dos fantasías memorables (two stories), Oportet & Haereses, 1946
Un modelo para la muerte (novella), Oportet & Haereses, 1946

Los orilleros-El paraíso de los creyentes (screenplays), Losada, 1955
Crónicas de Bustos Domecq (stories), Losada, 1967
Nuevos cuentos de Bustos Domecq (stories), Ediciones Librería La Ciudad, 1977

With José Edmundo Clemente:
El lenguaje de Buenos Aires, Emecé, 1952

With Delia Ingenieros:
Antiguas literaturas germánicas, Fondo de Cultura Económica (Mexico), 1951

With Margarita Guerrero:
El Martín Fierro, Columba, 1953
Manual de zoología fantástica, Fondo de Cultura Económica (Mexico), 1957
Enlarged and expanded into:
El libro de los seres imaginarios, Editorial Kier, 1967

With Betina Edelberg
Leopoldo Lugones, Troquel, 1955

With Luisa Mercedes Levinson:
La hermana de Eloísa, Ene, 1955

With María Esther Vázquez:
Introducción a la literatura inglesa, Columba, 1965
Literaturas germánicas medievales, Falbo, 1966

With Esther Zemboraín de Torres:
Introducción a la literatura norteamericana, Columba, 1967

With Alicia Jurado:
Qué es el budismo, Columba, 1976

With María Kodama:
Atlas, Sudamericana, 1984

3. Works in English. The *order* follows first publication in the United States; publication *details* refer to the first appearance of each title in the United Kingdom. Unless otherwise stated, place of publication is London. Asterisks denote volumes available in Penguin in the United Kingdom.

Ficciones (stories) Weidenfeld & Nicolson, 1962 (reissued by Everyman, with an introduction by John Sturrock, 1993)
Labyrinths (stories and short essays), Penguin, 1970*
Other Inquisitions (essays), Souvenir Press, 1973
Dreamtigers (fictions and poems), Souvenir Press, 1973
A Personal Anthology, Jonathan Cape, 1968
The Aleph and Other Stories, Jonathan Cape, 1971*
Selected Poems 1923–1967, Allen Lane, 1972*
A Universal History of Infamy (stories), Allen Lane, 1973*
Doctor Brodie's Report (stories), Allen Lane, 1974*
In Praise of Darkness (poems), Allen Lane, 1975
The Book of Sand (stories; also contains a selection of poems translated from *El oro de los tigres* and *La rosa profunda*, under the title 'The Gold of the Tigers'), Allen Lane, 1979*
Borges: A Reader (selected writings), eds. Alastair Reid and Emir Rodríguez Monegal, Dutton (New York), 1981
Evaristo Carriego (biography and other essays), Dutton (New York), 1984
Seven Nights (essays), New Directions (New York), 1984

In collaboration:

The Book of Imaginary Beings (fantasies), with Margarita Guerrero, Jonathan Cape, 1970*
An Introduction to American Literature, with Esther Zemboraín de Torres, Lexington (Kentucky), 1971
An Introduction to English Literature, with María Esther Vázquez, London, 1975

Six Problems for Don Isidro Parodi (stories), with Adolfo Bioy Casares, Allen Lane, 1981

Chronicles of Bustos Domecq (stories), with Adolfo Bioy Casares, Allen Lane, 1982

Atlas, with María Kodama, Viking, 1986

4. Books on Borges

In English (unless otherwise stated, place of publication is London):

The Cardinal Points of Borges, eds. Lowell Dunham and Ivar Ivask, University of Oklahoma, 1971

Conversations with Jorge Luis Borges, Richard Burgin, Souvenir Press, 1973

Jorge Luis Borges, J. M. Cohen, Oliver & Boyd, 1973

Borges: Irish Strategies, ed. Anthony Kerrigan, Dolmen Press, 1975

Paper Tigers: The Ideal Fictions of Jorge Luis Borges, John Sturrock, Clarendon Press (Oxford), 1977

Jorge Luis Borges: A Literary Biography, Emir Rodríguez Monegal, Dutton (New York), 1978

Borges at Eighty: Conversations, Willis Barnstone, *et al.*, University of Indiana, 1982

Jorge Luis Borges: An Annotated Primary and Secondary Bibliography, David William Foster, Garland (New York and London), 1984

Borges and the Kabbalah, Jaime Alazraki, Cambridge University Press, 1988

In Memory of Borges, ed. Norman Thomas di Giovanni, Constable, 1988

A Borges Dictionary, Evelyn Fishburn and Psiche Hughes, Duckworth, 1990

Borges Revisited, Martin S. Stabb, G. K. Hall & Co (Boston), 1991

Jorge Luis Borges: A Writer on the Edge, Beatriz Sarlo, Verso, 1993

With Borges on an Ordinary Evening in Buenos Aires, Willis Barnstone, University of Illinois, 1993

The Borges Tradition, ed. Norman Thomas di Giovanni, Constable, 1995

Miscellaneous volumes with essays or interviews:

The Old Patagonian Express, Paul Theroux, Hamish Hamilton, 1979

The Return of Eva Perón, V. S. Naipaul, André Deutsch, 1980

A Writer's Reality, Mario Vargas Llosa, Faber & Faber, 1991

Committed Observer, Andrew Graham-Yooll, John Libbey, 1995

In Spanish and French (unless otherwise stated, place of publication is Buenos Aires):

La nueva literatura III: evolución de la poesía 1917–1927, Rafael Cansinos-Assens, Paez (Madrid), 1927

Borges y la nueva generación, Adolfo Prieto, Letras Universitarias, 1954

Esquema de Borges, César Fernández Moreno, Perrot, 1957

La expresión de la irrealidad en la obra de Jorge Luis Borges, Ana Barrenechea, Colegio de México (Mexico), 1957

Jorge Luis Borges, Cahiers de L'Herne, L'Herne (Paris), 1964

Genio y figura de Jorge Luis Borges, Alicia Jurado, Editorial Universitaria de Buenos Aires, 1964

Entretiens avec Jorge Luis Borges (interviews), Georges Charbonnier, Gallimard (Paris), 1967

Entretiens avec Jorge Luis Borges (interviews), Jean de Milleret, Belfond (Paris), 1967

Diálogo con Borges, Victoria Ocampo, Sur, 1969

Jorge Luis Borges: bibliografía total, Horacio Becco, Casa Pardo, 1973

Siete conversaciones con Jorge Luis Borges, Fernando Sorrentino, Casa Pardo, 1973

Diálogos: Borges, Sábato, Emecé, 1976

Letras de Borges, Sylvia Molloy, Sudamericana, 1979 (published in English as *Signs of Borges*, trans. Oscar Montero, Duke University Press, Durham (USA) and London, 1994)

Borges y la crítica, Ana M. Barrenechea, Jaime Rest, John Updike, et al., Centro Editor de América Latina, 1981

Borges el memorioso, Antonio Carrizo, Fondo de Cultura Económica, 1982

Europe: Jorge Luis Borges, Monthly review published by Messidor/ Temps Actuels (Paris), 1982

Borges: sus días y su tiempo, María Esther Vázquez, Javier Vergara, 1984

Borges, Festschrift published by Biblioteca Nacional (Madrid), 1986

Cartas de juventud, ed. Carlos Meneses, Editorial Orígenes (Madrid), 1987

Jorge Luis Borges: manuscritos y fotografías, Miguel de Torre, Ediciones Renglón, 1987

Borges: biografía verbal, Roberto Alifano, Plaza y Janés (Barcelona), 1988

Borges a contraluz, Estela Canto, Espasa Calpe (Madrid), 1989

Diálogos, Jorge Luis Borges y Osvaldo Ferrari, Seix Barral (Barcelona), 1992

La metafísica del arrabal, Victor Farías, Anaya (Madrid), 1992

Cuadernos Hispanoamericanos 505/507: Homenaje a Jorge Luis Borges, Instituto de Cooperación Iberoamericana (Madrid), 1992

Oeuvres complètes, Pléiade, Volume I (1923–52), edited by Jean-Pierre Bernès, Editions Gallimard (Paris), 1993

El otro Borges, el primer Borges, Rafael Olea Franco, Fondo de Cultura Económica, 1993

Borges: una biografía, Horacio Salas, Planeta, 1994

Borges: biografía total, Marcos-Ricardo Barnatán, Temas de Hoy (Madrid), 1995

Borges: esplendor y derrota, María Esther Vázquez, Tusquets (Barcelona), 1996

5. Books of general interest (all publishing details are given):

Argentina, H. S. Ferns (in 'Nations of the Modern World' series), Ernest Benn, London, 1969

A House Divided: Argentina 1880–1980, Eduardo Crawley, C. Hurst & Co, London, 1984

Argentina 1516–1987, David Rock, Tauris, London, 1986

Sur: A Study of the Argentine Literary Journal and its Role in the Development of a Culture, 1931–1970, John King, Cambridge University Press, 1986

The Land that Lost Its Heroes, Jimmy Burns, Bloomsbury, London, 1987

Argentina 1943–1987: The National Revolution and Resistance, Donald C. Hodges, University of Mexico Press, 1988

Historia de los argentinos, Carlos Alberto Floria and César A. García Belsunce, Larousse, Buenos Aires, 1992

Breve historia de los argentinos, Félix Luna, Planeta, Buenos Aires, 1993

Traveller's Literary Companion to South & Central America, Jason Wilson, In Print, London, 1993

Memorias, Adolfo Bioy Casares, Tusquets, Barcelona, 1994

Index

330